Rural Settlement Structure
and
African Development

Rural Settlement Structure
and
African Development

EDITED BY

Marilyn Silberfein

WestviewPress
A Division of HarperCollins*Publishers*

Copyright © 1998 by Westview Press, A Division of HarperCollins Publishers, Inc.

Published in 1998 in the United States of America by Westview Press, 5500 Central Avenue, Boulder, Colorado 80301-2877, and in the United Kingdom by Westview Press, 12 Hid's Copse Road, Cumnor Hill, Oxford OX2 9JJ

Library of Congress Cataloging-in-Publication Data
Rural settlement structure and African development / edited by Marilyn
   Silberfein.
      p.   cm.
   Includes bibliographical references and index.
   ISBN 0-8133-8657-8 (hardcover)
      1. Land settlement—Africa.   2. Rural development—Africa.
I. Silberfein, Marilyn.
HD966.R87   1998
333.3′16—dc21
                                                                        97-30490
                                                                        CIP

The paper used in this publication meets the requirements of the American National Standard for Permanence of Paper for Printed Library Materials Z39.48-1984.

10   9   8   7   6   5   4   3   2   1

To the Memories of

My father, Ben Silberfein
and my advisor, David Sopher,
whose work inspired the kinds
of studies found in this volume

"States are not formed by elections. They are formed by geography, war, settlement patterns, and the literate bourgeoisies."

Robert E. Kaplan, "Democracy's Trap,"
New York Times, Dec. 23, 1995, p.E9.

Contents

Figures and Tables

* These maps were prepared by Gerry Krieg in the Temple University Cartography Lab. The lab is directed by Mark Mattson.

Tables

Preface

This volume is the result of a group of researchers applying their insights and experience to a common theme. All the authors are concerned with rural development in Africa and all have focused on the connection between the development process and the arrangement of people and their built environment in rural space. Both anthropologists and geographers have contributed to the dialogue on this subject and representatives of the two disciplines are included in this volume.

The members of this group have never all been in the same place at the same time, and so have utilized various electronic modes of communication to link their locations around the world. Two conferences were organized, however, among a subset of the whole, in order to generate a group discussion. One of these meetings was a symposium on African rural development held at Temple University while a second was organized at the African Studies Association Meetings in Toronto. Both opportunities helped raise issues that found their way into individual chapters. The audience in each case further stimulated our thinking.

All of the authors have been patient and persistent as the editor tried to weave these individual pieces into a coherent whole. So little has been written on our subject that everyone was highly motivated to add this volume and to the general discussion on rural development. We remain hopeful about the long-term viability of African rural areas, in spite of a litany of problems that have beset the continent in recent years.

The cartography lab at the Department of Geography and Urban Studies, Temple University, under the direction of Mark Mattson, played an important role in finalizing this manuscript. Initially, several graduate students were involved in map preparation, but the lead role was taken by Gerry Krieg who has continued his involvement with the project.

None of the chapters could have been written, however, were it not for the African academics, students, bureaucrats, farmers, and others who assisted the research effort of each author. We hope that many of them will get to see this volume and that they will find it to be both stimulating and useful.

PART ONE

Background to the Study of Settlement

1

Introduction

Marilyn Silberfein

This overview of rural settlement in Africa was first conceived to fill a gap in the literature and respond to development specialists who had complained that there were no sources for assessing the relative importance of settlement patterns. Their key question can be stated as follows: does settlement, or the arrangement of people and their built environment in rural space, have to be taken into account in evaluating development potential or in designing new programs, particularly those based on local participation? This book comes to grips with this issue but it has evolved further, focusing on such related themes as the evolution of settlement types and the efficacy of settlement schemes. It has also come to include many, if not most, of the geographers and anthropologists writing in English who have made the relationship of settlement and development one of their strong research interests.

The Nature of Settlements

Rural settlements are concerned principally, though not exclusively, with primary activities, particularly food production. They contrast with urban settlements in which the creation and/or distribution of goods and services become dominant. The interface of these two realms can be sharp or blurred. In some cases, settlements may defy categorization; in others, rural places gradually expand their range of activities and become increasingly urban over time, although they may continue to function socially as villages. The contact zone of rural and urban is an area of research in its own right but in this study it is a secondary theme, referred to in several of the chapters and at greater length in the conclusion.

Rural settlements are also landscape features. They include structures designed primarily to provide for shelter and storage as well as facilities for food preparation and the ancillary activities of the household or the larger community. The arrangement of all of these settlement components reflects the needs of the production system, but it also expresses

cultural values. Such attributes of settlements as the orientation of buildings or their exterior design and shape are not necessarily functional;
rather they may demonstrate aesthetic preferences or aspects of the local
cosmology. There is always a symbolic aspect to settlement structure that
is reflected in the built environment as well as in the existence of sacred
spaces that are set apart from those areas reserved for shelter and various
aspects of the production system.

There are two other aspects of rural settlement that need to be
addressed:

1. relative permanence and
2. the position of individual settlements with regard to each other.

Permanence is a particularly important issue in Africa where settlements often relocate because of environmental stress, soil exhaustion, or
political change. Furthermore, common building materials such as mud
brick or mud and wattle are not meant to last indefinitely; it may actually be more efficient to replace structures built with these materials rather
than to try to maintain them.

As for the second factor, relative position, settlements are usually
considered to be dispersed, clustered (nucleated), or intermediate.
Dispersed farmers live in homesteads (also referred to as farmsteads) on
the land they cultivate, often scattered across an interfleuve on an undu-
lating landscape (see Figures 1.1 and 1.2). Their homesteads are non-con-
tiguous and located more than 150 meters apart. This distance, which
varies according to local conditions, corresponds roughly to the maximum separation of neighbors who can still call to each other, the so-
called hailing distance. On the other hand, when settlements are clustered, farmers are grouped together in villages; their homesteads, often
less than forty meters apart, are located at some distance from their fields
(see, for example, Figure 6.7). There is no universal agreement as to how
many individuals living in adjacent structures constitute a village rather
than a dispersed homestead. Typically, up to fifty people can occupy a
homestead, whereas a village consists of more than 100. Distance
between homesteads, however, remains a more reliable way to establish
relative dispersion.

Between the two extremes of dispersed homestead and village is a
transition zone that is sometimes called a "hamlet" or described as "semi-
dispersed," with distances between homesteads as low as forty to fifty
meters and a populations, living in several homesteads, often in the range
of fifty to 100 persons. When this category is used in areas where there is
a tradition of agglomeration, any collection of fewer than 500 persons liv

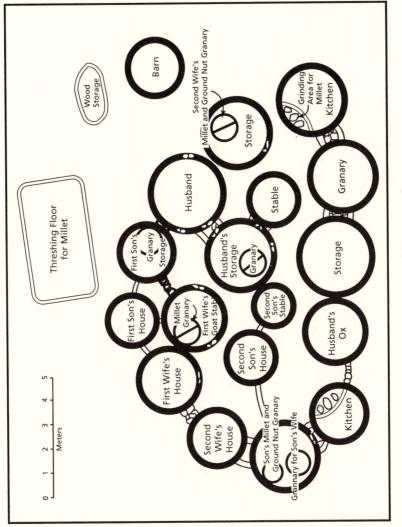

FIGURE 1.1   The Typical Structure of a Dispersed Homestead

Marilyn Silberfein

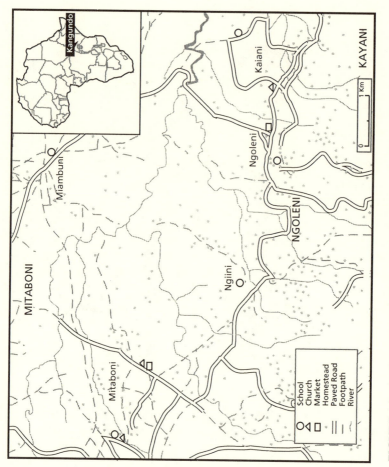

FIGURE 1.2 An Example of Dispersed Settlement : Kangundo, Kenya
Source: Kenya Topographic Maps - Series Y731; Government of Kenya, 1969

ing in homesteads more than thirty meters apart may be considered semi-dispersed.

Of course, reality is more complex than the above classification suggests. There are many variations on this theme, and actual settlement systems may include various intermediate types that fall between the extremes of dispersed and clustered. Descriptions of more complex or unusual forms are not always provided as part of the analysis of a particular social group, region, or country, but one exception to this rule is discussed at length by Massaro in his chapter on Tanzanian settlement. It should also be emphasized that the categories identified by the people actually living in a community may be quite different from those described by outsiders. Researchers are typically forced to use vocabulary from a very different cultural context than that which prevails in the area under analysis.

One of the more common variants on settlement form is the placement of homesteads along a road or the bluffs above a river. This linear arrangement facilitates access to a resource such as fish, alluvial soil, or markets and services. Linear and other geometric patterns) can be identified as either dispersed or clustered depending on the spacing of homesteads. The best description is usually semi-dispersed since the homesteads are located on the primary plot of cultivated land.

Although a particular settlement type may dominate a given area, individuals or families often depart from this norm in response to the needs of the local agricultural system, location within a market network, environmental stress, etc. For example, a village-based family may send selected members to occupy temporary homesteads that are either close to field crops during the period of peak labor demand or that are near a pasture where animals can be supervised. Similarly, in a region of dispersed settlement, clusters may be formed along a frontier. A single community can thus include both dominant and subsidiary settlement elements, a sign of adaptability in rural Africa.

The Sequence of Settlement Change

Despite these complications, it is possible to generalize about rural settlements, although the approach to the study of settlement processes may vary from one part of the world to another. Research in Europe and North America is often quite different from its African counterpart in terms of the nature of rural places as well as the problems investigated. In North America, for example, settlements may be treated as elements in geometric grids to be analyzed with quantitative techniques.

In Africa, however, it is important to look at settlements as spatial manifestations of changing adjustments to the environment, socio-economic variables, and the role of the elders in land allocation. For example, there is evidence that population growth and territorial expansion often leads to a sequence from dispersed to more clustered settlement forms. The sequence can be continuously interrupted, however, so that the ultimate formation of settlement clusters does not occur or only occurs temporarily.

The general trend toward nucleation is examined in Chapters 2 and 3 in this volume. It can be traced back to the first humans because early hominids were dependent on other members of their species for protection and mutual assistance. Additional circumstances are conducive to a sequence of settlement forms from homestead to village, as when a central source of authority develops within a society. A chief or other leading figure, then creates a land allocation systems that favors the clustering of members of the group near a designated point. Siddle, in Chapter 2, derives this view of rural settlement from the administrative version of central place theory. His model is based on optimizing population distribution so as to facilitate control.

Settlement clusters can also evolve as population growth leads to land subdivision, which, in turn, results in families utilizing several land parcels in different locations. In order to manage these disparate holdings, families may form a village that is accessible to all of the parcels. Finally, clustered settlements have developed when resources, such as water supplies, are extremely localized, when a society is characterized by strong mutual dependance, or when there is a need for defense during periods of conflict or along a frontier.

The theoretical sequencing of settlement from scattered to clustered has been used to support the concept, popular in some development circles, that there is an inevitability about the emergence of clusters, with villages as the natural end-product of an evolutionary process. This position, combined with a belief in the positive role of clustering in rural development, has been used to justify programs that relocate dispersed farmers into villages. Such programs, some of which are discussed in Chapters 4, 11, and 12, became popular in the 1960s and 1970s when independent African governments wanted to demonstrate their commitment to economic development in the countryside. Unfortunately, these efforts showed little sensitivity to the role of settlement systems in established modes of production and usually left a legacy of maladaptation wherever they were implemented.

In reality, despite the factors that favor nucleation, several circumstances usually intervene and disrupt the sequence from scattered to clustered in Africa so as to maintain a dispersed population or an alternation of dispersed and clustered stages. This process is sometimes referred to as settlement dynamism. The departure from the expected pattern requires an explanation. Two possible circumstances that might be responsible for interrupting the trend toward clustering are introduced in Chapter 3 by Newman: the emergence of a strong cattle-keeping tradition and the occupance of less fertile land. Cattle keeping has been conducive to dispersal because animals required considerable grazing and water supplies--both of which could be constrained in a village. In the same sense, low quality land pushed people further apart since more would be required per individual. Newman also suggests that the rise of patrilineal descent and residence as the dominant mode of social organization allowed families to break away from large, clan-based villages, although there is evidence that sometimes the opposite is true.

In addition, as African settlements evolved toward clusters, families often made a conscious decision to remain dispersed in the absence of severe security problems. Chapters 4 and 5 explain how dispersal was seen as a mechanism for minimizing pressure on farmland and other resources such as grazing land and firewood, while allowing flexibility in making land-use decisions. Dispersal also facilitated independence from centralized control without undermining the cooperative relationships that might be necessary for crop production.

All of the situations described above have been influenced by a combination of two factors that have become more important during the colonial and post-colonial period of this century: increasing population density and the spread of national and international markets. Both of these phenomena have a settlement-related dimension, discussed in Part 3 of this study. For example, as land becomes more valuable with both population growth and the spread of cash cropping, farmers may decide to protect their assets more carefully or spend more time and effort on their holdings (intensification). Either option can stimulate dispersal onto individual homesteads since the management and protection of resources is enhanced by proximity. This sequence is even more likely if the distribution of parcels is such that they can be managed from a single dispersed homestead.

Dispersal is also encouraged by other aspects of the spreading market economy. Members of rural communities tend to function more as individual actors then as group members with increasing reliance on cash-based production. Under these circumstances, village residents may actually move to dispersed homesteads to escape from the influence of traditional obligations or from the control of the local leadership.

When population growth is the major stimulus to change, new dis persed homesteads may be formed on land that was previously avoided-

-poorer quality land that cannot readily sustain the pressure of highly clustered settlements. Other homesteads emerge from village break-down due to the decline of resources in the vicinity of the village, sanita-tion problems resulting from large numbers of people in close proximity, or social conflicts. To use Stone's terminology (Chapter 5), the pull toward the land becomes increasingly strong as compared to the pull toward a location adjacent to other members of the social group.

Village Resettlement

There is a factor, however, that continues to attract individuals to cen-tralized locations: the need for goods and services. Indeed, villages have been promoted as places where produce can be picked up by trucks, where inputs such as fertilizer and tools can be delivered, and where other services such as agricultural extension and various essential goods are available. Some governments have carried this idea even further, maintaining that economies of scale favor groupings of farmers large enough to support equipment stations or ancillary activities.

Yet, in spite of widespread enthusiasm for the use of villages as ser-vice centers (see Parts 4 and 5), the provision of goods and services does not necessarily require the clustering of rural people . Services can be provided by individual farm families in an environment of dispersed homesteads, and several chapters in this book make reference to farmers that carry out secondary activities, functioning as part-time merchants or artisans. Farmers with particular skills, such as carpentry, can supple-ment their income by maintaining shops within their homesteads that service customers, particularly during the dry season. Other homesteads may be the site of a small shop that dispenses fertilizer or facilitates crop storage. Villages are also not necessary for group activities; there is con-siderable potential for dispersed families to function in this capacity. Examples abound in Part 3 of both individual enterprises and shared activities developed among scattered homesteads, including labor groups that participate in food production and other critical tasks.

In spite of this evidence, there have been many attempts by African governments to relocate scattered families in clusters, a process known as villagization. Some of these have been related to internal conflicts, but most have a strong ideological or developmental component. As was mentioned earlier in this introduction, many of these programs were part of the interventionist orientation that usually accompanied indepen-dence, although there are interesting examples of the use of resettlement during the colonial period as well.

One of the important themes to emerge from this book is that settle ment systems are intimately connected to various aspects of survival in both a subsistence and a commercializing economy. Thus, resettlement in villages or other forms of manipulation, should be a delicate process that must be treated gingerly. The consolidation of cultural values and adaptations to local environments represent long-term processes that need to be taken into account in any intervention. Several studies in this book, particularly Chapter 10 on Marsabit in Northern Kenya, show that relocation can be extremely stressful and can severely undermine both the local productive system and the social fabric. Under these circumstances, the value of villagization schemes and similar programs has to be questioned. While there are advantages that accrue to village residents, numerous studies show that most development goals can be achieved without extensive relocation or regroupment, but with close attention to and respect for the values and shared wisdom of rural communities.

2

The Geographical Study of Rural Settlements

David Grossman and David Siddle

In this chapter we present a review of the development of rural settlement theory and its relevance to tropical Africa. Because we do so against a background of approaches derived from experience in Europe and North America, we immediately make two major cultural assumptions. The first is that the terms used to describe and classify forms of settlement are transferable from one culture to another. The second is that settlement theory developed in the North can effectively be applied to other regions.

The search for structure and uniformity dominated rural settlement research in the 1960s and 1970s, as did the notion that settlement patterns tended to become regular over time. This applied to attempts to explain patterns of settlement throughout the world. In the case of Africa, however, these assumptions did not necessarily hold true. Acute awareness of this cultural limitation makes us sensitive to the fact that even common definitional terms are potentially controversial. One has only to observe that for many African people the terms "farm," "hamlet," and "village" could only be made meaningful if defined respectively as "an area of temporary cultivation," "a family compound," and "a lineage or kinship grouping." The notion of settlements may thus be based on such non-spatial elements as "activity at the time," "blood ties," and "where to build a shelter."

To a large extent, spatial interaction among settled communities in Africa has been and still is coterminous with lineage ties (real or assumed), not less than it is among nomadic and semi-nomadic peoples. Among the latter, the term "settlement" is clearly problematic. "Encampment" is more appropriate. Spatial interaction within and between camps is conditioned mainly by blood relations. Even though we are not dealing extensively with real nomads, it is worth noticing that low settlement stability among Africans tends to be associated with strong kinship ties.

In Euro-American terms, on the other hand, the shapes of the built-up areas of homesteads, hamlets, and villages readily lent themselves to spatial classification and explanation which accorded with cultural or economic attributes of Enlightenment thinking. For example, a persistent theme, particularly among the European continental scholars before World War II, was the close integration of physical patterns and forms of rural settlement with their social and economic function (Meizen 1895; Lefevre 1934; Demangeon 1927; see also Smith 1978).

However, even in Europe, this approach became increasingly problematic because many villages were already undergoing profound changes and a growing number of rural dwellers were no longer full-time farmers. The agrarian basis of the village community was slowly fading away, and the definition of rurality, which was based on the integrative nature of the village community and its land, was becoming less tenable. Although the impact of this transformation was felt on a large scale only after the 1940s, the centuries-old traditional settlement system in Europe was already crumbling when geographical analysis was taking shape.

So the scientific credibility of the descriptions of the forms and patterns of settlement was based, rather spuriously, on the physical appearance of the settlements. The permanence of the European structures, made of durable materials such as stone, timber, or brick, was an important component of the way settlement was studied. This permanence often stands in stark contrast to the relatively perishable structures of the African settlements, which were made mostly of grass, mud and wattle, or mud brick (Morgan 1983).

Similarly, the formal description of patterns--the way in which objects (settlements) are arranged in space, and their relationships to each other (Houston 1953: 80-85)--was based on the assumption (especially in early studies) that such objects were stable through time, and that the structures (houses or groups of houses) were not, in effect, actual or potential "ghosts." By the 1960s, the study of pattern had expanded to include concepts of settlement hierarchy, density, and spacing (Chisholm 1979; Haggett 1965), focusing on what Roberts (1977: 203) disparagingly refers to as "settlement geometry." This approach was, in his opinion, strong on description but not on explanation.

Most European settlement theorists who tried to model evolving processes over the next two decades were still confined by mechanistic assumptions of location theories and by the idea of intrinsic permanence. They followed the concept of "settlement" that was based on distinctions made by the earlier European taxonomists, such as the difference between nucleated and dispersed settlement (Roberts 1977: 82-84).

Roberts, at least, devotes a great deal of attention to patterns that are in various intermediate positions between dispersed and nucleated. He also attempts to illustrate the possible relationship between these patterns and the processes that may account for them (Roberts 1982; see also the discussion in Grossman 1992). Some effort was made by Roberts and others to take account of the dynamics of settlement evolution and the role of unstable structures, but European and North American geographers have found it difficult to incorporate temporary settlements within their frame of reference.

If the notion of fixed location was limiting in Western Europe, those who have tried to use maps or air photographs to chart all but the larger settlements, know how improper the term "permanence" is over much of rural Africa. As will be illustrated below, impermanence is, indeed, a common feature of rurality in many parts of the world, especially in the developing areas.

To add to the difficulty of finding proper terms to describe and interpret the multiplicity of patterns, one may add another problem which is no less difficult for students of African rural settlement: tracing and explaining processes by which patterns emerge and change. This difficulty stems from the very nature of the traditional rural structures and functions that--in comparison with urban ones--are under-recorded. In Africa, this problem is greater than elsewhere. Written records as well as archaeological remains are notoriously difficult to obtain. The availability of records depends on the development of a system of registration for rural populations and their activities. Bureaucracies that can carry out these surveys have been fairly common for some European rural areas and for parts of India and China, but they were almost unknown in Africa until the colonial period. Consequently, the researcher is forced to use informal oral sources and to try to understand uncodified land tenure practices and other agrarian systems by means of personal field studies.

Many factors account for the high spatial mobility and frequent shifting of dwellings among African farmers and pastoralists. These include the widespread use of perishable materials, the fragmented political systems, frequent local conflicts, as well as the poor resource base--especially the wide distribution of fluctuating, unreliable rainfall and poor soils. This complexity of partly known and often little understood forces stands in the way of pattern interpretation and an appreciation of the significance of rural processes. The absence of solid factual knowledge is also reflected in the lack of consensus among academics and planners concerning the proper strategy for African development.

Despite all the reservations that we have detailed here, we proceed in the following pages by using the European-derived concepts and theoretical approaches. The practical justification for taking this path is that the gap between African and non-African settlement forms and patterns is narrowing. Many rural settlements have become permanent and responses to recent external stimuli are taking place rapidly. The highly dynamic current processes are drastically changing the older patterns. So, while recognizing the constraints, we must try to struggle free from the more pervasive confinements of our cultural assumptions.

At the same time, we hope to get away from the preoccupation with measurement and spatial theory, and with structures and hierarchies, that led geographers to a rather restricted view of rural settlements as though they were molecules in some abstract space, far removed from the messy reality of human existence. The aim now should be to reveal settlement as a product of competing stimuli, a set of responses for which only much more varied (and changing) explanations are acceptable. Cultural forms and patterns of settlement emerge out of richly varied social, economic, and political contexts, representing both past and current attitudes.

Evolution of Euro-American Rural Settlement Studies

Scholars in Europe and North America have been particularly interested in the settlement changes that accompanied the diffusion of European arable farming. Although the exact occurrence and duration of this period varied by region, the time frame often coincided with the late Middle Ages. The typical patterns that emerged at this point were associated with the establishment of manorial vils (villages).

These villages, or grouped farming habitations, with their social and political structures, form what has been called the lower limb of a settlement hierarchy (Cowie 1983). They formed, in other words, the lower stratum of an established and stable system, and also provided the administrative and commercial framework of higher limbs, e.g., market towns, within a stabilizing, permanent settlement system. As European settlers moved from older core areas in Western Europe into new territories in the east and in the uplands, the clearing of land and the organization of agriculture around fixed locations, went along with a suitable defense. Quite soon it became a world of stone walls, brick-built habitations, and official buildings of church and state. Towns (burgs, boroughs) were often artificially created to provide structures of formal organization and protection.

For the most part, settlements, whether grouped homesteads, hamlets, or villages, were built around courtyards, greens, or squares and were protected by stone churches and castles. Often the shape of the settlement, with its gates and walls, reflected the primary preoccupation with security. In more peaceful times, the villages tended to string out along a roadway or dispersed homesteads developed in the fields, though the process of dispersal could also be affected by other factors. This was observed, in varying dimensions, in places that went through the parliamentary enclosures in Britain after the mid-eighteenth century.

The processes of change have intensified and become highly complex in the past decades, particularly since World War II. Yet, despite revolutionary developments, it has been unusual to encounter total desertion or abandonment of rural settlements within the European core regions (though desertion did occur in many marginal areas of Europe and America). The opposite process, that of establishing new agricultural colonies, has virtually been discontinued in the past half century in much of Europe and even North America.

The European tendency to live in nucleated villages was also the product of entrenched cultural values, traditions, and preferences. It was widespread, even where legislation freed people to hold and farm the land surrounding their homesteads and to house their families and their animals away from the security of the village. Furthermore, once the settlements were sited, the they continued to become more permanent. People built solid dwellings and in Europe at least, if not in North America, the rural dwellers replaced their wooden churches and thatch-roofed houses with brick and stone. This is the landscape, served by a pattern of local markets, that we still recognize in most of Europe today, even when farming is no longer the main way of life.

It was not surprising, therefore, that the European geographers who first began to classify the structure of rural settlements concentrated on fixed village forms. Indeed, the earliest scholarly attempts to study rural settlement in Europe followed this process of "settling down" quite closely. As we have indicated above, the first phase of this research work concentrated on descriptive taxonomy, though this was viewed as a necessary step towards explanation. The difference of opinion as to the relative significance of cultural, economic, or physical explanatory factors was one of the major pre-occupations of these early studies. Another focus of attention was the possible origin of settled places, their place-names, and the form and function of the built environment. The classification that came out of these studies formed the basis for many more elaborate and varied accounts of settlement patterns (Roberts 1982) as well as for numerous regional studies.

This phase of investigation allowed for a better understanding of the roots of European rural culture and its field and farming systems, but was relatively unconcerned with theory. Its main purpose was to explain local variations rather than seek common and general rules that would reveal forces of world-wide applicability. Researchers described the distinction between nucleated and dispersed settlements and attempted to explain these differences in terms of local physical conditions, farming and tenurial practices, modes of living, defense needs, and the ethno-cultural background of the settlers (Demangeon 1947).

The Quantitative Theoretical Approach

With few notable exceptions (Haining 1982; Grossman 1983; Cowie 1983; Coling 1984), rural settlement patterns and the theories associated with their development have attracted little attention during the two decades following 1975. The main reason for this was the replacement of the quantification phase of geographical research, dominant in the 1960s, by a less "mechanistic" approach to explanation. In addition, the research works of both scholars and planners moved from a focus on the explanation of evolutionary characteristics of rural settlements and their structures to a concern with purposive interventions for promoting "rural development." This approach is well represented in the chapters which appear in later sections of this volume.

The development of a settlement theory began in the 1950s with the translation of several works of German scholarship, and the publication of books in English that were based on the German theorists (e.g., Losch 1940, English translation 1954; Dunn 1954). The major impetus to Anglophone theoretical interest was provided by the rediscovery of Christaller's central place theory (1933, English translation 1966) which was concerned with defining spatial ordering principles for the settlement of South Germany in the 1930s, and the much earlier study by Von Thunen (1826), which dealt with the effect of distance from the market on the level of agricultural rent and on land use systems. Inspired by these works, Chisholm (1961) wrote of the relationship between economic functions and distance decay constraints, and Haggett (1965) related these concepts to alterations in settlement structure produced by environmental factors. These studies often focused on the way the rural population interacted with urban places, although rural settlements were sometimes examined as well.

The Application of Biological and Related Models

At the same time, a growing concern with spatial ordering and central places led scholars in several areas, e.g. England, the United States Mid-West, and Sweden, to explore the possible applications of principles derived from the works of plant and animal ecologists (Clarke and Evans

1954) to the evolution of human settlement. This was part of an attempt to identify and classify the patterns more precisely, to apply quantitative tools, to analyze them, and to use the analysis to derive the general principles that govern the spacing and, eventually, the diffusion processes of settlements.

The early studies of Dacey (1962) and Getis (1964) were followed by others (e.g., Singh and Singh 1975). They covered a range of geographical areas, from the Great Plains of the Midwestern states of the U.S. to the Ganga Plain of India. Focusing on areas which approximated isotropic plains (this assumption was considered vital to their analytical work), and treating the settlement systems as patterns of points in two dimensional space, they endeavored to explain how settlements have evolved since the inception of the colonization process. These studies have borrowed some basic methodological tools from biology which were later improved and extended to produce a number of statistical models and quantitative techniques, such as nearest neighbor theory and quadrant analysis.

Plant and animal behavior cannot be equated with human responses, but the new approach tried to overcome this difficulty by adapting the methods to the underlying assumptions and the logical principles of central place theory and distance decay, both of which are based on economic principles and concepts. The new methods were used, in fact, as means for verifying the classical theories. They were also expected to provide tools for measuring the degree of departure from theory as well as the stages leading to the expected evolution of spatial order (regularity) in settlement patterns. New categories of spacing (regularity, clustering, and randomness) were added to those early distinctions of distribution (dispersion or nucleation), as a means for improved quantification of settlement patterns.

It must be observed here that patterns are very much a function of scale. The degree to which settlements appear clustered or dispersed may reflect the scale at which the dots (homesteads, villages) are viewed. For example, dispersed single homesteads may form a regular pattern of evenly spaced dots, relatively grouped dots, or, more likely, a pattern of randomly distributed dots, depending on scale. If the number of farm structures is large enough, the homestead may even appear to be a hamlet. This is but one of the problems that challenges the claim to mathematical precision of this type of analysis.

While the quantitative studies injected fresh life into rural settlement research, many of them perpetuated older habits of thought. Much effort went into identifying patterns rather than processes. Thus, despite recognizing the significance of processes of diffusion and colonization, most of the studies considered rural settlements as fixed locations in static and theoretically isotropic space rather than as places of change and adaptation in real space. As pointed out earlier, this approach might work in areas with a long history of stable settlement, but it would be inappropriate for studying the highly dynamic, temporary, fluctuating, or seasonal rural settlements which prevail in Africa. Another major drawback of the models for our purposes is that isotropic plains, free of major variations in the resource base, are notoriously absent in tropical Africa.

If we are to use settlement theory for the understanding of African rural behavior, then it is necessary to focus on analyzing processes of change. A number of Euro-American theorists have moved towards meeting this requirement. A pioneering study by Bylund (1960) offered a simulated process of early colonization in the marginal areas of Northern Sweden based on principles which have close parallels in tropical Africa. As among the Swedish Lapps, many Africans have pursued a process of continuous colonization and recolonization, with related groups trying to avoid competition for space.

Bylund had defined colonization as a multi-stage model which began with a primary phase of long distance migration into a new territory and resulted in what he termed clone colonization or the branching of new offshoots from the original roots. This stage was then followed by a series of short distance expansions of the later generations in response to population increases. In Bylund's model, the final pattern is somewhat clustered in response to certain economic needs (proximity to markets and roads) and socio-religious needs (proximity to churches and selected relatives).

Hudson (1969) extended this approach, but introduced important changes into it. He placed great emphasis on competition rather than on its avoidance, and proposed a model which consists of three phases. The model was thus more akin to the diffusion approach that had been presented by plant ecologists and was, in addition, more mathematically based and less concerned with cultural factors than the Bylund model. Although the first two stages, "colonization" and "spread" are similar to those of Bylund, they are, in Hudson's schema, followed by a Darwinian stage of competition. Thus, when the increased density of the second phase leads to competition for space among rural dwellers, the less fit are forced out, and the final stage is a regular settlement pattern (Hudson 1969: 365).

Hudson's theory has stimulated additional studies based on similar assumptions and methodology. Olsson used Hudson's Iowa-based model and attempted to test it in Pite Lappmark. He defined the cloning stage as one where the number of points in the cluster increased faster that the number of clusters (Olsson 1968: 128). This assumption allowed him to equate each stage of settlement change with statistical hypotheses that have specific point-pattern associations (random = stage 1; clustering = stage 2; regularity = stage 3). Both Olsson and Hudson tested these models over a measurable time span, using statistics derived from Poisson (random), Negative binomial (cluster) and nearest neighbor (regular) distributions, but their studies don't extend beyond the recent past.

Criticism and Implications of the Quantitative Approach

One of the problems associated with the application of quantitative techniques to settlement studies has been the severe constraints imposed by the models. They assumed a once and for all migration, a colonization (settlement) phase with no room for further incursion by competing cultures with different requirements. Sampling grids which, as suggested above, are sensitive to scale, were largely arbitrary and bore little or no relation to the reality of economic experience. Hudson himself was quite aware of some of these shortcomings. He was careful to point out that not all rural settlement processes should pass through the stages he posited. Influences could shift, he argued, from clustering to competition and back according to exogenous variables (Hudson 1969: 380). It was the spatio-temporal indeterminacy of these models which created the most difficulty in any extension from the biological sciences to explaining human behavior. The models seem to be preoccupied with time as a progressive, linear continuum (a surrogate for progress).

North America was usually considered the ideal place to examine an isotropic surface with individuals making locational choices based on economic criteria. Yet, even there the evolving patterns were not free from deliberate outside interference, as in the case of the regular land subdivision of the Township and Range system. Furthermore, the so called "competition stage" is not so much endogenic to the process of settlement as largely the result of exogenous conditions: the complex spatial impact of modern technological and economic factors (Grossman 1971, 1983).

Modernization has often stabilized the highly volatile settlement processes, but not always in a way that was necessarily unidirectional. In the developed countries, particularly in North America, modernization has become a main source of rural instability and decline. It has, in fact, reversed earlier processes, and it accounts for widespread abandonment of farm areas in the very places which were, only a century ago, the main attractions for the expanding frontier.

The turnaround was not, as theory would like us to believe, the result of the onset of a new phase in a continuous process. It was, rather, the result of new factors which triggered new processes; those which accompanied the transition from traditional, horse-and-buggy culture, to one based on the internal combustion engine. Hart (1993) appears to be right, indeed, in singling out the combustion engine as the major factor which accounts for spatial restructuring in the twentieth century. It was responsible for both the transportation revolution and, through the diffusion of the trac-tor, for the most recent phase of the agricultural revolution. The com-bined impact of both was to reduce manual labor needs and increase space "consumption". Dispersal of the remaining farmsteads was, thus, strongly favored, but at the same time the expanding urban field has absorbed and profoundly altered former rural communities. The magni-tude of the abandonment process has led Coling (1984), to offer a model which extends Hudson's (1969) theory to take this abandonment into account.

The nature of rural processes is, obviously, varied, but nowhere in present day rural areas can one claim that rural settlements are inherent-ly stable. Clearly, this discussion has provided just a brief generalization of a very complex subject. The combustion engine is but one of many technological innovations which have affected all phases of life in devel-oped countries but which has hardly reached some parts of the world. The main point is, clearly, that the quantitative, biologically derived the-ory is ill fitted to deal with complex transformations of this kind.

The Process of Settlement in Tropical Africa

The first contributions to the study of rural settlement in tropical Africa were the work of colonial administrators. Their efforts reflect west-ern cultural conceptions and a preoccupation with fixed locations and linear progressions rather than with the multidirectional African process-es. The administrators were often confronted by a complex reality that included clans and tribal polities, polygamous households, groupings of impermanent dwellings, cattle-herders and shifting cultivators on com-munal lands, and pastoral nomads in temporary shelters. In order to make sense of all this, they had to define social and economic spaces of order and management, and they did so by using the preconceptions and terminology with which they were familiar.

The village was the social formation which European administrators took with them, in their mind's eye, as part of their cultural baggage. The term "village" became, therefore, the first construct imposed on most African societies by officials anxious to draw maps (to fix things in space) and to administer a territory. It was conveniently utilized even where no fixed villages existed. In some cases the colonial authorities ignored the existence of temporary or fixed offshoots which were located within a single clan area (village-group) or they administratively treated them as part of the mother settlement. Rural Africa was thus transformed into a system of "stable" landscapes of "villages". It must be stressed, however, that while most traditional African rural settlements are highly mobile, stable villages were not absent. Their presence is well documented in many densely settled areas, particularly in West Africa.

The initial research on African settlement gradually merged with work that was being done in other parts of the developing world. The wave of theory building of the 1960s became associated with research on settlement processes carried out in the Ganga Plain of northern India (Singh 1968; Singh and Singh 1976). But even though these studies have demonstrated an admirable ability to assemble, map, and analyze past records, their number is too small and their focus is too specific for meaningful testing of the abstract process models. They also tended to follow the European and American path, and have concentrated on methodological problems whose concern is pattern identification and description. The mapping of processes, e.g., in Singh (1968), focused on historical evolution, specifically, the preference for fortified towns in the face of warfare. Yet, the researchers did not acknowledge encountering any unstable or compound dynamic processes of the kind that prevail in tropical Africa.

Perhaps the only way to obtain some useful model of process-pattern relationships is by assuming that some unidirectional process had existed in a traditional subsistence system before the onset of modernization. In fact, although African traditional systems are, by nature, obscure and complex, local traditions can assist in tracing at least some of the perceived past processes and their spatial implication. In many areas, the only places of permanently fixed locations are those associated with the clan ancestors. For most rural Africans the social landscape of their known spaces were constructed and inhabited first by ancestors, then by men and women carrying out their economic and social lives. The social space can perhaps best be represented as a genealogical web of experience which takes place in space and is used for all purposes.

The ancestral sites can also be seen as starting points, marking the onset of the first of many processes of "clone colonization." At these sites there may have been several reversals and under severe conditions (such as military defeat), they were most likely abandoned to be replaced by new ancestral cores. The reverse process, that of extending the territory, was often achieved by violence, but, occasionally, peaceful expansion into fringe areas was possible. Bohannan (1954) showed this for the Tiv who "jumped over," beyond adjacent territories, in a form termed disjunction migration. This, however, may not have been a common traditional practice. It represents instead, a process that evolved under modern conditions as a response to acute population pressure and the suppression of violence.

Traditionally, the term "settlement" includes a range, a territory, or a clan grouping, with networks extending through various dwelling sites, some of them temporary. The fixing of such sites as semi-permanent to permanent locations for settlement reflects, first of all, the emergence of agriculture and an increasing capacity to draw sustenance from a limited territory (Roberts 1996: 21). Settlement fixation was, in addition, the result of three forces that overlapped with changes in productive systems: (1) the need for defensive protection, (2) demographic pressure and (3) modernization.

Demographic pressure may itself be the result of a process initiated by modernization, as the Tiv case illustrates. Typically, a combination of overlapping factors: better security, improved communication and transportation, better food supplies, and the availability of modern medicine, transforms demographic and even cultural processes. The result is that continuous demographic growth replaces the former fluctuations, reduces the amount of vacant land, and forces the farmers either to migrate (by disjunction migration or by moving to urban areas) or to intensify land use and fix their habitations (Boserup 1965).

Models of African Settlement Expansion

An approach which illustrates the possible patterns which can result from the traditional African processes has been offered by Siddle. His theoretical, quantitative approach was specifically designed for explaining subsistence economies, even though it was clearly inspired by the Eurocentric theories quoted above. Siddle attempted to explain rural settlement patterns in Sierra Leone (1970), an area of densely nucleated settlements. His assumptions were based on central place theory and on steady expansion within a unidirectional process.

In this model, a sequence of settlement processes is postulated. First, in the early subsistence stages, colonization is constrained by social and economic behavior. Whenever possible, natural increases in population are accommodated by establishing new colonies. Since the allocation of land is always regulated by the elders of the parent settlement, and since social ties remain strong between parent and colony, the second and the subsequent settlements are established at a point of equilibrium between the two competing sets of needs: economic space for subsistence and social proximity for interaction.

This "planned" radial process results in the formation of concentric circles of progressively younger settlements. The final outcome would be as follows: the growth of a series of evenly spaced colonies around a parent village, having a regular, hexagonal pattern, and following the Christaller k=7 administrative principle. Such an explanation seemed to fit the patterns of regularity revealed by nearest neighbor analysis (Siddle 1970). This orderly pattern could be disrupted, as when increasing population growth could not be readily accommodated but instead led to competition and warfare. This situation could, in turn, lead to defensive clustering. Similarly, increasing trade could encourage the development of a more linear pattern.

The way to verify Siddle's hypotheses is by collecting historical, empirical evidence on the nature of settlement change. Accurate data are rarely available, since even archeological records remain difficult to obtain. However, studies based on oral records, supplemented by intelligence reports from the early twentieth century, can provide some useful clues on this subject. Empirical work by Anglophone geographers, for example, reveals an awareness of African settlement fluidity. One of these researchers drew attention to the social roots of dispersed settlement in Ghana (Hunter, 1967). Others, working in Nigeria, established the relationship between increasing security during British rule and plateau settlements moving down onto the plains and assuming a more dispersed pattern (Gleave 1963).

On the basis of court records and oral information, Grossman (1971) reconstructed at least some of these processes in the northern Ibo area (southeastern Nigeria). His studies tend to confirm that the elders played a leading role in shaping the spatial pattern. They also confirm that warfare and violent activities, prior to the twentieth century, increased the tendency to cluster. However, these clusters (villages), as single points, were often arranged in regular patterns on a regional scale. The crescent shaped distribution of the villages located along the frontier, was meant to provide a buffer for the core zone, which consisted of a dense agglomeration of several villages.

These protection-generated patterns actually resembled the arrangement of settlement that resulted from clan expansion in an area of poor sandy soils on Nigeria's Udi Plateau. The extension of the frontier in this case, was meant to take advantage of better soil resources and was thus based on economic and ecological criteria (Udo 1965; Grossman 1971). It closely approximated the conditions postulated by Siddle's Sierra Leone example, since it was motivated by population pressure in a near subsistence economy. It also confirmed Siddle's hypothesis that social considerations and the elders' "planning" shaped the spatial expansion. However, the actual pattern was not hexagonal because of constraints related to landscape and soil conditions. Thus, while some patterns had a crescent shape, others were distinctly linear. In all cases, strips of farmland were carefully apportioned to each of the extended families in accordance with their land rights in the core zone.

This chapter has demonstrated, however, that it is difficult to reconstruct the process by analyzing a pattern that may be generated in several ways. It may originate in economic pressure under certain resource constraints but it may also be the result of security needs, as in the case of military posts whose role is to absorb an initial attack. It is likely that in the latter case, the pattern will be altered during peaceful periods when a new process will lead to dispersal. However, this process may, in turn, be halted by modernization or another exogenous factor or by a renewed period of uncertainty that reestablishes the original pattern, as discussed in Chapter 4 in this volume. Slave raiding or drought can also influence the evolution of settlements, as can the local cultural context. In the Kano area of Nigeria, for example, the Hausa Moslems live in villages, whereas the non-Muslims prefer dispersed dwellings (Mortimore 1989: 35). This is, in part, a result of the value that Islam places on creating communities for Friday services and other group activities.

In spite of this complexity, the more theoretical literature has usually adopted a unidirectional approach. Morgan (1957) based part of his model on the Euro-centric concept of the "block field" system when he tried to explain the movement from dispersed settlements associated with fallow systems to permanently settled nucleated villages in the savanna of Eastern Nigeria. However, even though Morgan used terminology previously applied in medieval southern Germany, he has to be given credit for being quite aware of the cultural and ecological differences between Europe and tropical Africa. In the former, the "block fields" were associated with non-communally operated forest lands, whereas Morgan found that in Nigeria, they were associated with the communally cleared savanna areas. The Eastern Nigerian forests, on the other hand, were found to have dispersed settlements, presumably because of the difficulty of performing communal clearing activities there.

Parallels with Non-African Processes and Patterns

Dynamic settlement systems are not totally unique to Africa. At present they are confined mainly to developing countries, but past records reveal that there were parallel processes in some marginal areas in Europe, particularly in mountain or high latitude zones. The practice of establishing permanent offshoot villages in former seasonal settlements such as the Scandinavian bod, the Scottish crofter, or the Irish clachan, even in modern times, is well recorded (Grossman 1992: 28-44). This process is not inherently different from the tropical African system in which many seasonal shelters have become fixed settlements. One may argue that the various transhumant systems, based on two, three, or four seasonally occupied settlements having varying degrees of permanency, are not too unrelated to the cyclical African patterns which evolve under shifting cultivation or bush fallowing practices. The custom of establishing an offshoot settlement in the forest, still common in Scotland in the eighteenth century, can be considered as equivalent to some tropical African practices which extended the village frontier.

Examples of processes of dynamic settlement evolution in the present century are more frequent in developing countries, especially where, as in parts of tropical Africa, there is still some unutilized land for expanding the frontier. In rare cases, the processes can be traced back for several centuries through historical records and travellers' literature. An example can be found in the West Bank and in other parts of former Palestine. This area has many ancient, permanent villages, some of them, as testified by their Biblical names, at least 3,000 years old. Yet, parts of the area have experienced active Arab colonization or frontier expansion for much of the past hundred years.

The most outstanding area of settlement instability in Palestine was found to exist on the flanks of Mount Hebron where agricultural resources are marginal, either because of aridity of because of rockiness. Some of the settlements in these zones consisted of (and still consist of in some isolated areas) caves, ruins, or tents. These dwellings were initially used as temporary or seasonal shelters, but have eventually become permanent villages. Significantly, the process of settlement fixation is largely the result of modern influences which have triggered population growth, improved security, and upgraded the economy.

The availability of documented cases that point to the existence of dynamic settlement processes outside of Africa makes the African case less unique but it is still difficult to construct widely applicable models. One generalization does hold up: the dynamism of traditional rural processes is, in part, conditioned by the nature of the resource base. The more marginal the resources, the greater the tendency to impermanence. Mountain areas and arid zones are two notable examples.

Conclusion

The various models of African settlement, like the quantitative, process-pattern, theoretical models, tend to treat settlements as the outcome of unidirectional processes. If we accept the "demographic determinism" which is implied in the "Morgan-Boserup school," then the flexible, unfixed, and dispersed settlement pattern is an expression of low density and an early stage of development. It may also be indicative of a situation in which security has not yet become a threat, or, at least, can be dealt with without resorting to modifications of spatial structure. For Western Europe and the Middle East, the existence of this stage of settlement evolution is supported by many archaeological findings and historical sources (Grossman 1992). For tropical Africa the evidence is less accessible, but there are some clues as to the existence of such a sequence, some of which are presented in Chapter 3 of this volume. Given these assumptions, the culmination of settlement evolution would be nucleated villages. Morgan (1957) makes the strongest case for a gradual sequence from dispersed homesteads to a "mature" phase of grassland towns.

Yet, settlement sequence is Africa seems very prone to disruptions. Several chapters in this book demonstrate that the removal of a security threat, land scarcities, and/or the intrusion of the cash economy, can draw farmers out of their villages. Such developments may also be accompanied by changes in tenure arrangements. One pioneering study by Jones (1949) showed that increasing population density favored the individualization and increased value of land, which, in turn, encouraged farmers to move directly onto their holdings.

Another factor that has to be considered is the impact of urbanization on rural patterns. Although most African settlements are still classified as rural, the character of villages and homesteads has been modified by non-farm employment opportunities, increased outmigration, and proximity to urban places. However, the impact in these cases, does not occur in just one direction. In the emerging cities, many communities continue to retain rural characteristics as they interact with and influence rural places.

It can be said that there are two contradictory forces at work in Africa. In some ways, due to structural imbalances, African settlement are moving toward less spatially organized and defined patterns. Yet, there are forces at work which reinforce stability. The spread of the market economy combined with government interventions are creating conditions for more stable settlements. Building materials are changing from mud, wattle, and thatch to concrete and corrugated iron which leads to more permanent locations. Although there are still many places where past processes continue to operate, it is highly unlikely that settlements established in newly accessible areas, close to main routes and towns, will be abandoned. Modern African settlement patterns may eventually not be too different from those evolving in other parts of the world.

References

Bohannan, Paul. 1954. "Migration and Expansion of the Tiv." *Africa* 24: 21-16.

Boserup, Esther. 1965. *The Conditions of Agricultural Growth*. Chicago: Aldine.

Buchanan, L. and J. C. Pugh. 1955. *Land and People in Nigeria*. London: University of London Press.

Bylund, Eric. 1960. "Theoretical Considerations Regarding the Distribution of Settlement in Inner North Sweden." *Geografiska Annaler* 42B: 365-381.

Chisholm, Michael. 1979. *Rural Settlement and Land Use*. Third Edition. London: Hutchinson.

Christaller, Walter. 1933. *Central Places in Southern Germany*. Jena, Germany: Fischer. (Translated from German by C. W. Baskin. 1966. Englewood Cliffs, NJ: Prentice Hall).

Clarke, P. J. and F. C. Evans. 1954. "Distance to Nearest Neighbor as a Measure of Relationship in Population." *Ecology* 35: 445-453.

Coling, Jerome F. 1984. "A New Approach to the Geographical Study of Settlement Morphology for Rural Settings." *Tijdschrift voor Economische and Sociale Geografie* 75: 263-272.

Cowie, W. J. 1983. "Towards a Normative Concept of Settlements: The Development Process and Theoretical and Conceptual Problems in the Lower Limb." *Geoforum* 14: 55-73.

Dacey, Michael F. 1962. "Analysis of Central Place and Point Patterns by Nearest Neighbor Method." *Lund Series in Geography* 24B: 55-76.

Demangeon, A. 1927. "La Geografie de l'Habitat Rurale." *Annales de Geografie* 36: 5-17.

____. 1947. *Problemes de Geographie Humaine*. Third Edition. Paris: Colin.

Dunn, E. S. 1954. *The Location of Agricultural Production*. Gainesville: University of Florida Press.

Getis, Arthur. 1964. "Temporal Land Use Pattern Analysis with the Use of Nearest Neighbor and Quadrat Method." *Annals of the Association of American Geographers* 54: 391-399.

Gleave, M. B. 1973. "Dispersed and Nucleated Settlement in the Yorkshire Wolds 1770-1850." In D. R. Mills, ed. *English Rural Communities: The Impact of a Specialized Economy*. Pp. 98-115. London: Macmillan.

Grossman, David. 1971. "Do We Have a Theory for Settlement Geography?" *Professional Geographer* 23: 197-203.

____. 1981. "The Bunched Settlement Pattern: Western Samaria and the Hebron Mountains." *Transactions of the Institute of British Geographers, New Series* 6: 491-505.

____. 1982. "Northern Samaria: A Process-Pattern Analysis of Rural Settlement." *Canadian Geographer* 26: 110-127.

____. 1983. "Commentary on 'Describing and Modelling Rural Settlement Maps' by Robert Haining." *Annals of the Association of American Geographers* 73: 298-300.

_____. 1992. *Rural Process-Pattern Relationships: Nomadization, Sedentarization, and Settlement Fixation.* New York: Praeger.

Haggett, Peter. 1965. *Location Analysis in Human Geography.* London: Arnold.

Haining, Robert. 1982. "Describing and Modelling Rural Settlement Maps." *Annals of the Association of American Geographers* 72: 211-223.

Hart, John F. 1993. "Rural Change in a Comparative Perspective." *Geography Research Forum* 13: 153-155.

Houston, J. M. 1953. *A Social Geography of Europe.* London: Hutchinson.

Hudson, John C. 1969. "A Location Theory for Rural Settlement." *Annals of the Association of American Geographers* 59: 365-381.

Hunter, John M. 1967. "The Social Roots of Dispersed Settlement in Northern Ghana." *Annals of the Association of American Geographers* 57: 338-349.

Jones, G. I. 1949. "Ibo Land Tenure." *Africa* 19: 309-323.

Lefevre, T. 1934. "L'Habitat Rural dans ses Rapports avec le Millieu Physique et Humaine." In *Comptes Rendus du Congres International de Geographie.* Pp. 269-272. Tome 3. Paris: Colin.

Losch, A. 1940. *The Economics of Location.* Jena, Germany: Fischer. (Translated from the German by W. H. Woglom. 1954. New Haven: Yale University Press).

Meitzen, A. 1895. *Seidlung und Agrarwesen der Westgermanen und Ostgermanen der Kelten, der Raemern, der Finnen und der Salven.* Berlin: Herz.

Morgan, W. B. 1957. "The Grassland Towns of the Eastern Region of Nigeria." *Transactions of the Institute of British Geographers* 23: 213-224.

_____. 1983. *Nigeria.* London: Longmans.

Mortimore, Michael. 1989. *Adapting to Drought.* Cambridge: Cambridge University Press.

Olsson, G. 1968. "Complementary Models: A Study of Colonization Maps." *Geografiska Annaler* 50B: 115-132.

Roberts, B. K. 1977. *Rural Settlement in Britain.* Folkstone, U.K.: Archon Books.

_____. 1982. *Village Plans.* Aylesbury, U.K.: Shire Publications.

_____. 1996. *Landscapes of Settlement.* London: Routledge.

Siddle, David J. 1968. "War Towns in Sierra Leone: A Study in Social Change." *Africa* 38: 47-56.

_____. 1970. "Location Theory and the Subsistence Economy: The Spacing of Rural Settlements in Sierra Leone." *Journal of Tropical Geography* 31: 79-90.

Silberfein, Marilyn. 1989. "Settlement Form and Rural Development: Scattered Versus Clustered Settlement." *Tijdschrift voor Economische en Sociale Geografie* 80: 258-26

Singh, K. N. 1968. "The Territorial Basis of Medieval Town and Village Settlement in Eastern Uttar Pradesh." *Annals of the Association of American Geographers* 58: 203-220.

Singh, K. N. and R.P.B. Singh 1975. "Some Methodological Components of Rural Settlement Research." In R. L. Singh and K. N. Singh, eds. *Readings in Rural Settlement Geography.* Pp. 26-40. Varanesi: National Geographic Society of India.

Singh, K. N. and R.P.B. Singh. 1976. "The Mechanism of Socio-Temporal Diffusion of a Clan-Settlement in a Part of the Middle Ganga Valley: Some Comparisons and Correlates." In R. L. Singh, K. N. Singh, and R.P.B. Singh, eds. *Geographical Dimensions of Rural Settlement.* Pp. 19-32. Varanesi: National Geographical   Association of India.

Smith, C. T. 1978. *An Historical Geography of Europe Before 1800.*   London: Longmans.

Stone, Kirk. 1965. "The Development of a Focus for Settlement Geography." *Economic Geography* 41: 346-355.

Udo, Ruben. 1965 "Disintegration of Nucleated Settlements in Eastern Nigeria." *Geographical Review* 55: 53-67.

Von Thunen, J. H. 1826. *Der Isolierte Staat.* Berlin: Rostock.

PART TWO

The Historical Perspective

3

The Origins of African Rural Settlement

James L. Newman

For much of this century, questions about cultural origins found an avid audience among American geographers and anthropologists, but today such interests have been superseded. Contemporary concerns are likely to be framed in a planning context or by critical social theories that run a gamut from traditional Marxism to feminism to postmodernism. The quest for cultural origins, however, has values beyond antiquarian interests and should not be left unattended by those engaged in social research. Rather, such a quest improves the chances of identifying the human needs and behaviors that have shaped present institutional edifices and whatever may be wrong with them. Moreover, directions of change—something easily blurred in efforts focused on the here and now—become more apparent, and these are crucial to the formulation of both meaningful critiques and problem-solving initiatives.

The matter of origins would seem to be particularly relevant to a study of the many relationships between settlement patterns and rural development since the settlements we inhabit today are all embedded in past experiences. They are the result of decisions taken about where and with whom to live in order to resolve two fundamental issues: how best to harness environmental resources and how to organize social life in advantageous ways.

Because Africa is the focus of this book, the search for settlement origins is based on a longer time-line than anywhere else in the world, starting with the experiences of our hominid forebearers. Their response to the needs of subsistence and security was to form small bands of adults and their offspring. Although the quest for food kept members on the move during daylight hours, each band apparently had favored sanctuaries where it assembled at night. These now barely discernible sites are called "living floors" by paleoanthropologists (Oliver 1991). From them it is possible to trace a direct line of descent to Stone Age semi-permanent camps, some of which may have evolved into the equivalent of home bases, to proto-villages, and then to full-scale agricultural villages.

More dispersed homestead-style living arrangements involving individual family units were a later development. They seem to have first appeared as the settlement norm in relatively undifferentiated sub-humid and semi-arid environments in which livestock, especially cattle, had become economically and socially important. A concurrent shift to social systems centered on patrilineal decent and patrilocal residence was possibly the final ingredient that made dispersed homesteads, as opposed to villages, a viable settlement option.

From Living Floors to Home Bases

Research findings in molecular biology indicate that our hominid lineage is about five million years old (Sibley and Ahlquist 1984). Although verifiable skeletal remains from this time have yet to be unearthed, the first members must have been very similar to the australopithecines that date from less than one million years later. Living about four million years ago, the variety called Australopithecus anamensis is now considered the oldest, but far more is known about its likely descendant, Australopithicus afarensis (Leakey et al. 1995).

A. afarensis was quite small, averaging only slightly above a meter in height and weighing about thirty kilograms. Its brain was no more than a few cubic centimeters larger than those of apes, both ancient and modern (Lambert and the Diagram Group 1987). As a means of compensating for the lack of any notable physical attributes, members of this species banded together for protection, perhaps in troops similar to those seen among chimpanzees. This behavior must have been the key to survival. Chimpanzee troops serve primarily defense and reproductive purposes, but it appears that A. afarensis may also have formed groups for the purpose of food-sharing (Schick and Toth 1993). If so, food-sharing would constitute the first distinctively human act and complement the first truly human anatomical feature of bipedalism. Many different reasons have been offered for the emergence of upright posture, but one of the most convincing is as follows: It allows individuals to forage over long distances and then carry food back to a designated site where it can be shared with others (Leakey and Lewin 1992).

This interpretation provides some insight into why the australopithecines emerged when and where they did. By five million years ago, eastern Africa had become a patchwork of forests, woodlands, and more open habitats, and a species able to move easily between them would have gained a competitive advantage over less mobile ones. In particular, band members could harvest what open country offered by day, and then retreat within the greater security of the forests to eat with others and sleep, probably in trees, at night. Still, a lengthy stay at any particular site would have meant the likelihood of attracting dangerous predators, such as hyenas and big cats, and, therefore, bands kept their stays short. Nevertheless, a few of the places where they congregated for lengthier periods have been preserved for the archeological record. These living floors confirm a grouping tendency at the heart of the human settlement experience.

The onset of the Stone Age some 2.5 million years ago marks the evolutionary arrival of Homo populations. The living floors of the first representative, Homo habilis, are distinguishable from those of A. afarensis, and all later australopithecines, only by the presence of stone tools and their associated debris. There is no indication of any extended period of habitation, although raw materials for making tools may have been cached at favored sites that were regularly revisited (Potts 1984).

In contrast, the transition to Homo erectus and then to Homo sapiens brings with it evidence of living floors that were occupied longer and which might qualify as temporary camps (Klein 1989). The harnessing of fire at a date and place that is still being debated, was probably the crucial event that made this possible. Fires allowed caves and rock shelters to be occupied, while in relatively open country, a night blaze could help keep predators at bay. The build-up of wastes and seasonal changes in food availability eventually made moves necessary, but stays at the same place for at least several months' duration became feasible.

Later, as these camps evolved, they gradually became complete home bases where such social events as finding mates and exchanging information took place (Isaac 1978). Home might be temporary, but it was home—a place where everyone in the group came together in comfort and with reasonable security.

In general, population sizes for the living floors cum camps seem to have been in the thirty to fifty range, which accords with the general totals recorded for surviving gatherer-hunter groups (Lee and DeVore 1968). If we can use such survivors as analogies, most camps would have consisted of several different family units, perhaps those of brothers and/or sisters, the exact composition probably changing rather frequently due to deaths, marriages, and personal preferences. Given prevailing technological limitations, even toward the close of the Stone Age, it is highly unlikely that individuals or even individual families could have survived on their own for very long. Everyone had to belong to a camp, and therefore it seems reasonable to define the groupings, whatever one wishes to call them, as villages-in-the-making.

For several million years there was little change in where African gatherer-hunters lived. They continued to be concentrated in more open country where game was abundant and the seasons produced a varying array of fruits, nuts, pods, and tubers to complement the diet. Some occupancy of denser woodlands and tropical rain forests may have taken place by 50,000 or so years ago, but the relative paucity of readily obtainable plant and animal foods made such habitats far less desirable than open country. Choosing a specific site at which to locate a camp meant balancing the need for security against that of proximity to water, a resource which could never be too far away. Access to land for foraging was also necessary, a factor that kept camps widely spaced except during more bountiful times of the year. The resulting population densities seldom amounted to more than one person per ten km².

The First Villages

The first truly significant settlement transformations occurred at various riparian sites, with Wadi Kubbaniya in Upper Egypt, just north of Aswan, being by far the oldest so far on record (Figure 3.1). Dated to about 18,000 years ago, excavations have revealed the presence of a highly intensified broad spectrum form of gathering, fishing, and hunting capable of supporting a comparatively large population, which may even have been resident year round (Hillman 1989). The times were hyperarid and we can envision people within and around the Sahara being progressively confined to the few productive places, e.g, Wadi Kubbaniya, that could still be found.

Archeology is quiet for approximately 8000 years, but the more sedentary settlement arrangement must have been becoming increasingly common. Beginning about 10,000 years ago, it can be observed at a number of sites, not only along the Nile, but in eastern Africa and across what is now the sahel and the southern margins of the Sahara desert (Sutton 1974; McIntosh and McIntosh 1981). A pluvial period had begun, leading to larger and more numerous lakes, swamps, and rivers. Lake Chad, for example, was many times its current size, as were the rift valley lakes of Nakuru and Elmenteita, which also contained much fresher water than they do at present. The rich fish and other aquatic food resources, including numerous roots and grasses, combined with an array of technological innovations—such as bone harpoons, hooks, grinding tools, basketry, and pottery—to support growing and increasingly sedentary populations. Ishango on Lake Edward and Old Khartoum appear to have been occupied for considerable lengths of time, at least on a seasonal basis, while the Kom Ombo complex near Aswan may represent the remains of several permanent villages (Phillipson 1993) (Figure 3.1).

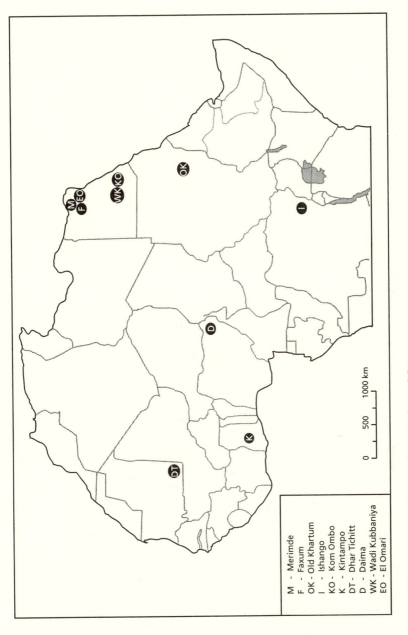

FIGURE 3.1 Location Map of Archeological Sites

M - Merimde
F   - Faxum
OK - Old Khartum
I   - Ishango
KO - Kom Ombo
K   - Kintampo
DT - Dhar Tichitt
D - Daima
WK - Wadi Kubbaniya
EO - El Omari

Along the Nile in Egypt, these riparian-oriented communities moved quickly into agriculture, with the first confirmed sites dated to about 7000 years ago in the Fayum depression. Local crops included barley, einkorn wheat, chickpeas, lentils, and flax complemented by tending cattle, sheep, goats, and pigs, and there is little doubt that this complex had come from sources in southwestern Asia. Its adoption only served to reinforce pre-existing settlement tendencies, as is evidenced by the fully sedentary farming villages at Merimde astride the Nile delta and at El Omari near present day Cairo by 5500 years ago (Figure 3.1). Within a few centuries numerous other villages made their appearance, prefiguring the Egypt of the Pharaohs (Trigger et al. 1983).

Elsewhere on the continent, events moved more slowly and with less uniformity. Around 8000 years ago, the climate had become drier again, but a thousand years later another wet phase ensued that replenished lakes, swamps, and streams. Although archeology has yet to uncover the necessary confirming evidence, findings from paleobotany and historical linguistics suggest that crop domestication was taking place across a broad zone from the Ethiopian highlands to the upper reaches of the Niger River. Included were sorghums, pearl or bulrush millet, African rice, fonio, eleusine, and teff among the grains and yams and ensete among vegetatively propagated species (Harlan 1971). Only further research will tell whether or not events had gone far enough to warrant a claim that full-fledged agriculture was being practiced at this time. However, it does seem fairly certain that a nomadic herding economy based on cattle, sheep, and goats had come into being within and around the Sahara. The evidence is in the form of animal bones, cultural remains, and rock art that come from the Khartoum area and the highlands of Dar Fur, Tibesti, Air, and Ahaggar (Williams 1984).

Around 4000 years ago, dry climatic conditions returned, leading to the pattern of desert, sahel, and savanna we are familiar with today. Under the press of a deteriorating environment, nomads began exiting the Saharan region. Although we cannot say that the combination of their arrival and increasing aridity served as the proximate causes, the first proven agricultural sites in Africa south of the Sahara date from shortly after this period.

The earliest such site is Dhar Tichitt in what is now southern Mauritania. This settlement started out as a series of lake-side fishing villages. Domesticated livestock were added to the subsistence inventory around 3500 years ago to be followed by the cultivation of pearl millet. Crop and livestock production was accompanied by an increase in the number of villages and the relocation of the villages from the lake basin onto an adjacent escarpment. The surrounding masonry walls suggest that the site changes reflected defensive concerns, not now centered on wild animals but rather on other humans. The threats could have come from sedentary populations or from invading nomads, who, along with the still intensifying aridity, brought an end to Dhar Tichitt's agrarian developments around 2500 years ago (Munson 1976).

A quite similar sequence of events can be documented near Lake Chad. Excavations of earthen mounds along the western side of the lake at Daima, have revealed the presence of a mixed economy involving fishing, hunting, gathering, herding, and cultivation, this time mainly of sorghums, by at least 2500 years ago (Connah 1981). Here, too, society had organized itself into villages, which ranged in size from 100 to 500 inhabitants, depending on their location. The larger ones have been found on fairly productive clay plains and apparently were occupied for many years, whereas the smaller ones were sited on lower fertility sandy soils and show less permanence.

A third area extends along the tropical rain forest/ savanna boundary from central Ghana to adjacent portions of the Ivory Coast and Togo. Under the eponym of Kintampo, it consists of a series of villages that bear considerable resemblance to contemporary ones, including the possibility of having quarters set aside for craft specialists such as potters and knappers (Figure 3.1). The earliest sites date from around 3800 years ago, and the largest so far excavated measures over 20,000 m2. Yam cultivation may have been practiced, although only cowpeas and dwarf (n'dama) cattle and goats have been positively identified (Flight 1976; Andah and Anquandah 1988).

The agricultural village thus seems to be a direct descendent of Stone Age living floors and camps—with the only real difference being one of size, as related to the change in subsistence from gathering, hunting, and fishing to agriculture. The alternative settlement type, which was later to become widespread in Africa, was the dispersed homestead consisting of several houses occupied by a man and his wife or wives and the families of their married sons (Figure 1.1). Surrounding the homestead, or only a short distance away, were its fields. In some areas, population growth gradually filled up much of the intervening space between the fields of individual homesteads but, initially, areas of uncultivated land, either virgin or in some stage of regrowth, tended to separate homestead units from each other.

The Conditions of Homestead Formation

Precisely when, where, and, more importantly, why homesteads first became the preferred settlement type remain mysteries that will probably never be totally solved. Nevertheless, I would like to offer a plausible scenario as a spur to further inquiry. It consists of three inter-related factors: (1) livestock, especially cattle, assuming a crucial role in the subsistence economy; (2) occupancy of relatively low potential agricultural environments having little internal variation in available resources; and (3) the adoption of a social system involving patrilineal decent and patrilocal residence.

We can begin by looking at the role played by cattle. Livestock became important to the farm economy wherever diseases, especially trypanosomiasis, posed little or no threat to their survival (Forde 1971). There was, however, considerable variability in terms of how important cattle would ultimately become to people's subsistence strategies. Although an early arrival throughout much of western Africa, cattle keeping was usually a subsidiary activity when compared first to gathering and fishing and later to crop cultivation. Owning cattle definitely accrued advantages to their owners, but farmers could survive reasonably well without them. In addition, as the Fulbe illustrate, tending livestock often became a specialist occupation (Stenning 1957). By developing what amounted to symbiotic exchange relationships with herders, many farmers could gain access to animal products without actually owning any. Alternatively, wealthy farmers could hire Fulbe or others to look after their herds.

The role of cattle became more important in Africa, however, as a result of environmental factors in areas of new settlement. As farmers expanded their range across the vast interior plateaus of the continent, they often found themselves working inherently low fertility soils derived from the ancient Gondwanaland crystalline shield. Furthermore, many of these same areas were also characterized by sub-humid to semi-arid climates, which led to highly uncertain crop yields. Occasionally harvests failed completely because of severe drought. Under such circum- stances, cattle provided a way for farmers to significantly broaden their subsistence options. While women cultivated, men herded. Cattle not only supplied milk and meat to the diet, they also allowed networks of dependency and obligation to be built through loan and marriage exchange. Indeed, the prominence of cattle within many African communities led Herskovits (1930) and others to identify them as the veritable centerpieces of culture and society.

Although much the same soil and climatic conditions prevailed in the sudan and sahel of western Africa, their impacts were mitigated by the possibilities of irrigation, particularly along the Niger River and its tributaries and within the Lake Chad basin. Furthermore, the associated alluvial and lacustrine soils possessed much greater natural fertility than

those on the interfluves. And, as we have seen, it was precisely these relatively rich sites that supported early villagized populations. But in less
advantageous circumstances, where agriculture was more uniform and
cattle-keeping important, villages did not constitute the most viable settlement option. At least two reasons can be given as to why this would
have been the case: (1) the potential for quickly exhausting nearby
sources of feed, thus leading to ever longer journeys to find new sources,
and (2) the inadequacy of most watering sites to support repeated visits
by large numbers of animals. Under such constraints, dispersed homesteads served as the more environmentally sensitive option.

There was, however, still one further requirement that needed to be
in place, namely a social system incorporating patrilineal decent and
inheritance rules and patrilocal residence. This combination appears to
be an almost "natural" accompaniment to livestock oriented economies,
and, indeed, the origins of patrilineality may well be found in the initial
appearance of pastoralism some 10,000 years ago (Quale 1988). A likely
explanation for this is the new division of labor in which men, as the
herders, found themselves in possession of the first really significant
means for accumulating wealth and its inevitable outcome, power. As a
result they were in a position to skew social relationships in their favor
by transferring livestock directly to sons (Reed 1975). The male lineage
had acquired the means for achieving dominance over the female one,
and among farming peoples, this usually meant the replacement of older
matrilineal or bilateral decent systems with those emphasizing patrilineal
ties.

Patrilineality, in turn, produced patrilocality, which proved to be a
possible factor in encouraging dispersed homestead formation. It served
to create a pool of adult males who could meet day-to-day labor and
defense needs, and each of these males had a vested interest in the overall well-being of the family. It was thus feasible for men to spread out
across the landscape, although extended family ties were sometimes
strong enough to ensure that the village structure remained intact.

In contrast, under a system of matrilineality/matrilocality, the number
of adult males within a household depended on the marriage of its
daughters, and, in addition, each man's primary loyalties lay with his
own matrilineage and not with that of his wife. By incorporating several matrilineages, villages resolved the adult male numbers dilemma, but
matrilocality would have made any attempt at residing in dispersed
homesteads a high risk venture.

Is there more than just speculation and inference to support this scenario? One promising place to look is among the Central Sudanic-speak-
ing peoples who inhabit the open woodland and savanna country of the

Central African Republic, southern Chad, and southwestern Sudan. Previously riparian-type gatherer-hunter-fisher folk, they appear to have abandoned their proto-villages for patrilineally/patrilocally structured homesteads as they made the shift some 4000 years ago to an agricultural economy featuring cattle (Ehret et al. 1974). However, archeological, ethnographic, and linguistic data are in short supply, and thus little more can be said.

Fortunately, another and better documented example exists, that of the Bantu. When their ancestors set out some 5000 years ago on the migrations that took them from an initial homeland in the vicinity of the Cross River valley near the present day border of Nigeria and Cameroon they subsisted by gathering, hunting, fishing, and cultivating yams while living in matrilineal/matrilocal villages (Vansina 1990). Those who moved southward into the equatorial rain forest—and then beyond through the vast expanse of dry brachystegia (miombo) woodlands—retained this basic form of settlement organization. If, at the outset, their ancestors had kept cattle, they would have been of marginal importance, but, in any event, the knowledge of doing so was lost because of the prevalence of trypanosomiasis and other livestock diseases in both habitats.

The Bantu who followed more easterly paths developed different socio-economic systems. Leaving heavily wooded and forested country behind, they entered the relatively tsetse-free savannas of the interlacustrine region west of Lake Victoria about 2500 years ago. Here they encountered other farmers who were probably of Central Sudanic affiliation (Ehret et al. 1974), For unknown reasons, Bantu identity prevailed, and from this new core, migrations fanned out both east and south (Oliver and Fagan 1978).

Except for certain locales, especially the highlands, such as the slopes of Mounts Kenya and Kilimanjaro, the migrants entered the kinds of plateau environments described earlier, but at the outset cattle do not seem to have been very important. Hunting, and in some instances fishing, supplemented cropping and pre-existing matrilineal/matrilocal traditions continued in force. This all began to change with the advent of the so-called New Iron Age some 1000 years ago. An important accompaniment was an increasing emphasis on cattle keeping, and with it came a shift to social systems built on patrilineality and patrilocality that was still in progress when the first ethnologists appeared on the scene earlier this century.

Elsewhere, conditions continued to favor villages. In fact, during the eighteenth and nineteenth centuries, villages appeared in areas of dispersed homesteads, primarily in response to the needs of defense. The following chapter will discuss at greater length, the types of violence that led to the emergence of large villages. Certainly, highly violent times and the presence of warriors, helps account for the huge villages of the Tswana and the kraals of the Zulu. In eastern and central Africa, the slave trade prompted the formation of numerous stockaded villages since anyone living in a homestead could be captured relatively easily.

Colonialism brought an end to warfare and the slave trade, and thus homestead living once again became possible. But it also brought something else that has made dispersal more likely—new ways of earning wealth. Land took on increased value, and labor could be sold for cash, a phenonemon which favored patrilocality and weakened the forces holding people together in villages.

References

Andah, B. W. and J. Anquandah. 1988. "The Guinea Belt: The Peoples Between Mount Cameroon and the Ivory Coast." In M. El Fasi, ed. *General History of Africa* III. Pp. 488-529. Berkeley: University of California Press.

Connah, G. 1981. *Three Thousand Years in Africa*. Cambridge: Cambridge University Press.

Ehret, C., T. Coffman, L. Fleigelman, A. Gold, M. Hubbard, D. Johnson, and D. Saxon. 1974. "Some Thoughts on the Early History of the Nile-Congo Watershed." *Ufahamu* 5: 85-112.

Flight, C. 1976. "The Kintampo Culture and Its Place in the Economic Prehistory of West Africa." In J. R. Harlan, J. M. J. DeWet, and A.B.L. Stemmler, eds. *Origins of African Plant Domestication*. Pp. 211-221. The Hague: Mouton.

Forde, J. 1971. *The Role of Trypanosomiases in African Ecology*. Oxford: Oxford University Press.

Harlan, J. R. 1971."Agricultural Origins: Centers and Non-Centers." *Science* 174: 468-474.

Herskovits, M. J. 1930. "The Culture Areas of Africa." *Africa* 3: 59-77.

Hillman, G. C. 1989. "Late Palaeolithic Plant Foods from Wadi Kubbaniya in Upper Egypt: Dietary Diversity, Infant Weaning, and Seasonality in a Riverine Environment." In D. R. Harris and G. C. Hillman, eds. *Foraging and Farming: The Evolution of Plant Exploitation*. Pp. 207-239. London: Unwin Hyman.

Isaac, G. L. 1978. "The Food-Sharing Behavior of Protohuman Hominids." *Scientific American* 238, 4: 90-99.

Klein, R. G. 1989. *The Human Career: Human Biological and Cultural Origins*. Chicago: University of Chicago Press.

Lambert, D. and the Diagram Group. 1987. *The Field Guide to Early Man*. New York: Facts on File Publications.

Leakey, M. G., C. S. Feibel, I. McDougall, and A. Walker. 1995. "New Four-Million-Year-Old Hominid Species from Kanapoi and Alia Bay, Kenya." *Nature* 376, 17: 565-571.

Leakey, R. E. and R. Lewin. 1992. *Origins Reconsidered*. New York: Doubleday

Lee, R. B. and I. DeVore, eds. 1968. *Man the Hunter*. Chicago: Aldine.

McIntosh, S. K. and R. J. McIntosh. 1981. "West African Prehistory." *American Scientist* 69: 602-613.

Munson, P. J. 1976. "Archaeological Data on the Origins of Cultivation in the Southwestern Sahara and their Implications for West Africa." In J. R. Harlan, J.M.J. DeWet, and A.B.L. Stemmler, eds. *Origins of African Plant Domestication*. Pp. 187-210. The Hague: Mouton.

Oliver, R. and B. M. Fagan. 1978. "The Emergence of Bantu Africa." In B. M. Fagan, ed. *The Cambridge History of Africa from c. 500 BC to AD 1050. Volume II*. Pp. 342-409. Cambridge: Cambridge University Press.

Oliver, R. 1991. *The African Experience*. New York: Harper Collins.

Phillipson, D. W. 1993. *African Archeology*. 2nd. ed. Cambridge: Cambridge University Press.

Potts, R. 1984. "Home Bases and Early Hominids." *American Scientist* 72: 338-347.

Quale, G. R. 1988. *A History of Marriage Systems*. New York: Greenwood Press.

Reed, E. 1975. *Woman's Evolution: from Matriarchal Clan to Patriarchal Family*. New York: Pathfinder Press.

Schick, K. D. and N. Toth. 1993. *Making Silent Stones Speak*. New York: Simon and Schuster.

Sibley, C. G. and J. E. Ahlquist. 1984. "The Phylogeny of the Hominoid Primates, as Indicated by DNA-DNA Hybridization. *Journal of Molecular Biology* 20: 2-15.

Stenning, D. J. 1957. "Transhumance, Migratory Drift, Migration: Patterns of Pastoral Fulani Nomadism." *Journal of the Royal Anthropological Institute* 87: 57-73.

Sutton, J.E.G. 1974. "The Aquatic Civilization of Middle Africa." *Journal of African History* 15: 527-546.

Trigger, B. G., B. J. Kemp, D. O'Connor, and A. A. Lloyd. 1983. *Ancient Egypt: A Social History*. Cambridge: Cambridge University Press.

Vansina, J. 1990. *Paths in the Rainforest*. Madison: University of Wisconsin Press.

Williams, M.A.J. 1984. "Late Quaternary Prehistoric Environments in the Sudan," In J. D. Clark and S. A, Brandt, eds. *From Hunters to Farmers*. Berkeley: University of California Press.

4

Cyclical Change in African Settlement and Modern Resettlement Programs

Marilyn Silberfein

Rural Africans have always used mobility as part of their strategy for survival. A range of problems can be dealt with by relocation: population growth, prolonged periods of low rainfall, and even the resolution or avoidance of conflict. One result of this high level of mobility has been a flexible settlement system. African settlement structures have long been modified as circumstances changed, in contrast to many areas of the world where settlement patterns have been a relatively stable element in the rural landscape.

At the same time that individual farmers have viewed settlement structures as part of their mode of survival, governments, and sometimes kinship-based organizations, have treated them as one mechanism for increasing control of the countryside. Although pre-colonial settlements were manipulated by the ruling elites, this chapter will focus on the interventions that took place in the colonial and post-colonial periods.

The Cycles of Settlement Change

The previous chapter has shown how an initial tendency toward clustering may have been disrupted, with dispersed settlements coming to dominate the landscape in the absence of specific constraints. Dispersal allowed for easy access to fields and, in turn, facilitated protection of crops against pests, thorough cultivating and weeding, timely planting and harvesting, and a more complete knowledge of the qualities of a particular piece of land. It also enhanced access to supplies of wood and pasturage as well as wild fruits, seeds, honey, and herbal medicines.

Dispersed settlements also had some capacity to provide protection against aggression or wild game. Homesteads were usually surrounded by a thorn-branch or euphorbia hedge, which served to deter cattle stealing or wild animal incursions. Scattered farmers also guarded against a

threat of land or cattle confiscation through a series of secondary strata-
gems. The Makonde of southwest Tanzania became very widely dispersed in the deep thickets of their plateauland when threatened with
invasion and thus removed any significant targets (Liebenow 1971: 41).
In Northern Tanzania, the Chagga and Pare cooperated in building elaborate tunnel systems in which whole communities could hide in the event
of invasion; one such system extended a distance of fifty meters underground (Denyer 1978: 68).

Africans have perpetuated the dispersed pattern by moving out of
their hamlets, usually when intergenerational families have grown large
enough to threaten the production system or when soil or weed problems
caused a decrease in yields after a few seasons of cultivation. Yet, even
when dispersed homesteads dominated within a given area, some settlements of different types and sizes were invariably present. At any given
time, some members of a community might be residing in temporary
camps near a remote field, grazing area, or permanent water source while
others had relocated alongside a river or road to form a quasi-dispersed
linear settlement.

Under some circumstances, the sequence leading to clustering was
not disrupted and villages were formed. Concentrated resources such as
water holes and strong social or political cohesiveness could lead families
to stay close to each other. The residents of such an incipient village
would have to find the means to support themselves on the arable land
within daily walking distance; often this was accomplished by intensifying their production system. There are numerous examples of societies
that developed a labor intensive approach that allowed them to prosper
in villages (Van Horn 1977; Vivian 1989: 110).

The most frequent rationale for clustering was insecurity, in circumstances ranging from frontier expansion to endemic warfare to threats
from wild animals and local thieves. The formation of villages for the
purpose of protection became fairly widespread during the nineteenth
century. Particularly important in this regard were the religious purifica-
tion movements (Jihads) that took place in West Africa, the expansion of
the Zulu-speaking people in east and south Africa (the Mfecane) and the
slave trade in east Africa.

If one traces changes from this period of endemic warfare (1800s) to
the present, it is possible to discern a cyclical pattern, alternating between
clustered and dispersed forms (Silberfein 1989). Many of the villages that
were formed during the conflicts of the first phase of the cycle broke up
with the peace imposed by colonialism. A dispersed pattern was reestablished as village walls were torn down and new homesteads were erected at some distance from one another. Exceptions included those areas

with strong indigenous governments or trading traditions, most of which were found in West Africa.

The colonial administrators initially reacted with indifference to the widespread movement out of villages. Gradually, however, they came to believe that a clustered rural population would be easier to measure, tax, conscript, and generally control. A new stage in the cycle began, usually early in the twentieth century, as colonial governments called for everyone in the countryside to reside in registered villages. Some of these clusters were located near the sites of old disintegrated villages, but the rural population was regrouped without much reference to kinship or even neighborhood relationships. As a result, there was a upsurge in social conflicts including witchcraft allegations.

Some of the best records of these two phases of the cycle, village break-up followed by reestablishment, were kept in Northern Rhodesia (Zambia). There are numerous reports from agents of the British South Africa Company who were amazed at the rapid movement out of villages once British authority had been established. Fearing that this process would undermine the role of the local chiefs, the agents finally tried to force the dispersing farmers back into villages. The results were often disastrous. The disruption caused by forced relocation, combined with sporadic efforts to modify local production systems, led to famines (Berry 1993: 37).

When the colonial government took over control of Northern Rhodesia, more modest efforts at villagization were implemented. Typically, everyone had to be registered as a resident of a village which could vary in size based on local conditions (Kay 1967). Once registration was complete, no relocation was supposed to be permitted, yet, within a few years, authorities were observing surreptitious movement out of these artificial entities. The sequence was predictable; initially a temporary home would appear beyond the village, followed by a more permanent structure.

Finally, by the 1920s, the government had stimulated the next phase in the cycle by modifying the settlement law and sanctioning the ongoing dispersal of the rural population. The policy change was gradual; first smaller settlement clusters were given official recognition, then the practice of identifying individuals by their location within a settlement was completely abandoned (Long 1968: 81). It had become clear that settlements established for primarily administrative purposes did not evolve into communities that were either socially cohesive or economically productive (Kay 1967: 19-20). There were some situations, however, as in the Belgian Congo, where centralized control was so tight that artificial villages continued to function in spite of social and production problems.

Colonial empires outside of Africa also created villages as a mechanism for controlling rural people, and these provide for some useful comparisons with the African situation. In Guatamala and southern Mexico, for example, the Spanish government grouped dispersed Mayan Indians together in villages that facilitated both administration and proselytizing. In Peru, a uniform design was developed for accomplishing the same purpose.

As they had done in Africa, peasants gradually moved out of newly created settlements and reestablished a more scattered arrangement. In the case of the Mayan villages, the process began within two generations of their founding, in part reflecting the tendency for officials to become less zealous in maintaining control. There were three mechanisms used by disaffected village residents: (1) escaping to areas that were not yet firmly in Spanish control, (2) moving to another town or village so as to avoid a current tax bill or labor requirement, and, (3) setting up a satellite settlement just beyond the edge of the official village (Farriss 1978: 203-204).

The relocation occurred in stages similar to those identified for African colonial villages. At first a family would set up a temporary shelter, usually returning to the home village on week-ends. Eventually, a more permanent house would be constructed at the new site and a complete transfer of people and possessions would take place. (Farriss 1978: 212). Within 150 years of the founding of the villages (usually by 1700), at least fifty percent of the population had deserted, although the authorities often continued to identify and map villages, even those that were no longer inhabited.

The Peruvian resettlement program caused similar problems, especially in areas where the old terraces and irrigation works had to be abandoned (Roberts 1996: 112). The new villages were often subject to floods, earthquakes, and the spread of disease which took a high toll of residents (Gade and Excobar 1982: 440). Records indicate that many officials recognized the need for farmers to be close to their land and they tacitly allowed outmigration to occur. Temporary satellite plots were occupied first, followed by more permanent relocation as farmers tried to protect their crops and cattle from thieves and pest damage (Gade and Escobar 1982: 441). In the 1800s, this movement accelerated, particularly in the areas where livestock became important. Yet, the formalization of title to land in the dispersed communities usually wasn't achieved until the 1920s.

In Africa, this type of dispersal continued into the early independence period. Families that had entered the cash economy wanted more of an opportunity to supervise their fields or expressed a desire to be free from control by traditional authorities (Grossman 1971). In some areas, such as Southeastern Nigeria, rural people who had lived in clusters for generations finally made the decision to relocate close to their fields.

Families with cattle dispersed out to better grazing areas while others located near improved supplies of firewood to provide for such needs as fuel and tobacco curing. Migrant farmers moving into new areas in search of decreasing supplies of arable land, as well as those who squatted illegally, also tended to reproduce a dispersed pattern (Bunce 1982: 133). These phenomena further corroborate Newman's ideas (Chapter 3) that cattle keeping and movement into areas of declining environmental quality are activities that are not conducive to agglomeration.

Villagization

While African farmers have spread out across the landscape as part of their adaptation to the environment, governments have used resettlement as a mechanism for the manipulation of rural people. Roberts discusses this phenomenon in terms of the the difference between the communality of assent, when people group together for their mutual benefit, and the communality of enforcement, when authorities cluster their subjects to enhance control (Roberts 1996:37). Many independent African states have now repeated this process, although the justification for the recent villagization efforts has been different than in the past.

Part of the new philosophical underpinning for resettlement is the proposition, discussed in Chapters 1-3, that villages represent the apex of an evolutionary process. Studies of settlement in several parts of the world do demonstrate a settlement sequence from farmstead to hamlet and then to village (Roberts 1985: 62), but this phenomenon is a limited basis for an interventionist policy. In much of Africa, the sequence has been interrupted too frequently--with the return of dispersed forms--for villages to be viewed as a culmination or sign of modernity. In fact, even in Europe it has become quite common for villages to disintegrate with technological change and in North America, dispersed farms have been the basis of farming since the colonial period.

Resettlement has also been justified in terms of improving conditions for economic growth or social cohesion. New villages are said to allow for the provision of services, inputs, and agricultural instruction, the formation of agricultural cooperatives or even communes, and the creation of economies of scale for mechanization and off-farm employment. Optimizing land uses (for example, putting residential areas on the poor land and crops and livestock on better quality land) and the promotion of conservation practices have also been put forth as part of the rationale

(Dewer et al. 1986: 152). The goal of greater control of the peasantry is usually not stated directly, as it runs counter to populist rhetoric. However, the authoritarian leadership in Rwanda (prior to 1994) did argue that a highly structured centralized government was required to maintain control over a dispersed rural population.

Resettlement has also been part of national spatial planning strategies, especially in countries that hope to achieve greater rural-urban and center-periphery equity. Yet, manipulating the settlement system and other forms of spatial restructuring, have often been used as substitutes for more difficult types of interventions such as land reform or the establishment of communal farms. Sometimes the modification of the settlement pattern is actually a mechanism for creating higher densities when the population is deemed to be too sparse as well as too scattered .

In general, expectations for spatial planning have been too high and results disappointing. Among the problems that have been encountered are the following: (1) the process is prone to standardization and to excessive bureaucratization, (2) spatial interventions tend to become politicized so that locational decisions don't represent the social or economic optimum, and (3) relatively few problems can be solved by spatial interventions alone (Dewer et al. 1986: 158-160).

In spite of a dearth of successful outcomes, spatial planning, particularly villagization, has frequently been undertaken in Africa. Overlapping the colonial and post colonial period are projects that range from security villages (such as Kenyan and Algerian villages built to isolate much of the rural population from anti-colonial insurrections), relocation schemes created in response to dam building (in independent Egypt and Ghana) and village projects introduced in many countries to stimulate agricultural development (See Figure 4.1 for place locations).

The rhetoric in favor of pulling people into clusters has reached all the way to the San people of Botswana. This is an unusual case since it involves a group of people who historically were not just dispersed into very small settlements, but were also nomadic gatherer-hunters, living in an extremely arid environment. Yet, the government has proposed bringing these people into new settlements that are large enough to support a range of services as well as employment opportunities. Several villages have actually been established, but income earning opportunities and water supplies are scarce and depression and alcoholism have been described as rampant (Daley 1996).

Another interesting example of villagization is a Zambian program that was part of the surge of development activities that followed independence in the late 1960s. By 1965, most rural Zambians were living in dispersed settlements but the government did not analyze the earlier,

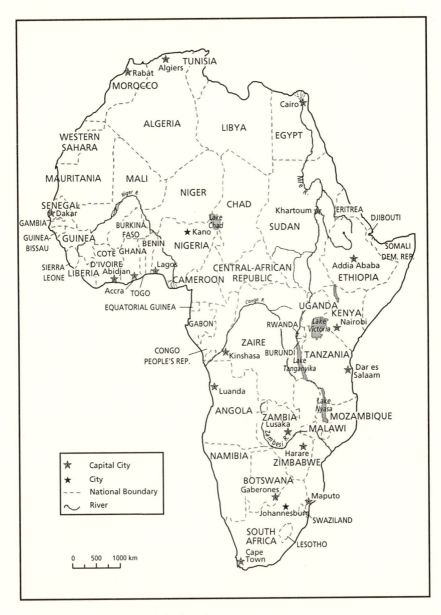

FIGURE 4.1 Political Map of Africa

unsuccessful colonial effort to stem the movement out of villages. Instead, officials took the position that productive activities and the delivery of services would be enhanced if people were regrouped into larger concentrations. The program included two approaches to achieving its goals. The more costly effort was based on designating a limited number of official village sites, and providing them with substantial assistance. At the same time, however, all dispersed farmers were encouraged to form "voluntary" villages on their own, in exchange for a government contribution of new services.

A large wave of exhortation swept across rural Zambia, as government and party officials pushed regroupment into larger settlements. The response was encouraging, in part because farmers with sufficient resources maintained both a homestead near their fields and a house in the largest accessible settlement. Yet, in spite of initial enthusiasm and flurry of activity, the regroupment strategy was abandoned by 1975. There are several reasons for this dramatic reversal:

1. Some farmers backed off of their original commitment when faced with the reality of leaving their established homes, field, burial sites, and even hunting grounds.
2. There were concerns about the soil quality and other physical attributes of the new location as well as the labor required to become established.
3. Many potential participants were aware that the provision of building material and services was behind schedule and that promised piped water or dispensaries might never be provided.
4. There was widespread fear of the negative attributes associated with village life: increased social conflict (including witchcraft) and loss of control over one's own productive activities (Bratton 1980: 172).

It is easy today to identify some of the mistakes of the Zambian regroupment program. The planning process was overcentralized; in spite of rhetoric to the contrary, few local communities were involved in choosing village sites. Promises of services were also unrealistic given limited resources, a situation that led to some serious problems. Dispersed farmers who regrouped and then did not receive piped water, for example, were worse-off then before relocating when they probably had access to a local water supply (Bratton 1980: 157). A very common and critical failing, and one that was also obvious in the San situation, was the lack of attention to increased productivity and improved income-earning potential as the ultimate goal of rural development.

These and other difficulties experienced in Zambia were to have their counterparts in resettlement problems in other parts of Africa. For example, the implementation of new villages often took place too rapidly and did not allow time for a thorough selection of sites or preparation of the population for change. Personnel might be dishonest or poorly trained or would interfere excessively in the lives of scheme members. Finally, a whole series of environmental and social problems could emerge as a result of imposing a new arrangement of people and farming activities on a prevailing system of settlement. Farmers in the villages were often too far from their fields, especially during periods of peak labor demand and resources such as firewood and grazing land came be in short supply.

The Zambian villagization program shared one attribute in particular with its counterparts in other African countries, at least those that began in the late 1960s: a strong development component with an emphasis on the provision of services to stimulate change. Yet, in other ways it was not typical. Most of the other large-scale programs shared two additional features: they were coupled with a call for communal farming as a mechanism for achieving socialism in the countryside (with the caveat that the transition to socialism could take place gradually), and they had at least an indirect association with defense against an internal security problem. All of these issues will be examined through several detailed examples of villagization programs on a state-wide scale.

Case Studies

Angola

When Portuguese rule in Angola was challenged by an independence movement between 1961 and 1975, villagization was used as a vehicle for controlling the rural population, isolating the guerilla movement, and encouraging development. Restructuring Angola's predominantly dispersed settlements was made easier by the colonial government's previous experience with creating rural concentrations as part of a sleeping sickness campaign.

The justification for the new program was familiar: villages would allow for the provision of medical, educational, agricultural, and other services and would improve rural productivity. In reality, a shortage of resources and personnel ensured that only a minority of villages were ever provided with water supplies, health centers, or other facilities. In 1971, more than fifty percent of all villages still lacked a primary school and even when schools were constructed, a teacher was not always available (Bender 1978: 173). Educators and other professionals were more likely to choose employment in established towns rather than in new villages that were often remote, makeshift, and lacking in amenities.

Although the process of creating villages varied from one region of Angola to another, a typical scenario involved rounding up dispersed farmers, screening them for guerilla sympathizers, and then preparing for relocation. When necessary, resistance was countered by the destruction of homesteads or by intimidation with guns and beatings. Resettlement took place in rapidly constructed "strategic hamlets" that were designed to isolate most of the rural population from the rebels. The hamlets were controlled by the military, and each was surrounded by a perimeter of barbed wire, bright searchlights, and guardposts (Roder 1973: 16).

In general, villages were distributed without much site analysis, resulting in predictable problems of land scarcity, poor soil, and inadequate grazing and water supplies. The settlements were supposed to be located along roads so as to enhance access by the military, but even this goal could not be achieved, and many villages were only reached by rutted dirt tracks that were seasonally inundated and subject to mining or guerilla attack.

In areas where the level of insurgency was low, the government initially refrained from forced resettlement. A few threatening guerilla attacks could undermine this resolve, however, and nervous officials would begin to collect reluctant farmers in hastily built security centers. In the less well endowed, sparsely populated areas, the creation of villages was particularly disruptive. In western Angola, for example, the resettlement program resulted in large areas being totally depopulated as up to seventy percent of the African rural residents were relocated. Sometimes movement into the villages meshed poorly with the growing season, and crops that were not yet harvested had to be left in the fields. This process made it more difficult for the guerillas to get food but it also undermined the survival system of marginal areas.

In the driest regions, where the dominant activity was herding, the government initially rejected the idea of fortified villages and allowed the pastoralists to remain in dispersed settlements (Niddre 1974: 72). Local officials later reversed themselves and ordered the construction of villages for the semi-nomadic population. The process resulted in the seizure of some land by Portuguese ranchers, an immediate economic decline within the African areas (grazing was inadequate near the villages), and an increase in anti-government activity (Bender 1978: 188-189).

By 1971, it is estimated that of a total African population of approximately 5,675,000 in Angola, about 1,500,000 were living in fortified rural hamlets. Life in these villages was hampered by restricted access to land, constant supervision, and the the ever-present threat of harassment (Roder 1973: 18). The villages were also associated with a drop in productivity and a loss of income due to the forced abandonment of animals, perennial crops, or land that had allowed for such specialized activities as riverain fish production. In extreme cases, settlers were not even permitted out of their village to farm and were forced to rely on sporadic food deliveries. Since shortages were common, families were motivated to escape just to ensure a reliable food supply (Roder 1973: 17).

The villages were also beset by health and social problems. Contagious diseases spread readily among people already weakened by malnutrition, while poor sanitary conditions encouraged gastro-intestinal infections. Centralized water supplies, once put forth as a positive feature of village life, were particularly subject to contamination. Crowding itself led to conflicts among unrelated people who had no tradition of living in contiguous houses.

All of the effort applied to resettlement was not sufficient to end the rebellion; in fact, support for the insurrection within the rural population increased. Yet, in spite of the negative experience of Portuguese resettlement, the civil war period that followed independence in 1975, saw a revival of similar practices. As two major organizations, the MPLA and UNITA, fought for control of Angola, manipulating the rural spatial structure became part of the overall strategy of each contender.

As soon as the MPLA was able to form a government, new villages were formed while old ones, colonial legacies, were prevented from breaking-up. These villages were viewed as both developmental, providing a setting for a more productive agriculture, and strategic, denying UNITA access to the uncommitted peasantry. They were also supposed to provide a setting for the emergence of communal farming systems, assuming the suppression of traditional farming methods as well as any residue of the free market system (Young 1988: 178-179). The MPLA did agree, however, that the shift to socialism should be gradual. Farmers could continue to cultivate their own plots, but they would also form associations that would be responsible for a collective field. Then, in time, the focus of the farmers' efforts was expected to shift to the group enterprise.

The government's ambitious goals were not realized; it proved impossible even to deliver material support, including hybrid seeds, fertilizers, and farm equipment. Nor could the government perform such basic tasks as purchasing output on designated days (Wolfers and Bergerol 1983: 142). Undaunted, officials continued to try to mobilize the peasantry, even making one effort near Luanda, in 1978, to forcibly villa gize urban migrants.

It wasn't until after food production fell to below fifty percent of national needs in the 1980s, that the government began to decentralize and decrease bureaucratic involvement in the rural sector. Gradually, market forces were allowed to return, plantations were reduced to family-sized farms, and resettlements were given less emphasis. This process was reinforced at the 1985 MPLA congress when the party secretary admitted that collectivization had been a mistake and agriculture was best left to individual peasant families.

As for the use of villages for strategic purposes, this phenomenon varied in importance during the course of the protracted Angolan civil war that continued into 1995 and may still be revived. The MPLA first tried to convince the opposition to join the government, but by 1977-1978 they had abandoned this approach and resumed the conflict. The MPLA's Cuban confederates continued to gather rural people into strategic settlements, especially in those locations where anti-government activities were likely to occur. Once again, though not on the scale of the Portuguese era, new villages were constructed adjacent to military installations (Bridgland 1984: 277). These entities were called by a new euphemism: "protected villages". Settlements were also constructed by UNITA, allegedly to provide protection and services to the rural population under their control, but they were very much like their MPLA counterparts (Heywood 1989: 60-61). The current movement toward a negotiated peace in Angola will probably curtail further village-building, but ongoing insecurity in the countryside will make it difficult to reoccupy many areas of the country with dispersed homesteads.

Mozambique

The situation in Mozambique has been very reminiscent of Angola to include a similar period of strategic villagization by the Portuguese. Both countries began the post-independence period with an emphasis on rural modernization and both embarked on a program that included both state farms and communal villages. The Mozambique government was probably more determined in pursuing these goals, even nationalizing all land resources and emphasizing the advantage of the state sector over the traditional sector.

The new villages were referred to as the "backbone of the country's rural development effort," integrating peasants and their local resources into the national economic system (Roesch 1984: 294). Moving the almost completely dispersed population of Mozambique into clusters was conceived of as the critical first step in stimulating communal farming and preventing exploitation in the countryside. According to a speech by President Samora Machel in 1975:

> The communal village is the political instrument which unites us and
> enables us to really exercise the power we have achieved--we must be
> very clear about this: we cannot exercise power in an unorganized or
> dispersed way" (Young 1988: 179).

In reality, both before and after independence, villages provided a mechanism for local control and for encouraging agricultural production for
urban and export needs (West and Myers 1996).

Convincing people to move into villages was to be accomplished by
a combination of exhortation and mobilization. Party members and government officials held sessions with "dynamizing groups" and publicized
the values of communal life (Isaacman 1983: 153-154). The government
offered to assist with loans or technical assistance and the village members, in turn, were to work together on improving local infrastructure,
schools, and clinics.

In one typical area that was subject to village promotion in the mid-
1970s (Baixo Limpopo), a few villages were founded during the first year,
but government efforts at surveying and recruiting could not stimulate
much local interest. By 1976-1977, only ten village-based agricultural
cooperatives had been formed with 100 members each, but these groups
were already retreating from their goals because of a lack of supplies and
insufficient technical expertise on the part of the members (Roesch 1984:
301).

The growth of the program would probably have continued at this
slow rate were it not for floods that disrupted farming in the area in 1977.
Over the following twelve months, all the farmers who had fled to higher ground were relocated into eighteen new villages. In other regions as
well, many of the new villages were settled by families uprooted by disasters. A few were also founded in matrilocal areas where men joined villages as part of a strategy to break the control of their wive's lineages.

In spite of the poor response, the following statement was made at
the third congress of the ruling party (Frelimo) in 1977:

> The villages permit a rapid growth in the revolutionary class conscious-
> ness in freeing the workers' immense creative capacity--the village
> should achieve self-sufficiency in food rapidly and also satisfy health
> and education and cultural needs and alleviate the pressure to migrate
> to cities (Isaacman 1983: 153).

The persistent civil war between the government's Frelimo party and its opposition, the MNR (Renamo), also caused dislocations that resulted in more villages being established. For instance, in southern Mozambique, villages were created to separate the rural population from the guerillas. In a particular irony, some of these war-zone villages were simply modifications, usually with additional fortifications, of the old Portuguese strategic hamlets.

There is considerable evidence that many of the settlements were established by force. Refugees leaving the country talked of houses being burned and the occupants being relocated at gunpoint (Young 1988: 182). The members of one new village claimed that they had been given two weeks to relocate and when they didn't comply, their homes were destroyed and they were forced to spend a cold night out-of-doors (Hanlon 1990: 129-130).

By 1978, problems in the villagization program were attracting attention from the international donor community. The FAO recommended that there be a moratorium on the creation of new settlements while past efforts were consolidated. Shortly thereafter, at a conference on spatial planning, a consultant confirmed the FAO position that resources were insufficient to carry out massive relocation. An alternative was advocated: district centers should be utilized to provide services while three model villages per district were created to show the advantages both of nucleation and cooperative production (Friedman 1980: 107). At this point, according to the consultant, the combination of service centers and mobile services would provide "a substantial margin for raising agricultural productivity (per unit of land) within the constraints of the existing dispersed settlement pattern" (Friedman 1980: 106).

In 1980 the government itself conducted a review of villages which acknowledged that the problems of isolation and lack of resources in the countryside had not been solved (Coquery-Vidrovitch 1988: 158). Within two years these reports and others had stimulated an increased level of government assistance to the approximately 1.5 million village dwellers (about fifteen percent of the population) (Roesch 1988: 76). The most advanced cooperatives (about forty-four) were provided with technical assistance while the remaining villages were aided by local authorities or state farms (Isaacman 1983: 157).

Shortly thereafter, it became clear that even these efforts were going to fall short. The familiar litany of excessive distance to fields, poor soil, and water scarcity were undermining the new production systems. Fertilizers, seeds, tractors, etc. did not arrive when expected and marketing remained so serious a constraint that spoilage of produce was widespread. At the same time, the delivery of consumer goods to the coun tryside was sporadic. As for participation in communal activities, it had continued to wane as poor bookkeeping and outright dishonesty reduced the profits of communal enterprises and convinced cooperative members to concentrate on their own holdings (Roesch 1984: 308).

In 1983, following the forth party congress, the government started to move cautiously toward privatization, decentralization, provision of consumer goods, and the improvement of the environment for productive activity (Bowen 1993: 349). For almost a decade, progress was stymied by the ongoing conflict with Renamo. However, the prospects became brighter in the mid 1990s with negotiations, elections and the replacement of Renamo's main source of support, the old apartheid state of South Africa, with a representative democracy.

Part of the opening up of the economy involved a government shift to an emphasis on the family homestead. Farmers were allowed to return to their former dispersed holdings, and, within a few years, some villages had lost one-third of their population (Roesch 1988: 80). Many village residents still lack the resources to reestablish themselves in a new location, but, in a reprise of dispersal during the colonial period, families will undoubtedly continue to trickle out of the artificial villages.

Ethiopia

The villagization that took place in Ethiopia up to the final decline of the Mengisto government in late 1991, was also multi-faceted. The most important component of the program was the creation of defensive villages, some going back to the 1970s and the Somalia-Ethiopia conflict over the Ogaden region. As in Angola and Mozambique, many of these villages were designed to separate guerillas from a potential source of support in an ongoing civil war. Some were also founded as a response to drought, as a source of rural development, or as a mechanism for furthering the goals of socialism in the countryside. One insightful analysis of the Mengisto regime in Ethiopia, indicated that the relocation campaign was undoubtedly used as part of a strategy for strengthening centralized government control.(Harbeson 1993: 209).

Ethiopia's resettlement program was different in one way from those already described: the location of many of the new villages was far removed from the home base of the participants. These source areas were suffering from a drought and a civil war that had begun in the mid 1970s after the miliary regime was established. The war and its side effects resulted in the occupants of the stricken regions being flown or sent by truck to resettlement sites in other parts of Ethiopia, sites that were deemed by the authorities to be underutilized. The response to this process was outrage of the part of the international community.

Particularly disturbing were the reports of hardships experienced during the process of resettlement and of inadequate health facilities, food supplies, and housing in the recipient areas.

One of the resettlement areas, the Metekel, was declared to be appropriate for the relocation of highland people in spite of having a physical environment that was hot, humid, and malarial with shallow soil, very different from that of the highlands. Furthermore, the area was already occupied by bush fallow farmers, the Gumuz, who had developed a complex production system that provided them with some income as well as a varied diet. The land and resource requirements of the Gumuz, taking the need for fallow into account, did not allow for a substantial influx of newcomers (Woldemeskel 1989: 372).

In spite of all these inhibiting factors, over 100 villages had been completed by June, 1985 with a total population of just over 100,000 persons. Within a short time, demands for housing and fuel for the immigrants depleted the Gumuz' wood supply at the same time that it undermined gum arabic collecting, an important local source of income (Woldemeskel 1989: 369-370). In effect, resettlement disrupted the survival system of the Gumuz while subjecting the new arrivals to difficult conditions in a remote area. Within a few years, there was a rise in mortality and erosion rates as well as a shortage of water and fuelwood.

Ethiopia also encouraged developmental villages based on the conviction, referred to earlier, that bringing scattered farmers together culminated a natural process leading from separate homesteads to clusters. Furthermore, villages were deemed necessary for the provision of services and security and for the promotion of more rational land use (Cohen and Isaksson 1987: 336). The unstated objectives once again included control of the countryside and the ultimate advancement of socialism through collective agriculture. There were similarities to Angola and Mozambique in that resettled farmers were supposed to be moving in the direction of communal agriculture even if they initially concentrated their efforts on their own fields.

Many of the developmental villages built in the mid 1980s were located in the Arsi region, an area that benefitted from a promising resource base and long-term foreign aid. In affect, the government was initiating its movement toward communal farming in a region likely to provide the fewest problems since it was characterized by good soil on gently sloping land, a paucity of permanent tree crops, and a land tenure system that was still flexible due to ongoing migration (Cohen and Isaacson 1987: 441-442).

One of the sources of inspiration and ideas for the Arsi villages was a 1970s project that had established a series of settlements in the Wabe area so as to relocate farmers displaced by new state farms. The Wabe region had been supplied with high quality housing, centralized water sources, extension, and other services, and so some positive outcomes had been achieved. Yet, these results could not be expected in the Arsi program, given the fact that investment per village was bound to be considerably less.

The Ethiopian government moved rapidly to relocate the Arsi farmers; almost one million were moved in 1985-1986. Technically, force was not applied in this effort but, in reality, the directives were taken very seriously by a rural population that had become used to receiving and obeying orders long before the Mengisto regime. The farmers were told to form peasant associations, select village sites, and prepare to move, all within six months. Then, when the transfer occurred, they were faced with insufficient shelter in cool weather and heavy work schedules. Although the peasant committees chose the relocation sites and used technical rather than political guidelines, the impetus for the whole operation was so obviously top-down that most participants were not sure why they were being told to move into villages (Cohen and Isaacson 1987: 448).

After the resettlement was well underway, it became clear that the promised services were not going to be available. Mosques and adult literacy classes were sometimes provided, but most people continued to travel to town to attend school, visit an infirmary, or purchases necessities not produced on the farm. The situation was made even worse by a prohibition on village shops which were considered antithetical to socialist values.

Environmental issues quickly came to the fore. Areas near the villages were subject to erosion and the depletion of wood supplies and pasturage. Some settlers established temporary cattle camps at some distance from the village, but others avoided this practice, convinced that the cattle kept at the camps would be collectivized. The government was also reluctant to allow temporary camps for fear that they would undermine the cohesiveness of the villages.

While the village structure created social and ecological constraints, the wider economic context played an even more important role in limiting the capacity to prosper. Official government crop prices, input supplies, and marketing conditions all acted to depress incentives to the producer, while opportunities to earn income outside of farming were almost nonexistent. There was also the omnipresent fear that at some point the next step would be taken and farming would be collectivized. All of these factors contributed to desertion from the villages whenever government surveillance weakened.

By 1990, Mengistu was making speeches that indicated a retreat from the concept of collectivization as well as hints of economic reforms. Evictions and forced relocations were terminated and some cooperative endeavors were dissolved (Rahmato 1993: 49). Within a year, most cooperatives had ceased to function and new villages had begun to be dismantled.

The process of reform accelerated with the fall of the regime in 1991 and the transfer of power to a transitional government. The role of the state was completely reappraised, based in part on the knowledge that excessive centralized control had contributed to the poor economic performance of the 1970s and 1980s (Hansson 1993: 302). In the past few years there have been several initiatives aimed at stimulating investment in agriculture, including the improvement of rural roads and the provision of farming support services and inputs. Gradually the government is moving toward a tenure system based on individual ownership. There is every expectation that artificial villages will decline in importance as relocated peasants continue to search for better prospects, in some cases returning to their areas of origin.

Tanzania

The established settlement mode in rural Tanzania was a primarily a scattered one, although, as discussed at length in Chapter 12, cultural and ecological diversity led to considerable variation in form. For example, in the Nyamwezi area of west-central Tanzania, intermediate size clusters often remained after villages began to come apart at the beginning of the colonial period. Gradually, a high level of mobility led to a looser pattern, with as few as six homesteads separated from other small groupings by 100 to 400 yards of open fields (Abrahams 1981: 57). This dispersion reflected the search for fertile land, as well as fear of social conflict (Abrahams 1981: 68).

It was these types of adjustments that were affected when the decision was made to implement a nation-wide policy of villagization. As in other resettlement efforts, this program went through several stages, starting with a reliance on the mobilization of volunteers, then reaching out to the victims of floods, droughts and other disasters, and, finally, shifting to forced relocation.

There was another major similarity to programs in Angola, Mozambique, and Ethiopia: resettlement in Tanzania was seen as part of a national mobilization, an effort to involve and energize the rural population so as to achieve economic, social, and national defense goals (Binns 1994: 11). Among these goals was communal farming, although, initially, the village members would cultivate their own holdings, spending only a limited amount of time on a jointly-managed field. The effort expended on the communal plot would then be expected to increase at the expense of individual enterprises.

However, most of the settlers remained disdainful of the collective farming aspects of villagization, in part because of insufficient preparation. The settlers were not sure how they would be compensated for different levels of skills, time inputs, or outside assets brought into the joint venture. Nor did they know how profits of joint enterprises were to be used -- whether they were to be plowed back into the village or shared equally (Bernstein 1981: 59-60). Ultimately, few settlers were willing to risk the their time or resources on such a questionable endeavor. They reacted to exhortations to collectivize by making only token efforts at cultivating a group field or by engaging in more direct sabotage (Kitching 1982: 120).

There was also one major difference between villlagization in Tanzania and other countries: rather than focusing on a few key areas, the government was determined to relocate the whole rural population by the late 1970s. To be sure, only about half of the population was actually moved, since high density regions were arbitrarily divided into villages without the necessity of resettlement (Van Donge 1992: 90). There was also a good deal of flexibility as settlement designs were adapted to fit local circumstances. Still, the undertaking was a very ambitious one, and much of the process had to be carried out without enough evaluation of new sites or farmer preparation (Kitching 1982: 112).

The first village locations were usually insect-infested, short of water, and based on questionable soil resources (Ergas 1980: 390). The site selection process did improve, but the rapid pace of resettlement made it difficult to always match up areas of origin with appropriate destinations. Farmers who were forcibly removed from an area where they understood the details of micro-climate and soil, might find themselves in a new location where none of their insights and experience were applicable (Nindi 1988: 179). Furthermore, some basic locational guidelines were applied everywhere rather than selectively. Proximity to a road or cooperative society was considered to be so important, that many villages were accessible to transport but not to good soil areas or a reliable supply of water, grazing land, or firewood (Moore 1979: 73). This orientation reflected the government's concern with control of the rural population (enhanced by a road) as well as with access to inputs and markets (Bernstein 1981: 58).

By trying to implement a state-wide transformation, the Tanzanian government overextended itself and could not fulfill its pledges to the new villagers. Some of the most serious problems were related to crop production. Fertilizers were advocated, but delivery of these inputs could be so sporadic that farmers were reluctant to commit themselves to new patterns of technology and input use (Bryceson 1988: 43). In a similar vein, both food supplies for the transition period and farm to market transport services might be too late to be of any use.

The dearth of resources that plagued the resettlement effort was compounded by administrative shortfalls. The program was overly central ized; local people were not involved in decision making so their expertise could not be utilized (McMaster1992: 205). Government officials could also be authoritarian, ineffective, or dishonest, sometimes because of a lack of training.

All of these issues can be examined by looking at a few areas of Tanzania in more detail. Iringa District (south-central Tanzania) is one such area that has been subject to several in-depth studies. Surveys were carried out in to determine the population that could be supported in selected villages in terms of the arable land within five kilometers, grazing land located within seven kilometers, and the water supply within one kilometer (UNDP 1976).

According to the survey, one-fifth of a total of over 400 villages in the district had either a deficient or polluted water supply. Shortage of land within reach of the villages was causing most members to look for better opportunities elsewhere, to excessively shorten fallow periods, or to cultivate land that, due to steep slopes, would better have been left as forest. Similarly, farmers with inadequate pasture were obviously overgrazing their land. In some cases, the villagers had already started to deal with these problems by improving the arrangement of dwellings and fields and a few had split into a main cluster with two or more satellites (UNDP 1976: 7).

Another study of the same general area reached similar conclusions after surveying both the physical resources of the villages and the technical capacity of the population (Thomas 1975: 185-186). More instances of excessive distance to water, land, and cattle were enumerated. It was clear that many families were maintaining their cattle at some distance from the village, a practice that relieved pressure on scarce local grazing supplies but which was at variance with a plan to provide centralized village cattle dips or with the need for milk in the villages (UNDP 1976: 30). The study also revealed signs of mobility; some village residents were earning wages elsewhere, some had moved from one village to another, and some, as in the first example, were forming small, semi-dispersed satellite villages. In the 1970s, no standardized procedures had been formulated to deal with these conditions (UNDP 1976: 9).

Another difficulty inherent in the process of relocation was a dearth of building materials. The widespread burning of land in preparation for construction of new villages wiped out the supply of wood for future building and fuel needs (Kalabamu 1989: 53). In the Nyamwezi area (central-west Tanzania), farmers in the new villages expressed fear of fire, epidemics, and witchcraft and several were convinced that they would not be able to control either the resources they had brought with them or those that they had developed since being relocated (Abrahams 1981: 46). There was also considerable dissatisfaction with distances to the fields; a typical villager would have preferred to walk further to the local dispensary while being better able to protect field crops from pests. As in the Iringa example, there was already evidence in 1980 of the formation of satellite hamlets and the seasonal occupation of huts located near to the fields (Abrahams 1981: 79).

These and other examples provide a picture of farmers adapting to new conditions through several distinct phases. Initially, villagization was rigidly enforced, although settlements were often too large, given ecological and social constraints. Within two years the second phase was underway, as satellite settlements were formed and temporary camps were occupied during the rainy season(s). This situation was accepted by the government in a 1983 policy change. Assistance was actually provided to farmers who wanted to realign their fields and central village to better fit local conditions (Barker 1985: 68). The government also tried to improve the tenure situation by providing longer land leases and agreeing that farmers should be compensated for improvements.

By 1985, the third phase had begun as families permanently relocated outside of the villages without government interference. While many villages continued to function, others were clearly disintegrating. The most likely clusters to break apart were those that were much too large to begin with and so had generated environmental problems without developing much of a sense of community. Also at risk were villages in tree crop regions, such as the cashew-growing area in the southeast. Members of these villages deserted as soon as they could and tried to salvage the tree plantings that had been neglected following villagization.

It would seem that another sequence in the settlement cycle has come full circle as the dominant pattern in Tanzania shifts toward dispersal. It should be mentioned that the villagization experiment has faltered not just because it was contrary to the established mode of adaptation, but also because it did not bring about production increases that could compensate for the negative features of resettlement. The government never focused on the issue of productivity, so positive changes in output were not forthcoming. Rather than raising yields, the disruption caused by villigization led to a decline in production.

Conclusion

One persistent theme in the evolution of African settlement patterns is the recurrence of dispersal. It continues to function as an important mechanism for reducing the negative impact of farming and grazing on the environment. This has been especially true in areas of low intensity agriculture, such as those based on bush fallow systems. Dispersal has also reduced the labor requirements for working on and protecting field crops. Over a range of settings, and through a long historical sequence, scattered homesteads have frequently reappeared following periods of clustering.

Under these circumstances, governments have shown unusual arrogance in attempting to create new arrangements of rural people so as to satisfy their own priorities. Villagization programs, especially as they have evolved during the last two decades, may make sense in the abstract, but they tend to fail in a real world context. In all the examples discussed in this chapter, governments have lacked the resources to bring about their vision of a rural utopia. By making promises that couldn't be kept and raising false expectations, they only heightened frustration level among the settlers. By neglecting the planning component of villagization, governments have had to deal with unprepared settlers and sites that were poorly selected in terms of soil, water supplies, and other relevant factors.

In virtually all cases, the implementation of resettlement programs has been a top-down process. Participants have been recruited, cajoled, and often forced into relocating, but usually without being convinced of the efficacy of the entire process. They have had to endure various hardships: adjustment to a new setting, an inadequate food supply during the transition, makeshift shelters, and often the loss of some element of their livelihood, such as access to fishing grounds or tree crops. All these accommodations have not necessarily resulted in any improvement in their economic status and sometimes only marginal improvements in the availability of services.

Through all of this manipulation, resettled population have waited for an opportunity to assert their own alternative economic priorities and spatial arrangements. In examples from both Africa and the Americas, from periods of colonial control to that of political independence, village residents have looked for openings that would allow them greater flexibility. They have resisted the rigidities of the planned village, not with direct mass protests, but with a slow, inexorable reshaping of the settlement system. Sometimes they have formed sub-villages which, in turn, have disintegrated into individual homesteads. Sometimes they have sent family members to other areas, both rural and urban, to supplement their local productive capacity. They have found ways of pasturing their cattle, obtaining water, and decreasing the distance to their fields, often by creating small scale, temporary hamlets at some distance from village centers. Invariably, official positions have changed as government functionaries have been forced to react to ecological damage, economic diffi culties, and the realities on the ground. Although another program on the scale of Tanzania's Ujamaa villagization is not likely to be initiated, there is still a shared perception in many parts of Africa that villages are required to span the wide gap between rural and urban places. There is also an imperative in Africa to increase the viability of newly formed states, in part through tighter control of the countryside. Given this reality, it is likely that spatial planning, particularly the clustering of dispersed settlements, will continue to be incorporated into national development strategies.

References

Abrahams, R. G. 1981. *The Nyamwezi Today: A Tanzanian People in the 1970s.* Cambridge: Cambridge University Press.

Barker, Jonathan. 1985. "Gaps in the Debates About Agriculture in Senegal, Tanzania, and Mozambique." *World Development* 13: 59-76.

Bender, Gerald J. 1978. *Angola Under the Portuguese: 2The Myth and Reality.* Berkeley: The University of California Press.

Bernstein, Henry. 1981. "Notes on the State and Peasantry: The Tanzanian Case." *Review of African Political Economy* 21: 44-62.

Berry, Sara. 1993. *No Condition Is Permanent.* Madison: University of Wisconsin Press.

Binns, Tony. 1994. *Tropical Africa.* London: Routledge.

Bowen, Merle L. 1993. "Socialist Transitions: Policy Reforms and Peasant Producers in Mozambique." In Thomas J. Bassett and Donald E. Crummey, eds. *Land in African Agrarian Systems.* Pp. 326-353. Madison: University of Wisconsin Press.

Bratton, Michael. 1980. *The Local Politics of Rural Development: Peasant and Party-State in Zambia.* Hanover, NH: University Press of New England.

Bridgland, Fred. 1984. *Jonas Savimbi: A Key to Africa.* Edinburgh: Mainstream Publishing.

Bryceson, Deborah. 1988. "Household, Hoe, and Nation: Development Policies of the Nyerere Era." In Michael Hodd, ed. *Tanzania After Nyerere.* Pp. 36-48. London: Pinter Publishers.

Bunce, Michael. 1982. *Rural Settlement in an Urban World.* London: Croom Helm.

Coquery-Vidrovitch, Catherine. 1988. *Africa: Endurance and Change South of the Sahara.* Berkeley: University of California Press.

Cohen, John M. and Nils-Ivar Isaksson. 1987. "Villagization in Ethiopia's Arsi Region." *Journal of Modern Africa Studies* 3: 435-464.

Daley, Suzanne. 14 July 1996. "Botswana is Pressing Bushmen to Leave Reserve." *New York Times International.* P. 3.

Dewar, D., A. Todes, and V. Watson. 1986. *Regional Development and Settlement Policy.* London: Allen and Unwin.

Denyer, Susan. 1978. *African Traditional Architecture.* London: Heinemann.

Ergas, Zaki. 1980. "Why Did the Ujamaa Policy Fail? Towards a Global Analysis." *The Journal of Modern African Studies* 18: 387-410.

Farriss, Nancy M. 1978. "Nucleation Versus Dispersal: The Dynamics of Population Movement in Colonial Yucatan." *Hispanic-American American Historical Review* 5: 187-216.

Friedmann, John. 1980. "The Territorial Approach to Rural Development in the People's Republic of Mozambique." *International Journal of Urban and Regional Research* 4: 97-116

Gade, Daniel and Mario Escobar. 1982. "Village Settlement and the Colonial Legacy in Southern Peru." *Geographical Review* 72: 430-449.

Goldman, Abe. 1993. "Agricultural Innovation in Three Areas of Kenya: Neo Boserupian Theories and Regional Characteristics." *Economic Geography* 6: 44-71

Grossman, David. 1971. "Do We Have a Theory of Settlement Geography? The Case of Iboland." *Professional Geographer* 23: 197-203.

____. 1992. *Rural Process-Pattern Relationships.* New York: Praeger.

Hanlon, Joseph. 1990. *Mozambique: The Revolution Under Fire.* London: Zed Press.

Hansson, Gote. 1993. "Ethiopia: Away from Socialism." In Magnus Blomstrom and Mats Lundahl, eds. *Economic Crisis in Africa.* Pp. 288-321. London: Routledge.

Harbeson, John W. 1993. "The Future of the Ethiopian State after Mengisto." *Current History* 92: 208-212.

Harden, B. "Ethiopians Risk Lives Fleeing Resettlement." *Washington Post.* March 10, 1986.

Heywood, Linda M. 1989. "Ethnic Nationalism in Angola." *Journal of Modern African Studies* 27: 47-66.

Hitchcock, Robert K. and John D. Holm. 1993. "Bureaucratic Domination of Hunter-Gatherer Societies: A Study of the San in Botswana." *Development and Change* 24: 305-338.

Isaacman, Alan and Barbara Isaacman. 1983. *Mozambique: From Colonialism to Revolution 1900-1982.* Boulder, CO.: Westview Press.

Kalabamu, Fuastin T. 1989. "Some Effects of Tanzania's Villagization Programme on Traditional Building Materials." *Geoforum* 20: 51-56.

Kay, George. 1967. *Social Aspects of Village Regrouping in Zambia.* Lusaka, Zambia: Institute for Social Research.

Kitching, Gavin. 1982. *Development and Underdevelopment in Historical Perspective.* London: Methuen.

Liebenow, Gus J. 1963. *Colonial Rule and Political Development in Tanzania: The Case of the Makonde.* Evanston, IL.: Northwestern University Press.

Long, Norman, 1968. *Social Change and the Individual.* Manchester, U.K.: Manchester University Press.

McMaster, D. N. 1992. "Agricultural Development." In M.B Gleave, ed. *Tropical African Development*. Pp. 192-222. New York: Longman.

Mehretu, Assefa. 1989. *Regional Disparities in Sub-Saharan Africa: Structural Adjustment to Uneven Development*. Boulder, CO.: Westview Press.

Moore, J. 1979. "The Villagization Process and Rural Development in the Mwanza Region of Tanzania." *Geografiska Annaler* 61B: 65-80.

Morgan, W. B. 1957. "The Grassland Towns of the Eastern Region of Nigeria." *Transactions of the Institute of British Geographers* 23: 213-224.

Morgan, W. B. and Jerzy Solarz. 1994. "The Agrarian Crisis in Sub-Saharan Africa: Development Constraints and Policy Problems." *Geographical Journal* 160: 57-73.

Niddre, David L. 1974. "Changing Settlement Patterns in Angola." *Rural Africana* 23: 47-77.

Nindi, Benson C. 1988. "Issues in Agricultural Change: The Case of Ismani, Iringa Region, Tanzania." In Peter Little and David Brokensha, eds. *Anthropology, Development and Change in East Africa*. Pp. 161-182. Boulder, CO.: Westview Press.

Rahmato, Dessalegn. 1993. "Agrarian Change and Agrarian Crisis: State and Peasantry in Post-Revolution Ethiopia." *Africa* 63: 36-54.

Roberts, Brian K. 1989. "Nucleation and Dispersion: Distribution Maps as a Research Tool." In Michael Aston, David Austin and Christopher Dyer, eds. *The Rural Settlements of Medieval England*. Pp. 59-75. Oxford: Basil Blackwell.

____. 1996. *Landscapes of Settlement: Prehistory to the Present*. London: Routledge.

Roder, Wolf. 1973. "Effects of Guerilla War in Angola and Mozambique." *Antipode* 5: 14-21.

Roesch, Otto. 1984. "Peasants and Collective Agriculture in Mozambique." In Jonathan Barker, ed. *The Politics of Agriculture in Tropical Africa*. Pp. 291-316. Beverly Hills, Ca.: Sage Publications.

____. 1988 . "Rural Mozambique Since the Frelimo Party Fourth Congress: The Situation in the Baixo Limpopo." *Review of African Political Economy* 41: 73-91.

Silberfein, Marilyn. 1989. "Settlement Form and Rural Development: Scattered Versus Clustered Settlement." *Tijdschrift voor Economische en Sociale Geografie* 80: 258-268.

Tandap, Lucas. 1976. "The Evolution of Rural Settlements in Cameroon" *Ekistics* 249: 106-108.

Thomas, Ian D., et. al 1975. *Physical Planning and Resource Evaluation*. Follow-up Studies, *Iringa Region. Preliminary Report.* Norwich, U.K.: The Overseas Development Group for U.N.D.P.

U.N.D.P. 1976. *Physical Planning and Resource Evaluation*. Follow-up Studies, Iringa Region. Volume 2. Norwich, U.K.

Van Donge, Jan Kees. 1992. "Agricultural Decline in Tanzania: The Case of the Uluguru Mountains." *African Affairs* 91: 73-94.

Van Horn, Laurel. 1977. "The Agricultural History of Barotseland, 1840-1964." In Robin Palmer and Neil Parsons, eds. *The Roots of Rural Poverty in Central and Southern Africa*. Berkeley: University of California Press.

Vivian, R. Gwinn. 1989. "Kluckhohn Reappraised: The Chacoan System as an Egalitarian Enterprise." *Journal of Anthroplogical Research* 45: 101-113.

West, Harry G. and Gregory W. Myers. 1996. "A Piece of Land in a Land of Peace? State Farm Divestiture in Mozambique." *The Journal Modern African Studies* 34: 27-51.

Wolfers, Michael and Jane Bergerol. 1983. *Angola on the Frontline.* London: Zed Press.

Woldemeskel, Getachew. 1989. "The Consequences of Resettlement in Ethiopia." *African Affairs* 88: 359-374.

Young, Tom. 1988. "The Politics of Development in Angola and Mozambique." *African Affairs* 87: 165-184.

PART THREE

The Evolution of Settlement Types: Some Case Studies

5

Settlement Concentration and Dispersal Among the Kofyar

Glenn Davis Stone

The stretch of twenty-five kilometers between the Jos Plateau and the edge of the Namu Plains in central Nigeria has long been an area of rich diversity in settlement patterns. Near the edge of the Jos Plateau, the Kofyar traditionally lived in small, dispersed farmsteads. Immediately to the south reside the Njak, who share the Kofyar language, origin myth, and other cultural features, yet live in small clustered hamlets. Further south, on the fertile plains of the Benue Valley, are nucleated towns of the Goemai, formerly walled against slaving and raiding.

Since mid-century, Kofyar farmers have been moving from their relatively crowded homeland and establishing farms in the Benue Valley, especially in the broad stretches of savanna between the Goemai towns, such as Lafia and Shendam, on the Namu Plains (Figure 5.1). Moving into this frontier, the Kofyar had few constraints on settlement form; land was cheap and abundant, and external meddling in the settlement process was negligible. Kofyar pioneers were free to replicate the dispersed settlement pattern of their homeland, form concentrated settlements like other plains groups, or develop alternative settlement forms.

In describing how the Kofyar settlement pattern has developed, this chapter provides insight into several issues in settlement theory, in particular, how phenomena often associated with nucleated settlement may occur in dispersed systems. The focus of attention is initially on the factors favoring the dispersal of Kofyar frontier settlement and the relationship between settlement structure and communal labor groups. It will then be demonstrated that dispersed settlement can support a considerable density of activities that are usually considered to be central functions in nucleated communities. The final discussion will examine those factors which are associated with the rudimentary forms of aggregation found in the Kofyar landscape.

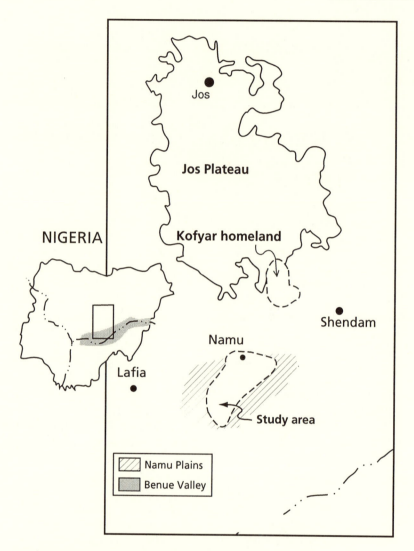

FIGURE 5.1 Nigeria and the Kofyar Study Area.
Source: American Anthropologist 92:1 (March, 1990). Reprinted by permission of the American Anthropological Association.

Background

The Jos Plateau of north-central Nigeria is a remnant of the Precambrian Gondwanaland surface. Deep weathering and erosion along joints have produced dramatic hills along the Plateau's southeastern edge where the Kofyar lived. South of the Plateau, the Benue Piedmont forms an expanse of thin soils dotted with inselbergs. Just north of Namu, the Benue Piedmont gives way to the Benue Valley—actually a deep trough filled with sedimentary deposits. Here, beneath a vast tree savanna, fertile soils formed in sandstones and shales offered great opportunities for the farmer, but the threat of slaving and raiding kept out most small groups of the Nigerian Middle Belt.

In the Namu Plains, the military threat in the sixteenth and seventeenth centuries could have come from the Jukun Empire, based in Wukari. The Jukuns are believed to have extracted tribute from the Goemai, who in turn raided the Kofyar for slaves. Jukun influence had waned by the late eighteenth century, but the jihad of the early nineteenth century left the Plateau ringed by Fulani dynasties that kept many groups in the defensive hills of the Jos Plateau.

The Kofyar were one such group. When first studied in the 1960s by Robert Netting, this population of around 50,000 lived in the hills of the plateau's southeastern corner and in a band of dense settlement around the escarpment base (Netting 1968). Population density exceeded 200/km in places (Stone et al. 1984), and agriculture was highly intensive, with annually fertilized and cultivated plots of millet, sorghum, and cowpeas (Netting 1968). Settlement took the form of contiguous farmsteads, averaging around .5 hectares in size, with residential compounds located near the center. If we define dispersed settlement as having households located on their fields and nucleation or concentration as the removal of population from agricultural plots to villages or towns, we would classify the Kofyar as a textbook case of dispersed settlement.[1]

Away from the plateau, settlement was quite different. In the early twentieth century, the very old Goemai (Ankwe) towns of Shendam, Kurgwi, and Kwande had populations in the thousands; the smaller town of Namu and the hamlets of Njak and Shindai had populations in the dozens or hundreds. These settlements were nucleated for defense; all save Njak and Shindai were walled and crops were grown outside the walls. There were attacks on these towns and villages until the "Pax Britannica" in the first decades of the twentieth century (Stone 1988: 116-118).

By the 1940s, many Kofyar had built residences on the Benue Piedmont south and east of the homeland, Then, in the early 1950s Kofyar settlement leapfrogged over the farmlands of Namu onto the frontier along the northern edge of the Benue Trough. Encouraged by the abundant and fertile soils and by the growing market for cash crops, seasonal migration began to increase steadily. In 1961, around twenty-five percent of the households had frontier farms, although few had abandoned their home farms. By the 1980s, the homeland was sharply depopulated, and thousands of Kofyar farms had been established on the Namu Plains.

Emerging Patterns of Settlement

Visiting the new Kofyar community south of Namu in 1961, Netting saw a settlement pattern of mainly farmsteads, with less substantial dwellings than in the homeland. Frontier farms were arranged along roads and paths in contrast to the homeland settlements which were scattered irregularly across the landscape and connected by a network of paths. A reconstruction of the residential pattern in 1963, based largely on aerial photographs, is shown in Figure 5.2.

Although there were no concentrated settlements, the Kofyar did recognize named areas called ungwa.[2] Each ungwa had a headman, or mengwa (from the Hausa mai ungwa, neighborhood head), who handled administrative functions such as tax collection and announcements, but he often was also the most influential member of the ungwa.[3] Some ungwa were named for the homeland village of the first pioneers to settle a particular area of the frontier (e.g., Ungwa Goewan, Ungwa Dunglong, Ungwa Kofyar) while others were named for a feature of the local landscape (Kwallala, Dangka). Their boundaries were never marked in the landscape.

By 1985, the population density of the area shown in Figure 5.2 had risen from around 10/km to 100/km. Average farm size was around 5.5 hectares. The ungwas had increased in number and in some cases subdivided; their boundaries had taken on the form of bush neighborhoods shown in Figure 5.3. There is little sign of settlement concentration; with few exceptions, the Kofyars' residential compounds were located near the centers of rectangular or oblong farms, as in Figure 5.4.

To understand this pattern of settlement, we might first ask whether the Kofyar have essentially reproduced the homeland settlement pattern. After all, the pattern of contiguous farmsteads was present in the homeland, and it may appear that frontier settlement has been driven by the power of tradition. For several reasons, this does not appear to be the case. Although traditional practices undoubtedly provide a baseline with which to approach new situations, the Kofyar have shown a consistent willingness to adapt to the economic and physical environment on the

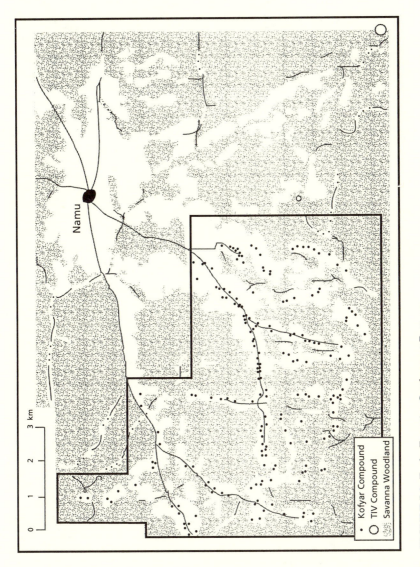

FIGURE 5.2 Early Frontier Settlement Patterns

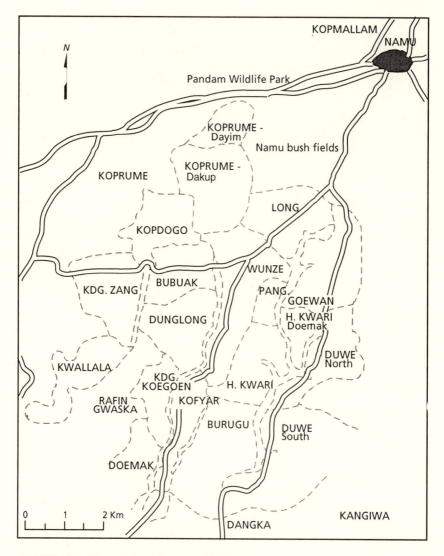

FIGURE 5.3 Ungwa Boundaries in 1984

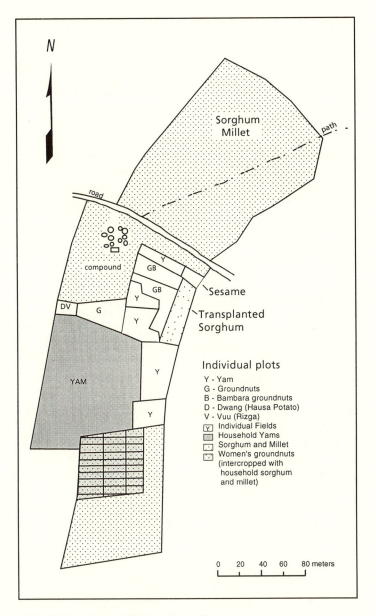

FIGURE 5.4 Typical Kofyar Farm, Namu Area

frontier. These are, after all, people who enthusiastically amended their household size and composition, agricultural strategy, and some fundamental aspects of their economy in response to new conditions on the frontier (Netting 1965; Stone et al. 1984; Netting et al. 1993).

The frontier and homeland settlement patterns also differ in numerous respects, including size and shape of farm, relationship of residences to roads, and abandonment practices (Stone 1996). These sorts of settlement changes are common in cases of "downhill movements" in Nigeria (Udo 1966: 135-136; Gleave 1965). Moreover, there were instances in which early settlers devised new forms of concentrated settlement that had no antecedent in the homeland (discussed below). I believe that the similarities in homeland and frontier settlement result less from tradition than from similarities in farm production in the two areas.

Agriculture and Settlement Dispersal

The agricultural system of the Kofyar is critical to the evolution of settlement patterns. Farm plots generally experience declining yields after several years of cultivation, which promotes shifting cultivation and homestead relocation. However, in certain situations, farmers elect not to relocate but to stay put and adjust their farming methods. This approach, intensification, mitigates the effects of worsening fertility, weeds, and other problems. To understand rural settlement, it is necessary to understand when intensification is and is not selected over relocation.

Some areas of the Namu frontier have seen abandonment rather than intensification (Stone 1996). Abandonment after a few years of cultivation is becoming increasingly common where shale-derived, clayey soils develop impeded drainage. But in other areas, there are well drained, fertile, sandy soils that farmers almost never abandon; they intensify their agriculture instead (Stone 1993a).

Intensification is generally understood to involve harder work, but the nature of the added work varies in important ways in different ecological settings. Among the Kofyar, intensification has taken the following forms:

1. The roster of crops has changed. Some traditional grains have been dropped, while yams and rice have been added. These are valuable cash crops but they are expensive of human labor and they pose potentially serious problems in labor scheduling (Stone et al. 1990).

2. Crops have come to be cultivated more densely, both in space and in time. Spatial density is increased by intercropping, and it is

now common for millet, sorghum, and groundnuts to be growing in a field simultaneously. Temporal density is increased by lengthening the agricultural calendar, leaving only a brief dry season break. At the same time, various cropping strategies are used to absorb labor during slack times, evening out the profile of labor inputs across the seasons.

3. Human intervention in the cultivation process has increased in myriad ways. For instance, in a sample of fifteen households, the amount of time devoted to weeding was 431 hours per person across the agricultural cycle (out of a total of just under 1600 hours spent on agriculture). This emphasis on weeding is very unusual in extensive systems, and certainly did not occur in the early days on the Kofyar frontier. The use of animal dung fertilizer is also on the rise. Baskets full of pig or goat dung are dumped on the land closest to the compound where the kitchen garden is located and where many of the crops are perennial.[4] Chemical fertilizers are also likely to be used more frequently. As a result of these developments, the average annual labor input into agricultural work has gradually increased to around 1600 hours, which is quite intensive by African as well as global standards (Cleave 1974; Clark and Haswell 1967).

The relationship between agricultural intensification and settlement pattern has sometimes been misunderstood. On one hand, nucleation raises local population density and can force agricultural intensification (e.g., Nichols 1987: 596). However, intensive farmers often tend to disperse rather to nucleate. The nature of intensification is such that more time is spent on one's field in contrast to the relatively infrequent field visits of extensive cultivators. Most Kofyar are on their fields virtually every day from March through October. As this process of intensification amplifies the time and energy spent in commuting to the field, it raises the premium on residing near-by. If the pull towards the plot is not diluted by field fragmentation, it favors locating the residence close to the center of the farm (Brookfield 1972: 32; Stone 1993b; Drennan 1988).[5]

The pull of the farmer towards intensively cultivated land results from a fundamental principle consistent with both Central Place Theory and von Thünen's theory of land use: residences are "pulled" towards landscape features in proportion to the frequency that any landscape feature is accessed. Since causality runs both ways, this relationship can be stated in more general terms: the value of distance minimization increases with the frequency that the distance is traversed. In farming systems, intensification's pull toward the land is usually coincident with develop ment of more enduring rights to land (Boserup 1965; Netting 1993), a factor which also encourages the physical presence of the farmer. Residence on the plot can be a physical concomitant of land tenure as well as a means of reducing travel costs (Smith 1972: 415)

Settlement Concentration

Intensification may encourage settlement dispersal but it obviously does not determine it. Various factors that favor settlement concentration may override the pull towards dispersion, especially if agriculture is not especially intensive and/or land is fragmented. I will consider three factors that promote concentration: (1) coercion and defense, (2) labor pooling, and (3) central functions.

Coercion and Defense

Both African and non-African colonial governments have created settlement concentrations to facilitate taxation and control of indigenous populations (Udo 1966). Independent African governments promote or force settlement concentration as well, usually out of the belief that it will stimulate "development" (Silberfein 1989). In the Kofyar region of Nigeria, the colonial administration did not force nucleation, but it did bestow economic and political rewards on nucleated settlements. The district administration was headquartered in the Goemai town of Shendam where the Goemai chief was mandated to collect taxes from the neighboring Kofyar, symbolically subordinating the dispersed Kofyar to the nucleated Goemai.

Small pockets of concentrated Kofyar settlements at the foot of the Plateau escarpment were rewarded as well. Kwa, an area with a diminutive concentration around a market, saw its chief elevated to the paramount chieftaincy of the Merniang Kofyar, a title traditionally held by the chief of the (dispersed) hill village of Kofyar. The small towns at Kwa, Doemak, and Kwalla have expanded somewhat in recent years, as more Kofyar have taken up nonagricultural pursuits, but these changes have been voluntary. Kofyar settlement has never been forcibly concentrated, even, in 1930, when several hundred households were run out of the hills as punishment for assaulting an assistant district officer.

Defense is probably the most prevalent factor that can override the pull towards dispersion, and there is little doubt that defense needs provided the primary motive for the formation of Namu, Kwande, Kurgwi, and other early plains settlements. Other Nigerian settlement concentrations also resulted from a threat to security; otherwise, dense population and intensive agriculture would have produced a strong impetus for dispersal. In many cases, dispersal did occur soon after pacification (Bohannan 1954; Udo 1965,1966; Mortimore 1967). Among the Kofyar, any military threat had been virtually eliminated once movement began onto the Namu Plains. At this point, there were few dangers other than the occasional run-in with an elephant and thus, no strong defensive impetus to concentrate settlement.

Labor Pooling

The notion that settlement concentration results from the need for a localized, coordinated labor pool occurs in geographical, historical, and anthropological writings. Labor may be needed for defense (Ogundele 1989: 87) or agriculture (e.g., Cordell and Plog 1979: 417; Hamond 1981: 222), or even to deal with ecological challenges such as flooding (Huang 1990: 65). It is often held that agricultural intensification is especially important in promoting concentration. For instance, Vivian (1989: 109) stresses how the need for a large, coordinated work force to meet the demands of "horticultural intensification" promoted prehistoric nucleation in Chaco Canyon the Southwest, and Farriss (1978: 190) sees intensification as both requiring and permitting settlement nucleation in Yucatan. By the same token, Thompson (1973) writes that "where settlement is dispersed, it is difficult if not impossible to maintain an elaborate system of cooperative labor" (see also Trigger 1968).

One of the major goals of the Kofyar research was to explore the relationship of settlement concentration and the labor demands of the agricultural system. A considerable body of data was collected which indicated that the Kofyar rely heavily on pooled, supra-household work forces, and that they have the ability to mobilize labor from dispersed compounds. In fact, a principal function of the ungwa appears to be in the organization and mobilization of agricultural labor. To study the Kofyar agricultural system, we collected detailed records of labor inputs of a sample of fifteen households in three separate ungwa for the 1984 farming season. These records reveal an instrumental role for supra-household labor in agricultural production. The primary mechanism for mobilizing group labor is called mar muos ("beer farming" or "farming for beer"). During much of the agricultural season, mar muos are a near-daily occurrence. Parties comprising workers from most or all households in the ungwa convene to work for several hours or half a day on a farm. After (and sometimes during) the work, all participants are given millet beer, brewed during the preceding week by the resident women and their friends (M. P. Stone et al. 1995). There are also other mechanisms for mobilizing labor, including *wuk* labor exchange groups which do not require beer (Stone et al. 1990).

There are several reasons for forming supra-household labor groups. One is that some agricultural operations demand the applications of many hands at once, or what has been called simultaneous labor (Wilk and Netting 1984).[6] Mar muos also permits "banking" agricultural labor in the form of millet, a crop that provides a particularly advantageous ecological complement to the staple sorghum. Labor invested during the short growing season of penisetum millet can be "withdrawn" by brewing millet beer for mar muos whenever the household farm requires a major amount of labor. Festive labor parties are common throughout West Africa (Saul 1983), and essential to the Kofyar agricultural system. Our sample worked almost one hour on neighbors' fields for every four hours worked on their own farms.

The ungwa are directly related to mobilization of this communal labor. Out of 2,616 recorded bouts of work on other farms, ninety-four percent occurred on farms within the worker's own ungwa. The pattern holds for farmsteads located near ungwa edges as well as ungwa centers, confirming that ungwa are agricultural labor pools. Thus, mobilization of supra-household labor normally occurs within ungwa boundaries. As one might expect, the size of the ungwa does reflect the size of labor parties, although this requires some explanation.

Mar muos size is difficult to measure because of an ongoing fluctuation in the number of worker.[7] But based on farmers' recalled estimates, the median size is fifty, and sixty-three percent of all mar muos were in the thirty-seventy range in size. Ungwa populations are much larger than this; even if exclude those too young to participate fully in group labor (forty-four percent are under the age of fifteen), the median ungwa population is 238.

However, we shouldn't expect the size of mar muos to correspond to the adult population of the ungwa. Since the household's commitment to group labor mobilization must not jeopardize the operation of its own farm, no household is required to send its entire adult population to any mar muos; except for special occasions, one may skip a mar muos in favor of pressing chores at home. Yet, no household can withdraw from the communal labor pool. A household's repeated absence would be noted, and those who repeatedly skip mar muos could be fined by the community (generally payable in millet beer). This ensures reliability in the communal labor groups without endangering the household farming enterprise.

In the long run, the household contribution to a single mar muos within the ungwa probably averages out to around one worker, but most or all adults can be counted on if the mar muos is for a close neighbor, friend, or relative. This explains the correspondence between communal labor group sizes and the number of households rather than individuals within the ungwa: our sample of ungwas had a median of 35 households. The ungwa does operate as a labor pool, but distribution of ungwa sizes reflects a solution to the tension between communal and household labor. This case shows how communal labor mobilization promotes the existence of, and shapes the size of, formal settlement entities which can be based on dispersed patterns. Communal labor mobilization can play a central role in food production without the administration of that labor having to be concentrated.[8]

Central Functions

Secondary functions are non-agricultural activities in rural areas that are conducted by part-time farmers or by individuals who are no longer involved in farming. Many of these secondary economic activities depend on customers travelling to the purveyor, a process which encourages population concentration and the growth of localized markets. Thus, many secondary functions are also central functions. They promote settlement concentration by the same logic that agricultural intensification promotes dispersal: the residence is pulled towards those points on the landscape that people most frequently access.

There is certainly evidence, for example, that the location of Kofyar homesteads has been influenced by the central functions of the town of Namu, particularly the small clinics and large weekly market. But, since the pull to the central functions of Namu is less than the pull to the agricultural plot, the overwhelming majority of Kofyar live on dispersed farmsteads rather than in town. Under these circumstances, some secondary functions may be adopted even as the residence remains near the fields. When agriculture is already relatively intensive, the marginal returns to further intensification can be easily surpassed by the returns to a part-time secondary activity.

In effect, when the pull to the farm plot that results from agricultural intensification is balanced by increasing monetization, the means exist to initiate or to patronize nonagricultural functions (Stone 1991b, Netting et al. 1989). The result of the concurrent pull towards central functions and the farm plot is the rise of secondary functions within dispersed settlements.

I became intrigued with the notion of non-centralized central functions after a trip to the farmland surrounding Nsukka, an area of exceedingly dense agricultural settlement in the Ibo heartland in south-central

Nigeria. There one finds mile after mile of contiguous farmsteads practicing highly intensive agriculture. Quite a number of the farms also offer secondary functions; they sell food or palm wine, bush meat, medicine, clothes, and a multitude of other wares. They seem, as M. J. Mortimore puts it, to be "urbanizing in situ" (personal communication 1984).

The same process is beginning in Namu District. By 1984, several ungwa were beginning to hold small periodic markets. Like the periodic markets held in all towns in the area, these ungwa markets took place on a designated day of the week and in a designated location. But, whereas town markets meet year-round and may have several hundred vendors proffering a wide variety of merchandise, ungwa markets offer only a few goods and services and are mainly restricted to the dry season. Most are located along roads with a lot of foot traffic. They are usually marked by an isolated stall, which falls into disrepair during the agricultural season.

The small dry season market near our compound in Dadin Kowa consisted of a tailor with an old foot-pump sewing machine, a sundries merchant from Namu with batteries, candies, and kola nuts, and a few girls with millet beer for sale by the jug or by the calabashful. A little market was also starting up in Ungwa Long, beside the dirt road to Namu. It was to be held on Namu's market day, to cater to the considerable foot, bicycle, and taxi traffic.

Diverse secondary functions were appearing in individual compounds as well. Several farmers acted as beer retailers in the dry season, importing caseloads of bottled beer to be resold at a profit in the bush. One man even constructed a saloon next to his compound where he sold bottled beer from Namu. This unshaded aluminum box with no windows did not provide an attractive setting for eating and drinking. Yet, since Kofyar social life traditionally revolved around the pe muos (beer place) where people talk and drink beer from calabashes (as a perpetual pe muos), the miniature saloon was able to turn a profit. Other secondary functions included gasoline-powered grinding mills and churches.

That agricultural intensification may be accompanied (or replaced) by investment in nonagricultural pursuits is discussed in the literature of economic anthropology (Smith 1975; Dow 1985). Archaeologists have explored this phenomenon as well, with a singular focus on ceramic production (e.g., Arnold 1985). What I find interesting about the Kofyar's nonagricultural functions is that so many of them are "central" functions in the sense that patrons must come to where they are offered. The spatial organization of these "non-central places" are obviously not explained by central place theory; they are embedded within the "agricultural settlement pattern" to which, as Christaller (1933) pointed out,

Central Place Theory does not apply. Since these enterprises are widely scattered in space, they do not benefit from the "shopping mall" effect of one business's pull contributing to other businesses (except for the periodic markets). Although such enterprises would improve their performance given a more aggregated forms of settlement, a much higher priority is agricultural production, and the prevailing Kofyar settlement pattern remains dispersed.

Population Change

I have analyzed the Kofyar responses to land pressure and found a marked tendency to abandon farms in areas offering particularly low marginal returns to intensified agriculture (Stone 1996). Other parts of the frontier, however, do offer increased returns for more concentrated labor inputs, and these areas are characterized by intensive agriculture and the pull of the household to the plot. This raises the question of what settlement form to expect under less crowded and less agriculturally intensive conditions. If we eliminate the pull of the household to the plot, would we be left with forces holding the households together?

The longitudinal Kofyar database allows this sort of comparison. For the past four decades, Kofyar population has flowed from the homeland in the Jos Plateau into the Benue Valley frontier. Crowded hills and a sparsely settled frontier have given way to the reverse: sparsely settled hills and a crowded frontier. On the early frontier and in the present-day hills, cultivation should be less intensive and there should be less pull of the compound to the plot. Interestingly, there was aggregation of households in both situations, although the conditions of aggregation were different.

Aggregation on the Frontier

The Kofyar movement onto the plains south of Namu was spearheaded by Doedel, the chief of Kwa, in the early 1950s. The first settlers resided in Ungwa Long (ungwa of the chief). Doedel's own compound was near the northern end of the ungwa. It has long since been razed, but the location is still marked by a borrow pit (from mudblock construction) several times the size of other borrow pits. During the early phase of frontier settlement, the chief's compound housed his own large household and numerous other households and household fragments. This "macro-compound" functioned in some ways as a unit of production (Stone 1988). Across the path was another large compound; the two together probably comprised a population of over fifty, around ten times the population of a homeland farmstead.

A few years after people began to move into the chief's compound, a group of a dozen households, all from the homeland village of Goewan, broke away to form a macro-compound of their own on the other side of the Gbokgbok River. Whereas the chief's macro-compound had grow by accretion, the Goewan compound was a planned multi-household settlement from the beginning, probably with a population in the thirties. They called the settlement "Goewan gari," using the Hausa word for a town. One reason for forming the gari was said to be political. The virtually uninhabited east bank of the Gbokgbok was obviously going to be a prime area for agricultural settlement, and the Goewanians, by establishing the first settlement of any size and duration, could dominate the area. This strategy echoed the geographers' concept of the "First Viable Settlement" (Jordan and Kaups 1989). Since the initial migration, the residents have responded to the pull of farmers to their plots, forming a new ungwa of dispersed households in less then a decade. The settlement is now called Ungwa Goewan, and it is indeed dominated by Goewan households (Stone 1992).

Aggregation in the Homeland

As the Kofyar diaspora has populated the Namu frontier, it has drained population from the homeland villages. The village of Bong, high in the hills of the Jos Plateau, is where Netting lived during much of his fieldwork with the Kofyar in the 1960s (Netting 1968). Although it is characterized by a somewhat greater reliance on outfield farming and on the cultivation of maize (because of the high elevation) than other Kofyar settlements, the basic Kofyar homeland pattern of individual farmsteads with intensively cultivated infields is very much in evidence. Bong is relatively large for a homeland village; in 1966, its fifty-four households had an adult population of 165.

Bong is one of several hill villages with its own primary school, which acts as a settlement anchor, but it has still suffered a sharp decline in adult population. Our 1984 census showed forty-eight households and a total adult population of 103; in 1990 the adult population was down by over a third. This brings the modern population density down to the range of the early frontier. Cultivation has indeed become less intensive, with less reliance on permanent infield cropping and increasing use of abandoned infields for shifting cultivation.

A new settlement form had appeared on the Bong landscape. Six households have abandoned their farmsteads and forged a new aggregated hamlet, or macro-compound, which they call by the English term

"Company." Figure 5.5 compares the Company with the ground plan of a typical Bong compound. While it is not a large settlement concentration, the Company is still quite notable on a landscape where other settlement is relentlessly dispersed.

Company residents cite religion as the cause behind the settlement change. A small faction of Protestants in the community grew through the 1960s and 1970s, eventually leaving their dispersed compounds to form a new social and settlement entity. Company members say that an important factor pulling compounds together was the need to appear in church every morning for prayers. Morning prayers were held before sunrise to keep from interfering with the work day, and walking the rugged terrain in the dark was both time-consuming and hazardous. Although company households still retain at least some economic autonomy (some cultivate their abandoned infields as extensive outfield plots), the company in many ways acts as a unit of production and consumption. Company members sometimes attend traditional mar muos, but drink a non-alcoholic grain beverage that the beer drinkers prepare for them.

There is also a compound cluster on the frontier today. This is a group of four compounds which is also a Protestant enclave adjacent to its church. It is located in the Kwande ungwa of Mangkogom, which is one of the ungwa that has been depopulated in recent years (due to the quality of the soils).

Discussion

The demands of agricultural labor places a premium on residing on the land where that labor is concentrated; the question is which factors can override this "pull" towards the field. On the Kofyar frontier today, the advantages of a localized communal labor pool do not override the premium on dispersion. Over three-fourths of all agricultural labor is invested in the household plot, and this, along with the other advantages of on-site residence, reinforce the farmstead pattern more than the fact that dispersed farmsteads are traditional. The communal labor pools, however, are important enough to have been a factor in the establishment of ungwas which are formal (albeit invisible) settlement entities serving as forums for labor mobilization.

In three separate situations there has been less need for highly intensive labor focused on the farmstead: the pioneering phase on the frontier, the depopulated homeland village, and the depopulated frontier ungwa. In each case there are examples of compounds coalescing into larger settlement units and greater reliance on communally-worked outfield plots

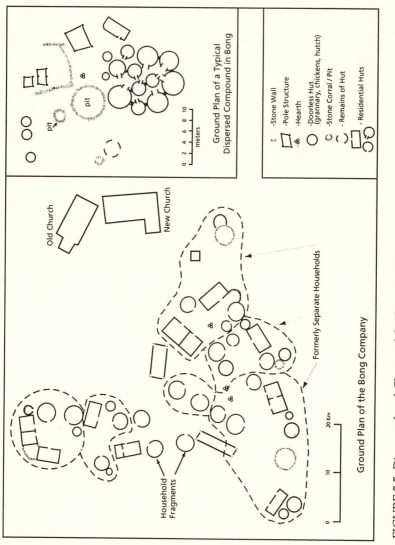

FIGURE 5.5 Dispersed and Clustered Settlements in Bong

than there is on the more crowded frontier today. Yet, residents of macro-compounds still have had to trek to their plots on a regular basis. Thus, although the "pull" to the plot has been less, it has still been a factor that had to be overridden.

These relationships among population, intensification, and settlement dispersal have general applicability, but the causes of aggregation are more particular to the Kofyar case. The first (Doedel's) macro-compound on the frontier had developed a sizable population of Goewanians, and they found themselves acting as a unit and wanting to look after Goewanian interests. The Protestant groups found that as they came to have more in common with each other than with the Catholics and traditionalists; they wanted to become an actual enclave rather than a dispersed subset of the local population. They also wanted their churches to be more accessible.

It appears that when conditions of agricultural regime and land tenure do not pull settlements to their land, aggregation may be prompted by relatively weak forces; households may express relations of production by their settlement, may want to cluster with those most like them, or may seek the sociability of aggregation.

Notes

1. This simple and intuitive definition of dispersal is used widely in settlement geography (e.g., Chisholm 1968: 113) and I will use it here without elaboration. However, I should at least point out that in infield-outfield systems, farmers live on their agricultural plots at the same time they are removed from other plots. In fact, hill Kofyar could have their residential plot (futung; cultivated intensively), separate plots within the village, usually a short walk (mar lang; cultivated extensively), plots between villages, often several kilometers away (mar goon; cultivated extensively) and frontier farms, sometimes 50 km away (wang, cultivated by seasonal migration). Details are in Netting (1968).

2. Unguwa is a Hausa term with no direct English equivalent, referring to a settlement grouping, neighborhood, or town ward, and implying a certain formality and distinct identity. Dictionaries define it as a quarter of town, town ward, or village near a town. The "ungwa" spelling I use in this paper reflects the Kofyar pronunciation of the word.

3. The role in some ways paralleled that of the chief in homeland villages. Only a few chiefs managed to garner considerable power and wealth. The most notable example was Doedel, the paramount chief of the large population to the east of the escarpment, who had 80 wives at the time of his death. His position had been invested with abnormal influence by the colonial government. On the other hand, the chief of the large hill village of Bong had a small household, no unusual wealth, and practically no authority beyond that of any elder in the community.

The authority of mengwas on the frontier varied in similar ways. When we visited mengwas to seek permission for our census, some unilaterally okayed our work and instructed all ungwa household heads to cooperate; others called a meeting of the ungwa elders to discuss the matter. In one particularly democratic ungwa, before the group was satisfied, we had to attend a later meeting of the elders to answer questions about our research.

4. In 1984, 42.5 percent of 595 farms questioned on the Namu Plains used dung. On the Jangwa Plains, where abandonment rather than intensification is the rule, the rate was 10.5 percent of a sample of 181 farms.

5. The relationship between intensification and dispersal is discussed more fully in Stone (1996).

6. The best example of this is the process of storing millet after the harvest (lang maar), in which an assortment of tasks are conducted concurrently. Grasses are gathered for ropes and thatching; ropes are braided to tie bundles of seed heads while thatch mats are woven; workers throw the bundles up to a high wooden rack, where others arrange them in a conical heap, around which the thatching mat is wrapped. Millet storage parties can put away millet for several households in one day, often beginning early in the morning and working into the late afternoon. Whereas millet can be harvested piecemeal, mostly by household labor, over 72 percent of the hours spent storing millet occurred in mar muos (Stone et al. 1990).

7. The first mar muos I attended began with 21 workers, of whom 10 were working in the field while the rest were working their way through the muos (millet beer) prepared for the occasion. The size of the group fluctuated considerably over the next 3 hours, reaching a size of 47 before I left.

8. The larger question of the conditions which promote mobilization of labor across non-aggregated settlements is beyond the scope here; it is presently a topic of debate among students of agricultural systems (Chibnik and de Jong 1989; Guillet 1980). For present purposes, it will suffice to note that agricultural collaboration among nonaggregated settlements occurs in such diverse areas as the West African savanna (Saul 1983), Indonesia (Chibnik and de Jong 1989, the Andes (Guillet 1980), Amazonia (Chibnik and de Jong 1989), northern Argentina (Eidt 1977), and 17th Century America (Boatwright 1941).

References

Arnold, Dean E. 1985. *Ceramic Theory and Cultural Process.* Cambridge Univ. Press, Cambridge.

Boatright, Mody. 1941. "The Myth of Frontier Individualism." Southwestern Social Science Quarterly 22: 12-23.

Bohannan, Paul. 1954. *Tiv Farm and Settlement.* HMSO, London.

Boserup, Ester. 1965. *The Conditions of Agricultural Growth.* Aldine, New York.

Brookfield, H. C. 1972. "Intensification and Disintensification in Pacific Agriculture." Pacific Viewpoint 13: 30-48.

Chibnik, Michael and Wil de Jong. 1989. "Agricultural Labor Mobilization in Ribereo Communities of the Perivian Amazon." *Ethnology* 28: 75-95.

Christaller, Walter. 1966. (orig. 1933) *Central Places in Southern Germany*, translated by C.W. Baskin. Prentice-Hall, Englewood Cliffs NJ.

Cordell, Linda S. and Fred Plog. 1979. "Escaping the Confines of Normative Thought: A Reevaluation of Puebloan Prehistory." *American Antiquity* 44:405-429.

Dow, Malcolm M. 1985. "Agricultural Intensification and Craft Specialization: a Nonrecursive Model." *Ethnology* 24: 137-152.

Drennan, Robert D. 1988. "Household Location and Compact Versus Dispersed Settlement in Prehispanic Mesoamerica." In *Household and Community in the Mesoamerican Past*, edited by R. R. Wilk and W. Ashmore, pp. 273-293. University of New Mexico Press, Albuquerque.

Farriss, Nancy M 1978. "Nucleation vs. Dispersal: the Dynamics of Population Movement in Colonial Yucatan." *Hispanic American Historical Review* 5: 187-216.

Gleave, Michael B. 1966. "Hill Settlements and Their Abandonment in Tropical Africa." *Transactions of the Inst. of British Geographers* 40: 39-49.

Guillet, David. 1980. "Reciprocal Labor and Peripheral Capitalism in the Central Andes." *Ethnology* 19: 151-167.

Hamond, Fred. 1981. "The Colonisation of Europe: the Analysis of Settlement Process." In *Pattern of the Past: Studies in Honor of David Clarke*, edited by Ian Hodder, G. Isaac, and N. Hammond, pp. 211-248. Cambridge Univ. Press, Cambridge.

Huang, Philip. 1990. *The Peasant Family and Rural Development in the Yangzi Delta, 1350-1988*. Stanford Univ. Press, Stanford.

Jordan, Terry G. and Matti Kaups. 1989. *The American Backwoods Frontier: An Ethnic and Ecological Interpretation*. The Johns Hopkins Univ. Press, Baltimore.

Mortimore, Michael J. 1967. "Land and Population Pressure in the Kano Close-Settled Zone, Northern Nigeria." *The Advancement of Science* 23: 677-686. Reprinted in *People and Land in Africa South of the Sahara*, edited by R.M. Prothero, pp. 60-70. Oxford Univ. Press, New York.

Netting, Robert McC. 1965. "Household Organization and Intensive Agriculture: the Kofyar Case." *Africa* 35: 422-429.

____. 1968. *Hill Farmers of Nigeria: Cultural Ecology of the Kofyar of the Jos Plateau*. Univ. of Washington Press, Seattle.

____. 1993. *Smallholders, Householders: Farm Families and the Ecology of Intensive, Sustainable Agriculture*. Palo Alto: Stanford University Press.

Netting, R. M. Stone, G .D. and Stone, M. P. 1993. "Agricultural Expansion, Intensification, and Market Participation among the Kofyar, Jos Plateau, Nigeria." In Turner ,B. L. II, Hyden, G. and Kates, R., ed. *Population Growth and Agricultural Intensification in Africa*, pp. 206-249. Univ. of Florida Press, Gainesville.

Netting, Robert McC., Stone, M. Priscilla and Stone, Glenn D. . 1989. "Kofyar Cash Cropping: Choice and Change in Indigenous Agricultural Development." *Human Ecology* 17: 299-319.

Nichols, Deborah L. 1987. "Risk and Agricultural Intensification During the Formative Period in the Northern Basin of Mexico." *American Anthropologist* 89:596-616.

Ogundele, S. Oluwole. 1989. "Settlement Archaeology in Tiv Land: A Preliminary Report." *West African Journal of Archaeology* 19: 83-92.

Provinse, J. 1937. "Cooperative Ricefield Cultivation Among the Siang Dyaks of Central Borneo." *American Anthropologist* 39: 77-102.

Saul, Mahir. 1983. "Work Parties, Wages and Accumulation in a Voltaic Village." *American Ethnologist* 10: 77-96.

Silberfein, Marilyn. 1989. "Settlement Form and Rural Development: Scattered Versus Clustered Settlement." *Tijdshrift Voor Economishe en Soc. Geografie* 80 :258-268.

Smith, Carol A. 1975. "Production in Western Guatemala: a Test of von Thunen and Boserup." In *Formal Methods in Economic Anthropology*, edited by Stuart Plattner, pp. 5-37. *American Anthropological Association Publication 4.*

Smith, Philip E. L. 1972. "Land-use, Settlement Patterns and Subsistence Agriculture: a Demographic Perspective." In *Man, Settlement and Urbanism*, edited by Peter J. Ucko, R. Tringham and G.W. Dimbleby, pp. 409-425. Schenkman, Cambridge MA.

Stone, Glenn Davis. 1988. *Agrarian Ecology and Settlement Patterns: An Ethnoarchaeological Case Study.* PhD. Dissertation, Dept. of Anthropology, University of Arizona. University Microfilms, Ann Arbor.

____. 1991a. *Settlement Ethnoarchaeology: Changing Patterns Among the Kofyar of Nigeria.* Expedition 33(1): 16-23.

____. 1991b. "Agricultural Territories in a Dispersed Settlement System." *Current Anthropology* 32: 343-353.

____. 1992. "Social Distance, Spatial Relations, and Agricultural Production Among the Kofyar of Namu District, Plateau State, Nigeria." *Journal of Anthropological Archaeology* 11: 152-172.

____. 1993a. "Agricultural Abandonment: A Comparative Study in Historical Ecology." In *Abandonment of Settlements and Regions: Ethnoarchaeological and Archaeological Approaches*, ed. C.Cameron and S.Tomka, pp. 74-81. Cambridge Univ. Press, Cambridge.

____. 1993b. "Agrarian Settlement and the Spatial Disposition of Labor." In *Spatial Boundaries and Social Dynamics: Case Studies from Food-Producing Societies*, ed. A.Holl and T.Levy. International Monographs in Prehistory, Ethnoarchaeological Series 2, pp. 25-38.

____. 1996. *Agrarian Settlement: The Spatial and Social Organization of Kofyar Agriculture.* Univ. of Arizona Press, Tucson (forthcoming).

Stone, Glenn Davis, Johnson, M. P. and Netting. R. M., 1984 "Household Variability and Inequality in Kofyar Subsistence and Cash-Cropping Economies." *Journal of Anthropological Research* 40: 90-108. Reprinted in *Household Economies and Their Transformation*, edited by M.D.Maclachlan, pp. 173-197. Univ. Press of America, Lanham.

Stone, Glenn Davis, Netting, R. M. and Stone, M. P. 1990. "Seasonality, Labor Scheduling, and Agricultural Intensification in the Nigerian Savanna." *American Anthropologist* 92: 7-23.

Stone, Priscilla, M., Stone, G. D. and Netting, R. M. 1994. "The Sexual Division of Labor in Kofyar Agriculture." *American Ethnologist* 22: 165-186.

Thompson, Stephen I. 1973. "Pioneer Colonization: a Cross-Cultural View." Addison-Wesley Module in *Anthropology* 33.

Trigger, Bruce. 1968. "The Determinants of Settlement Patterns." In *Settlement Archaeology*, edited by K.C. Chang, pp. 53-78. National Press, Palo Alto.

Udo, Reuben K. 1965. "Disintegration of Nucleated Settlement in Eastern Nigeria." *Geographical Review* 55: 53-67.

____. 1966. "Transformation of Settlement in British Tropical Africa." *Nigerian Geographical Journal* 9: 129-144.

Vivian, R. Gwinn. 1989. "Kluckhohn Reappraised: the Chacoan System as an Egalitarian Enterprise." *Journal of Anthropological Research* 45: 101-113.

Wilk, Richard R. and Netting ,Robert McC. 1984. "Households: Changing Forms and Functions." In *Households: Comparative and Historical Studies of the Domestic Group*, edited by Robert M. Netting, R. R. Wilk and E. J. Arnould, pp. 1-28. Univ. of California Press, Berkeley.

6

The Role of Villages and Ecological Constraints in Botswana

R.M.K. Silitshena

In most of Africa, the trend since the time of the imposition of colonial rule has been for rural settlements to scatter. One of the exceptions is Botswana, where nucleated settlements have continued to be part of the landscape. The largest of these settlements, varying in population from 10,000 to over 30,000, are concentrated in the southeastern, central, and northwestern parts of the country (Figure 6.1). They are referred to as "large villages" or "agro-towns." The most substantial of these, also known as "primary centers," are usually district headquarters; the relatively smaller ones are sub-district centers, sometimes called "secondary centers."

This chapter has two main objectives. The first is to discuss the functions of villages that have changed through time. Beginning as agricultural and administrative centers, they are now also important for commerce and industry. The second is to explain how the people of Botswana, living in a semi-arid environment, have been able to sustain a system of large settlements.

Ecological Considerations and Settlement

The arid and semi-arid environments of Africa are usually fragile, characterized by poor soil and low, variable, and unpredictable rainfall. The precarious nature of existence in such areas is brought into sharp focus during periods of severe environmental stress. When a drought strikes, for example, individuals, and, later on, entire households, may relocate in search of subsistence (Mortimore 1987). During the drought of the early 1970s in northern Nigeria, many villages were abandoned and pastoralists had to change their patterns of movement (Afoloyan 1992).

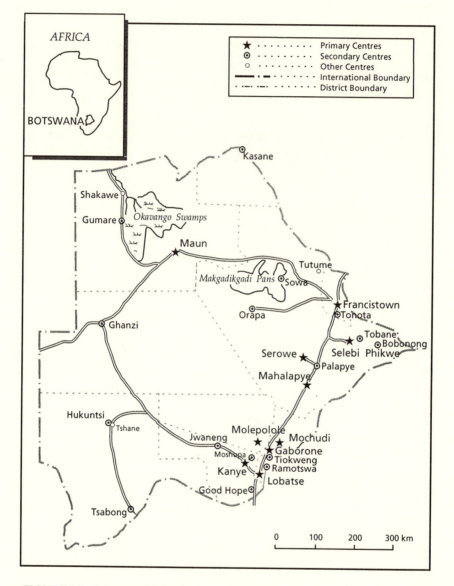

FIGURE 6.1 Botswana: Major Settlements and Roads

Arid and semi-arid environments have, therefore, traditionally supported small and mobile populations. In pre-colonial Africa, settlements
were moved frequently as a result of diminishing soil fertility and water
resources (Morgan and Pugh 1969; Siddle 1971). Sometimes social conflicts caused part of a settlement's population to relocate, which was also
a mechanism for balancing population with limited resources. Yet, the
need for small and dispersed settlements was sometimes in conflict with
the need for defense or labor mobilization (Schapera 1943).

Modern resettlement programs do not appear to take into account
the fragility of arid and semi-arid areas or the adaptations of farming and
pastoral communities to difficult environments. Mascarenhas (1979) has
argued that the planners who organized Ujamaa villages in Tanzania did
not fully appreciate the difficult environment of much of the central part
of the country or the relationship between permanent large settlements in
inappropriate locations and land deterioration. Thus, in many areas, the
creation of Ujamaa Villages resulted in deforestation when trees were cut
for fuelwood, the depletion of pasturage when animals were overcon-
centrated, and serious soil erosion (Mascaren has 1979; Mlay 1982).
These changes were observed by Mascarenhas in the Dodoma Region of
Tanzania:

> Changes in the traditional pattern of activity have brought about envi-
> ronmental stress. When a dense settlement is introduced into a fragile
> environment, pressure is brought to bear on local vegetation.
> Regeneration of his vegetation was easy when settlement was dispersed
> and fluid but repeated use of land by people who are no longer mobile
> requires a change in agricultural practices. Increased use of water has
> raised the specter of a lowered water table which could be a local disas-
> ter if not controlled (Quoted in Mlay 1982: 104).

One further example will illustrate the problematic nature of arid and
semi-arid environments. After a drought period in northeast Kenya, a
decision was made to sedentarize some of the Turkana nomads, giving
them better access to boreholes and services. Dense permanent settlements were created that disrupted the fragile environment, resulting in
severe deforestation, overgrazing, and poverty. Hogg (1987) examined
the area after resettlement and found that it was no longer self-sufficient.

The Structure and Role of Large Villages in Botswana

In spite of a difficult environment, the typical settlement systems of
Botswana are dominated by villages. In order to understand this anom-

aly, it is necessary to consider such factors as social organization, physical conditions, the nature of settlement structure and some relevant government policies. Each of these will be discussed in turn.

The Social Organization of the Tswana

Large villages are typical of the Tswana (or Setswana-speaking) people. The Tswana belong to the Sotho sub-group of the Bantu language family that is found in much of interior southern Africa (Kuper 1975). More specifically, the Tswana area covers parts of the northern Cape and western Transvaal in South Africa and the country of Botswana.

The Tswana were divided into groups and during the pre-colonial period, each of these constituted a kingdom led by a ruling dynasty.[1] This centralized political system was led by chiefs who, for the most part, have ruled with the consent of their people and who resided in the capital (Schapera 1955). The society was stratified into four groups which, in descending order, include nobles, commoners, immigrants, and serfs (Schapera 1955: 36-37).

The kingdom boundaries, or frontiers in some instances, were likely to change over time as was the location of the capital city. These cities would relocate because of a number of factors such as wars or the outbreak of disease but the major factor was apparently ecological problems. Capital cities, which constituted the main settlement, could have populations of over 15,000 but most villages in the kingdoms ranged in size from 100 to a few thousand each. The larger villages were divided into wards, each ward with its own kgotla (council place), under the supervision of a headman.

The Tswana have traditionally lived in nucleated settlements. The origin of this pattern is not clear, but the settlements have evolved over a long enough period to have become accepted as the ideal form of spatial organization. The arrangement has also been sustained by the centralized political leadership that has used nucleation to facilitate administration and defense. Travelogues from the nineteenth century abound with references to these large settlements. The goal in virtually all Tswana kingdoms was for everyone to live in one settlement (Schapera 1943: 270; Silitshena 1976). At the very least, residence in a village was made mandatory:

> Tswana law in regard to residence is emphatic on one point: no one may build a house wherever he pleases. All members of the same ward or family group are expected to live together in one settlement (Schapera 1943: 59).

The villages were the centers of Tswana social and economic life. Each of them was surrounded concentric by zones of land use: areas of crop cultivation (usually referred to as "lands") surrounded by grazing areas (focused on stations called "cattleposts"), and then zones for hunting. The cycle of agricultural activities--when to go to the lands to plant, to weed, and to harvest, and when to let the cattle into the fields to eat the stubble--was controlled by the chiefs (Schapera 1943).

The colonial period had a differential impact on the Tswana population. In South Africa, the colonial government removed the power of the chief through a system of direct rule, a process which contributed tremendously to the disintegration of nucleated settlements among the Tswana (Pauw 1960; Dachs 1975). In Bechuanaland (Botswana), however, the chiefs exploited the system of indirect rule and continued to enforce village residence (Silitshena 1983).

The Physical Environment

Botswana's physical environment is unfavorable to productive activity (Cooke 1982). The rainfall is meager, averaging only 450-500 mm per year in the more favored and densely populated eastern part of the country, and declining to a mere 250 mm in the near-desert southwest. The area with the highest rainfall receives only 600 mm of rainfall per year. In addition, rainfall is highly variable and drought is endemic (Hinchey 1978). Much of the paltry precipitation is lost to evaporation as a result of high daytime temperatures (mean maxima, thirty to thirty-five degrees celsius).

The soils of Botswana are generally poor. More than two-thirds of the country is covered by the Kalahari semi-desert with its sandy soil. As for natural vegetation, it is composed mainly of deciduous shrub savanna with scattered trees and tufted perennial grasses. Even these indigenous plants have been seriously disturbed by grazing and burning.

There is not much surface water except along the Chobe and the Okavango River systems in the north (Figure 6.1). However, where some seasonal rivers and streams occur, the sand beds can be a good source of water during the dry season. More than seventy-five percent of the rural water supply comes from underground water. Before the introduction of boreholes, the location of a reliable surface water supply exerted a considerable influence on the choice of settlement sites (Schapera 1943). Whether this factor has also been partially responsible for the development of nucleated settlements has been a moot point. Monica Wilson has argued that the limited water supply has not been a cause of village formation:

It has been suggested that concentration was due to shortage of permanent water, but settlements moved, showing that there was more than
one spring in their territory, and each cattlepost had a water supply. In
fact, concentration results in long queues of women waiting for
water, a problem which might be obviated if settlements split up.
Moreover, the largest of the ancient settlements was in well-watered
country (Wilson 1969:154).

The Settlement Structure of Botswana

Although this chapter has emphasized the village, it is important to
realize that other types of settlement also exist including the following:
seasonally-changing settlements, farmsteads, dispersed homesteads, and
modern commercial and industrial towns (Silitshena 1982a). The first
type is disappearing and is common only among the Basarwa
(Bushmen). The farmstead is connected with the few commercial farming areas, based mainly on ranching, which were originally set aside for
Europeans.

As for dispersed settlement, it is most relevant in such areas as the
Kalanga-speaking Northeast District. Many reasons have been given to
explain this dispersal, including lack of centralized political institutions
and aspects of the social and agricultural system (Silitshena 1982b).
Dispersed settlements have also been common among the non-Tswana
peoples in the northwest (Campbell 1982). Currently, some dispersal is
found even among the Tswana, especially in the lands areas, a subject
which will be discussed later. However, in most parts of the country, concentration (nucleation) continues to be the dominant form (Silitshena
1993).

The contemporary commercial and industrial towns include a variety
of modern centers. Four of the towns--Selibe-Phikwe, Jwaneng, Orapa,
and Sowa--are mining towns and three--Gaberone, the capital;
Francistown; and Lobatse--are commercial/industrial. For a settlement
to qualify for urban status, it is supposed to have a minimum population
of 5,000 with at least seventy-five percent of the economically active population engaged in non-agricultural activities. Urban status may also be
conferred through a special legal arrangement. This has taken place in
the case of the mining settlements which are classified as towns even
though their populations are below the stipulated minimum.

The distribution of population across different size settlements has
changed substantially between 1971 and 1991. Large villages have generally gained in population, with many achieving urban status.

Consequently, the population classified as urban has jumped from 9.5 percent in 1971 (when there were only five urban centers), to 45.7 percent in 1991.

At the same time, the population of the lands and cattle posts has progressively shrunk although there has been a small increase in the numbers of people in settlements with fewer than 500 persons. A settlement must have 500 people to be considered a village in the more densely settled eastern part of the country; in the sparsely populated west, 250 is the minimum for village status. In general, the large villages have experienced phenomenal population growth in recent years (Ngcongco 1990). In 1971 there were no villages with a population of 20,000, while in 1991 there were six. Some of the factors behind this growth are given in the next section.

The Government Impact on Large Villages

The present status of large villages is, in part, the result of government policies from the colonial era to the present. After Botswana was declared a British protectorate in 1885, one of the first acts of the colonial government was to terminate the frequent movement of settlements, especially the large villages where colonial headquarters were located (Schapera 1943). Shortly thereafter, services such as post offices and schools began to be provided in the larger centers.

The people of Botswana were not passive bystanders at this point. They started to adopt new building technologies involving the use of durable materials and to erect bigger and better structures. The process was facilitated by participation in the cash economy and a shortage of traditional building materials that occurred just as relatively cheap manufactured materials were becoming available.

Settlements were also influenced by indirect rule which allowed the chiefs to be less accountable to their people and to exercise tight control on population movements (Silitshena 1983: Chapter 4). Village residence was strictly enforced and anyone who built a home at the lands or cattleposts was severely punished (Schapera 1943). The perpetuation of nucleated settlements was justified to the colonial government on the grounds of tradition and administrative and service needs.

The chiefs had become so powerful by the 1960s that the first independent Botswana government which came to power in 1966 enacted legislation aimed at reform. Some of the chiefs' power over land and economic life was taken away and vested instead in new institutions, notably landboards. These were committees composed of representatives of the district councils, the chief and his assistant, and elected mem

bers. The landboards have introduced new rules relevant to the allocation of land in rural areas and these have affected the structure and
growth of large villages, as will be shown below. Change has also
occurred because the movements of people are no longer regulated to the
extent that prevailed before independence. Some families have used the
greater flexibility to settle permanently at the lands and cattlepost areas
(Hitchcock 1978a; Silitshena 1983), a phenomena which began impercep-
tibly during the colonial period.

Post-independence economic policies have also been significant in
stimulating settlement change. In 1966, Botswana, in the grip of a severe
drought, had become dependent on British grants-in-aid to balance its
budget. Since agriculture, including livestock production, was central to
improving economic performance, the government concentrated on raising output in this sector. During this crisis period, villages actually came
to be viewed as a stumbling block to upgrading agricultural productivity. The first president of the country even called for the dismantling of the
"anacronistic" villages and the movement of people close to their fields
where they could concentrate on effective farming. A sociologist with the
Ministry of Agriculture made a case for the "hamletization" of the country:

> The country, both the electorate and their chosen leaders must abandon
> the idea of big villages getting bigger and bigger and being given a dis-
> proportionate share of the available services, education, water, electrici-
> ty and the like. Rather, such scarce resources must be concentrated on
> opening up and developing new centers of population, large enough to
> provide minimal social services but small enough to enable the cultiva-
> tor to remain within reasonable reach of his land and stock (Fosbrooke
> 1971: 198).

Before any new policies could be enacted, however, the economic situation changed following the discovery and exploitation of diamonds.
The Gross Domestic Product (GDP) was raised from $125 million in 1966
to $1,995 million in 1988/89, a sixteen fold increase (Republic of
Bostwana 1991), The revenues from the mining sector were augmented
by revenues from the customs pool, following the revision of the customs
agreement with South Africa, Lesotho, and Swaziland, and grants and
loans provided by donor finance.

Since the mining industry was capital intensive and did not create
many jobs, the government adopted the twin strategy of maximizing
returns from mining and investing them in rural areas (Republic of
Botswana 1973a). In 1972, rural development emerged as a focus of

national planning with the publication of a white paper and the appointment of a consultancy team (Republic of Botswana 1972, 1973b).

At this point, the government again reviewed the role of villages in the national economy. It was decided that villages should be viewed not as obstacles to improved agriculture, but as instruments of rural development:

> It is already apparent, however, that the large traditional villages are a major asset to the rural development effort. As centers of population, commmunications, purchasing power, production, and services, they can serve as focal points for the development of their rural hinterland. The major villages will, therefore, be primary targets for the provision of social and economic infrastructure and the creating of income-earning opportunities (Republic of Botswana 1977: 197).

A few examples will illustrate efforts at village improvement as part of rural development. During the period 1973-1976, the government launched the "Accelerated Rural Development Program" (ARDP) which focused on making improvements in classrooms, clinics, and roads. Further developments have been instituted under the "Major Village Infrastructure Program" which includes the servicing of sites, upgrading of roads, water supplies, housing, and sanitation, and the strengthening of local administration.

In the current (1991-1997) Development Plan, $64 million has been set aside for village infrastructure upgrading which deals with roads, sewerage works, power, water supply, and tele- communications (Republic of Botswana 1991). One important intervention has been the paving of roads, particularly those linking villages to the modern towns such as Gaborone and Francistown. The road improvements have contributed to the development of commuting within a radius of fifty kilometers. Villages like Molepolole, Mochudi, Ramotswa, Gabane, Tlokweng, and Thamaga, which are within easy reach of Gaborone, have been dormitorized and have experienced very rapid population growth. There are two types of commuters: local people who are finding it cheaper to stay at their homes and commute daily and migrants from the countryside who cannot find or afford accommodation in town.

The impact of government economic policies on rural settlements has been felt mainly in the area of social and physical infrastructure. In the income generating sectors, especially in agriculture, the effect has been more limited because of continuing problems of poor soils, low rainfall, and inadequate technology. One exception is the tourism industry which has experienced rapid growth in recent years. The industry has followed the high-cost, low-volume model, attracting most of its customers from the region, particularly South Africa, but with an increasing number coming from further afield. The main centers for tourism have been the towns of Maun and Kasane, and both have expanded in recent years. One of the main consequences of government policies has been the growth of large villages. Most villages have more than trebled their population since 1971 with growth rates much higher than the national rate of 3.4 percent per year. It is obvious that the large villages are the focus of in-migration. This is the result, in part, of the stagnation of arable production that has encouraged migration in search of employment and social security benefits such as drought relief (Republic of Botswana 1992; Silitshena 1993).

Finally, we should note the attempt by the government to incorporate rural settlements into national settlement planning through the National Settlement Policy (NSP). The main goal of NSP is to provide a framework for the distribution of investment in a way that reflects settlement size, population, economic potential, level of infrastructure, and the role of service centers in the surrounding regions (Republic of Botswana 1992). The specific objectives of the NSP include the following: (1) Control of excessive migration to urban areas, (2) Provision of guidelines and long-term strategy for the development of settlements, (3) Rationalization and promotion of the optimal use of land and the preservation of the best arable land, (4) Conservation of natural resources for the benefit of present and future generations, and (5) Provision of guidelines for the development of transportation networks to strengthen the functional linkages between settlements.

According to the NSP, settlements are classified into three categories: primary, secondary, and tertiary. The six largest villages--Molepolole, Maun, Kanye, Serowe, Mahalapye, and Mochudi--belong to the primary category as do the leading modern towns--Gaborone, Francistown, Selibe-Phikwe, and Lobatse. Therefore, for the purpose of investment, these villages are treated as towns.

The Evolution of the Tswana Village

The village in Botswana has always performed a number of roles. It has been a home for farmers but it has also been a social and political hub and a central place. Now some villages are being transformed into industrial centers. As already noted, some of the villages near the big modern towns have been turned into dormitory settlements for urban workers. As these changes have taken place, there has also been some continuity. In this section we shall discuss the village from a historical perspective.

The nucleated villages in Botswana traditionally had populations varying from 500 (or 250 in the dryer areas) to more than 30,000 (Schapera 1955: 8). The center of the village was the main meeting place (the Kgotla), situated near the chiefs house, while the rest of the village was divided into wards (Figure 6.2). The ward developed as a social and administrative unit, and each had a population ranging from 100 to 1000 persons who were related by blood or marriage. The wards were administered by headmen who owed allegiance to the chief and virtually all had their own kgotla near the headman's home. Wards were distributed over space in such a way as to reflect the social divisions in society (Tlou 1974) (Figure 6.3).

During the colonial and post-colonial periods, the processes discussed above brought about some changes in the character of the villages. One of the earliest of these, following the stablilization of villages, was architectural (Schapera 1943; Hardie 1982). The round huts with conical thatched roofs gave way to a variety of designs, including European-style buildings constructed with imported materials. The new houses took more space which, along with population growth, caused the villages to gradually spread outward. During the colonial period, the chiefs occasionally had to relocate wards to create space for expansion (Gardener 1974).

Independence came with new institutions and new rules concerning spatial organization. Residential stands were no longer allocated according to membership in a ward, but on a first-come, first-served basis. Even single women were allocated stands, which was uncommon before independence. According to Hardie (1982), during the first eight years of its operation, the Kgatleng Land Board allocated all the stands that it had available, most at the periphery of the village. Generally, the ward system has not been reproduced in these newly developed areas.

The rapid expansion of the periphery contrasts with the decay at the center of the villages (Hardie 1982). This is the result of a preference for the larger stands near the edge of the village and a reluctance to give empty stands at the center to strangers. The decay is also demographic as most of the heads of households near the center are female, many of them widowed and elderly. The disintegration at the center is symptomatic of the breakdown of the power of the chiefs and the former system of land allocation:

> No longer does the kgosi (chief) have the authority to direct the people as to where they should live. No longer is the status of ward or individual reflected in a person's residential location in town. No longer is security and protection required and water, which once was available

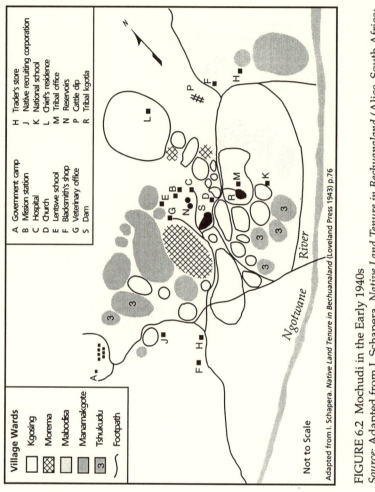

FIGURE 6.2 Mochudi in the Early 1940s
Source: Adapted from I. Schapera, *Native Land Tenure in Bechuanaland* (Alice, South Africa: Loveland Press, 1943), p.76. Reprinted by permission

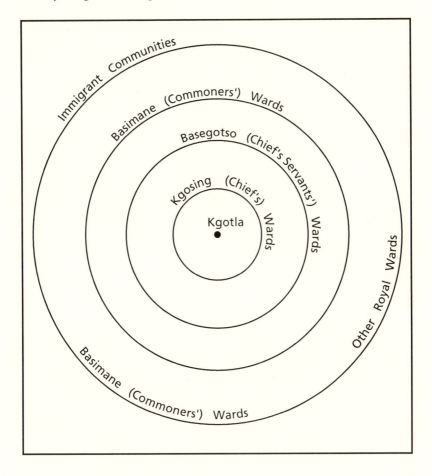

FIGURE 6.3 Ward Location at the Batawana Capital (Diagramatic)
Source: T. Tlou, *Botswana Notes and Records 6* (1974), P. 73. Reprinted by permission.

only in the center of town, is now equally available to the houses on the periphery. The control of land has moved from a centralized authority to a democratically elected one and the former rules of status and precedence, reflected in the spatial expression, have now been swept aside. The ease with which land is attainable makes the disintegration and spread of the town that much more rapid and Mochudi, for example, has experienced tremendous growth (Hardie 1982: 210).

Although the villages became permanently fixed to specific locations, agriculture remained relatively extensive. With continuous cultivation, the land nearer the village became exhausted and the fields, which had become bigger on average with the use of the plough, began to "migrate" further away from the village. The increase in distance between the villages and the lands was also a natural consequence of population growth (Silitshena 1983). In time, people established second homes at the lands which they used during the period of peak labor demand.

During the early part of the agricultural season, (November-January), the husband, wife and preschool children would move with a few possessions to the lands. The school-age children remained at the main village and joined the family on weekends. The husband had to spend much of his time traveling, since he was responsible for supervising activities at the cattleposts, lands, and in the village. Other members of the family might visit the village as well in order to obtain supplies, to use health facilities, or to attend social occasions. They might also visit the cattlepost to fetch some milk. At the end of the agricultural season (July/ August), after harvesting was completed, members of the household moved back to their village home with their produce. This respite provided an opportunity for house renovation and for organizing social events.

Evidence suggests that long before independence, some individuals were already dissatisfied with this system and were settling at their lands (Silitshena 1983). However, with the demise of the chiefs, following the post-independence legislation, the process became more open and widespread and some of the second homes were converted into permanent residences.

There are several motives behind this change, the most important of which is supervision and protection of livestock (Arntzen 1989: 174). The herd owners, especially those with small herds, cannot afford to keep their animals at the cattleposts because most of the herdboys are either in school or seeking paid employment in town. Movement to the lands has also resulted from lack of space in the villages, lack of transport, and insufficient resources to afford a house in the village and near the fields. Some farmers believe that proximity to the lands will improve product ivity and, at least, make water, firewood, and milk more accessible. Figures 6.4a and 6.4b show the modifications in land use that reflect all of these socio-economic developments.

Although permanent movement to the lands is now an option, there are still many farmers who continue to be involved in seasonal movements between village and fields, a distance that usually averages about 12.2 kilometers (Kgatleng District) but which will vary with the size of the village. Thus, in the primary center of Mochudi, the average farmer must travel 17.3 kilometers to the family fields, while the average for a small village may be closer to five kilometers. The Mochudi figure is comparable to Molepolole (Silitshena 1983). Distances to cattleposts are invariably long but are influenced by the location of the villages in relation to the grazing area.

A great deal has been written about the administrative role of Tswana villages in the context of the Tswana political system (Schapera 1943; Tlou 1974; Campbell 1982; Parsons 1982). The pre-colonial Tswana chiefs controlled relatively large states with diverse ethnic groups. Elaborate systems of local government had developed to ensure security and to extract tribute and various forms of service from the non-Tswana subject peoples, some of them located at the periphery of the state. Campbell has described the Tawana system, which was centered on Maun village as follows:

> The whole areas under Tawana thraldom was divided into "counties" with senior Tawana in charge of each. These were subdivided and were nominally under the charge of the senior local person, normally Yei of royal descent, to supervise the areas and to ensure that Tawana property, cattle, ivory, and furs, was properly guarded. Several times a year they would visit their countries; then the local Yei headmen had to give a reckoning of the property under their charge, produce children to be used as serfs at the capital, and take instructions for the following months (Campbell 1982: 134).

The nineteenth century was a momentous period for the Tswana village, as a result of intensive culture contact. The first groups of Europeans to come to Botswana were missionaries and traders. The missionaries, among them the famous David Livingstone, started by converting the chiefs. The traders set up their stores in the villages and exchanged some of their merchandise, which included guns and ammunition, first with Tswana nobles and then with the rest of the community. The nobles, in turn, used subject peoples to procure local trade goods, particularly ivory and ostrich feathers. The village was thus evolving

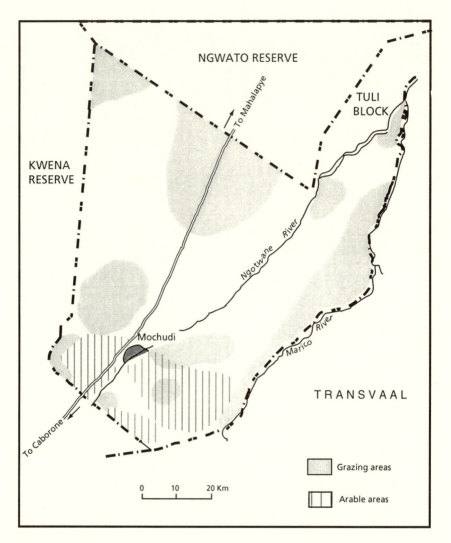

FIGURE 6.4a Pre-Independence Rural Land Use, Mochudi Area
Source: Adapted from J. Arntzen. *Norsk Geografisk Tidsskrift 36* (1984) p. 97.
Reprinted by permission

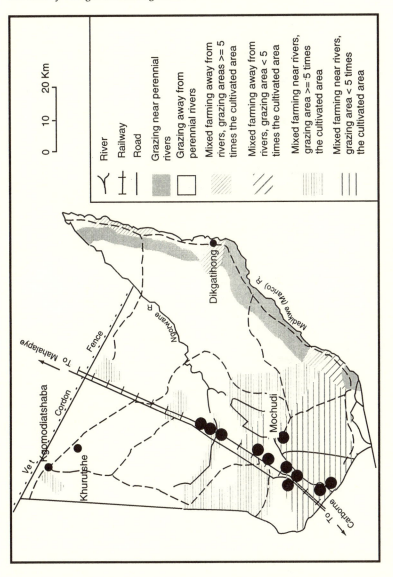

FIGURE 6.4b Post-Independence Rural Land Use, Mochudi Area

Source: Adapted from J. Arntzen. *Norsk Geografisk Tidsskrift 36* (1984) p. 97. Reprinted by permission

into both a central place where goods were traded, and a center of diffusion of new ideas. Parsons (1982), who showed how Shoshong was the center of development in the Ngwato State during the nineteenth century, observed the following:

> At the center of the state stood the capital town or city, Shoshong. The town was the administrative, trading, and cultural center of the kingdom and a crossroads of major wagon routes (Parsons 1982: 120).

The colonial era was an important formative period for settlements in Botswana. It was a period when pre-existing "capital" villages were stabilized and started to grow. Under the new regime, they became headquarters of the native reserves, a demotion from being state capitals. They also began to provide educational and health services in addition to performing commercial and administrative functions. Some of the fastest growing settlements were located along the railway, such as Mahalapye (population 28,078) and Tonota (population 11,129). A new commercial type of village with a transport function had thus come into existence.

At the time of independence, the former native reserve headquarters were adopted as the capitals of the new districts, each to contain district councils and a number of other local and central government offices and services. An example of the range of activities found at one primary center is shown in Table 6.1The Department of Town and Regional Planning (Republic of Botswana 1983) also identified a five order central place hierarchy in one district (Table 6.2). Such a distribution of government and economic activities over settlements of different sizes was seen to maximize access to needed goods and services.

The range of central place activities included in Table 6.1 are not typical of African rural settlements since the provision of services in Botswana is unusually decentralized. Some of the functions offered by the district centers are available, but at a lower level and for smaller catchment areas, in the sub-district centers. This is in line with the National Settlement Policy, whereby such centers are expected to provide services to their immediate hinterlands. In fact, sub-district offices have been established in some villages as part of the decentralization of district council authority.

The large villages have played a particularly important central place role. People who have migrated to the lands continue to visit former villages, primarily to shop and use medical services (Silitshena 1983). One interesting study of the central place functions of a large village was carried out in Mahalapye and its surrounding region (HHC Team Consultants 1984). The study found that Mahalapye had the following

TABLE 6.1 Some Central Place Activities Found at Mochudi

Facilities	Number	Facilities	Number
Hospitals	1	Clinics	2
Primary Schools	9	Secondary Schools	2
Tech. Training	2	Banks	5
Posts/telecomm.	2	Museums	1
Public Library	1	Chemist	3
Government Dept. (Central)	13	Government Dept. (Local)	8
Tribal Admin.	8	General Retailers	38
Wholesalers	1	Garage, Gas Stations	4
Bars, liquor	12	Restaurants	14
Fresh Produce/ Butcher	24	Churches	25
		Undertakers	1
Manufacturing	8	Sports, Soc. Organ.	30

Source: Central Statististics Office. 1983. *Guide to the Villages of Botswana.* Section 4. Pp. 101-102. Gaberone: Government Printer

TABLE 6.2 Settlement Heirarchy in the Kweneng District

Settlement Type	No. of Settlements	Range of Functions
District Center	1	Over 70
Sub-District Center	3	31-37
Regional	6	23-26
Local	23	11-20
Sub-Local	51	1-9

Source: Department of Town and Regional Planning, 1983. *Kweneng District Spatial Plan*. Molepolole: Kweneng District Council.

characteristics: (1) it accounted for at least sixty-five percent of all the cattle marketed in the region for the previous six years, (2) it was the main regional commercial center (fifty percent of total sales), (3) it was a major rail and road transport center where transport was considered the "key to growth and development in the area," (HHC Team Consultants 1984: 18), and (4) it was the leading manufacturing center accounting for sixteen of the seventeen businesses established region-wide.

Yet, in spite of commercial success, villages in Botswana are not yet fully engaged in income generating activities, especially manufacturing. The exceptions are the villages close to modern towns and those involved in tourism. Industrial stands remain undeveloped (Sebina 1990). According to Modibetsane (1990), villages do not satisfy the minimum conditions necessary to attract manufacturing.

Ecological Constraints on Botswana's Large Villages

The Tswana, with their relatively high level of social organization, were able to maintain large nucleated settlements. However, the hostile environment described above has always imposed some constraints on development and the formation of villages. We can identify two phases of the evolution of the Tswana village in the context of environmental interrelationships: the pre-modern period during which the village was almost totally dependent upon local resources and subject to the vagaries of the physical environment, and the modern period during which the village has increasingly become divorced from local resources as a result of the intervention of the modern economy and new technologies. It is not easy to fix dates for these periods but generally, we can say the modern village starts to form during colonial times.

The Pre-Modern or Traditional Village

There were three major considerations in the choice of a site for traditional Tswana settlements: water supply, proximity to arable land, and potential for defense (Schapera 1943). A location among hills with good soil and a river nearby was therefore favored. However, as Parsons has observed, "Tswana centralization in large agro-towns promoted a cycle of depletion of local grasslands" (Parsons 1982: 120). Therefore, villages had to keep changing their sites to combat water shortages, famines, outbreaks of disease, and soil exhaustion.

Schapera (1943) has documented movements of such Tswana groups as the Bakwena, Bangwato, and Batawana. The Bakwena moved their capital no fewer than ten times in the space of about twenty-five years

(c1827-1852). The Bangwato relocated their capital about five times during the period c1810-1825, while the Batawana, between 1883-1916, occupied six different sites. The reasons given above were responsible for
these movements, as well as occasional flooding or conflict. In times of
severe drought, people were reduced to foraging and village locations
had to be within easy access of wild plant resources (Hitchcock 1978b).

Sansom (1974) has a slightly different approach to explaining land
use and settlement among the Tswana. He contrasts the scattered settlement patterns of the Nguni, whose country is composed of "small-scale
repetitive configurations that contain a variety of natural resources" to
the uniform terrain of the Sotho-Tswana country (Sansom 1974: 140) .
The uniform ecological environment militates against the concentration
of land uses-- residence, agriculture, and pastoralism--in one place, as
would occur in dispersed settlement systems. He has argued that:

> On the inland plateaux one is often confronted with large expanses of
> relatively uniform country. To move from one type of plant to another
> or to find different soil types, one must travel over larger distances.
> There is a general problem of finding a constant water supply and water
> resources are often far apart. Because people need to exploit variations
> of terrain, they much range over an extensive area. To accommodate a
> ranging and open strategy, the tribal territory replaces the district in sup-
> plying the self-contained area in which the variety of its inhabitants'
> requirements will be satisfied (Sansom 1974: 142-143).

The combination of nucleated settlements (with arable fields and grazing
at some distance from the residence) and frequent relocation, could
accommodate the need for access to varied resources.

By the turn of the century, Pax Britannica was firmly entrenched and
the scourge of tribal wars had ended. This situation allowed for new
solutions to the problems of population/ resource imbalance. Thus, in
1898, Chief Kgama of the Bangwato decided to break up some of the large
villages, particularly his capital, because of scarcity of water and the
increasing distance to the fields (Schapera 1943). He also felt that his people "could not live huddled up as their fathers used to do, and leave the
vast majority of the country unoccupied" (Schapera 1943: 269). His other
goal was to improve sanitation. He wrote to the British High
Commissioner in Pretoria as follows:

> "Your excellency may know that since the Matabele War, I have aban-
> doned the policy of having all my people in one large town, thinking it
> better for the people that they should live in smaller communi-

ties. We Bechuana people do not know how to keep large towns healthy as you white people do, though we were formerly obliged to live in large towns for protection" (quoted in Schapera 1943: 270).

It is clear, then, that the deterioration of sanitation and its association with disease, must have been one of the causes of settlement movement in the past, although the resulting deaths would probably have been attributed to witchcraft. The answer this time was found in the creation of smaller settlements in the outlying regions of the state, where they could be positioned to guard the frontiers (Silitshena 1976; Parsons 1982). The pre-modern village had thus come to an end.

The Modern Village

As already noted above, colonial rule, combined with new technologies and economic changes, brought about the stabilization of major villages. The dilemma surrounding the movement of the Bangwato from Phalatswe illustrates the interplay of these factors. By 1896, Phalatswe's water supply had dwindled and the vegetation around the village had been devastated (Parsons 1982). The option of moving to another site was initially rejected because of the capital investment that had gone into a local school and church buildings. Alternative water supply sources were then sought and the construction of a dam and a kilometer of water piping was proposed. Finally, when this option proved to be too expensive, the dilemma was resolved by moving the population to the large village of Serowe (Parsons 1982).

Boreholes turned out to be the new technology that did the most to remove the restraint of water supplies and, in turn, stabilize settlements. It was a development that was initially undertaken and paid for by the people of Botswana themselves, without any assistance from the colonial government (Silitshana 1983: 126). However, population continued to increase and, as boreholes began to dry up, deeper ones had to be drilled. In some places, such as in Mahalapye, it was necessary to tap aquifers at a distance of fifty kilometers and to have the water transported by pipe to the village. In other large settlements, including Molepolole, limited water supplies have been a constraint on development (Republic of Botswana 1990).

For boreholes to be viable, ground water resources have to be protected from pollution by pit toilets. This has been done by restricting village growth in the direction of boreholes (Government of Botswana 1986). However, according to the 1981 census, more than sixty percent of rural households had no private toilets. A recent survey carried out in

Molepolole showed that seventy-seven percent of households had no access to a toilet of any kind and only thirteen percent had access to private toilets (Government of Botswana 1990). Conditions in large villages were indeed considered unsanitary during the colonial period and there were occasional calls for the dismantling of settlements on this account (Schapera 1943: 267).

In addition to limited water supplies, the other major constraint on village permanence or expansion was the availability of natural vegetation for construction materials and fuel. Hardie (1982) has shown how the architecture at Mochudi has evolved from a building style based on local materials, to one incorporating foreign styles and using imports. This transformation has been facilitated by the increasing participation of Batswana in the cash economy, starting with labor migration to the South African mines. According to Hardie's study of Mochudi, seventy-four percent of those questioned intended to pay for the construction of new homes with wages earned outside of the area (Hardie 1982: 208). It is clear, therefore, that the Tswana village can no longer be understood only within the context of its local environment and resources.

Vegetation around the villages is also used for feulwood, and supplies have become either scarce or procurable only at long distances. Most of the vegetation is now composed mainly of thorn bushes, a reflection of environmental degradation (Van Vegten 1983). Finally, since the removal of vegetation exposes the soil to rain and wind, erosion have become a serious concern.

Ameliorating Environmental Stress

One way of combatting the decline of the ecosystem has been to make the production of village physical plans a legal requirement. This has been facilitated by extending the operation of the Town and Country Act to rural settlements. The landboards and the Department of Towns and Regional Planning (DTRP) of the Ministry of Local Government, Lands, and Housing, are the main institutions involved in the physical planning of villages. Figure 6.5 shows the current land use in Molepolole where planning has facilitated balanced growth.

The Department of Town and Regional Planning is responsible for the enforcement of the Town and Country Planning Act. A number of village development plans have been produced with the following objectives: (1) anticipating future demand for land, (2) providing and upgrading services and infrastructure, (3) avoiding socio-economic polarization, (4) preserving certain village traditions, (5) protecting the environment, and (6) decentralizing planning and implementation functions and

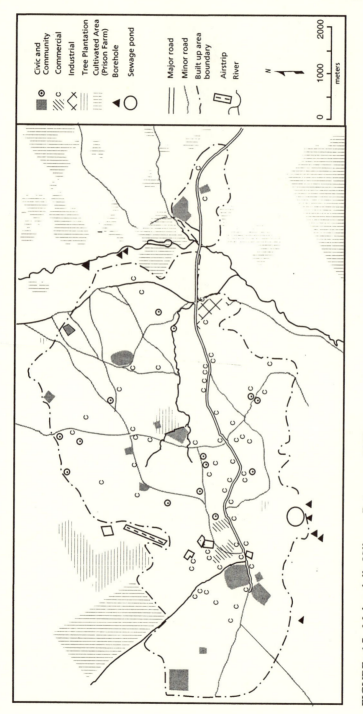

FIGUREe 6.5 Molepololle Village - Botswana, 1990s
Source: Dept. of Town and Regional Planning, Gaberones, Botswana (1990), Map 8.3

encouraging local participation (Republic of Botswana 1986; Sebina 1990). Earlier in the chapter it was mentioned that the government has set aside a considerable amount of money for the improvement and upgrading of village infrastructure. Priority is being given to primary centers and "infrastructure standards applied in urban areas will be adopted for rural areas to enable these villages to become alternative locations for commercial and industrial investment" (Republic of Botswana 1991, Part II: 44).

One important innovation has been the provision of sewers in some large villages, although it will take some time before this measure impacts on a substantial number of people. A recent study has shown that it is possible to install a series of communal septic tanks that could serve groups of homes (Baldwin et al. 1993). Perhaps a more affordable sanitation option for most people is the pit toilet. During the 1985-1990 development plan, the government launched a UNICEF-funded self-help Environmental Sanitation Project in which 7,000 toilets were built; 22,000 toilets are to constructed during the current development plan that ends in 1997 (Republic of Botswana 1991).

Finally, it is important to show that people are not just helpless victims; they can design adaptive strategies to cope with difficult circumstances. One example would be the approaches people have used to address the fuelwood problem. A few households have switched to alternative sources of energy (Kgathi 1992) The overwhelming majority that still collect firewood for themselves have responded to fuelwood shortages in several ways such as: (1) increasing the labor time spent on fuelwood collection, (2) switching to collecting less preferred species, (3) abandoning taboos surrounding the collection of certain plants, and (4) conserving firewood through such devices as cooking fewer meals and protecting open fires (Kgathi 1992)

Conclusion

The Tswana village has been a persistent feature of the Botswana landscape and is rooted in the culture of the people. Nucleated settlements have facilitated administration and mobilization of people for defense. In more recent times thay made it possible for relatively large numbers of people to enjoy educational and health facilities. The latter argument was used extensively by the chiefs during the colonial period in support of villages. At this point, when the chiefs were at the height of their power, some individuals occasionally disobeyed the rule of not having permanent homes at the lands. In such cases, the chiefs could send their army to burn the homes and crops of recalcitrants who were then brought back to the village by force (Schapera 1943).

Yet, the existence of large, nucleated settlements in a fragile, semi-arid environment has always posed serious challenges to survival and the forces favoring nucleation were continuously at odds with those that favored dispersal. Environmental problems were further complicated by social conflicts, such as those over witchcraft and succession, which might lead to fission. The traditional compromise was to build villages, but to relocate them as often as possible, usually when signs of environmental or social stress became evident. The average period spent in one area rarely exceeded five years, although the settlement might move because of other reasons such as war.

Since colonial days, the large villages have become fixed and they have grown in size. This has been made possible largely by the introduction of new technology to tap ground water and the spread of the cash economy. The processes that started during the colonial period have accelerated. Some of the policies pursued by the independent government have entrenched the large villages and increased their attractiveness. Thus, two current trends now overlap; some of the population is redistributing itself into smaller settlements to gain access to fields and cattleposts while aggregation in the largest villages continues.

The government of Botswana is trying to use the large villages as nodes of development and in so doing avoid urban primacy and the uneven distribution of resources between rural and urban areas. Various programs have been implemented to help villages improve their physical infrastructure, although social infrastructure has not been neglected. While the government and commerce continue to provide the most jobs, there is a need to develop some productive activities that will be income generating and stimulate new types of employment in rural areas.

The fixation of settlements has had serious environmental consequences: depletion of vegetation, dwindling water supplies, and the problems arising from all forms of waste disposal. The benefits of large villages have to be weighed against the costs of overcoming these problems. The Botswana example shows that when there are adequate resources, it becomes possible to ameliorate environmental concerns and increase the range of choices available for the arrangement of people in rural space.

Notes

1. It is not easy to reconstruct the actual size of a kingdom. The boundaries were fluid and, in some instances, not clearly defined. One of the largest kingdoms was Ngwato, which roughly corresponded with the boundaries of the present Central District. In fact, the native reserves were created roughly out of the kingdoms. We can use the data on reserves to get an idea of the size of these kingdoms. In 1947, Schapera gave the following figures.

Reserve	Area (square miles)	Population est.	Density
Ngwato	40,000	110,000	2.8
Tawana	34,500	35,000	1.0
Kwena	10,000	33,000	2.2
Ngwaketse	9,000	31,000	3.4
Kgatleng	3,600	18,000	5.0
Malete	178	8,500	47.8
Tlokwa	67	2,000	29.9

Source: I. Schapera. 1947. *Migrant Labor and Tribal Life*. London: Reprinted by permission of Oxford University Press. P. 4.

References

Afolyan, A. A. 1992. "Environmentally Induced Population Mobility in Africa." In *Population and Environment in Africa*. Pp. 172-184. Dakar: The Union for Population Studies.

Arntzen, J. 1984. "Crop Production, Cattle Rearing and Land-Use in Kgatleng District, Botswana." *Norsk Geografisk Tidsskrift* 38: 95-   108.
____. 1989. *Environmental Pressure and Adaptation in Rural Botswana*. Amsterdam: Free University of Amsterdam.

Baldwin, M., P. Cole, P. Graham, C. Kuan, J. Osiowy, A. Pike, and L. Rasesigo. 1993. *Tradition and Change: The Ramotswa-Taung Development Proposal*. Winnipeg: University of Manitoba, Department of City Planning.

Campbell, A. C. 1982. "Some Aspects of Settlement in Northwestern Botswana." In R. R. Hitchcock and M. R. Smith, eds. *Settlement in Botswana*. Pp. 129-139. Gaberone: Botswana Society.

Chambers, R. and D. Feldman. 1973. *Report on Rural Development in Botswana*. Gaberone: Government Printer.

Central Statistics Office. 1983. *Guide to the Villages and Towns of Botswana*. Gaberone: Government Printer.

Cooke, H. J. 1982. "The Physical Environment of Botswana." In R. R. Hitchcock and M. R. Smith, eds. *Settlement in Botswana*. Pp. 1-12. Gaberone: Botswana Society.

Cooke, H. J. and R.M.K. Silitshena. 1986. "Botswana - An Environmental Profile." Unpublished Report Prepared for the United Nations Environmental Program. Nairobi, Kenya.

Dachs, A., ed. 1975. Papers of John McKenzie. Johannesburg: Witwatersrand University Press.

El-Bushra, El Sayed. 1967. "The Factors Affecting Settlement Distribution in the Sudan." *Geografiska Anneler* 49: 10-24.

Fosbrooke, H. A. 1971. "The Role of Tradition in Rural Development." *Botswana Notes and Records* 3: 188-198.

Gardner. R. 1974. "Some Sociological and Physiological Factors Affecting the Growth of Serowe." *Botswana Notes and Records* 6: 77-88.

Hardie, G. 1982. "The Dynamics of the Internal Organization of the Traditional Capital, Mochudi." In R. R. Hitchkock and M. R. Smith, eds. *Settlement in Botswana*. Pp. 205-219. Gaberone: The Botswana Society.

Henderson, W. 1974. "A Note on Economic Status and Village House Types." *Botswana Notes and Records* 6: 228-230.

HHC Team Consultants, Inc. 1984. *Mahalapye Upgrading Feasibility Study*. Volumes 1-3. Gaberone: Ministry of Local Government and Lands.

Hinchey, M., ed. 1978. *Drought in Botswana*. Gaberone: The Botswana Society.

Hitchcock, R. K. 1978a. *Kalahari Cattle-Posts*. Gaberone: Ministry of Local Government and Lands.

_____. 1978b. "The Traditional Response to Drought in Botswana." In M. Hinchey, ed. *Drought in Botswana*. Pp. 91-97. Gaborone: The Botswana Society.

Hogg, R. 1987. "Development in Kenya: Drought, Desertification, and Food Scarcity." *African Affairs* 86: 47-58.

Kgathi, A. 1992. "Household Response to the Fuelwoood Scarcity in Southeastern Botswana: Implications for Energy Policy." Unpublished Ph.D. Thesis, University of East Anglia.

Kuper, A. 1975. "The Social Structure of the Sotho-Speaking Peoples of Southern Africa." *Africa* 45: 67-81 and 138-149.

Mascarenhas, A. 1979. "After Villagization - What?" In C. Pratt and B. U. Mwansasu, eds. *Towards Socialism in Tanzania*. Pp. 145-165. Toronto: University of Toronto Press.

Mlay, W.F.I., 1982. "Environmental Implications of Land Use Patterns in the New Villages in Tanzania." In J. W. Arntzen, L. Ngcongco, and S. D. Turner, eds. *Land Policy and Agriculture in Eastern and Southern Africa*. Pp. 100-106. Tokyo: United Nations University.

Modibetsane, D. 1990. "Urbanization as a Concept for Development." *Report on the Proceedings of the National Settlements Policy Workshop.* Prepared by the Department of Towns and Regional Planning. Pp. 108-115. Gaberone: Government Printer.

Morgan, W. B. and J. C. Pugh. 1969. West Africa. London: Metheun.

Mortimore, M. 1987. "Shifting Sands and Human Sorrow: Social Response to Drought and Desertificiation." *Desertification Control Bulletin* 14: 1-14.

Ngcongco N. 1990. "Population Distribution and Settlement Patterns." *Report on the Proceedings of the National Settlement Policy Workshop.* Prepared by the Department of Town and Regional Planning. Gaberone: Government Printer.

Pauw, B. A. 1960. "Some Changes in the Social Structure of the Tlhaping of Taung Reserve." *African Studies* 19: 49-76.

Parsons, N. 1982. "Settlement in East-Central Bostwana c. 1800-1920." In R. R. Hitchcock and M. R. Smith, eds. *Settlement in Botswana.* Pp. 115-128. Gaberone: Botswana Society.

Republic of Botswana. 1972. *Rural Development in Botswana.* Gaberone: Government Printer.

_____. 1973a. *National Development Plan 1973-78. Part 1.* Gaborone: Government Printer.

_____. 1973b. *National Policy for Rural Development: The Government Decisions on the Report of Rural Development.* Gaberone: Government Printer.

_____. 1977. *National Development Plan, 1976-81.* Gaberone: Government Printer.

_____. *Department of Town and Regional Planning.* 1983. Kweneng District Spatial Plan. Molepolole: Kweneng District Council.

_____. *Department of Town and Regional Planning.* 1986. Serowe Development Plan. Gaberone: Government Printer.

_____. *Department of Town and Regional Planning.* 1990. Molepolole Development Plan - Report of Survey. Gaberone: Department of Town and Regional Planning.

_____. 1991. *National Development Plan: 1991-97.* Gaberone: Government Printer.

_____. 1992. *National Settlement Policy.* Gaberone: Government Printer.

Sansom, B. 1974. "Traditional Economic Systems." In W. D. Hammond-Tooke, ed. *The Bantu-Speaking Peoples of Southern Africa.* Pp.135-176. London: Routledge and Kegan Paul.

Schapera, I. 1940. "The Political Organization of the Ngwato of Bechuanaland Protectorate." In M. Fortes and E. E. Evans-Pritchard, eds. *African Political Systems.* Pp. 60-82. London: Oxford University Press.

_____. 1943. *Native Land Tenure in Bechuanaland Protectorate.* Alice, South Africa: The Lovedale Press.

_____. 1955. *A Handbook of Tswana Law and Custom.* London: Cass.
Sebina, M. 1990. "Village Planning: The Palapye Experience." *In Report of the Proceedings of the National Settlement Policy Workshop.* Prepared by the Department of Town and Regional Planning. Pp. 99-107. Gaberone: Government Printer
Siddle, D. J. 1971. "Some Rural Settlement Forms." In D. Davies, ed. *Zambia in Maps.* Pp. 60-61. London: Hodder and Stoughton.
Silitshena, R.M.K. 1976. "Notes of the Origins of Some Settlements in the Kweneng District." *Botswana Notes and Records 8*: 97-103.
_____. 1982a. "Population Movements and Settlement in Contemporary Botswana." In R. R. Hitchcock and M. R. Smith, eds. *Settlement in Botswana.* Pp. 31-46. Gaberone: The Botswana Society.
_____. 1982b. "The Regrouping Policy in the North East District of Botswana." In L. A. Kosinski and J. I. Clarke, eds. *Redistribution of Population in Africa.* Pp. 202-208. London: Heinemann,
_____. 1983. *Intra-Rural Migration and Settlement Changes in   Botswana.* Leiden: African Studies Center.
_____. 1993. "Where Will Batswana Live in the 21st Century." paper presented to the Botswana Society Symposium on Botswana in the 21st Century. Gaberone, October 19th-22nd.
Tlou, T. 1974. "The Nature of Batswana States: Towards a Theory of Batswana Traditional Government: The Batawana Case." *Botswana Notes and Records 6*: 57-75.
Van Vegten, J. A. 1983. "Thornbush Encroachment in a Savanna Ecosystem in Eastern Botswana." *Vegetatio 56*: 3-7.
Wilson, M. 1969. "The Sotho, Venda, and Songa." In M. Wilson and L. Thompson, eds. *The Oxford History of South Africa.* Volume 1. Pp. 131-182. London: Oxford University Press.

7

Settlement Structure and Landscape Ecology in the Sahel: The Case of Northern Yatenga, Burkina Faso

Robert E. Ford

Settlement patterns visible across a landscape reveal to the careful observer a complex interaction of dynamic forces--sociocultural, political, economic, demographic, and environmental--within a specific geographical and social space. Africa, like many Third-World regions, is experiencing dramatic settlement change; nowhere is this more evident than in zones of strong cultural and ecological transition which some have called "cultural frontiers" or "ecotones." The Sahelo-Sudanian (semi-arid) zone of northern Yatenga, Burkina Faso, is such a zone (Figure 7.1). The patterns of interaction observable in Yatenga are particularly fascinating due to an inherently complex social, ethnic, and religious history, which, in turn, has been altered by dramatic post-colonial political and economic change, intensified by recent ecological deterioration. All this has greatly affected the region's potential for long-term sustainable development as well as its settlement structure (Milleville and Serpantié 1993; Ford 1982, 1992).

This chapter describes general patterns of settlement evolution in northern Yatenga as illustrated by the experience of three distinct communities--Banh, Toulfe, and Sodin (Figure 7.1). In all three cases, a combination of socio-economic and other forces have produced dramatic land-use intensification and even possibly "agricultural involution" (Geertz 1963; Marchal 1977, 1983; Benoit 1982). The issue of the "environmental nexus", (Cleaver and Schreiber 1993) or the relationship between population pressure and environmental degradation, has become the focus of considerable debate (Honadle, Grosse, and Phumpiu 1994; Grosse 1994a,b; Turner II and Benjamin 1994; Ford 1995). (See also Repetto and Holmes 1983; Falloux and Mukendi 1988; Lele and Stone 1989; Shaikh and Snrech 1993; Williams 1991; King 1993; Falloux and

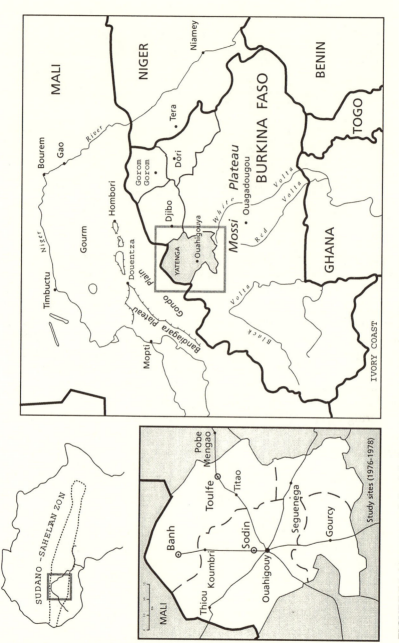

FIGURE 7.1 Yatenga and the Sahelo-Sudanian Region of Burkino Faso

Talbot 1993;   Milleville and Serpantié 1993; Meillassoux et al. 1991; English et al. 1994). This chapter will attempt to elucidate the links between settlement structure and cultural-ecological and agricultural change.

Historical-Political Backgrounds of Yatenga

The Kingdom of Yatenga is the most recently founded of the major Mossi States that occupy much of the Voltaic shield area in the headwaters of the Red and White Volta rivers. The Mossi peoples originally migrated from present northern Ghana somewhere between the late fourteenth and early fifteenth centuries (Figure 7.2). Those who migrated into the Sahelian fringe of the Mossi Plateau in Yatenga did not achieve control over its present territory until the reign of King Naaba Kango (1757-1787) (Skinner 1964; Hammond 1966; Izard 1985).

Naaba Kango is still remembered for his ruthless and despotic reign as well as the numerous wars of conquest he led against surrounding peoples. In the process, many Kurumba and Dogon, the autochthonous people of the region, were assimilated as sub-castes within Mossi society. Those who resisted assimilation were generally pushed back into isolated northern and eastern fringe areas on the Senno dunes or granitic peneplaine (Figure 7.3). Naaba Kango also founded Ouahigouya, the region's capital, and established a strong hierarchical social structure that fostered increased trade and agricultural production as well as population growth (see population distribution of the Mossi in Figure 7.3).

During the 1800s direct military and diplomatic conflict came to a head between the expanding, animist Yatenga Mossi kingdom and the Islamic Fulani empire of the Macina based in the interior delta of the Niger. One of those Fulani leaders, Cheiku Amadou, set out to unite all the Fulani peoples of the Niger Bend region under a Jihad against the Mossi animist kingdoms that controlled the land routes over which kola nuts and gold, among other goods, were shipped between the Asante kingdom and the Djenne/Timbuctu centers via Bandiagara.

Both Banh and Toulfe became heavily embroiled in these conflicts. For many reasons, the Fulani clans of Banh, known as the Foynabe, refused to join Cheiku's jihad. Instead they formed an alliance with the animist Mossi Naaba to resist the invaders. These actions reflected a desire, on the part of the Fulani, to maintain longstanding social and economic ties with many of their subject peoples, i.e., Rimaaybe, who were of Kurumba and Dogon descent as well as being animist. There is also some dispute as to when the Foynabe of Banh became truly Islamicized. It appears that their full integration into Islam did not solidify until the

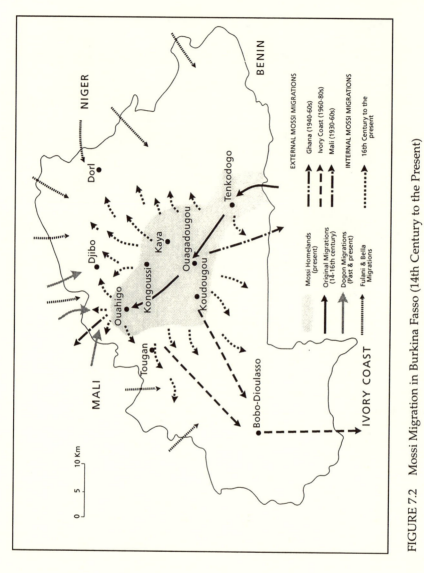

FIGURE 7.2   Mossi Migration in Burkina Fasso (14th Century to the Present)

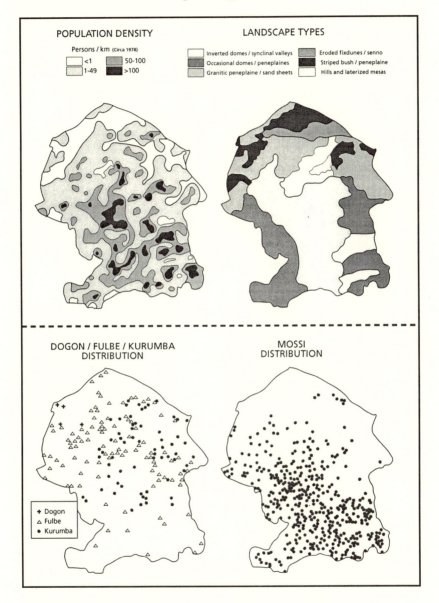

FIGURE 7.3   Population, Ethnicity, and Landscape in Yatenga

establishment of a marabout (Islamic missionary community) in Banh late in the nineteenth century. The result of these struggles for power was that the Foynabe of Banh were able to remain relatively independent and in control of their lands and subjects through most of the nineteenth and even into the twentieth century. The Foynabe achieved this independence through an astute shifting of alliances as well as strategic assertion of power when necessary. The situation was later perpetuated by the French.

The case of the Kurumba (Dogon) was quite different. Never as strong politically as the invading Fulani or Mossi peoples, their preferred survival strategy was to assimilate or melt into the countryside in times of conflict. Oral history in Toulfe confirms that during the middle 1800s, a Mossi military expedition passed through their territory on the way to Djibo to confront the invading Muslims of the Macina (Schweeger-Hefel and Staude 1972). The Mossi won that encounter (Riesman 1977; Izard 1985). In this instance, the Kurumba around Toulfe had sought protection for themselves by subordinating their chieftancy to a Mossi overlord. This event integrated the Kurumba into the orbit of the Yatenga kingdom as a frontier vassal community, though they have fiercely attempted to preserve their distinct language, religion, and customs.

By the late 1870s, the exterior Muslim threat to the Yatenga Mossi Kingdom had subsided. Political ties between the victorious Yatenga Mossi and their Kurumba and Fulani allies were consolidated. Unfortunately, internecine conflict among rival Mossi clans for the throne in Ouahigouya now posed threats to the region's stability--particularly when the French became embroiled in the region's politics. In 1885, Baogo, the eldest son of Naaba Yemde became ruler; Bagare, a rival from a different royal line contested the succession. Nine years later, in an attempt to hold onto power, Baogo sought assistance from Captain Destenaves, the head of the French garrison in Bandiagara. Subsequently, Bagare's supporters defeated Naaba Baogo with the strategic assistance of several Fulani clans of Yatenga, in spite of Destenaves offer to mediate the conflict. The tables now being turned, the usurper became Naaba. He quickly reversed his position by negotiating a treaty with Destenaves that established Yatenga as a protectorate of France. This act is still seen by some as treachery. The French, in turn, imposed a new political/administrative structure that attempted to enforce a Pax Franca. With peace a reality, settled farming villagers saw a dramatic decrease in the inter-ethnic raiding and feuding which had long occurred in this frontier region.

Primary Forces Affecting the Precolonial Settlement Structure

Most pre colonial settlements in Yatenga as well as housing patterns were designed, sited, and constructed with landscape ecology as well as defense and other cultural factors in mind. There are five principal factors involved:

First, Yatenga's settlement pattern strongly reflects landscape and disease ecology, i.e., population density is inversely related to distance from disease-ridden lowlands. In fact, this holds true for Burkina Faso as a whole as well as within Yatenga proper. This pattern--established early by the autochthonous peoples as well as the later arriving Mossi--reflects the need to avoid the disease vectors and seasonal flooding common to the wetter Sudanic zone. Recent attempts to control Onchocerciasis and Schistosomiasis in these river bottom lands has spurred a major government sponsored "new lands" resettlement effort there. If successful, this effort may lead to a major redistribution of population in Burkina Faso (McMillan 1986, 1995). Most of the migrants to these new lands are Mossi who come from the higher density plateau lands of central and northern Burkina such as Yatenga--areas where drought has hit hardest in recent years.

Secondly, trade and geostrategic/political attempts--principally by the Mossi--to control key commodity markets, e.g., grain, cattle, gold, and kola nuts, favored agglomeration in the settlement system of central Yatenga. Ouahigouya, the center of the frontier Mossi Yatenga kingdom, was on a major trade route linking the gold and kola trade from the kingdom of Asante to the south with the interior kingdoms and market centers of Djenne and Timbuctu near the Saharan fringe. A periodic market near Ouahigouya (at the town of Yuba), for example, is still one of the largest cattle and grain market centers in Burkina Faso where both licit and illicitly traded goods show up from across the nearby borders. Therefore, it is not surprising that defense, trade, and sociopolitical locational factors such as the need to control captive peoples and protect the region's trade arteries and marketing nodes, became crucial factors in Yatenga's settlement history. It is also understandable that many of the oldest and largest villages in Yatenga are sited high on outcropping crusts, rocky hills, or along easily defended escarpments.

Thirdly, environmental factors associated with the practice of agriculture and animal husbandry in the environmentally risky, semi-arid Sahelo-Sudanian zone, also influenced settlement structure. Specifically, there was the need to adapt to: (1) high precipitation variability, (2) groundwater distribution problems, (3) patchy soil-vegetation catena patterns, (4) the ancient custom of practicing both farming and herding on the same landscape (often by different ethnic groups), (5) agricultural technology limitations, (6) household labor allocation bottlenecks, and (7) low population density to list the more important factors. Ford (1982) describes the farming systems of northern Yatenga in more detail elsewhere and shows how and why settlement clustering tended to support farming system adaptation and resource exploitation, as well as labor allocation and social customs.

Fourthly, the French colonial experience accelerated trends in settlement structure in the direction of clustering or agglomeration. The French, like the British and Belgians elsewhere in Africa, often found it to their advantage to require that taxes be paid in cash. The goal was to foster capitalist market penetration as well as to increase control over the traditional political systems. As might be expected, the highly structured "direct rule" colonial administrative practices of the French were easier to implement among those peoples who already had strongly agglomerated settlement patterns, e.g., among the Mossi of central Yatenga. The least impact was seen among the more isolated and dispersed farming or pastoral peoples, e.g., the Fulani and Kurumba. Consequently, the French colonial impact on settlement structure and housing patterns is most visible in the Mossi areas around the regional capital--Ouahigouya--and sub-regional administrative centers such as Titao, Seguenega, and Gourcy. French colonial influence at the village level is less visible but nevertheless observable. For example, older villagers frequently point out stately lines of mahogany trees that were planted by corvée labor along main roads or around government installations.

In sum, the French colonial experience favored the accelerated development of a select few central places within the urban hierarchy, and, on the other hand, it froze in place many other historical, political, and cultural patterns such as clustered settlements. The French also perpetuated a system of power relations that marginalized certain groups such as the more dispersed pastoral Fulani and the reclusive Kurumba farmers. Many French political and economic policies also set the stages for later hyper-urbanization, as seen in the primate capital city, Ouagadougou, regional centers such as Bobo-Dioulasso and Ouahigouya, and other African cities such as Abidjan (Le Pape 1993).

Fifth, the greatest socioeconomic change associated with the French colonial experience was the expansion of long-distance seasonal and permanent migration as a Mossi economic coping pattern. By the 1910-1920s, under the Pax Franca, thousands of Mossi migrated seasonally or permanently to Mali, Ghana, and the Ivory Coast to work on rice, banana, cotton, or other plantations (Le Pape 1993). Yatenga became one of West Africa's most important labor reserve areas--essential to the colonial economies of several West African states--and the pattern continues today in many respects. Currently, remittances from expatriate Burkinabe from the Ivory Coast, for example, remain crucial to the country's economic survival.

Settlement Evolution at the Village Level

The Settlement of Banh

When the movements of Foynabe Fulani herders are traced from their ancestral home near Douentza (in Mali) to present-day Banh, it is evident that both their livelihood and settlement patterns changed as they interacted with different ethnic groups and as they faced the unfamiliar ecological circumstances found around Banh (Ford 1982, 1992). Prior to the 1900s, the Foynabe practiced nomadism and long-distance transhumance in the vast Plain of Gondo (in Mali) and northern Yatenga--a region dominated by extensive brousse tigrée (banded vegetation or bushlands) and senno (longitudinal dune fields covered with grassy steppes) (Figure 7.3). Extreme specialization of livelihood was the norm as was high spatial mobility and settlement dispersion. The only agglomerated settlements were those, like the Banh core settlement, where Rimaaybe (former slaves of the Fulani) provided grain and other needed services, e.g., blacksmithing or pottery-making, to the Fulani pastoralists through a longstanding feudal, reciprocal economic system. The Fulani overlords maintained this pattern through intimidation and force as well as the tradition of complementary herder-farmer reciprocal economic relations that included manuring contracts. In the case of Banh, land tenure was also controlled by the Fulani clan elders, whereas in Toulfe and Sodin, Kurumba or Mossi "earth priests" maintained ritual and customary control over land resources (including access to and usufruct rights to trees).

With the arrival of the French, the Foynabe began to sedentarize due to the imposition of peace, the pressures to integrate into a state system and market structure, as well as the general anti-pastoralist attitudes of the colonial administrators and later Burkinabe government bureaucrats. Mobile herding peoples such as the Fulani have long been distrusted by both the colonialists as well as newly arriving Mossi settled farmers. It also appears that the arrival in Banh of Islamic missionaries known as marabout, accelerated processes toward sedentarization. In hindsight, it seems clear that the forces for change began during the early colonial period and then accelerated after independence--particularly after the droughts of 1968-1973 and the latest one of 1984 (see Adamou 1990; de

Verdiere 1988). The rise to power of the Sankhara revolutionary regime in the mid-1980s was also influential in undermining the political power of the Fulani clan chiefs. The Mossi-dominated Sankhara regime greatly limited the Fulani chiefs' customary right to control access to grazing and farming lands in northern Yatenga; the consequence has been an accelerated movement by Mossi peoples into former grazing lands controlled by the Foynabe. The Fulani also found themselves less able to control their former vassals, the Rimaaybe, who now tended to frequently side with the Mossi-dominated government. In other words, the old rules of ethnic economic cooperation were destroyed or altered and the balance of power had now tipped toward settled peoples and against pastoralists.

In these reversed circumstances, the formerly enslaved Rimaaybe found themselves better able to confront their erstwhile masters and take advantage of new opportunities in the changed political and socioeconomic landscape. Like the Mossi, they improved their position vis-à-vis herders through better access to health, education, and other services, as well as by becoming active in trade and politics. Demography also played a role as population growth rates are considerably higher among the settled peoples, especially the Mossi.

The Rimaaybe have been particularly attracted by the economic potential of irrigated market gardening projects promulgated by the government agriculture services as well as a local Mossi-led NGO or nongovernmental organization (Association 6-S 1990; Milleville and Serpantié 1993). When a new source of irrigation water was to be provided by damming the Nimbaru River at Banh, a major political confrontation occurred between herders and farmers over land, water use, ecological deterioration, and herder/farmer relations. The conflict eventually required presidential intervention and has yet to be resolved. Some environmental organizations have even become involved (Elsasser 1990; Ford 1992). In fact, due to dramatically changing inter-ethnic power relations, many pastoral Fulani now practice some permanent agriculture along with herding. This is because they can no longer count exclusively (if at all) on grain for milk exchanges and other herding services and manuring contracts--much less tribute--as they could when the previous herder-farmer reciprocal relations prevailed. These changes have meant that herder households must divide labor in highly inefficient ways to cover subsistence activities. Part of the Fulani household now stays permanently at their dry-season camps adjacent to Banh to plant crops, trade, and become involved in other sedentary economic activities: gardening, craft production, education, government service, and trade. Other members of the household--often young men--still follow the herds into the bush. Increasingly, the Fulani don't own all the animals they herd; rather the owners are the former vassal Rimaaybe farmers who entrust cattle to Fulani herders for a price. It should be pointed out that the Fulani who have had to do more farming, frequently lack motivation, experience, and the knowledge necessary to practice farming effectively in this high-risk semi-arid zone. It is not surprising, therefore, that agricultural yields and efficiency differs significantly between Fulani and Kurumba or Rimaaybe farming households (Ford 1982).

What has been the ultimate effect of these multiple changes on settlement structure and even house construction styles in Banh? Up to the 1950s there was a clear differentiation between the typical dispersed Fulani round woven grass-hut camps and the agglomerated, mud-walled, fortress-like Rimaaybe settlements of Banh, e.g., the quartiers of Tougounongou and Tanguile (Figure 7.4). These patterns show up clearly in the aerial photo reconnaissance mission performed by the French in 1955. Extreme agglomeration is observed for the settled vassal farmers and high dispersion among the Fulani pastoralists. But, even by 1955, some settlement and housing change had already begun. For example, the marabout quartier (compound) of Yallaré became one of the first permanent outlier Fulani-dominated hamlets to be established in Banh (Figure 7.4). Curiously, some of its housing structures were constructed in the manner of the central core Rimaaybe settlement (square, massive, mud-walled, flat-roofed structures). This was a radical departure from the extremely agglomerated pattern that had been typical for generations.

By the late 1970s many more Fulani households in the satellite camps began to copy the building styles of their former Rimaaybe serfs, first for granaries and later for houses. Many adopted the square instead of round design and used more permanent mud/adobe (or even tin roofs), all indicating an increasing trend toward sedentarization. When people were asked about this practice in the mid-1970s, most Fulani, especially women, would still vociferously extol the relative comfort and other virtues of the traditional, round Fulani hut. Yet, the trend continued due to such factors as the influence of returning migrants (mainly Rimaaybe) who had traveled to Ghana, the Ivory Coast, and other urban areas and the increasing difficulty of finding native plant materials to build the traditional grass hut.

In the 1980s it became clear that the increasingly important role of the Rimaaybe in economic and political life had significantly affected settlement and housing patterns. For several reasons the forces for dispersal were becoming more dominant in the once heavily agglomerated core settlement: (1) the desire for more economic and social freedom--particularly by the Rimaaybe, (2) the need for access to new government services

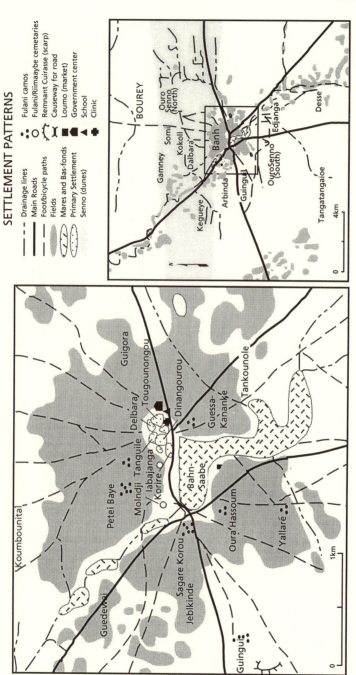

SETTLEMENT PATTERNS

- – – – Drainage lines
- —— Main Roads
- –·–·– Foot/bicycle paths
- Fields
- Mares and Bas-fonds
- Primary Settlement
- Senno (dunes)

- •:° Fulani camos
- O Fulani/Riimaaybe cemetaries
- (Remnant Cuirasse (scarp)
-)(Causeway for road
- ■◖ Loumo (market)
- ◀ Government center
- ✚ School
- ✚ Clinic

FIGURE 7.4   Bahn Settlement Patterns, 1950s - 1970s

such as the agricultural extension and credit office or MCH (Maternal and Child Health) clinic and schools which were built outside of the old, core settlement (Figure 7.5), and (3) environmental concerns such as the higher frequency of disastrous flooding associated with upstream erosion and deforestation on the Mossi Plateau that had forced many families in the core settlement to rebuild elsewhere. Most chose to build in new, dispersed compounds or hamlets farther upslope and closer to the main road. The most recently constructed government facilities are near the main road on more open, upslope lands, and none have been built within the old core settlement (Figure 7.5).

Other general land use changes have also impacted settlement structure. The unique agrosylvopastoral system practiced by Fulani, Dogon, and Kurumba peoples is being altered due to both market penetration and environmental degradation. Currently, the farming systems around Banh are the subject of intense study by several researchers who hope to describe and better understand this almost extinct livelihood pattern (D'Aquino 1991; Adamou 1990; de Verdiere 1988; Elsasser 1990; Medina 1991; Ogier 1991; Ouedraogo 1988; Perez 1990; Serpantié 1989). Several trends in farming systems are clear: transhumance in all forms is decreasing, mixed-farming is increasing, Fulani herders are being forced to do more farming, and non-Fulani farmers are doing more herding (particularly with small ruminants). In 1991, for example, a Rimaaybe farmer had become the largest cattle owner in the region, a fact that caused considerable controversy.

Outside agencies, such as the Ministry of Agriculture, have been implicated in the alteration of these traditional livelihood and cultural patterns through the implementation of often misguided, misinformed, or even deliberately destructive investment and extension policies that benefit settled farmers at the expense of herders. Many of the policies reflect failed, production-oriented agricultural policies, inherited from the French colonial era, that were started during an earlier, abnormally wet period--a climatic aberration. Of course, those practices generally failed when the drought years of the 1970-80s came (Figure 7.6). Unfortunately, most outsiders, including many central government extension agents and even researchers, have a very rudimentary and frequently unflattering perception of the form of agrosylvopastoralism practiced around Banh. This is unfortunate because it now appears that this unique, extensive farming-herding system was quite adaptive to a high risk environment. One of the goals of the research project mentioned above was to learn from the past and integrate useful, traditional ecological knowledge systems into modern mixed-farming practices. It is still unclear whether this is possible, given the radically changed political,

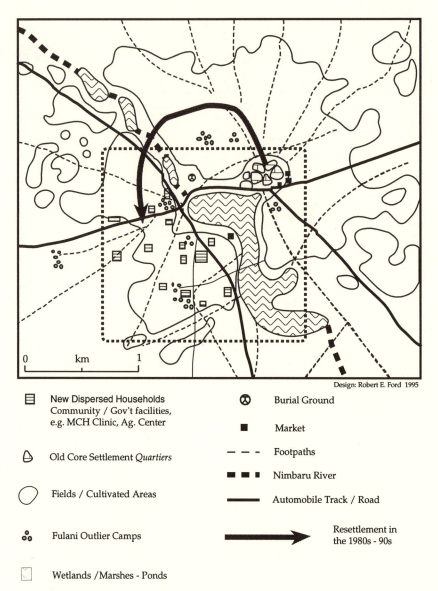

New Dispersed Households
Community / Gov't facilities,
e.g. MCH Clinic, Ag. Center

Old Core Settlement *Quartiers*

Fields / Cultivated Areas

Fulani Outlier Camps

Wetlands / Marshes - Ponds

⊗   Burial Ground

■   Market

– – –   Footpaths

■ ■ ■   Nimbaru River

Automobile Track / Road

Resettlement in
the 1980s - 90s

FIGURE 7.5 Settlement Changes in the 1980s-90s

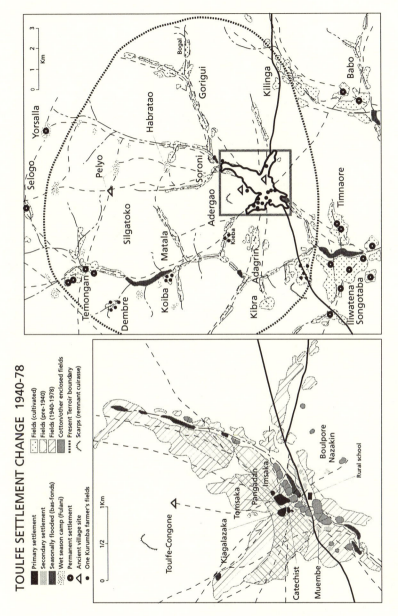

FIGURE 7.6 The Settlement of Toulfe, 1940-78

economic, and demographic situation.

Toulfe Settlement Evolution

Toulfe's settlement structure and history were also affected by the Mossi/Macina conflicts of the mid-nineteenth century. Several times the Kurumba were forced to abandon their settlements and flee to the bush--the vast, impenetrable brousse tigrée or banded/striped vegetation formations of northeast Yatenga (Figure 7.3). Oral history in Toulfe claims that they originally migrated to this part of Yatenga from the east in today's Niger (Figure 7.1).

The largest concentration of Kurumba in Burkina Faso is located on the senno (longitudinal dune-field system) centered on Aribinda in the province of Soum; this region is plainly in the Sahel and has a very high risk from climatic drought episodes (Dupré 1991). Toulfe itself is located in a large bush area of banded vegetation on the granitic peneplain to the southwest of the senno dunes, on the Soum/Yatenga border. In this region, year-around groundwater is very difficult to access. Even where available, it is very deep, and the spatial distribution of perennially-accessible, shallow surface-groundwater aquifers is sparse. As a consequence, villages in this zone have tended to become heavily agglomerated around the very few favored groundwater sites accessible by traditional water-lifting technology. Central Yatenga, by contrast, has many easily accessible, shallow, surface-level aquifers. This fact relates to past geological history, i.e., the presence of sub-surface indurated ferruginous crusts related to an inverted landscape and other factors (Ford 1982).

Consequently, Kurumba farming communities developed as heavily agglomerated, fortified, intensive (infield) farming "island" communities within a vast "bush-sea" where extensive (outfield) bush-fallow farming and pastoralism were practiced. Perennial groundwater availability--essential for human and animal survival during the latter parts of the long dry season--is only accessible around these few strategic settlements. As a consequence, herders and farmers were forced to cooperate and share crucial dry-season groundwater resources. Ford (1982) describes the traditional Kurumba mixed-farming system and all its many adaptations to climatic risk, including the essential herder-farmer interaction patterns.

The agrosylvopastoral farming system found around Toulfe contrasts significantly in one way with that found around Banh: herder-farmer interaction around Toulfe has been more egalitarian and cooperative. True transhumance is still practiced by the pastoralists living in Toulfe's hinterland, and the ethnic division of labor is largely intact. The explanation for this pattern is as follows: the Kurumba remained largely independent of both Mossi and Fulani sociopolitical control; land tenure around Toulfe is still controlled by the Kurumba customary "earth priest" (tengsoba), not the Fulani or Mossi hierarchy. In addition, the Toulfe Kurumba were never assimilated as a slave caste as were the Rimaaybe around Banh; the historical reasons for this are explained in detail elsewhere (Ford 1982).

In sum, the agrosylvopastoral system of the Kurumba has been highly touted for its adaptability to the risky Sahelian environment (Ford 1982; Dupré 1991). The Kurumba subsistence strategy exploited a diversity of micro-habitats scattered over a wide territory (Figure 7.7). They farmed both shifting, bush-fallow outfields scattered in the outlying bush and permanent infields (heavily manured) under the Acacia albida "tree parks" located adjacent to the core settlement and close to accessible groundwater. This complex extensive/intensive mixed-agricultural system originally included a thirty-fifty year fallow cycle, and it dealt with spatial climatic risk quite effectively. Traditional Kurumba farmers would minimize subsistence risk through dispersal of bush-fields over a wide territory. Note the spatial distribution of one Kurumba farmer's fields in Figure 7.7. The infield intensive farming zone where the permanent settlement was located, supported a sizeable population concentration of up to several thousand inhabitants. The core settlement structure was characterized by a few adjacent agglomerations of large, extended-family compounds, some numbering in the hundreds, that were formed around clan structures. The village's appearance was highly fortress-like. Recall that Toulfe, frequently exposed to periodic raiding, has been isolated on the Mossi/Fulani frontier until a new road was built in 1983 that connected it to the larger world.

The Kurumba agroforestry system has also produced a highly visible vegetative imprint on the landscape quite apparent on aerial photos. Most noticeable are the dense "tree parks" and other economic species, planted or protected through selective weeding, around the heavily agglomerated settlements. Under these parks, farmers would plant their most productive crops. The preferred tree--the Acacia Albida--is leguminous and leafs out in the dry season, providing shade to animals. During the rainy season, the leaves fall and crops can be cultivated beneath the trees. In addition, the animals drop manure under the shade trees during the dry season, further enhancing the fertility of these permanently farmed agroforestry parks. A description of a similar system in Senegal is presented by Dommen (1988) and Stomal-Weigel (1988).

Unique social interaction patterns were also essential for this agropastoral system's success. Traditionally, Fulani and other herders would camp on the village infield lands after the harvest period so their

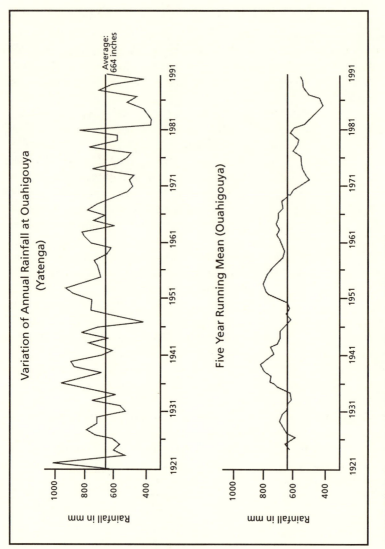

FIGURE 7.7 Precipitation Patterns in Yatenga 1920s - 1991

cattle could graze the stubble. The cattle, in turn, would drop their urine and manure on the fields. Herders would then trade with the settled farmers, exchanging milk and other animal products for grain. Farmers and herders would also cooperate in digging shallow, dry-season wells to access the spatially limited, shallow aquifers found in this arid peneplain region. These complex "manuring contracts" have existed for generations between Fulani herders and Kurumba farmers and were but one of many essential human adaptations and coping strategies engineered over time to maximize survival. Few outsiders, be they French colonial adminis-trators or post-independence bureaucrats, have understood or cared much about learning how this system worked. Kurumba farmers were notorious among Ministry of Agriculture extension agents for being "dif-ficult, suspicious, and very traditional" (personal communication, Toulfe Agricultural agent).

By contrast, when the Mossi moved into the region--less than 400 years ago--they tended to interact less with the herders (most often they were at war with them). Furthermore, the Mossi practiced a more Sudanian form of agriculture (which was adapted to a wetter savanna environment) and they demonstrated a preference for different tree species, e.g. Butyrospermum paradoxum. Mixed farming and intensive farmer/herder interaction have gradually been learned by some Mossi farming communities--particularly those with larger numbers of assimi-lated peoples such as the Karumba. But overall, their agricultural prac-tices are still not as effective in coping with the north Yatengan environ-mental risk as compared to the more traditional Kurumba.

Even today, at the micro-scale, there are significant observable differ-ences in agricultural productivity between these two ethnic groups that reflect a differentially adaptive response to coping with the risk of farm-ing on the Sahelian fringe (Ford 1982). The Mossi system has been more exploitative and inefficient in its use of land, water, and plant resources, while the Kurumba focused on perfecting and practicing intensive sus-tainable agriculture. The Mossi have more frequently preferred to cope with economic risk through migration and trade. It is significant, I believe, that the historic front of Mossi migration into the Sahelian zone was halted fairly close to the outer limits of Sudanian vegetation forma-tions and plant species distribution. Thus, the knowledgeable observer can not only identify Mossi, Fulani, or Kurumba cultural landscapes by their housing and settlement structures, but also by their vegetative imprints. Monique Marchal (1983), uses great detail in describing and comparing rural settlement patterns from all over Burkina Faso; her work illustrates well the differing interactions between culture, environment, and settlement observable in the region.

On the other hand, Kurumba adaptation to political and economic change has not been as effective as the Mossi. This may reflect the fact that they were never a very aggressive people, were rarely involved in long distance trade or migration, did not live on the better soils of the region, and had to deal with groundwater accessibility patterns that varied greatly. The Kurumba never integrated into the colonial economy well, in part because their territory was too dry for the favored cash crops, cotton and peanuts. Therefore, when Islamic Jihads would occur--or other feuds including the arrival of the French--the Kurumba were frequently marginalized. It is no wonder their preferred response to conflict was to assimilate to invading groups or flee to the bush. Most Kurumba have also remained staunchly animist rather than converting to Christianity or Islam, as was more common among the Mossi. They would probably have continued to practice the "old ways" but for accelerated migration by Mossi into their territory in the recent wetter years. Mossi migration northward did slow significantly during the dry period of the mid-1970s and 80s, due to their inability to handle desertification. However, with the return of the rains, the advance will probably continue and land encroachment will begin to impact even the Kurumba. It is too soon to know what these changes will mean to the settlement system.

Settlement Evolution in Sodin

The effects of early market penetration, economic migration, and integration among the Mossi is most evident in central Yatenga around villages such as Sodin (Figure 7.1). Located close to Ouahigouya, Sodin gained ready access to more profitable regional and local cash-driven markets controlled by the Naaba and later the French. Central Yatenga had also attained the highest population density in the region, due partly to favored economic and political characteristics and such positive landscape features as easier access to groundwater and distance from river bottom lands. But as early as the 1920s, the region began to show signs of disequilibrium or "agricultural involution" according to some observers (Marchal 1977, 1983). The plant, aquifer, and soil-catena relations typical of many Mossi villages on the Central Plateau are described in Figure 7.8 and 7.9.

The environmental consequences of combining rapid demographic growth, the application of a less-adaptive agricultural strategy to this risky Sudano-Sahelian zone, and the French push for cash crops, almost guaranteed the crisis in food production that began as early as the 1930s. Numerous colonial schemes are found in the historical literature which document attempts to solve or avert famines on the Mossi Plateau and in Yatenga (Marchal 1977, 1983). Some of these famines resulted from peo-

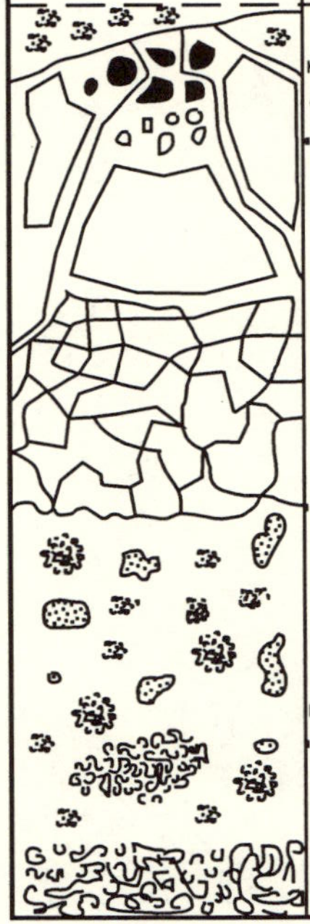

LAND USE PATTERN — Heavily Clustered Settlement Pattern (Extended Family Units)	FIELD TYPES	PLANT COVER — Parkland to Bush	SOILS & CATENA — Valley Bottom / Uplands / Hills	LAND TENURE	DIVISION OF LABOR	CROPS — Major Cultivars & Soil-Crop Associations	CULTIVA. RESTOR. TECHN.	TRADIT. LANDUSE TERMIN.
	INFIELDS — Kitchen Gardens Intensively Cultivated Plots e.g. Tobacco	PARKLAND — Acacia albida Dominant	Clays to Sandy-Clay Soils	COLLECTIVE EXTENDED FAMILY FIELDS	WOMEN & CHILDREN of Household	Maize "greens" e.g. okra Long-maturing Cereals, e.g. Red Sorghum	Plant Mounding & Gen. Weeding Composting of Household Wastes	BAONGO
	PERMANENT FIELDS	Mixed Trees & Shrubs / Grasses; Acacia albida Adansonia sp. But. paradoxum Sclerocarya sp. Parkia biglobosa Lannea oleosa Etc.	Thicker "Good" Soils; Sandy-Clays to Fine Sandy & Gravelly Soils	COLLECTIVE FIELDS OF QUARTIER — Pug Keena or "Great Field"; COLLECTIVE FIELDS — Buud ziise or Beolse; Common Fields of Quartier Extended Family	ALL MEMBERS of Household or Quartier; EXTENDED FAMILY — Yiri or Sub-groups, i.e. Zaske	Pluvial Rice in Bas-fond; White Sorghum w/ Cowpeas & Long-maturing Millet; POLYCROPS: Sorghum Millet Cowpeas Cotton; Occasionnally Fonio	2-3 Weedings per Season Occasional Plant-Thinning & Mounding; Household & Animal Manure on Fields; Same as Above but with less Manuring & more Mulching with Crop Residues	ZIPELLE
	TEMPORARY OUTFIELDS; Bush Fallows; Pasture Lands; "Wild Foods" & Medicinal Plants Collection	Bush-Fallows & Shrublands w/ Combretum sp. Dominant	Gravelly Soils w/ Sandsheet Deposits; "Mediocre" Soils	PERSONAL FIELDS or Beolse; Dispersed in Bushlands & Commonlands	INDIVIDUAL LABOR Male & Female; Occasional Group Work (e.g. age-sets)	SPEC. CROPS: Peanuts & Bambara Groundnuts (e.g. Seeds); OTHER CROPS: Short-maturing Millet, sesame, Fonio (on Sandsheets)	1-2 Light Weedings; No Manuring	TENGA
	Non-Cultivated Bush Reserve; Firewood	Bushlands	Ferruginous Crusts with Gravel / Rocks				Bush-fallow Cycle of Regrowth (15-20 years)	ZENGADEGA

FIGURE 7.8 Model of Settlement Structure in Mossi Central Yatenga Circa 1910

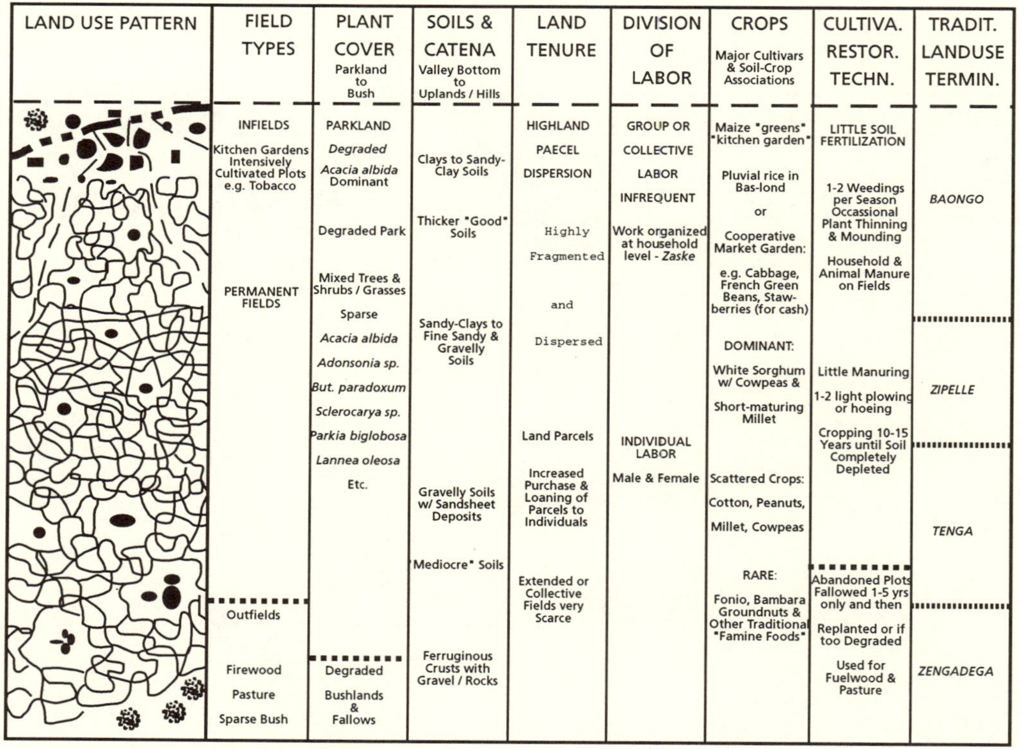

LAND USE PATTERN	FIELD TYPES	PLANT COVER Parkland to Bush	SOILS & CATENA Valley Bottom to Uplands / Hills	LAND TENURE	DIVISION OF LABOR	CROPS	CULTIVA. RESTOR. TECHN.	TRADIT. LANDUSE TERMIN.
	INFIELDS Kitchen Gardens Intensively Cultivated Plots e.g. Tobacco	PARKLAND *Degraded* Acacia albida Dominant	Clays to Sandy-Clay Soils	HIGHLAND PAECEL DISPERSION	GROUP OR COLLECTIVE LABOR INFREQUENT	Major Cultivars & Soil-Crop Associations Maize "greens" "kitchen garden"	LITTLE SOIL FERTILIZATION 1-2 Weedings per Season Occasional Plant Thinning & Mounding	*BAONGO*
						Pluvial rice in Bas-fond		
	PERMANENT FIELDS	Degraded Park Mixed Trees & Shrubs / Grasses Sparse Acacia albida Adonsonia sp. But. paradoxum Sclerocarya sp. Parkia biglobosa Lannea oleosa Etc.	Thicker "Good" Soils Sandy-Clays to Fine Sandy & Gravelly Soils	Highly Fragmented and Dispersed	Work organized at household level - Zaske	or Cooperative Market Garden: e.g. Cabbage, French Green Beans, Staw-berries (for cash) DOMINANT: White Sorghum w/ Cowpeas & Short-maturing Millet	Household & Animal Manure on Fields Little Manuring 1-2 light plowing or hoeing Cropping 10-15 Years until Soil Completely Depleted	*ZIPELLE* *TENGA*
	Outfields Firewood Pasture Sparse Bush	*Degraded* Bushlands & Fallows	Gravelly Soils w/ Sandsheet Deposits Mediocre* Soils Ferruginous Crusts with Gravel / Rocks	Land Parcels Increased Purchase & Loaning of Parcels to Individuals Extended or Collective Fields very Scarce	INDIVIDUAL LABOR Male & Female	Scattered Crops: Cotton, Peanuts, Millet, Cowpeas RARE: Fonio, Bambara Groundnuts & Other Traditional "Famine Foods"	Abandoned Plots Fallowed 1-5 yrs only and then Replanted or if too Degraded Used for Fuelwood & Pasture	*ZENGADEGA*

FIGURE 7.9   Model of Settlement Structure in Mossi Central Yatenga Circa 1990

ple being forced into commercial agriculture without sufficient food reserves to weather the periodic "normal" droughts common to the Sahel.

Given the need to increase agricultural production (for both cash and food), as well as the relative peace of colonial times, Mossi villagers began to spread out on the landscape. They started to farm marginal, upland, lateritic soils that had once been left as bush. The better-than-average rainfall years of the 1930-1970 period, made that kind of land expansion feasible. It should be noted that many areas opened up for cotton or peanuts would not have been farmed by Kurumba subsistence farmers. Unfortunately, when the drought years came, the expansion onto marginal lands brought about rapid soil degradation.

It also appears that very early in the colonial period (possibly even before), the Mossi approach to coping with population pressure had also changed. In essence, the Mossi strategy was not to improve productivity through fertility-increasing "intensification" techniques, or through interacting with the Fulani herders as did the Kurumba, but, rather, to cope by out- migration and involvement in such non-farm activities as trade, and joining the civil service. So the French political-economic system, which emphasized market penetration, fit in well with the Mossi approach to agricultural. As long as the rainfall was above average, central Yatenga could absorb its population growth (Figure 7.6), but, when the drought-years inevitably hit, it became quickly apparent that the traditional Mossi agricultural system had exceeded its ecological and social limits. Even after Independence, while an economic boom occurred in places like Nigeria and the Ivory Coast, Yatengan Mossi peoples by the thousands survived by outmigration. In retrospect, the migration solution made sense for the Mossi, as long as the boom in the coastal economies continued. When the boom ended in the late 1980s, many migrants were forced to return home.

By then, unfortunately, the land base was heavily degraded, and many social signs of disequilibrium were evident. There was a great increase in landlessness, land borrowing, and land sales, for example. In other words, all the forms of evidence of agricultural involution were now present: reduced fertility, decreasing yields, increasing degradation of soils, increased labor requirements per unit of output from the land, as well as disruptions to the social fabric. All this has produced either stagnant or declining yields (Marchal 1983; Rochette 1988; McMillan 1986, 1995). Even in the early 1990s, after some economic rebound in Ghana and elsewhere, the traditional safety valve of emigration and non-farm economic activity did not completely take up the slack. Only a lucky few, those who literally struck gold in the 1980s gold rush in Burkina Faso, were able to cope effectively (Le Pape 1993).

The result of all these negative driving forces on settlement structure has been dramatic.   Sodin, for example, has completely lost its once extensive outfield system of bushlands (Figure 7.9). The settlement itself, once heavily agglomerated, somewhat analogous to Toulfe's structure, is now much more dispersed.   There is little if any bushland separating Sodin from adjacent village lands (Figures 7.8 and 7.9).   Nevertheless, a clarification is in order.   Even a hundred years ago, Mossi settlements were already somewhat less agglomerated than those of the Kurumba because, as explained earlier, groundwater access is easier and more dispersed on the Mossi plateau.   Furthermore, the political structure of the Mossi state could protect dispersed settlements better than could the more isolated groups in frontier areas such as Toulfe. Mossi social systems have also tended to splinter households into smaller units.

Today, Sodin is comprised of more than ten separate settlement clusters or hamlets spread over the entire village territory with a population of 200-300 each. One can also see the formation of many small incipient hamlets from dispersed household compounds that are often sited on the fringes of the village lands. Many of the latter are located on marginal uplands beyond the reach of easily accessible groundwater bottomlands or mid-catena soils; these incipient hamlets have populations of fifteen to thirty people each. Yet, fortress-like house construction patterns remain beyond their original "defensive" role with only minor changes; the mammoth fences enclosing compounds are now made from sun-dried brick because there is a dearth of vegetative material. Fuelwood is also much more scarce. Dispersal of the population is also a logical approach to dealing with the increasing scarcity of land and plant resources.

In sum, though settlement dispersal is becoming more common, some agglomerative tendencies remain. Social interaction patterns common to the large extended family units still encourage people to live closer together.   Villages are also perceived to be preferable for the marshalling of agricultural labor, and there are increasing concerns for a new type of security threat--the increased incidence of thievery. Other social needs reinforce this pattern: the desire for a threshold number of people to build a small mosque or the need to share grinding platforms and extended-family granaries. Another priority that can inhibit complete dispersal is better access to shops and to public services such as clinics and schools. Government infrastructure being built near recently constructed roads or near central market areas is frequently becoming the focus of new dispersed hamlets. As facilities are made available, they are not commonly located within the older crowded core settlement areas.

As mentioned earlier, after the 1980s economic downturn in the coastal economies, thousands of Mossi migrants who had always assumed they could survive by seeking off-farm employment, found they were without jobs or land resources. Many who came back discovered that survival depended on intensifying the agricultural system and even considering previously ignored land conservation and restoration techniques (Batterbury 1993, 1994). The World Bank and other agencies, after the early 1960s "land degradation" scare, had tried to implement some expensive, capital intensive, soil erosion control projects. Unfortunately, these programs failed miserably, partially due to "top-down" approaches and technology-dependent techniques (Dugué 1989; Milleville and Serpantié, 1993). Furthermore, there was little incentive to invest in agricultural intensification, much less land restoration, until the economic "bust" of the late l980s provided the needed impetus for change.

Recently, more enlightened approaches to sustainable development, implemented by several grass-roots NGO agencies such as OXFAM and Association Six-S, began to succeed where the big agencies had previously failed. These newer "small is beautiful" approaches have focused on appropriate technologies for conservation and water-retention, e.g., small dam construction, stone-lines, and plant barriers. Some of the innovations were also introduced with the post-1970s growth of dry-season, irrigated market-gardening of such export food crops as green beans, strawberries, and onions (Ouedraogo and Rideout 1980; Wright and Bonkoungou 1985; Rochette 1988, 1989; Milleville and Serpantié, 1993; Batterbury 1994). Some of these "rediscovered" traditional conservation methods have come from people like the Kurumba. Foreign aid programs have also become more effective in recent years, after learning from the failures of the earlier programs; many newer approaches in development encourage "learning" from traditional indigenous knowledge systems (Engberg-Pedersen 1995; Batterbury 1994; Goumandakoye and Bado 1991).

As a consequence, these new and old driving forces have indeed focused attention on the potential for agricultural intensification. Many people now see value in being closer to their fields where they can provide both better supervision and more of the intensive labor required for land restoration. Off-farm economic pursuits and involvement in the informal sector are still important coping strategies, but not the only ones. Diversification of economic activity within the Mossi household has increased. This result should have been expected, given the creativity and long history of adaptation of Sahelian peasant peoples. A geographical farming systems study carried out on the Mossi Plateau (Batterbury 1994), found evidence of people being willing to apply intensive effort to back-breaking land restoration. Batterbury's goal is to better analyze the practical conditions necessary to make intensification pro grams more effective.

How has all this affected settlement structure in the 1990s? First, it appears that settlement expansion is continuing unabated, though at a decreasing rate. Most available land in central Yatenga has been occu pied. In fact, there is considerable evidence that even undesirable lands are now being filled in (in some cases even lands originally degraded during the 1930-1970 period). As a consequence, instead of high population density being concentrated on the best lands only, the traditional pattern in Yatenga, population and settlement density is more equalized over the entire landscape.

What does Sodin look like today from the air? For one, it is difficult to distinguish the infield from the outfield system as is still possible in the case of Toulfe or Banh. In fact, there is now an almost continuous pattern of fields and hamlets extending out from the oldest settle- ment cluster into the next village's territory. Fallow cycles are way down (two-three years at most on scattered plots) while composting is, of necessity, up. Meanwhile, the broad expanses of starkly-eroded ferruginous crust areas--many of which were first degraded during the colonial era--now appear to be stabilizing. Some of the fragile upland areas expanded significantly after the 1984 drought, but since 1991-1992, when better rains returned, incipient efforts at land restoration have actually been succeeding. Yet, some experts believe that these positive changes are not occurring at a pace sufficient to counter the forces causing dryland degradation.

The final outcome is still uncertain, though troubling signs persist. Bushland areas which once separated village territories are essentially non-existent, except in a few favored sites. Collecting fuelwood and wild plants is now a time-consuming or even impossible task. Many economic plant species have become impossible to find. The only remaining natural forest observable from the air around Sodin is a small forest plot (two-three acres) that is an animist burial and ceremonial ground. It stands out on the landscape in a most bizarre manner. The other remaining trees on the landscape are almost exclusively very old, i.e., economic species such as Acacia albida and Baobab (Adansonia digitata) scattered through the more productive bottom land soils of the catena. But even these scattered trees are diminishing as fewer young trees are replanted or protected than the number being lost. There is also evidence that the decline in mixed-farming that came with the Mossi hegemony in Yatenga, reduced reseeding rates of trees such as the Acacia albida that reproduce best when their seeds pass through the gut of domesticated animals. Some reforestation success in selected villages is occurring, but generally the efficacy of government-run programs has been low because they emphasize exotic species (e.g., Eucalyptus, Neem) that local people dislike. Newer, more successful NGO reforestation efforts in Yatenga, e.g., the OXFAM agroforestry project, emphasize planting native tree species.

Environmental Degradation and Settlement Structure Change

In hindsight, it is not surprising that by the end of the 1970s, most outside experts saw in Yatenga a clear example of agricultural involution--a true Malthusian disaster in the making (Repetto and Holmes 1983; Falloux and Mudendi 1988; Williams 1991; Shaikh and Snrech 1993; King 1993). But the worst case Malthusian scenario did not occur, although it still could. As Grosse (1994a,b) and Ford (1995) have shown, Malthusian analyses are often too simplistic and mechanistic to account for the full range of factors which increase or decrease "vulnerability" in societies like those in Yatenga (Bohle et al. 1994).

Since the late 1980s, contrary evidence has begun to accumulate which suggests that it is too early to write-off Yatenga. Newer approaches which call for more nuanced "contextual" analyses of population-environment relationships provide more satisfying explanations of both past and present patterns in Africa (see Honadle, Grosse, and Phumpiu 1994; Grosse 1994a). This is not only the case for humid regions like Rwanda (Ford 1993; Turner II, et al. 1993; Turner II and Benjamin 1994) but also the semi-arid regions such as the Sahel (Ford 1992; Milleville and Sepantié 1993; Batterbury 1993, 1994).

Although accelerating population growth and environmental degradation have encouraged land use expansion and intensification, one cannot automatically label this process desertification as has been done by journalists and lay people. Such a simplistic assessment does not explain the complex economic, political, social, and ecological picture one sees in the Sahel. Using an historical perspective, it appears that during much of the 1930-1970s period, rainfall patterns were above normal in the Sahel; at least that is now the conclusion by most authoritative sources (Figure 7.7). The colonial imposition of a market-oriented cash-cropping system, for instance, actually worked quite well because these interventions were being tried out during a favorable rainfall period. Starting in the early 1970s, however, population went through a rapid growth phase that coincided with a long, cyclical drought, making market-oriented cash-cropping interventions unsustainable.

This "Sahelian Drought", in the late 1970s to early 1980s, was perceived to be a "natural" disaster and thus the use of the term "desertification" to denote an aberration from "normal" climatic patterns. This disaster was often cited as the primary cause for most social, political, and environmental ills besetting the newly independent Sahelian states. But with the longer view of recent research, it seems clear that this region has always had to deal with both short and longer-term climatic drought cycles. The difference in this case, is that the situation had been compounded by "human" forces including the need for political reform (Mabogunje 1995). In other words, the cultural and political-economic response system had become out-of-balance, not the natural system per se (Campbell and Olson 1991; Bohle et al. 1994; Ford 1994).

Economic restructuring also played a role in intensifying the problem of land degradation. By the 1980s, when the coastal economies began to succumb to global recession, many of those who had earlier used the migration solution to cope with land scarcities, were forced to return to places such as Sodin. Thus, internal migration became increasingly important, adding to urban crowding and unemployment and putting pressure on rural land as well. At about the same time, the very severe drought of 1984 added further stresses to traditional coping patterns. The political instability of the Sankhara revolution of the 1980s also caused problems, essentially destroying traditional conflict resolution and resource allocation systems without installing effective new ones (Engberg-Pedersen 1995). The migrants were left with one promising option as a result of the discovery of gold in Burkina Faso in the mid 1980s. This phenomenon spawned an overnight growth of many ephemeral settlements, some of which have recently taken on the trappings of permanency.

Sociocultural Forces and Settlement Change

The dominant forces affecting settlement structure today appear to be those favoring dispersal in contrast to clustering or agglomeration. This tendency to dispersion is not driven by ecology alone; sociocultural factors are highly significant. The following are some tentative observations and conclusions,

First of all, religion seems to be a significant sociocultural variable encouraging dispersion. This is an interesting phenomenon, because in those regions where dispersion is initially dominant, religion is often a factor which brings people together in villages. When Islam arrived in Toulfe, many of the first converts left (or were forced out) to establish their own separate quartier (hamlet) away from the animist central core settlement. This was particularly the case for those who followed a specific marabout founder of a reformed sect. A similar pattern occurred when Christianity arrived, first Catholicism in the 1920-1930s, and then Protestantism. It appears that whenever the social cohesion of the community was stressed by differences over such issues as politics, religion, or attitudes toward polygamy and women's work, those who abandoned the old ways found it more congenial to relocate, often to new hamlets of under 100-150 in population. This pattern shows how powerful social forces are in settlement change; religious conflict no doubt accelerated or at least facilitated the breakup of many heavily agglomerated core settlements. Several villagers specifically cited discord over social issues as a major cause for relocation.

A second source of settlement and house style change has been new ideas introduced by returning migrants from the Ivory Coast or the capital city, especially those who joined the civil service or who became involved in itinerant commercial pursuits. One successful returned migrant in Toulfe has set up a thriving business (trading grain and cattle) out of a new compound modeled after homes built in the elite quartier of Ouahigouya or Ouagadougou. His European-style house is placed along the main road, removed from the older core settlement. He owns several trucks and has established a small store near the highway. In addition, he is known as El Hadj, having made a pilgrimage to Mecca. All of the above has elevated his social status, particularly among young people, many of whom have converted to Islam or Christianity.

In Banh, similar trends have been observed. One of the most visibly grand outlier compounds has been constructed by a retired, male government nurse. He also established a commercial mango orchard adjacent to his house, an innovation which spawned a considerable flurry of mango and guava tree planting a few years ago. Unfortunately this venture was not as profitable as expected due to the poor road and marketing connections with Ouahigouya. Settlement changes in Banh were also brought by the marabouts (holy men) mentioned earlier as well as other important local personages (Figure 7.5). During a 1991 visit to Banh, I observed that a clan of blacksmiths and griots (oral historians) had also established their own dispersed outlier compounds near the main road away from the old central settlement. In this case, one of the blacksmith's wives is credited with influencing the move; she is the midwife at the new government MCH (Maternal and Child Health) clinic built in the outskirts of Banh (Figure 7.5).

Many more examples of this type could be cited. It is obvious that changing social relationships or conflict over them is a prime cause of settlement change. New style preferences for housing also impact settlement structure. Some of the older homes in the core are now being abandoned for their perceived "oldness" and lack of space. Newer homes are usually bigger, with more yard space, and tin roofs. Another element in the process of change is the increasing role of women involved in NGO service projects and informal market sector activities (note the case of the midwife above). Social differentiation, accelerated by the 1984 drought, is also a factor. Several former Rimaaybe vassals who have become better-off financially than some of their former Fulani masters, have built new compounds, either to gain more freedom and show their success, or to take advantage of proximity to government facilities.

The proximity factor has more widespread application, especially with regard to government and non-governmental agency interventions. The physical structures and the institutions they represent, are not only altering the physical landscape and settlement system, but they are altering community decision making, landuse and land tenure patterns, and social class relations (Engberg-Pedersen 1995). In Toulfe, for instance, the building of a rural school as well as a clinic near the major road, away from the central settlement, led several people to build nearby. An NGO working in Banh set-up a small-credit scheme for women as well as a grain-bank. Those projects, which dramatically increased the influence of NGOs and formerly dis-empowered groups such as women, have also led to new construction and increased settlement dispersion.

The effects of government policy can be important as well. In the late 1980s, Banh lost out on being selected for a new cattle market to Nogodoum, a village closer to the Mali border. One reason that itinerant cattle traders preferred Nogodoum, was the decision by the government to establish a tax and customs office in Banh. Not surprisingly, many merchants stopped trading in Banh; the region is close to the Mali border and is known for smuggling. Of course, most smugglers avoided the higher visibility that a location in Banh would have provided.Other government policy-related changes stem from the abolition or curtailment of the traditional political structure by the Sankhara Revolution (Ela 1990; Savonnet-Guyot 1986; Politique Africaine 1989). Even an isolated and traditional community such as Toulfe, which once prided itself on not cooperating with the government apparatus, and attempted, wherever possible, to solve its own problems through application of customary laws, now finds itself more and more dependent on outside political structures--courts, police, and extension services.

Finally, a continuing source of settlement change is still the increasing pressure on resources. Some of this problem is due to population growth, but more, in my opinion, is due to market penetration and other forces transforming African societies and resource management systems. Toulfe, which is located in one of the least densely populated regions of Yatenga, has even experienced a dramatic increase in itinerant pastoralists, e.g. new Bella and Fulani groups who go there for the dry season. The most recent arrivals do not, however, have the longstanding contractual herder/farmer ties which have typified previous relationships. Many Mossi settlers have also built communities nearby and gradually impinged on the Kurumba terroir or traditional communal land base, e.g., Timnaore and Songotaba in Figure 7.7.

With the increased encroachment on each other's lands, and particularly with the intensified herder/farmer contact, there has been a greater frequency of cattle predation of standing crops. I observed (and even mediated) a few of the resulting palabres. Yet, in 1991 when I interviewed several longtime, older informants, their greatest concern was how their bushlands--the brousse tigrée to the north of Toulfe--had become a source of fuelwood for the urban markets. They particularly decried the fact that many of their returning youth from the Ivory Coast have deliberately joined this cash-driven fuelwood trade dominated by outside Mossi merchants. So competition over land and resource rights between the youth and the old tengsoba (earth priest) has made intergenerational conflict a new and serious reality.

One event which exacerbated this most recent phenomenon was the 1983 Italian government reconstruction of the former highway linking Djibo with Ouahigouiya (Figure 7.1). Its goal was to increase access to the cattle markets in the Sahelian zone with coastal West Africa as well as to facilitate commercial penetration of the zone (Zida 1991). In my opinion, the presence of that road has done more to break down traditional patterns of livelihood than anything in the fifteen years of research I have carried out in Toulfe. Whether the changes are for the better remain inconclusive. What is clear is that even the most isolated and traditional communities now find it impossible to remain aloof from the external world.

Conclusion

In summation, it is evident that the general process of settlement dispersion is most advanced in Mossi Sodin and least so in the very traditional Kurumba settlement of Toulfe. Isolation from regional market and political power centers seems to be a significant explanatory variable. That situation is changing rapidly, particularly as many youth return with new ideas from the major cities and coastal regions of West Africa. While it is clear that current settlement systems have their antecedents in the pre-colonial period, the colonial and post-colonial forces have had the most impact. Yet, the influence of these processes varies considerably among the three villages.

Toulfe, the most traditional village, retains many of the settlement and livelihood characteristics which have disappeared in other areas. It

is the most agglomerated and its village land area shows the least degradation. The outside world is beginning to impinge, however, through
increased accessibility to markets (which has brought in the cash-driven
fuelwood trade) and through behavioral modification engendered by
returning migrants. NGO and government interventions have also
brought change, as has social and religious competition and conflict.
Though the production system around Toulfe is still functionally intact, it
may not remain that way for long. The influence of immigrants is important here, particularly Fulani and other herder groups and the Mossi who
are encroaching on Kurumba lands. Only the future will demonstrate
whether these tradition-bound Kurumba peoples can hold back or channel change in ways that preserves some of their uniquely sustainable
agrosylvopastoral practices.

Banh is the more intermediate case. Again, isolation and distance
from the regional capital kept the region very traditional for a longer
time. The Fulani have been reticent to travel, join the civil service, or get
an education, though the drought of 1984 appears to have taught them
the necessity of interacting with the outer world's economy and political
structure. Banh has also experienced a dramatic increase in outside intervention; it now boasts a rural credit banking program, a government livestock and farming systems center, school, MCH clinic, and other ventures
by NGOs. As mentioned earlier, one agency even attempted to build a
dam for irrigated horticulture. That plan was backed by the local
Rimaaybe farmers, but widely disparaged and fought against by the
Fulani herders (Association 6-S 1990; Elsasser 1990). See also the article
by Ford (1992) for a discussion of the resource conflict that has ensued.

Sodin, the dominantly Mossi community, has experienced the most
drastic dispersion and overall population growth. This was to be expected given its location at the center of the region's economic and political
life, the high population density and growth rate, and the traditional
Mossi coping pattern which focused on migration. Certain patterns of
house/quartier siting, dictated by ecological factors, still hold true.
Permanent year-round wells can only be dug in specific places on the
catena in order to attain the perched water-tables common to these ferruginous soils, and there is still the need to avoid flooding. But other concerns now have become important as well; land scarcity and the expansion of agriculture to once marginal areas, as well as the increase in thiev-
ery--a new type of security threat--has accelerated settlement dispersal.
As a result of this dispersal, it has been possible to make more efficient
use of a shrinking land resource base. This is particularly true for women
who find it necessary to scavenge ever farther afield for fuelwood or fodder for stall-fed animals.

In many areas of Yatenga, a small but visible trend toward increased land conservation and even restoration has begun. The changing economics of the 1990s has encouraged this process. As for the overall pattern of settlement and landuse change in central Yatenga, it can be characterized as an almost complete occupation and humanization of the landscape (Figure 7.8 and 7.9). Even formerly ignored marginal uplands are now scavenged for fodder and firewood--see the very moving story of Mossi women described in a special edition of the London Times/Observer (1988).

In hindsight, we now realize that by the mid-1960s, central Yatenga had already become a severe example of "involution" (Marchal 1977, 1983). Early hi-tech approaches to deal with land degradation failed, but recent low-tech grassroots methods appear to have a better chance at success. All of these development programs as well as informal socioeconomic trends and driving forces have left their imprints on the landscape. What these trends portend for the future in political economy, culture and settlement structure are slowly becoming clearer, but by no means is the final outcome assured. Yet, I am encouraged overall that the people of this region, and the social systems as well as settlement structures represented, are continuously adjusting. This fact behooves us to avoid simplistic answers to complex issues of vulnerability and to learn from the context of each case. Then, maybe, we can possibly influence change in a more positive direction.

One lesson is clear: rural settlements like these cases in Yatenga are no longer isolated. They are now part of the global rural-urban, political, and economic continuum that transcends national and even transnational units. These villages are integral elements in complex open-systems that span "local to global" scales. In this regard, the "new ecology" approach is a very appropriate analytical tool (Zimmerer 1994). The global village is a reality, and Yatenga, too, is part of it!

References

Adamou, Djibo. 1990. *Etude des Systèmes de Culture en Milieu "Eleveurs": Cas du Territoire de Banh*. Febuary. Montpellier, France and Ouagadougou, Burkina Faso: CNEARC/CIRAD/INERA.

Association Internationale Six S. 1990. *Barrage de Ban*. Dossier, Resume, and Conclusion. May. Ougadougou: Sahel Consult.

Batterbury, Simon. 1993. "Roles for Farmers' Knowledge in Africa." *ODI Agricultural Administration (Research and Extension) Network*. Network Paper No. 42: 18-30.

____. 1994. "Changing Ecological and Social Dynamics of Mossi Livelihood Systems: Assessing the Impacts of Soil and Water Conservation and 'Village

Land Use Management' Schemes." Paper presented at the Annual Meeting, Association of American Geographers, San Francisco.

Benoit, M. 1982. "Nature Peul du Yatenga: Remarques sur le Pastoralism en Pays Mossi." *Travaux et Documents de l'ORSTOM*. No. 143. Paris: ORSTOM.

Bohle, Hans G., Thomas E. Downing, and Michael J. Watts. 1994. "Climate Change and Social Vulnerability: Toward a Sociology and Geography of Food Insecurity." *Global Environmental Change* 4: 37-48.

Campbell, David and Jennifer Olson. 1991. *Framework for Environment and Development: The Kite*. CASID Occasional Paper No. 10. East Lansing, Michigan: Michigan State University. Center for Advanced Study of International Development.

Cleaver, K. M. and G. A. Schreiber. 1993. *The Population, Agriculture and Environment Nexus in Sub-Saharan Africa*. Agriculture and Rural Development Series, No. 9. Washington, D.C.: World Bank, Technical Department, Africa Region.

D'Aquino, Patrick. 1991. *Viabilité d'une Exploitation Pastorale plus Intensive (Parcours et Fourrage) d'un Ligneux Sahélien: Pterocarpus Lucens*. Premieres Etudes et Experimentations sur le Departement de Banh, Province du Yatenga, Burkina Faso. Montpellier, France and Ouagadougou: INERA/DSA-CIRAD.

de Verdière, P. Colin. 1988. *L'Elevage Peul au Nord du Yatenga-Burkina Faso: Système Actuel et Perspectives d'Avenir*. Sèptembre. Montpellier, France: CNEARC/CIRAD/ESAT.

Dommen, A. J. 1988. *Innovation in African Agriculture*. Boulder: Westview Press.

Dugué, Patrick. 1989. "Possibilités et Limites de l'Intensification des Systèmes de Culture Vivriers en Zone Soudano-Sahèlienne: Le Cas du Yatenga (Burkina Faso)." *Département Systèmes Agraires du CIRAD, Collection: Documents Systèmes Agraires*. No. 9. Monpellier, France: CIRAD.

Dupré, Georges. 1991. "Les Arbres, le Fourré, et le Jardin: Les Plantes dans la Societé de l'Aribinda, Burkina Faso." In *Savoirs Paysans et Développement*. Paris: Karthala/ORSTOM.

Ela, Jean-Marc. 1990. *Quand l'État Penètre en Brousse: Les Riposts Paysannes a la Crise*. Paris: Karthala.

Elsasser, Konrad. 1990. *Le Terroir Agrosylvopastoral de Banh: Synthèse du Diagnostic sur les Systèmes de Production*. May. Burkina Faso: INERA (Institut d'Études et de Recherches Agricoles).

Engberg-Pedersen, Lars. 1995. *Creating Local Democratic Politics from Above: the "Gestion des Terroirs" Approach in Burkina Faso*. Issue Paper No. 54. London: Drylands Programme, IIED (International Institute for Environment and Development).

English, J., M. Tiffen, and M. Mortimore. 1994. "Land Resource Management in Machakos District, Kenya 1930-1990." *World Bank Environment Paper No. 5*. Washington, D.C.: World Bank.

Falloux, F. and A. Mukendi, eds. 1988. *Desertification Control and Renewable Resource Management in the Sahelian and Sudanian Zones of West Africa*. Technical Paper No 70. Washington, D.C.: World Bank.

Falloux, F. and L. M. Talbot. 1993. *Crisis and Opportunity: Environment and Development in Africa*. London: Earthscan.

Ford, Robert E. 1982. "Subsistence Farming Systems in the Semi-arid Northern Yatenga (Upper Volta)" 2 Vols. Ph.D. Dissertation, University of California, Riverside. University Microfilms: University of Michigan.

____. 1992. "Human Environment Interaction in Sahelian North Yatenga." *Research and Exploration*. National Geographic Society 8, 4: 460-475.

____. 1993. "Marginal Coping in Extreme Land Pressures: Ruhengeri, Rwanda." In B. L. Turner II, Robert Kates, and Goran Hyden, eds. *Population Growth and Agricultural Change in Sub-Saharan Africa*. Pp. 145-186. Gainesville, Fl: University Press of Florida.

____. 1995. "The Population-Environment Nexus and Vulnerability Assessment in Africa." *GeoJournal* 35, 2: 207-216.

Geertz, Clifford. 1963. *Agricultural Involution: The Process of Ecological Change in Indonesia*. Berkeley: University of California Press.

Goumandakoye, Mounkaila and Jean Babou Bado. 1991. *L'Aménagement des Terroirs: Concept et Opérationnalisation*. Ouagadougou, Burkina Faso: CILSS.

Grosse, Scott. 1994a. "More People, More Trouble: Population Growth and Agricultural Change in Rwanda." Draft report prepared for EPAT/USAID. Department of Population Planning and International Health, University of Michigan, School of Public Health.

____. 1994b. "The Roots of Conflict and State Failure in Rwanda: The Political Exacerbation of Social Cleavages in a Context of Growing Resource Scarcity." Draft report prepared for EPAT/USAID. Department of Population Planning and International Health, University of Michigan, School of Public Health.

Hammond, P. 1966. *Yatenga: Technology in the Culture of a West African People*. New York: Free Press.

Honadle, G. Scott Grosse and P. Phumpiu. 1994. "The Problems of Linear Project Thinking in a Non-Linear World: Experience from the Nexus of Population, Environmental and Agricultural Dynamics in Africa." Draft Report. EPAT Policy Paper Series.

Izard, Michel. 1985. *Gens de Pouvoir, Gens de la Terre. Les Institutions Politiques del'Ancien Royaume du Yatenga (Bassin de la Volta Blanche)*. Paris and Cambridge: Cambridge University Press and Éditions de la Maison des Sciences de'Homme.

King, Maurice. 1993. "Demographic Entrapment." *Transactions of the Royal Society of Tropical Medicine and Hygiene* 87 (Supplememt), 1: 23-28.

Le Pape, M. 1993. "L'Attraction Urbaine--Soixante-Cinq Ans d'Observation sur Abidjan." *Cahiers Sciences Humaines* 29: 333-348.

Lele, Uma and S. W. Stone. 1989. *Population Pressure, The Environment and Agricultural Intensification: Variations on the Boserup Hypothesis*. MADIA Discussion Paper 4. Washington, D.C.: World Bank.

London Times/The Observer. 1988. "Fragile Future." Special Edition. Pp. 5-29. London: OXFAM in Association with the Observer.

Mabogunje, Akin L. 1995. "The Environmental Challenges in Sub-Saharan Africa." *Environment* 37, 4: 4-10.

McMillan, Della E. 1986. "Distribution of Resources and Products in Mossi Households." In Art Hansen and Della E. MacMillan, eds. *Food In Sub-Saharan Africa*. Boulder, CO: Lynne Rienner Publishers.

_____. 1995. *Sahel Visions: Planned Settlement and River Blindness Control in Burkina Faso*. Tucson: The University of Arizona Press.

Marchal, J. Y. 1977. "The Evolution of Agrarian Systems in Yatenga." *African Environment* 2 & 3: 73-85.

_____. 1983. "Yatenga, Nord Haute-Volta: La Dynamique d'un Espace Rurale Soudano-Sahèlien." *Travaux et Documents de l'ORSTOM*. No. 167. Paris: ORSTOM.

Marchal, Monique. 1983. "Atlas des Structures Agraires au Sud du Sahara." *Les Paysages Agraires de Haute-Volta: Analyse Structurale par la Methode Graphique*. No. 18. Paris: ORSTOM.

Martinelli, B. and G. Serpantié. 1987. *Deux Points de Vue sur la Confrontation des Paysans aux Aménageurs dans le Yatenga (Burkina Faso)*. February. Ouagadougou: ORSTOM.

Meillassoux, C., B. Schlemper, F. Gendreau, and M. Verlet, eds. 1991. *Déséquilibres Alimentaires, Déséquilibres Démographiques*. Paris: EDI ORSTOM, CEPED.

Medina, Maria do Livramento. 1991. *Les Réssources des Parcours dans l'Alimentation des Animaux Domèstiques. Les Cas du Campement d'Hivernage de Gassenaye et du Village de Banh-Burkina Faso*. November. Centre Montpellier, France: ENGREF.

Milleville, P. and G. Serpantié. 1993. "Intensification et Durabilité des Systèmes Agricoles en Afrique Soudano-Sahèlienne." Paper presented at the seminar: Promotion de Systèmes Agricoles Durables. Montpellier, France: ORSTOM.

Ogier, Joseph.1991. *Liste Bibliographique des Publications de l'INERA ed du DSA/CIRAD dans le Cadre du Programme RSP/Nord Yatenga depuis fin 1987*. Burkina Faso: INERA.

Ouedraogo, B. L., and W. M. Rideout Jr. 1980. "Traditional Modalities of Participation and Self-Development: Indigenous Age-Set Groups and Rural Development in Upper Volta." In N. Colletta and R. Kidd, eds. *Tradition for Development: Indigenous Structures and Folk Media in Non-Formal Education*. Pp. 150-193. Berlin: International Council for Adult Education and German Foundation for International Development.

Ouedraogo, Ignace Marie Omer. 1988. *Contribution à un Projet d'Aménagement de Territoire Cartographié et Analyse Phyto-Écologique d'un Milieu Soudano-Sahélien. Cas du Terroir Agropastoral de Banh au Nord Yatenga, Burkina Faso*. November. Montpellier, France: CNEARC/ESAT/DSA-CIRAD.

Perez, Frédéric. 1990. *Utilisation de l'Espace et des Ressources par Deux Implantations Humaines dans le Département de Banh (Province du Nord Yatenga-Burkina Faso). L'exemple du Campement d'Hivernage de Gassenaye et du Village de Diendié*. October. Montpellier, France: CNEARC/ESAT/DSA-CIRAD.

Politique Africaine No. 33. 1989. *Retour au Burkina*. Paris: Karthala.

Repetto, R. and T. Holmes. 1983. "The Role of Population in Resource Depletion in Developing Countries." *Population and Development Review* 9: 609-632.

Riesman, Paul. 1977. *Freedom in Fulani Social Life*. Chicago: University of Chicago Press.

Rochette, R. 1988. "Migration and Settlement of New Lands." In F. Falloux and A. Mukendi, eds. Technical Paper No. 70. Washington, DC: World Bank.

____. 1989. *Le Sahel en Lutte contre la Désertification: Leçons d'Expériences.* CILSS (Comité Inter-état de Lutte contre la Secheresse au Sahel) and GTZ (Deutsche Gessellschaft für Technische Zusammenarbeit).

Savonnet-Guyot, Claudette. 1986. *État et Societés au Burkina: Essai sur le Politique African.* Paris: Karthala.

Schweeger-Hefel, A. and W. Staude. 1972. *Die Karumba von Lurun.* Monographie Eines Volkes aus Ober Volta. Wien: Verlag A. Schendl.

Serpantié, G. 1989. "Transformations d'un Système Agropastoral Soudano-Sahélien. Bidi, Nord Yatenga, Burkina Faso." *Cahiers de la Recherche-Développement.* No. 20. Montpellier, France: ORSTOM/CIRAD.

Shaikh, A. and S. Snrech. 1993. "Managing Change: The Population Environment, and Development Nexus in the Sahel." Slideshow Presentation, International Resources Groups. Washington, D.C.: The World Bank.

Skinner, E. P. 1964. *The Mossi of the Upper Volta: the Political Development of a Sudanese People.* Palo Alto, CA: Stanford University Press.

Stomal-Weigel, B. 1988. "L'évolution Récente et Comparée des Systèmes de Production Serer et Wolof dans Deux Villages du Vieux Bassin Arachidier (Sénégal)." *Cahiers Sciences Humaines* 24: 17-33. Paris: ORSTOM.

Turner II, B. L., Robert Kates, and Goran Hyden, eds. 1993. *Population Growth and Agricultural Change in Africa.* Gainesville, Fl: University Press of Florida.

Turner II, B. L., and Patricia A. Benjamin. 1994. "Fragile Lands: Identification and Use for Agriculture." In Vernon W. Ruttan, ed. *Agricultural, Environment, and Health: Sustainable Development in the 21st Century.* Pp. 105-124. Minneapolis: University of Minnesota Press.

Williams, G. 1991. "What Disequilibria? People, Land and Food in Nigeria." In C. Meillassoux, B. Schlemper, F. Gendreau, and M. Verlet, eds. *Déséquilibres Alimentaires, Déséquilibres Démographiques.* Paris: EDI ORSTOM, CEPED.

Wright, P. and E. G. Bonkoungou. 1985. "Soil and Water Conservation as a Starting Point for Rural Forestry: the OXFAM Project/Ouahigouya, Burkina Faso." *Rural Africana* 23-24.

Zida, Gabriel. 1991. Personal Communication. Extension Agent Working with the PAE Project at the CRPA/Yatenga, Ouahigouya, Burkina Faso.

Zimmerer, Karl. 1994. "Human Geography and the 'New Ecology': the Prospect and Promise of Integration." *Annals of the Association of American Geographers* 84, 1: 108-125.

8

Settlement Structure and Landscape Ecology in Humid Tropical Rwanda

Robert E. Ford

Africa's settlement patterns include examples of both extreme clustering as well as dispersion. Until very recently, parts of Rwanda, Burundi, Uganda, and eastern Zaire along the Great Western Rift Valley (Figure 8.1) have been noted for some of the most extreme cases of settlement dispersion and high rural population density in Africa and the world (Sirven 1984; Charlery et al. 1989, 1993; Ford 1990; Rossi 1991; Bart 1993; Clay 1993; Honadle et al. 1994; Grosse 1994a,b). Rwanda's population, ninety-four percent rural, has had the highest density on the African continent--about 300 persons/km2 prior to the 1994 genocide and mass migrations--while its internal population growth rate for the period 1978-1991 was 3.1 percent.

Rwanda's population-environment status has been debated by numerous authorities.[1] Some see a clear doomsday Malthusian scenario playing out, while others theorize that it may exemplify a more optimistic Boserupian case of population-induced "intensification" (Ford 1993, 1995; Honadle et al. 1994; Turner II et al. 1993; Turner II and Benjamin 1994). At the very minimum, it is seen as a case of severe "agricultural involution" as Geertz (1963) and others have defined the concept. One point is clear, Rwanda is an excellent case for observing and testing diverse ideas and theories concerning nature-society relationships and sustainable development in humid tropical montane agroecosystems (Figure 8.2a). This chapter then, will explore the applicability of the Rwandan case to current theoretical ideas and practice in respect to settlement structure, population dynamics, resource management, and sustainable development in the region. Out of this analysis, one hopes, will come a clearer understanding of the fundamental ecological, historical-political, and demographic forces that have shaped settlement processes in pre-colonial, colonial, and post-independence Rwanda.[2]

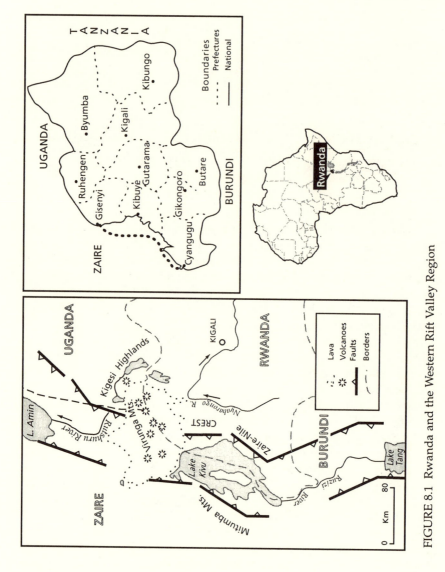

FIGURE 8.1 Rwanda and the Western Rift Valley Region

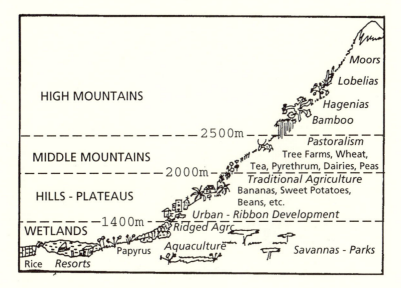

FIGURE 8.2a Vertical Belts in Rwanda

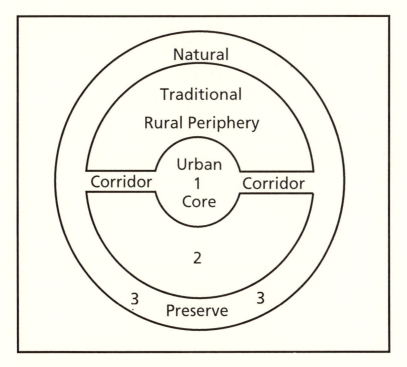

FIGURE 8.2b Spatial Accessibility Zones in Rwanda

Robert E. Ford

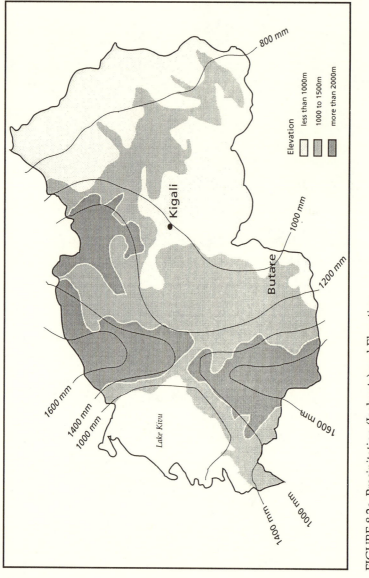

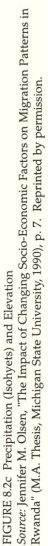

FIGURE 8.2c Precipitation (Isohyets) and Elevation
Source: Jennifer M. Olsen, "The Impact of Changing Socio-Economic Factors on Migration Patterns in Rwanda" (M.A. Thesis, Michigan State University, 1990), p. 7. Reprinted by permission.

Ethnic, Socioeconomic, and Ecological Background

Rwanda is a small mountainous country; the appellation *pays de mille collines* (land of a thousand hills) is quite appropriate. Furthermore, it is characterized by a high level of landscape diversity and complexity, to include substantial variations in altitude, relief, precipitation, agroecology, geology, hydrology, and so on. Rwanda is also a country with an active tectonic and volcanic history: the Great Rift Valley's spectacular escarpment that drops precipitously from the Zaire-Nile Divide to Lake Kivu is indeed a world-class natural wonder. Finally, the area is renowned for its rare flora and fauna, as celebrated in the work of Dianne Fossey and others (Fossey 1983).

The ethnic history of the region is frequently cited as an explanation of many sociocultural as well as ecological patterns in Rwanda. Examples include the assumed ninth-century arrival of the Bantu BaHutu farmers (eighty-three to eighty-seven percent of the population), followed later in the fourteenth or fifteenth century by the BaTutsi pastoralists (fourteen to sixteen percent), whose ancestors can be traced to the Ethiopian/Somali region. The third ethnic group found in Rwanda, the BaTwa, are a pigmoid group who represent only about one percent of the population. They have not had as visible an effect on Rwanda's settlement structure due to their reclusive tendencies and small numbers.

In terms of settlement pattern and population distribution, some have suggested that it was the overlord Tutsi pastoralists and their feudalistic state who forced the Hutu population into one early concentration in the northern highlands (around Gisenyi and Ruhengeri) and another in the southern foothills (Figure 8.1). Some observers have suggested that the Tutsi feudal overlords deliberately enforced an extreme dispersion of households outside of the royal palace centers in order to divide and conquer their Hutu serfs. Rwanda's political-ethnic history has indeed been a significant factor in settlement structure. The above thesis is plausible considering the very close and long period of interaction between the three groups, although there are credible theories to the contrary as well. Though dramatically different in livelihood patterns and many social customs, all three groups speak the same language: *Kinyarwanda* (LeMarchand 1970).

Prioul (1981) and Cambrezy (1984), as well as others, have cast some doubt on any exclusive role for Tutsi feudalism in determining pre-colonial population distribution and settlement structure. There may have been, in fact, a significant pre-Tutsi (Hutu) pattern of landscape ecology and economy that was simply reinforced by the Tutsi political-economic system. Cambrezy (1984), utilizing a very unique cartographic method to study population change as it relates to agriculture, particu larly *marais* (marshland) development, has suggested that the original patterns are still present, though muted by dramatic post-World War II changes.

It is clear, however, that settlement patterns now visible on the landscape have been most affected by the dramatic post-World War II population growth and land use restructuring, and by the tumultuous political events of the post-independence era (Figure 8.3). Most significant are the developments that followed the start of the civil war in 1990 and particularly, the massive displacement that occurred after the downing of President Habyarimana's airplane in April 1994 and the subsequent conflict. These events will seriously affect population and settlement in Rwanda, and though some would say they were "serendipitous", they actually reflect the concatenation of numerous forces which were building up for some time in Rwanda and Burundi. Some of the most significant historical, political, and social factors involved are as follows:

First, the region was not known to westerners until after the famous journeys of such explorers as Speke, Burton, and Stanley in the late nineteenth century, well after most other regions had become embroiled with the colonial powers (Moorehead 1983; Burton 1862; Stanley 1878). Furthermore, neither western nor Arab slave raiding had much impact in Rwanda. In this regard, Ford (1990) states the following:

> Due to historical and ecological factors, the ravages of the slave trade did not devastate these core mountain areas (the "interlacustrine" region) as much as the peripheral East African coastal belt. Part of this was due to the development of militarily powerful, feudalistic, and socially stratified kingdoms, such as the Buganda, Bunyoro, and Ankole kingdoms of east-central Uganda....The Ruanda and Urundi kingdoms, located on the Rwandese Central Plateau, were related historically and politically to Ankole and Bunyoro. In fact, inter-lacustrine Central Africa may have achieved the highest rural population density on the African continent outside of the Nile Delta as early as the eighteenth or early nineteenth century (Vancina 1962; Ford 1990: 47).

Secondly, the two dominant ethnic groups--Tutsi and Hutu--share more intensely, often to an extreme level, the memory of past ethnic and political rivalries as well as mutual recriminations surrounding current disputes which were aggravated by the colonial and post-colonial experience. Because ethnic cleavages in Rwanda and Burundi are not diffused among many competing groups, as is the case in surrounding countries

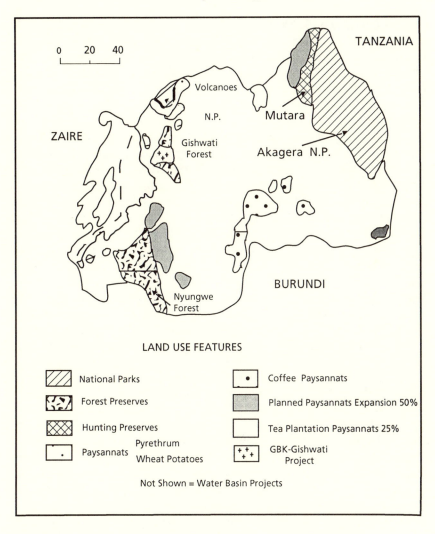

FIGURE 8.3 Major Colonial And Post-Colonial Land Use Features
Source: Adapted from Sirven et al. (1974).

such as Tanzania or Zaire, ethnic conflict has often become magnified out of proportion. It should be noted that the impact of German and Belgian colonialism was less direct and onerous in Ruanda-Urundi--the pre-independence League of Nations mandate. The result was that traditional political structures--and cleavages--remained intact, and, unfortunately, were intensified by the brief colonial experience rather than diffused by it (Grosse 1994a,b).

Third, the geopolitics of the Cold War in Africa, with its creation or support by western powers of one-party states (often military-style regimes) to serve their own "proxy" interests, helped establish and perpetuate corrupt, and often monolithic, authoritarian regimes that suppressed any political pluralism or democratic institutions. Most of these governments, including the Habyarimana regime in Rwanda, became entrenched and unwilling to face change--economic or political. Many utilized their monolithic power to favor narrow tribal, regional, or even class interests, often with the tacit acquiescence of the Big Powers. Furthermore, in Rwanda, the Hutu-dominated government came to be perceived by many external donor agencies as being a rather effective regime with a good record for development-project implementation. Therefore, few outsiders challenged the use of undemocratic methods to maintain its power base as long as the perception of stability, effectiveness, and a pro-western tilt was maintained.

Fourth, class/clan and north-south regional economic conflicts were aggravated by a late 1980s drought and local famine in southern Rwanda and a precipitous drop in global coffee prices, events which put pressure on the political-economic system beyond its ability to cope. These problems were compounded by growing resource scarcity, rising unemployment among landless youth, and land degradation. All of these factors fed into the cauldron which erupted in the mid-1994, genocidal civil war.

Fifth, in late 1990, the long-term question of what to do with the increasingly militant refugee Tutsi in Uganda and elsewhere came to a head. When this political and population crisis arose, President Habyarimana's unwillingness to compromise and deal with the Tutsi refugee issue and the ensuing invasion by the RPF--the Tutsi dominated guerrilla army--was the final straw that may have precipitated the chaos culminating in the genocide of 1994. It should also be made clear that this tragic conflict was not simply an "old ethnic fight." The RPF had found allies among many increasingly disenchanted "moderate Hutus" who had become caught up in the democratization movement sweeping across Africa. That situation, as mentioned previously, was further aggravated by the post-Cold War vacuum (and UN ineffectiveness) created by western unwillingness to directly counter nascent ethnic extremism when it first appeared in places like Liberia, Somalia, Sudan, and finally Rwanda and Burundi.

The use of ethnic hatred to precipitate a "final solution" by hardline Hutu elements within the Rwandan government was not an aberration. It was planned deliberately and was essentially successful because the rest of the world did not wish to become involved until it was too late to avoid disaster. Grosse (1994a,b) Olson (1995) Ford (1995) and Percival and Homer-Dixon (1995) point out that, though it is tempting to see in Rwanda a Malthusian "demographic" doomsday scenario at work, the reality is much more complex than such a simplistic explanation would allow. In hindsight, it seems clear that the pre-conditions for a political and ecological explosion in Rwanda were long in the making. Some refer to this type of societal-wide collapse as the "failed state" syndrome (Wunsch and Olowu 1990).

Pre World War II Population and Settlement Patterns

The dominant settlement pattern during the pre World War II era was one of extreme settlement dispersion centered on the traditional nuclear household enclosure or *urugo*, each of which exploited a soil-slope sequence extending from the relatively rolling to flat hilltops to the marshy lowlands (Figure 8.4). It should be noted that this extreme pattern of dispersal was also found in other East and Central African regions, except for certain areas directly affected by local and regional conflict, e.g., slave raiding. Therefore, defensive villages were not as necessary here as in some other areas of Africa.

Very early in the pre-colonial period, this inter-lacustrine zone of Africa became one of the most significant high population-density "islands" within Africa, an arrangement which facilitated feudal control by the Tutsi hierarchy without requiring forced agglomeration of the population into clustered settlements. The high population concentration in these highlands developed because of numerous favorable ecological factors as well as the ethnic and political history discussed previously. The following ecological factors were among the most important: (1) opportunities to avoid exposure to diseases such as malaria which were more common in the lowlands; (2) the more fertile soils, particularly along the volcanic rift zone; (3) reliable and abundant rainfall which allows for up to two growing seasons per year; and (4) high floral and faunal biodiversity.

In sum, the population and settlement structure inherited from the pre-World War II era could be characterized as a bipolar concentration of dispersed settlements in the northern highlands and southern foothills.

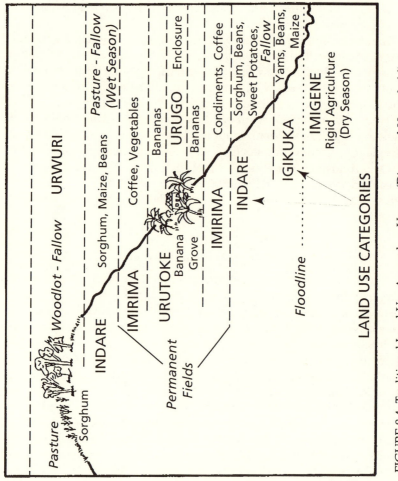

FIGURE 8.4 Traditional Land Use Around an Urugu (Dispersed Household)

This spatial pattern was enforced for generations by the Tutsi pastoralists and was later perpetuated by German and Belgian colonial administrators (Scaetta 1932; Harroy 1949; Tondeur 1949; Gourou 1952; Neesen 1956; Bart 1993). Some critiques of both the pre-colonial Tutsi feudal period and early Belgian-occupation suggest that the rationale for imposing a strongly dispersed settlement structure was to "divide and conquer" the majority Hutu settled-farmer peoples. The Belgian colonial administration was often accused by Hutu groups of being pro-Tutsi.

Thus, for generations, Hutu settled-farmer expansion into the Central Plateau, the Eastern Lowlands, and some of the higher altitude regions was greatly restricted (Figures 8.1, 8.3). Even temporary farming in the local wetlands--*marais*--was restricted by the Tutsi. These lowland zones were utilized primarily by transhumant Tutsi pastoralists for seasonal grazing lands as were the Eastern savannas. Later park and forest preserve development along the Tanzanian border--Akagera National Park and near-by areas--further restricted settled-farmer movement and expansion. The first national park in Africa--Volcanoes National Park--was established by King Leopold in the Virunga volcanic chain where the mountain gorillas are located (Figure 8.3).

For both the Hutu and Tutsi, much of the Central Plateau region and Eastern Lowlands, with its larger number of lowland marais and semi-arid savannas, were simply not the most desired location for either permanent or transitory occupance. Higher altitude regions over 2000 meters (Figure 8.2c) were also undesirable. The limiting factors in both these zones included: disease, e.g., Trypanosomiasis and East Coast Fever, dense bamboo belts and other impenetrable vegetation, soil/hydrology factors, e.g., dense papyrus swamps and peat deposits, and time-distance socioeconomic factors. Therefore, pre-colonial and early colonial land use/population preference patterns focused on a narrow altitudinal belt between 1400-2000 meters. Colonial governments throughout East Africa frequently referred to these zones as "high potential" zones. Significant permanent expansion down into local valley bottoms or upwards into the higher altitudes did nor occur, or was unnecessary, prior to the dramatic population growth which occurred in the post-World War II period (Cambrezy 1984; Bart 1993).

Nevertheless, though the German and then the Belgian influence under the Ruanda-Urundi mandate was relatively short, many aspects of life as well as the landscape were altered significantly. Some of the most visible effects were produced by soil-erosion control projects, e.g., contoured bunding (Figure 8.5). Early colonial administrators railed frequently over the "backwardness" of local agricultural and livestock development practices (Scaetta 1932; Harroy 1949; Tondeur 1949). Old

FIGURE 8.5 Contoured Bunds on Steep-Slopes in Ruhengeri Prefecture

photos of the landscape as well as written records--particularly from missionaries--portray a landscape that in many respects was indeed more degraded than today. Attempts to institute reforestation--usually with corvee (forced) labor--started quite early in Rwanda under the Belgians. Later, post-colonial mass campaigns by the Habyarimana regime to control erosion, build roads, and plant trees with communal free labor (umaganda) were undermined by the negative memories of earlier Belgian forced labor, a major barrier to community participation (Nyamulinda and Ngiruwonsanga 1992). Organizing a highly dispersed population could also be difficult without a centralized and often coercive state apparatus. The Habyarimana regime often rationalized its use of a Chinese-style, one-party centralized, state structure on the basis of the need to impose order in the dispersed settlement and social context inherited from the Belgians and feudal Tutsi.

From a settlement perspective, the arrival of Catholic White Father missionaries, and later Protestants such as the Seventh-Day Adventists, was probably most significant in starting new patterns that would change the settlement structure. They established rural mission stations which impacted health, nutrition, education, and culture in significant ways (Heremans et al. 1982). Many of these early mission stations grew into nascent agglomerations (service centers) often referred to as *Bourgs*, e.g., Byumba, Gitarama, Nyakinama (Figure 8.1, 8.6b). This nascent pre-urban process has been cited by Sirven (1984) as a most significant colonial impetus to clustering and break-up of the "*sous-urbanization*" (under-urbanization) that characterized Rwandan settlement history until recently (Bart 1989, 1993; Ford 1993). Rwanda and Burundi were until recently the least urbanized countries in Africa.

Post World War II Population and Settlement Change

Pre-1980 Population Growth

Cambrezy (1984) has described post World War II population changes as an "in situ densification of the landscape." In fact, up to the time of independence in 1961, when the Hutu gained political control over their former feudal overlords, population growth and migration were indeed very local and did not affect significantly the pre-colonial bipolar distribution of the population. However, starting as early as the 1940s, but accelerating after World War II, rapid population growth lead to significant changes in the distribution of people and settlements.

In the post-war period, Rwandese farmers were required to significantly intensify agricultural production. They first achieved this by

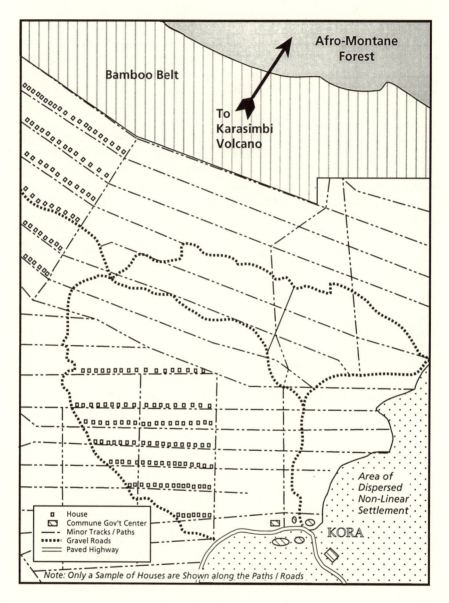

FIGURE 8.6a Paysannat - Rectilinear Pattern

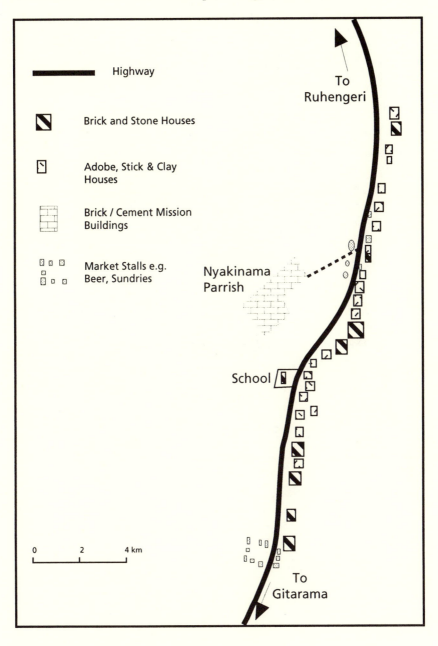

FIGURE 8.6b Ribbon / Strip Settlement - Niakinama
Source: F. and A. Bart (1989)

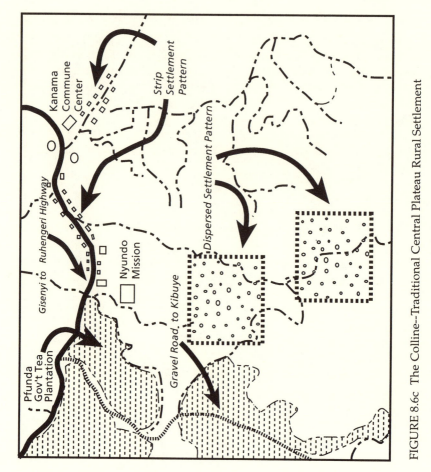

FIGURE 8.6c The Colline--Traditional Central Plateau Rural Settlement

adopting new crops such as white potato, soybeans, and maize. Later improvements in yield per unit of land accelerated the process of "agricultural intensification" (Martin 1987; Turner II et al. 1993; Ford 1993; Charlery 1993). The post-war period also brought an increase in lands devoted to export crops that included pyrethrum, coffee, tea (Figure 8.3). Unfortunately, due to the land locked-up in reserves and parks or inaccessible because of other cultural restrictions, land available for food production was limited. These factors together produced a state of "agricultural involution" and reduced productivity per unit of labor, a negative condition which came early in Rwanda. One need recall that Rwanda has had few options other than agriculture for generating foreign exchange. Thus, "land scarcity" has long been a critical factor in the Rwandese human-environment equation, though much of the scarcity was initially the result of ethno-political restrictions. Martin, in 1987, theorized about a Boserupian explanation of population-agricultural change in Rwanda (see also Ford 1993).

By the time of the census of 1978, population growth and distribution had changed significantly in Rwanda. Now a third center of high density was formed in the Kigali region (center-east of the country) besides the early bipolar high-density areas of north and south (Ruhengeri/Gisenyi in the north and Butare in the south). As might be expected, changes in migration patterns have been significant in altering the post-World War II population distribution. Olson (1990, 1992) and Cambrezy (1984), describe the first phase in Rwanda's dramatic post-World War II population realignment as one which was largely a local "rural-rural" migration phenomenon. It was characterized by modest intensification of agricultural outputs and inputs in those areas already under high population density on the *collines*--the hills of the Central Plateau--where most peasants live (Olson 1990; Ford 1990, 1993; Grosse 1994a,b). Most new lands added to the system in this pre-1961 period fit into a pattern of localized "extensification"--that is, it was primarily a short movement upslope or downslope (Figure 8.7).

The second phase began in 1962--after a bloody post-independence ethnic conflict--when the now ascendent Hutu government began an aggressive campaign to open up "new lands" in once banned areas in the Central Plateau and Eastern lowlands. This phase was also characterized by extensification and lasted until about 1971. But the increasing scarcity of locally available free land, the diminishing returns from cropping intensification, as well as the diminishing farm sizes, meant that serious "population pressures" began to be felt. A critical difference to this second phase was that the migrant's decision to move and choice of destination were heavily controlled by the government's efforts to direct

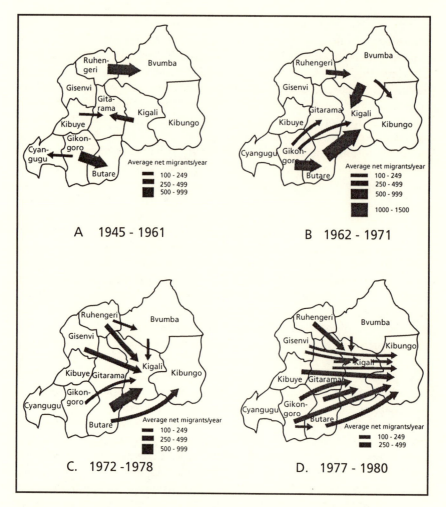

FIGURE 8.7 Rural-Rural Migration
Source: Jennifer M. Olsen, "The Impact of Changing Socio-Economic Factors on Migration Patterns in Rwanda" (M.A. Thesis, Michigan State University, 1990), p. 134. Reprinted with permission.

investment and migration toward planned "new settlements" called *paysannats* (Figure 8.3, 8.6a) whose primary purpose was the expansion of export agriculture--particularly coffee and pyrethrum   (Olson 1990; Grosse 1994a,b; Ford 1993).   Note the rectilinear pattern of households and farm plots in this new but still highly dispersed settlement type in contrast to the traditional pattern on the *colline* (Figure 8.6c). Unfortunately, besides increased deforestation, one of the impacts of opening up new lands along the apron of the Virunga Mountains, as well as in the Gishwati Forest, was the stress put on the mountain gorilla's habitat. This is described in the discussion of the Belgian-funded pyrethrum project in Ruhengeri and Gisenyi in the 1960s, as well as the coffee projects in Bugesera (Prioul 1989).

The next two phases (1972-1976 and 1977-1980), as described by Olson (1990), continued to be characterized by rural-rural population growth and settlement change (Figure 8.7). But once the better lands for these government-organized projects were exhausted--particularly the lands in the southern part of the Kigali prefecture as well as near the city itself--migration focused on the last remaining low-density region in the eastern prefecture of Kibungo (Figure 8.1, 8.3). The net effect of these intensification and extensification phases of migration was to: (1) decrease the national variance in population density, (2) all but eliminate the availability of "non-preserved land" outside the major parks as a source of new land, and (3) dramatically "humanize" the landscape, from the lowest *marais* (flooded lowlands) to highest hilltops (Figure 8.5).

Political instability continued in post-Independence Rwanda and eventually culminated in the political crisis of 1973 which propelled a Hutu-dominated military group into power. President Habyarimana-- who died in the plane crash of April 1994--came to power as a result of that mid-1970s ethnic and regional political upheaval. Until this second political crisis, government rural settlement, population, and develop- ment policy focused on creation of the rural *paysannats* (Dumont 1960) or the servicing and control of the highly dispersed rural population on the *colline*. In sum, the dominant process in rural settlement structure up through the early 1980s, was one favoring extreme dispersion of house- holds on the landscape.

Urban growth was also minimal before 1980; under the colonial regime, urban commercial and administrative functions had been con- centrated in Bujumbura south on Lake Tanganyika and within Ruanda, at places such as Chyangugu at the southern end of Lake Kivu. Kigali, throughout that period, was only a small, isolated regional administra- tive center (Sirven 1981). But, at the time of independence, and with the end of the first major ethnic conflict in 1959-1962, Ruanda-Urundi became two separate countries. Burundi came under control of the Tutsi and Rwanda, the Hutu. In addition, the early ethnic wars forced significant numbers of the former Tutsi elite and some Hutu to flee to surrounding countries, e.g., Zaire, Uganda, Tanzania, and Burundi. Collectively these groups have been called the *Banyarwanda* (see report by the U.S. Committee for Refugees 1991).

Post-1980 Population Growth

Around 1980, when there was limited scope for additional rural-rural migration, the urban phase of settlement and population change began in earnest. Until 1973, the country's major urban center--Kigali--had grown at a significant rate (Nwafor 1981) but the impact was muted by the fact that it had started with a very small population base. Thus, it took time for symptoms of "hyperurbanization" to become visible in Rwanda. Other African cities, such as Dar es Salaam or Kinshasa, were already experiencing severe pressures (Nwafor 1981; Sirven 1981).

Government settlement and development policies up to the mid-1980s tended to reinforce each other. In the countryside, the Habyarimana regime attempted to limit and control urban growth by means of rudimentary urban planning and a very centralized authoritarian state structure that utilized such techniques as an internal passport/I.D. card system (Sirven 1981). There were also attempts to decentralize government services, in part by encouraging urbanization in certain growing regional centers or *Bourgs*, e.g., Ruhengeri, Gisenyi, and Butare. For instance, the national university was split into two campuses, one at Nyakinama (near Ruhengeri) and the other near Butare. This plan was partly the result of regional political rivalries--a desire to benefit the President's clan and home region--and partly a reflection of decentralization policies. Most new rural infrastructural improvements were located around *commune* offices which were frequently based in nascent pre-urban *bourgs*. The *commune* with its *bourgmeister* (mayor) was the basic political and administrative unit of the one-party Hutu state structure known as the MRND (Mouvement Revolutionaire Nationale pour le Développement). On the positive side, this centralized state structure--using *umuganda* community labor--was able to achieve quite impressive results in reforestation, health service delivery, agricultural extension, and immunization coverage during the early 1980s.

In hindsight, it is clear that this efficient state apparatus was also used to control and monitor political opposition right down to the household level. It later even became the structural means by which extremist paramilitary gangs--the *Interahamwe*--were able to so swiftly control the population, focus its organized hate campaign, and carry out the "final solution" in mid-1994 which nearly succeeded in the eliminating the Tutsi ethnic group as well as opposition Hutu. As Olson (1995) and others point out, the rise of these gangs and the manipulation of ethnic hate by extremist within the elite, had a direct bearing on the increase, in the late 1980s, of a "land scarcity" problem in Rwanda. This situation, in turn, created thousands of jobless youth--from whose ranks many of the *Interhamwe* were drawn (Percival and Homer-Dixon 1995).

As might have been expected, this "top-down" approach to governance did not continue to receive public favor in the late 1980s when the economy stagnated and when democratization fever swept across Africa. The resulting political impasse and "deligitimization of the regime" led to a severe economic and political crisis (Olson 1995; Grosse 1994a,b; Ford 1995; Percival and Homer-Dixon 1995). Those Hutu disaffected groups who were not included in the inner circle of the MRND--primarily moderate Hutu from the southern region, as well as Tutsi in and outside of Rwanda--used the opportunity to actively seek reform. The RPF actually carried their demands to the battlefield in the guerrilla invasion of 1990, which eventually led to the drafting of the Arusha Accords. In hindsight, it is clear that the pressures built up were too much for a fragile society to bear and the result was the tragedy of April 1994 (Olson 1995).

Other developments during the early 1980s should be noted. Tourism had became the major source of foreign exchange. To service this new economic sector, the government focused on improving its road network and the national airport so as to better access hotels and national parks from the capital city. These tourist-oriented developments were a significant boost to the economy by the mid-1980s--particularly after the notoriety garnered from the film *Gorillas in the Mist.* Many formerly isolated bourgs expanded--those at major road junctions and particularly those servicing tourism, export agriculture, or development project activities (Figure 8.3).

Towns in the northwestern region of Rwanda benefited more than the southern region. This perceived "regional tilt" in political favor added to the discontent which erupted in the late 1980s. Ruhengeri, for instance, benefited from its location along a newly paved road that led to the lakeside resorts in Gisenyi. It became the prime jumping-off place for visitors to the gorilla habitat in Volcanoes National Park. Ruhengeri also became a service center for various commercial and research facilities, such as the CIAT bean-research center, as well as for the new campus of the National University in the nearby *Bourg* of Nyakinama (Figure 8.6b).

Predictably, many formerly dispersed rural peoples moved closer to the major roads and growing service centers in order to better access the power and wealth trickling-down through the expanding urban hierar-chy. One of the results, was the creation of a new settlement type--*ribbon or strip-settlements* (Figure 8.6b).[3]   This restructuring of the rural and urban landscape and economy in Rwanda followed patterns seen else-where by Chambers (1983) and others. The smaller centers also attracted significant informal-sector economic growth, though most new job cre-ation occurred in the larger towns or around government development projects. Many households, caught-up in this economic and settlement restructuring, continued to live in nearby dense rural areas while com-muting to the growing service centers. As a result, rural density around towns such as Butare, Ruhengeri, Gisenyi, and Kigali, and along new paved roads, increased to well over 1500 persons/km[2].

All this was evidence of a major agglomeration trend in Rwanda's settlement system. Ultimately, of course, Kigali itself became the prime focus of the migration and growth which resulted in nascent symptoms of hyper-urbanization.   Clay (1993) and Clay and Reardon (1994) describe the 1980s growth in the informal sector and its impact on the economy.   Olson (1990) summarizes the late 1980s migration and settle-ment restructuring in this manner:

> The composition of the urban in-migrant stream has undergone a change due to decline of agricultural options. Although earlier urban in-migrants had relatively high levels of schooling, the educational level has declined as young men with little or no education, those who previously sought land in rural areas, now migrate to the city. The rural-urban movement is composed pri-marily of single young men, not young families as was the case with the rural-rural movements. Their permanency in the city is not known. An implication of this change in the composition of migrants is that increasing numbers of households in the rural areas are headed by women and these households will be among the poorest, with the smallest landholdings and particular vul-nerability to food security problems (Olson, 1990).

There was some disagreement among authorities as to the implica-tions of these settlement trends. Sirven (1984), for instance, had stated that because Rwanda had been so long "under-urbanized" it's high poten-tial for urban growth could be a "safety valve" to absorb excess popula-tion for some time. Sirven's thesis became the underlying assumption of many policy-makers and planners. Other authorities predicted a collapse of some kind in Rwanda as early as the 1930s (Scaetta 1932; Harroy 1949; Tondeur 1949).   Though the collapse, when it did come in 1994, did not occur as predicted, or for the reasons most assumed would be paramount.

Looking back at the two decades of the Habyarimana regime (1973-1994), it would seem that, at least for the rural areas, decentralization of services has been a useful policy (from the perspective of a centralized state) as long as the economic pie was expanding and political dissent could be curtailed. It allowed most rural households to remain highly dispersed and yet be located within close walking distance of clinics, communal administrative offices, credit bureaus, schools, and commercial services. This dispersal of services, of course, was only possible because of the high population density; otherwise it would have not been economically feasible in most cases. On the other hand, the tiered structure of the political system down to the sub-communal level (to groups of 100 households), allowed the regime to exert exorbitant control over nascent opposition groups and thus restricted the growth of a true civil society. In essence, Rwanda had gone from two forms of authoritarian, non-democratic government--Tutsi feudalism and then Belgian colonial "divide and conquer" rule--to a post-independence, Hutu-dominated, one-party state.

By the late 1980s, and particularly after the 1990 RPF (Rwandese Patriotic Front) invasion, a severe economic and political crisis was erupting. Several specific events and conditions contributed to the impasse including a downturn in the pyrethrum and coffee markets and the effects of a major drought. In hindsight, it seems that the 1989-1990 drought and famine in southern Rwanda was probably the most significant "triggering" event that led to the deligitimization of the Habyarimana regime. Curiously, only a few months prior to this, the regime had officially stopped PL-480 food aid programs, ostensibly because of success in moving toward "food self-sufficiency." These problems contributed to the rising discontent which resulted in the invasion of November 1990 by the RPF and the subsequent events which created a "failed state" situation. The final outcome of the 1994 genocide, as of 1997, is yet unclear. But certainly we are entering another major phase in settlement change as well as development policy implementation. What the final result will be depends much on whether peace and reconciliation occurs between the many alienated groups within Rwanda's civil society.

Theories of Mountain Development and Rwanda

Overview

A spirited debate in *Mountain Research and Development* has explored what might be called the "Troll-Allan controversy" (Ives 1986). In essence, the debate revolved around the relative merits of geoecological, accessibility, and other socio-economic or altitudinal zonation models in the explanation and analysis of human-environment relations in mountain regions (Troll 1968; Troll and Lauer 1978; Allan 1986; Uhlig 1986; Soffer 1986; Greenland 1986; Guillet 1986). Each of these terms reflects diverse philosophical and disciplinary traditions in the analysis of mountain social and ecological systems. The debate is not inconsequential though, because understanding the multi-factoral relationships in mountains is crucial to informed and effective management of induced development activities in these regions.

Until very recently, much of the literature on mountain development has focused on the "the Himalaya-Ganges problem" (Ives and Ives 1987) and the Andes (Johnson 1983; Guillet 1986; Troll 1968) or the Swiss Alps (Messerli and Ives 1984) to cite a few examples. Mountains in Africa have not received equal attention in the literature though some recent work is beginning to fill the void (Bart 1993; English, Tiffen, and Mortimore 1994). Unfortunately, explanatory models of mountain development based on the experience garnered in the more popular mountain regions, e.g., the Alps, Andes, or Himalaya, cannot provide a sufficiently broad framework from which to test theory. Therefore, it is imperative that current models be tested in lesser known mountain regions such as the montane ecosystems of Rwanda.

From a theoretical perspective, a key question arises when one tries to explain and understand land-use patterns in mountain regions. To what degree do these patterns reflect "adaptation" to relatively unchanging environmental and altitudinal forces? Or, do they reflect a more dynamic interaction with such changeable human-induced forces as time-distance, economic, cultural, and historical forces--in other words, "accessibility"? Chambers (1983), among many has shown how cases of "spatial bias" related to differential "accessibility" to wealth and power can occur in the economic development process. This leads to regional inequities in economic development (a situation that did occur in Rwanda).

The *accessibility model* of mountain development proposed by Allan (1986) and particularly by Guillet (1986) is one attempt to better integrate human and environmental/ecological processes in one model.

Accordingly, increased access to markets and political power centers facilitates the construction of modern transportation networks which alters long-standing patterns of land-use in mountains. Allan and Guillet suggest that established subsistence and economic patterns that were seen by some cultural ecologists as a sort of "climax cultural adaptation" may in fact reflect temporary time and distance-bounded economic and sociopolitical relationships (Figure 8.2b).

Soffer (1986), reflecting a more traditional cultural-ecological perspective, has described mountain development in terms of socio-economic vertical belts (Figure 8.2a). He attributes most of what is observed in mountains to the assumed paramount influence of altitude and physical environment or verticality. Soffer's perspective has been criticized by Allan and Guillet and others as a holdover from the widely debunked environmental determinism of an earlier era in geography. The question this section of the chapter will explore is the following: does the case of Rwanda shed any light on the relative merits of the above models of mountain development? Both approaches, in fact, are relevant as can be better understood by applying the two approaches to the specific case of Rwanda.

Accessibility Zones in Rwanda

Rwanda exhibits three "accessibility" zones on the landscape (Figure 8.2b). The first is a central Urban Core/Corridor zone, where modern industrial and other monetarized economic activities are developing within easy access to external (international) sources of power, technology, and finance. This zone has expressed itself on the landscape in new point and linear patterns of activity, e.g., the new service centers--*Bourgs*, tea plantations, the *paysannat* settlements, lake-side resorts, and the ribbon/strip settlements described earlier. This pattern of settlement structure appears to have been influenced heavily by planned colonial and post-independence development policy as well as unplanned ecological, demographic, and social driving forces. The net effect has been to favor a trend toward agglomeration.

The second zone, the Traditional Periphery, predominates where the rural, highly dispersed subsistence-system on the *colline* continues to function. This zone began to fall behind economically quite early in the modern era due to unequal access to the power and wealth emanating from the core. Much of this has occurred because of well-known problems associated with trickle-down economic development theory and practice. This marginalized zone in Rwanda continues to use dispersion as a means of copomg with spatial, cultural, and ecological forces.

The third Natural Preserve zone is spatially removed, but increasingly accessible because of its links to the core via a corridor of modern roads and airplane routes created to accommodate tourists. Curiously, this region's natural resources were previously perceived as uneconomic and inaccessible, e.g., mountain wilderness and wetlands containing exotic plant and animal resources. In Rwanda, this zone became the focus of government development initiatives during the 1970-1980s, e.g., dairies, tree farms, pyrethrum, wheat and potato cooperatives. Even traditional peasant agriculture and pastoralism was heavily controlled or pressured to modernize. Some suggest that the application of a new law to ban freely wandering cattle herds, which disproportionately affected Tutsi herders, had a hidden ethnic objective as well as a development policy goal.

Vertical Zonation in Rwanda

Soffer's perspective on mountain development can also be seen in Rwanda. Four distinct vertical zones or belts are apparent on the landscape (Figure 8.2a). The lowest wetlands belt (below 1400 meters) was largely empty in pre-colonial times due to its high incidence of disease and uncomfortable climate. Until recently, this zone of savannas, lakes, drowned river-valleys, and papyrus swamps of the eastern and southern border areas was used only seasonally and by relatively few people. The second hills and plateau belt (1,400-2,000 meters) was the permanent preferred site for early settlement by both the pre-colonial pastoralists and farmers, and during colonial times it became the preferred site for the new urban core. The third middle mountains belt (2,000-2,500 meters) was also under-utilized during pre-colonial times. Some seasonal upslope movement by traditional farmers and herdsmen did occur, in some respects similar to the *Alpwirtschaft* system cited by geographers (Rhoades and Thompson 1975).

It was really the advent of a monetarized agriculture, based on pyrethrum and other highland products, that gave the middle mountain belt its modern economic value. Unfortunately, these more intensive forms of agriculture came into direct conflict with traditional Tutsi pastoralism. The competition was definitely unequal, and the latter lost out- -at least during the Habyarimana years (Bart 1993; Rossi 1991). One of the most dramatic changes in Rwandan agriculture prior to 1994 was the increase in small ruminants and decrease in cattle; zero-grazing was a prime objective of the Hutu-dominated Habyarimana regime.

The fourth high mountain belt (above 2,500 meters) was the domain of uneconomic natural Afromontane and Afroalpine forests, moorlands, and permanent or occasional snow and ice. Not until colonial days-- when much of this zone was integrated into natural reserves and parks--

did it become recognized as a prime asset (Figure 8.3). In the mid-1980s, when tourism, primarily in the Volcanoes National Park, became the country's main source of foreign currency, the perceived value of parks changed dramatically.

The Models Compared

In each of the "vertical" or "accessibility" zones not only have economic relations changed but so has the settlement structure. Overall, the trend has been toward increased clustering in response to the deteriorating security situation. By mid-1995, clustering became extreme in the border regions because of fear of guerrilla incursions by former Hutu militias. Also important was the breakdown of economic and social infrastructural outside of major centers served by the UN and other groups, e.g., Kigali. And of course, the concentration of thousands of refugees in camps created some of the world's most agglomerated, non-urban settlements in Zaire, Burundi, and Rwanda (around Kigali). Within Rwanda, it is not yet clear whether the new Tutsi-dominated regime will foster dispersion or agglomeration in its policy. The country is essentially penniless and much of its population continues to depend on outside donor assistance. No doubt, Rwanda's new situation will initiate another phase change in population/landscape ecology relations that will further alter settlement structure.

In summary, both models recognize that the impact of the modern, monetized urban economy--often driven by "accessibility" factors related to external market demands--changed the perceived value of resources in the formerly isolated low wetlands and high mountain forest zones. The lowland increased in value because of their potential for irrigated rice, hydro-electric power generation (the Kagera Dam Project), aquacultural, and as wildlife reserves for tourists. At the same time, population growth pushed many traditional farmers into the lowlands where they could supplement a declining land resource base. Perception and use of the high mountain zones changed in similar ways. Even the second altitudinal zone--the hills and plateau belt--changed because of accessibility. Those areas, without strong links to the new superimposed Urban Core, sunk into marginalization within the Traditional Periphery while the better linked locations prospered from new development initiatives.

It is clear that human forces that relate to accessibility, such as politics and technology, have become dominant. Yet, this does not mean that the older "vertical-ecological" factors have no importance. Disease patterns, agricultural and resource management limitations, settlement and housing styles, and other phenomena still reflect underlying altitudinal/ecological relationships. I am convinced therefore, that explanation of the

observed differences is   strengthened by
using both perspectives. An eclectic approach helps achieve a more "con-
textualized" view of human-environment relations in Rwanda (see also
Campbell and Olson 1991; Zimmerer 1994; Blaikie et al. 1994; Bohle et al.
1994; Ford 1995).

Boundary Zone Interactions

From a development policy and theoretical perspective, boundary-
zone interactions are also of great interest. For instance, interaction
between the second and third accessibility zone--the Traditional
Periphery with the Natural Preserves--has come to be increasingly characterized by confrontation in the post-colonial era. Examples of this phenomenon include the rising rate of wildlife poaching, unauthorized tree-
cutting, and pastoralist incursions into formerly protected reserves, e.g.,
the Gishwati Forest and Akagera National Park. In early 1995, hundreds
of thousands of cattle brought in by former refugee Tutsi herders from
Tanzania and Uganda began wandering over the once off-limits savannas
of the Akagera region. Attempts to control these incursions were essentially meaningless given the political and economic collapse of the country.

Even before the 1994 civil war, there had been an increase in strident
political pressure by peasant representatives to open more preserved
lands for pioneering. The government (with assistance from the World
Bank) did open up a large portion of the Gishwati Reserve for modern
dairy production while other lands were opened for pyrethrum, tea, and
coffee production. In hindsight, land scarcity and its role in the radical-
ization of a bitter, unstable group of landless youth--many of whom
became easy prey to join extremist Hutu factions--was a major factor in
the genocide of 1994. There were also political pressures to drain certain
wetlands for agriculture, e.g., the high altitude Rugezi swamp which is a
critical nesting habitat of the crested crane. The way in which government manages these confrontations in the transitional borderlands
between zones, will largely determine the future of rare natural vegetation and wildlife resources.

Interaction between the traditional periphery and the urban core
zones will also continue to generate conflict; the interchange has seldom
been equal or congenial and will probably get worse. The periphery
wants the benefits accruing from an urban-industrial society but often
decries the political and social disruptions impinging on traditional subsistence systems. It is currently not clear whether the right balance can
be found between achieving sustainable development and perpetuating
a trend toward accelerated degradation and misery.

Optimism or Pessimism for Rwanda

After the 1994 tragedy in Rwanda--and to a lesser degree the equally tragic events in Sudan, Somalia, Liberia, and Bosnia--interest has grown in the purported causal links between population, environment, and security.[4]   In all cases, philosophical opinions and theoretical perspectives fall along a continuum stretching from those taking negative (Malthusian) to more optimistic (Boserupian) perspectives (Ford 1995).

Some have seen in Rwanda, data that supports the classic technology-oriented Boserupian hypothesis of "intensification of agriculture" being triggered by population pressure--the optimistic scenario (Ford, 1993). Sirven (1983) essentially supported this hypothesis by suggesting that urban growth could be a "safety valve" allowing time for the success of Green Revolution, biotechnic agricultural change coupled with family planning implementation. USAID's investments in agriculture and family planning were largely predicated on that hope as were most other donor investments. There has certainly been an improvement in crop production to support this scenario. Some food crops were gradually becoming the new "cash crops" as had been envisioned by Horowitz and Little (1987). In fact, many former *paysannats* that had once produced coffee or pyrethrum had been able to refocus on food crops for an expanding urban market. There is also evidence that, prior to 1994, Rwanda's family planning program had finally begun to "take-off." USAID officials who participated at a special session at the African Studies Association meetings in 1995, touted Rwanda as one of its best examples of success in Africa (see also Ford 1995).[5]

In a related vein, some within the NGO (non-governmental organization) community felt that it was possible to make development more "user-friendly" by trying to understand the traditional coping mechanisms and risk-averse subsistence strategies utilized by Rwanda's herders and farmers. The goal was to build from the "bottom-up" toward a more sustainable and participatory approach to development and resource management. Included in this agenda were those who emphasized democratization, public sector reform, promotion of private sector growth, as well as the need to improve health care, literacy, and access to capital, particularly for women.

Others have seen a negative scenario at work in Rwanda in spite of well-intentioned development efforts (Geertz 1963). According to this perspective, excessive population growth leads to "agricultural involution", followed by environmental scarcity, and finally, ecological collapse. In this situation, agricultural productivity is cancelled by population growth, thus negating the resource generation and other changes that are assumed necessary for sustainable development (Martin 1987). Actually, it became quite common for authorities, in and out of government, to attribute numerous current and past problems to a massive population-resource imbalance (Munyenbaraga 1985; ONAPO 1982; Rossi 1991; Bart 1993). The problems most often alluded to were the following: stagnating economic growth, ethnic strife, hyper-urbanization, deforestation, poaching, and reduction of available arable land per household unit.

The recurring theme of adaptation and disequalibrium has long been a favorite topic of cultural ecologists looking at mountain regions around the world--not just at Ruanda. The above-mentioned perspectives were central themes in early twentieth century environmental determinist literature and in the more recent "geoecological" approaches focused specifically on mountain regions (Guillet 1986: 207-8; Rhoades and Thompson 1975; Hewitt 1983). For an excellent discussion of earlier conceptions of mountain ecosystems see Messerli and Ives (1984).

Certainly the land scarcity problem in Ruanda has remained a critical issue. In 1990 and 1995, Olson conveyed the gravity of the situation in Rwanda by pointing out that National densities have gone from around seventy-seven persons/km^2 in 1948, to 188 in 1978, and to an estimated 355 in 1991 (Ford 1992). The average size of farms has diminished dramatically: from 2.7 hectares in 1965 (Nwafor, 1981) to 1.2 hectares in 1984 (MINAGREF/SESA 1986). Projections were that by the year 2000, farms would be 0.6 hectares or less (Futures Group 1990; Olson 1990; Grosse, 1994a,b). In very few other countries in Africa were such seemingly alarming population and settlement trends occurring at such a rapid rate, with such visible impact on the landscape and environment, and in spite of ongoing intensification (Figure 8.5).

What does the Rwandan case teach us about human-environment theory in densely populated tropical montane regions? It is my assessment that both the traditional cultural ecological and newer "geoecological" perspectives, espoused by Troll (1968) and Troll and Lauer (1978) do provide important insights on the (internal) micro-system level. But the modern problems of mountain development in Rwanda are so dynamic and multifaceted, we need better tools of analysis. Specifically, we can no longer ignore the fact that (external) macro-system factors have assumed great significance for the average peasant whose life depends on these supposedly isolated humid tropical montane ecosystems. Therefore, an eclectic approach--one that is more "political ecological"--may be the more productive (Blaikie and Brookefield 1987; Bryant 1992; Campbell and Olson 1991; Zimmerer 1994).

This has become even more the case following the genocide of 1994. The question that now haunts analysts is this: to what degree was the genocide caused by ecological/demographic forces, or political/ social ones, or both? Percival and Homer-Dixon (1995) conclude that though there was an element of environmental scarcity involved in the crisis, that explanation alone was insufficient considering the magnitude of the conflict and its outcome. They also state that political factors were equally important: elite insecurity; a failed transition from authoritarian rule; the manipulation of ethnic identity for political ends; increased mass grievances linked to both political problems, economic crises, and a society-wide stagnation; an external post-Cold War geopolitical vacuum, and a lack of international political will to counter internal ethnic conflicts after the failed Somalia intervention by the United Nations.

Overall Conclusions

By no means is the final outcome for Ruanda clear; the deaths of hundreds of thousands of Tutsi in 1994 was certainly significant enough to alter the demographic profile of the country. Furthermore, the thousands of Hutu who for two years resided in extremely agglomerated refugee camps have to be reabsorbed into Ruandan society. The impact of these new human forces on the settlement structure in the post-1994 period will depend on whether there is peace or not and who the "winners" and "losers" are.

Most settlement and population processes begun earlier in Rwanda can still be observed there. Land use and crop intensification will probably continue out of necessity, though much of the progress occurring up to April 1994 has been put temporarily on hold. There is even some minor extensification going on, particularly by the reintroduction of cattle by former refugee Tutsi pastoralists into the wilderness preserves. But that trend does not make long-term economic or ecologic sense. Even the new Tutsi dominated government recognizes that tourism to parks and preserves is a major source of foreign currency for the country. Yet, it is still an open question whether the political will and capability exists to protect these ecologic assets from encroachment and degradation. The solution to this latest "confrontational process" in land management will give strong indications of the future of Rwanda.

With regard to settlement structure, clustering has become the more dominant process in Rwanda today, especially in light of the "unresolved" refugee and security crisis in Rwanda and in the surrounding countries. How far this process will go in breaking down Rwanda's historically dispersed rural settlement pattern is unclear. It is possible--if peace can be established--that the old cultural preferences for dispersion will reassert themselves but that hopeful future is yet in doubt.

What is so remarkable, particularly as one compares the rural situation is Rwanda with the Yatengan case in Burkina Faso (Ford 1992) is how modern economic and political reality in Rwanda has forced settlement structure in seemingly opposite directions from that affecting Burkina Faso. (See Chapter 7). In the latter case, settlement change appears to be dominated by a stronger trend to dispersion while in Rwanda agglomeration is becoming more important. Is this a case of "convergence", an attempt by these African societies to attain a new equilibrium located between purely dispersed or completely agglomerated? If that is the case, what would be the right balance? And what about trends in urbanization? Both Rwanda and Burkina Faso are facing problems associated with hyper-urbanization, a situation common to many African states. Obviously there are many unanswered questions, yet Rwanda will continue to offer opportunities to test ideas and research methods as well as evaluate policy interventions in an arena that calls out for solutions to grave human dilemmas.

Notes

1. See also: Scaetta 1932; Harroy 1949; Tondeur 1948; Gourou 1952; Neesen 1956; Boserup 1965; Prioul 1981; Pagni 1982; Martin 1987; Harrison 1987; Lewis and Berry 1988; Lele and Stone 1989; Ford 1990, 1993, 1995; King 1993; Cleaver and Schreiber 1993; Clay 1993; Clay and Reardon 1994; Honadle, Grosse, and Phumpiu 1994; Grosse 1994.

2. For more background on the dynamics of human-environment interaction in the most densely settled mountain regions of Rwanda see: Gourou 1952; Trewartha and Zelinsky 1954; LeMarchand 1970; Canbrezy 1984; Sirven 1984; *Colloque de Bujumbura* 1988; Lewis and Berry 1988; Byers, E. A. 1991; Byers, A. C. and B. Hastings 1991; Byers, A. C. 1988 a,b,c; Byers and Nyamulinda 1988; Olson 1990, 1992; Bart 1993; Ford 1990, 1993. An excellent study of a similar high population density mountain environment was done in Machakos District Kenya by English, Tiffen, and Mortimore (1994).

3. An excellent description of the spatial dynamics of the urban growth of Kigali through 1980 is presented by Sirven (1981). For a more detailed discussion of the housing style changes affecting settlement see Ford (1990) and Bart and Bart (1989).

4. See the various reports by the AAAS Program on Science and International Secturity. The work by Percival and Homer-Dixon (1995) is one example. Others include case studies of South Africa, Chiapas in Mexico, and Pakistan. A special 1994 issue of *Human Ecology Review* (Vol 1, 2) included many articles debating various perspectives on population-environment relationships that ranged from Malthusian to Cornucopian. Also of interest is the 1995 special issue of *Geojournal* (Vol. 35, 2) which does much the same but with more of a focus on Africa. See also the so-called "NEXUS Studies" by the World Bank in the early 1990s and work by USAID's EPAT Project (Honadle, Grosse, and Phumphiu 1994) among several relevant sources.

5. For a more in-deapth analysis of agricultural change in Ruanda see Delepierre and Prefol 1974; Zaag 1980; LeMarchand 1982; Reintsma 1982; Durr 1983; Gotanegre 1983; Vis 1984; Charlery et al. 1986, Charlery 1989; Moeyersons 1989; Chapuis 1986; Balasubramanian and Egli 1986; Rossi 1991; Lewis 1992; Bart 1993; Ford 1990, 1993, 1995; Clay and Lewis 1990; Honadle, Grosse, and Phumpiu 1994; Grosse 1994 a,b.

References

Allan, Nigel J. R. 1986. "Accessibility and Altitudinal Zonation Models of Mountains." *Mountain Research and Development* 6, 3: 185-194.

Allan, Nigel and Gregory. W. Knapp. 1988. *Human Impact on Mountains.* Totowa, NJ: Rowman & Littlefield.

Bart, Annie and François Bart. 1989. "Niveau de Vie et Habitat Rural: le Cas des Terres de Lave du Rwanda." In *Pauvreté et Développement: dans les Pays Tropicaux.* Pp. 155-174. Hommage a Guy Lasserre. Sous las Direction de Singaravelou. Talence, France: Université de Bordeaux III. CEGET-CNRS.

Bart, François. 1993. *Montagnes d'Afrique, Terres Paysannes. Le Cas du Rwanda.* Bordeaux: Presses Universitaires de Bordeaux.

Blaikie, P. and Harold Brookfield. 1987. *Land Degradation and Society.* London: Methuen.

Blaikie, P., Terry Cannon, Ian Davis, and Ben Wisner. 1994. *At Risk: Natural Hazards, People's Vulnerability and Disasters.* London and New York: Routledge.

Bohle, Hans G., Thomas E. Downing, and Michael J. Watts. 1994. "Climate Change and Social Vulnerability: Toward a Sociology and Geography of Food Insecurity." *Global Environmental Change* 4, 1: 37-48.

Boserup, Ester, 1965. *The Conditions of Agricultural Growth: The Economics of Agrarian Change under Population Pressure.* Chicago: Aldine.

Bryant, Raymond L. 1992. "Political Ecology: An Emerging Research Agenda in Third-World Studies." *Political Geography* 11: 12-36.

Burton, R. F. 1862. *Voyages aux Grands Lacs de l'Afrique Orientale.* Paris: Hachette.

Byers, E. A. and B. A. Hastings. 1991. "Heterogeneity of Hydrologic Response in Four Mountainous Watersheds in Northwestern Rwanda." *Mountain Research and Development* 11, 4: 319-328.

Byers, A. C. 1988a. "Catastrophic Rainfall, Landslides and Flooding in Nyakinama and Nyamutera Communes, Ruhengeri Prefecture." *RRAM Technical Report #2.* Kigali, Rwanda: USAID.

____. 1988b. "A Comparative Analysis of Soil Loss in Three Ecological Zones of Ruhengeri Prefecture, Rwanda, 1987-1988." *RRAM Technical Report #3.* Kigali, Rwanda: USAID.

____. 1988c. "Geomorphological Effects of Catastrophic Rainfall in the Parc National des Volcans, Ruhengeri Prefecture, Rwanda." *RRAM Technical Report #4.* Kigali, Rwanda: USAID.

____. 1991. "Mountain Gorilla Mortality and Climatic Factors in the Parc-National-des-Volcans, Ruhengeri Prefecture, Rwanda, 1988." *Mountain Research and Development* 11, 2:   145-151.

Byers, A. C. and V. Nyamulinda. 1988. "Soil Loss in Nyarutovu." *RRAM Technical Report #1.* Kigali, Rwanda: USAID.

Campbell, David and Olson, Jennifer. 1991. *Framework for Environment and Development: the Kite.* CASID Occasional Paper No. 10. Michigan State University, East Lansing, Michigan: Center for Advanced Study of International Development.

Cambrezy, L. 1984. "Le Surpeuplement en Question: Organisation Spatiale et Écologie des Migrations au Rwanda." *Travaux et Documents de l'ORSTOM.* No. 182.

Chambers, R. 1983. *Rural Development: Putting the Last First.* London: Longman.

Chapuis, O. 1986. "La Théiculture Rwandaise." *Cahiers d'Outre-Mer* 154: 117-142.

Charlery, Barlery de Masseliere, Francois Bart, O. Barbary. 1986. "La Répartition Régionale des Cultures Vivrières au Rwanda." *Cahiers ORSTOM, Sciences Humaines* 3/4: 453-477.

Charlery, Barlery de Masseliere. 1989. "Systèmes de Culture et Surfaces de Densités dans le Nord-ouest du Rwanda." *Géographie et Aménagement dans l'Afrique des Grands Lacs.* Pp. 92-116. (Colloque du Bujumbura, 25-29 Janvier, 1988). Bordeaux: CRET, Institut de Géographie, Université de Bordeaux III.

____. 1993. "Du Versant-Terroir aux Territoires Fragmentés. Organization, Dynamique, et Crise de l'Espace Agraire au Rwanda." *Cahiers Sciences Humaines* 29: 661-694.

Clay, D. C. 1993. "Fighting an Uphill Battle: Demographic Pressure, the Structure of Landholding, and Land Degradation in Rwanda." Michigan State University, Department of Agricultural Economics. Mimeo.

Clay, D. C. and L. A. Lewis. 1990. "Land Use, Soil Loss and Sustainable Agriculture in Rwanda." *Human Ecology* 18: 147-161.

Clay, D. C. and T. Reardon. 1994. "Determinants of Farm-level Conservation Investments in Rwanda." Contributed Paper. Michigan State University, Dept. of Agricultural Economics.

Cleaver, K. M. and G. A. Schreiber. 1993. *The Population, Agriculture and Environment Nexus in Sub-Saharan Africa.* Agriculture and Rural Development Series, No. 9. Washington, D.C.:   World Bank, Africa Region, Technical Department.

Colloque de Bujumbura. 1988. "Pays Enclaves." *Géographie et Aménagement dans L'Afrique des Grands Lacs.* Collection No. 3. Talence, France: CRET (Centre de Recherches sur les Espaces Tropicaux), Université de Bordeaux III.

Delepierre, G. and B. Prefol. 1973. *Disponibilité et Utilisation des Terres au Rwanda, Situation Actuelle et Perspective.* Rubona, Rwanda: Instituts des Sciences Agronomiques du Rwanda.

____. 1974. "Les 12 Régions Agricoles du Rwanda." *ISAR, Note Technique* No. 13.

Dumont, R. 1960. "Décolonisation et Développement Agricole au Centre-est de l'Afrique, (Kigali), le Ruanda-Urundi." *Tiers-Monde* 1, 4: 421-445.

Durr, G. 1983. "Potato Production and Utilization in Rwanda." Working Paper No. 1, Social Science Dept. International Potato Center.

English, J., M. Tiffen, and M. Mortimore. 1994. "Land Resource Management in Machakos District, Kenya 1930-1990." *World Bank Environment Paper No. 5.* Washington, D.C.: World Bank.

Falloux, F. and L. M. Talbot. 1993. *Crisis and Opportunity: Environment and Development in Africa.* London: Earthscan.

Ford, Robert E. 1990. "The Dynamics of Human-Environment Interactions in the Tropical Montane Ecosystems of Rwanda: Implications for Economic Development and Ecological Stability." *Mountain Research and Development* 10: 43-63.

_____. 1992. "Human Environment Interaction in Sahelian North Yatenga." *Research and Exploration.* National Geographic Society 8: 460-475.

_____. 1993. "Marginal Coping under Extreme Land Pressures: the Case of Ruhengeri." In B. L. Turner II, Robert Kates, and Goran Hyden, eds. *Population Growth and Agricultural Change in Africa.* Pp. 145-186. Gainesville, FL: University of Florida Press.

_____. 1995. "The Population-Environment Nexus and Vulnerability Assessment in Africa." *GeoJournal* 35: 207-216.

Fossey, D. 1983. *Gorillas in the Mist.* Boston: Houghton-Mifflin.

Futures Group. 1990. *Population et Environnement au Rwanda.* Washington, D.C.: The Futures Group.

Geertz, Clifford. 1963. *Agricultural Involution: The Processes of Ecological Change in Indonesia.* Berkeley: University of California Press.

GeoJournal. 1995. "Questioning Development: Growth, Destruction, Sustainability?" (Special Issue) 35, 2.

Gotanegre, J. F. 1983. "La Banane au Rwanda." *Cahiers d'Outre-Mer* 36, 144: 311-342.

Gourou, P. 1952. *La Densité de la Population du Ruanda-Urundi.* Brussels: Institut Royal Colonial Belge.

Greenland, David. 1986. "Comments on: Accessibility and Altitudinal Models of Mountains, by Nigel J. R. Allan." *Mountain Research and Development* 6, 3: 195-197.

Grosse, Scott. 1994a. "More People, More Trouble: Population Growth and Agricultural Change in Rwanda." Draft Report Prepared for EPAT/USAID. Department of Population Planning and International Health, University of Michigan, School of Public Health.

_____. 1994b. "The Roots of Conflict and State Failure in Rwanda: The Political Exacerbation of Social Cleavages in a Context of Growing Resource Scarcity." Draft Report Prepared for EPAT/USAID. Department of Population Planning and International Health, University of Michigan, School of Public Health.

Guillet, David. 1986. "Towards a Cultural Ecology of Mountains: the Central Andes and the Himalaya Compared." *Mountain Research and Development* 6: 206-214.

Harrison, Paul. 1987. *The Greening of Africa.* London: Paladin Grafton Books.

Harroy, J. P. 1949. *Afrique, Terre qui Meurt.* Brussels. Publisher Unknown.

Heremans, R., Annie Bart, and Francois Bart. 1982. "Agriculture et Paysages Rwandais à Travers   des Sources Missionnaires (1900-1950)." *Cultures et Développement* 14, 1: 3-39.

Hewitt, K. 1983. "Human Geography and Mountain Environments." *Canadian Geographer* 27:   96-102.

Honadle, G., Scott Grosse, and P. Phumpiu. 1994. "The Problems of Linear Project Thinking in a Non-Linear World: Experience from the Nexus of Population, Environmental and Agricultural Dynamics in Africa." Draft Report. EPAT Policy Paper Series.

Horowitz, M. M. and P. D. Little. 1987. "Subsistence Crops are Cash-Crops: Some Comments with Reference to Eastern Africa." *Human Organization* 46: 254-258.

Ives, Jack D. 1986. "Editorial." *Mountain Research and Development* 6, 3: 183-184.

Ives, Jack D. and Pauline Ives, eds. 1987. "The Himalaya-Ganges Problem: Proceedings of a Conference." Mohonk Mountain House, New Platz, NY. April 6-11, 1986. *Mountain Research and Development* 7, 3: 181-344.

Johnson, Dennis V. 1983. "Agriculture on Slopelands of Tropical America: Problems and Prospects." *Culture and Agriculture*. Newsletter of the Anthropological Study Group on Agrarian Systems 18: 1-8.

King, Maurice. 1993. "Demographic Entrapment." *Transactions of the Royal Society of Tropical Medicine and Hygiene* 87, Supplement 1: 23-28.

Lele, Uma and S. W. Stone. 1989. *Population Pressure, the Environment and Agricultural Intensification: Variations on the Boserup Hypothesis.* MADIA Discussion Paper No. 4. Washington, D.C.: World Bank.

LeMarchand, R. 1970. *Rwanda and Burundi.* London: Pall Mall Press.

____. 1982. "The World Bank in Rwanda." *African Studies Program.* Bloomington: Indiana University.

Lewis, Laurence and Leonard Berry. 1988. *African Environments and Resoures.* London: Unwin/Hyman.

Lewis, Laurence, Daniel Clay, and J. Dejaeher. 1988. "Soil Loss, Agriculture, and Conservation in Rwanda: Toward Sound Strategies for Soil Management." *Journal of Water and Soil Conservation* 43, 5: 418-421.

Lewis, Laurence. 1992. "Terracing and Accelerated Soil Loss on Rwandian Steeplands: A Preliminary Investigation of the Implications of Human Activities Affecting Soil Movement." *Land Degradation and Rehabilitation* 3: 241-246.

Martin, Susan. 1987. "Boserup Revisited: Population and Technology in African Agriculture, 1900-40." *Journal of Imperial and Commonwealth History* 16, 1: 109-123.

Meillassoux, C., B. Schlemper, F. Gendreau, and M. Verlet, eds. 1991. *Déséquilibres Alimentaires, Déséquilibres Démographiques.* Paris: EDI ORSTOM, CEPED.

Messerli, Bruno and Jack D. Ives. 1984. Mountain Ecosystems: Stability and Instability.   Proceedings of a Workshop, Berne-Riederalp, Switzerland, September 14-19, 1982. *International Mountain Society.*

MINAGREF/SESA. 1986. *Resultats de l'Enquête Nationale Agricole. Rapport I, II, et III.* Kigali, Rwanda: République Rwandaise, Ministère de l'Agriculture, de l'Elévage, et des Forêts. MINAGREF/SESA.

_____. 1987. *Description Sommaire des Principales Caracteristiques de l'Agriculture au Rwanda. Report No. 2.* Kigali, Rwanda: République Rwandaise, Ministère de l'Agriculture, de l'Élévage et des Forêts. MINA-GREF/SESA.

_____. 1987. *Plan Forestier National (1987-1997).* Kigali, Rwanda: République Rwandaise, Ministère de l'Agriculture, de l'Élévage et des Forêts. MINA-GREF/SESA

MINIPLAN. 1983. *Stratégie Alimentaire au Rwanda: Objectifs Chiffrès et Programmes d'Actions. Document No. 3.* Kigali, Rwanda: République Rwandaise, Ministère du Plan.

_____. 1985. *Bulletin de Statistique. Supplement Annual No. 12.* Direction Générale de la Statistique. Kigali, Rwanda: République Rwandaise, Ministère du Plan.

_____. 1985. *Troisieme Plan de Développement Socio-Èconomique et Culturel (1982-1986): Èvaluation 1982-1984.* Kigali, Rwanda: République Rwandaise, Ministère du Plan.

_____. 1986. *Enquête Nationale sur le Budget et la Consommation des Ménages: Milieu Rural.* Kigali, Rwanda: République Rwandaise, Ministère du Plan.

_____. 1987. *Troisième Plan de Dévelopment Économique, Social, et Culturel 1982-1986.* Kigali, Rwanda: République Rwandaise, Ministére du Plan.

Moeyersons, J. 1989. *La Nature de l'Érosion des Versants au Rwanda.* Tervuuren, Belgium: Musée de l'Afrique Centrale.

Moorehead, A. 1983. *The White Nile.* London: Penguin Books.

Munyenbaraga, Narcisse. 1985. "Développement Socio-Économique: Problèmes et Perspectives." *Vivant Univers* 357: 10-17.

Neesen, V. 1956. "Aspects de l'Économie Démographique du Ruanda-Urundi." *Bulletin de Recherches Èconomiques et Sociales* 22, 5: 473-504.

Nwafor, J. C. 1981. "Some Aspects of Urban Developement in Tropical Africa: The Growth Toward Urban Status of Kigali, Capital of Rwanda." *African Urban Studies* 9: 39-56.

Nyamulinda, V. 1988. "Èrosion Agricole Accélerée et Techniques Biologiques et Méchaniques de Conservation des Sols Applicables en Prefecture Ruhengeri." *RRAM Technical Report.* Kigali, Rwanda: USAID.

Nyamulinda, V. and V. Ngiruwonsanga. 1992. "Lutte Anti-Érosive et Stratégie Paysanne dans les Montagnes du Rwanda." *Réseau Erosion Bulletin* 12: 71-82.

Olson, Jennifer. 1990. "The Impact of Changing Socioeconomic Factors on Migration Patterns in Rwanda." M.A. Thesis. Lansing, Michigan: Michigan State University.

_____. 1992. "Projet des Enquêtes Agricoles et Analyse des Politiques Économiques du Secteur Rural (ASAP)." Kigali, Rwanda: Rapport du Mission.

_____. 1995. "Behind the Recent Tragedy in Rwanda." *GeoJournal* 35, 2: 217-222.

ONAPO. 1982. "Population et Énvironnement." *Actes du Colloque: Famille, Population et Développement.* Kigali, Rwanda: République Rwandaise, Office National de la Population. Pp. 144-175.

_____. 1983. *Rwanda 1983: Enquête Nationale sur la Fecondité.* Vol. 1. Analyse des Résultats. Kigali, Rwanda: République Rwandaise, Office National de la Population.

Pagni, L. 1982. "L'Ombre de Malthus Face à l'Espoir Réel du Progrè Économique." *Courrier Afrique-Caraïbes-Pacifique* 72: 8-15.

Percival, Valerie and Thomas Homer-Dixon. 1995. *Environmental Scarcity and Violent Conflict: the Case of Rwanda.* Toronto: University of Toronto Press.

Pingali, P. L. and H. P. Biswanger. 1984. *Population Density and Agricultural Intensity.* Report No. 22. Washington, D.C.: World Bank, Agriculture and Rural Developmentstian.

Prioul, Christian. 1981. "Les Densites de Population au Rwanda: Leur Évolution entre 1948-1978." In *Les Milieux Tropicaux d'Altitude: Recherches sur les Hautes Terres d'Afrique Centrale (Rwanda, Burundi, Kivu).* Pp. 61-80. Travaux et Documents de Geographie Tropicale. CEGET, No. 42. Talence, France: Centre d'Ètudes de Géographie Tropical.

_____. 1989. "Bugesera - 1965-1975 (Rwanda)." *In Pauvreté et Développement: dans les Pays Tropicaux.* Hommage a Guy Lasserre. Sous las Direction de Singaravelou. Pp. 397-419. Talence, France: CEGET-CNRS, Université de Bordeaux III.

Reinstma, M. 1982. "Land Tenure in Rwanda." *AID Research and Development Abstracts* 10314: 56-67.

Repetto, R. and T. Holmes. 1983. "The Role of Population in Resource Depletion in Developing Countries." *Population and Development Review* 9: 609-632.

Rhoades, R. E. and S. I. Thompson. 1975. "Adaptive Strategies in Alpine Environments: Beyond Ecological Particularism." *American Ethnologist* 2: 535-551.

Rossi, G. 1991. "Croissance de la Population, Mise en Valeur et Équilibre des Versants: Quel Avenir pour le Rwanda.?" *Cahiers d'Outre* Mer 44: 29-47.

Scaetta, H. 1932. *Les Famines Périodiques dans le Ruanda. Contribution à l'Étude des Aspects Biologiques du Phénomène.* (Memoires in-4. Tome 1, Fasc. 4), Brussels: Institut Royal Colonial Belge. Section des Sciences.

Sirven, P., J. F. Gotanegre, and C. Prioul. 1974. *Géographie du Rwanda.* Brussels: A. De Boeck.

Sirven, P. 1981. "Kigali: Etude de la Croissance Urbaine. Recherches sur les Hautes Terres d'Afrique Central." No. 42. In *Travaux et Documents de Géographie Tropicale* Pp. 109-126. Talence, France: CEGET.

_____. 1984. "La Sous-Urbanisation et les Villes du Rwanda et du Burundi." *Thèse de Doctorat d'État en Géographie Soutenue a l'Université de Bordeaux III* 2 Sèptembre 1983.

Soffer, Arnon. 1982. "Mountain Geography: a New approach." *Mountain Research and Development* 2, 4: 391-398.

_____. 1986. "Man-Made Altitudinal Belts in the Mountains-the Result of Plain-Mountain Interaction." *Mountain Research and Development* 6, 3: 199-204.

Stanley, H. M. 1878. *À Travers le Continent Mystérieux.* Paris: Hachette.

Tondeur, A. 1949. "Surpopulation et Déplacement des Populations." *Bulletin Agricoles du Congo Belge* 40, 3-4: 2325-2352.

Trewartha, G. and Wilbur Zelinski. 1954. "The Population Geography of Belgian Africa." *Annals of the Association of American Geographers* 44, 2: 163-193.

Troll, Carl. 1968. "Geo-Ecology of the Mountainous Regions of the Tropical Americas." *Colloquium Geographicum* 9. Bohn: Ferdinand Dummlers Verlag.

Troll, Carl and W. Lauer, eds. 1978. *Geo-Ecological Relations Between the Southern Temperate Zone and the Tropical Mountains.* Wiesbaden: Franz Steiner.

Turner II, B. L., Robert Kates, and Goran Hyden, eds. 1993. *Population Growth and Agricultural Change in Africa.* Gainesville, FL: University Press of Florida.

Turner II, B. L. and Patricia A. Benjamin. 1994. "Fragile Lands: Identification and Use for Agriculture." In Vernon W. Ruttan, ed., *Agricultural, Environment, and Health: Sustainable Development in the 21st Century.* Pp. 105-124. Minneapolis: University of Minnesota Press.

Uhlig, Harald, 1986. "Do Accessibility Models Make Altitudinal Models Obsolete?" *Mountain Research and Development* 6, 3: 197-198.

U.S. Committee for Refugees. 1991. *Exile from Rwanda: Background to an Invasion.* Issue Paper (February). Washington, D.C.: American Council for Nationalities Service.

Vansina, J. 1962. *L'evolution du Royaume Rwanda des Origines à 1900 (XXVI).* Brussels: Academie Royale des Sciences d'Outre-Mer, Classe des Sciences Morales et Politiques.

Vis, H. L. 1984. "Analyse de la Situation Nutritionnelle dans la Région des Grands Lacs d'Afrique Centrale." In *Rapport du Seminaire sur la Santé Familiale.* 16-18 April. Kigali, Rwanda: République Rwandaise, Office National de la Population.

Watts, Michael and Hans G. Bohle. 1993. "The Space of Vulnerability: the Causal Structure of Hunger and Famine." *Progress in Human Geography* 17, 1: 43-67.

Wisner, Ben. 1988. *Power and Need in Africa.* London: Earthscan Press.

Wunsch, James S. and Dele Olowu. 1990. *The Failure of the Centralized State: Institutions and Self-Governance in Africa.* Boulder: Westview Press.

Zaag, P. van der. 1980. "Strategy for Developing a National Potato Program for Rwanda." In *Root Crops in Eastern Africa.* Proceedings of a Meeting held in Kigali, November 23-27, 1980. IDRA-177e. CIP/PNAP, ISAR, Ruhengeri, B.P. 73.

Zimmerer, Karl. 1994. "Human Geography and the "New Ecology": The Prospect and Promise of Integration." *Annals of the Association of American Geographers* 84,1: 108-125

PART FOUR

Rural Development Programs: The Role of Settlement Structure

9

Participatory Development and Settlement in Southern Africa

Edward C. Green and Raymond T. Isely

It is widely accepted by development planners and administrators in Africa that the nucleation of populations into permanent villages is a prerequisite to development programs, especially those that depend on active participation by the populations concerned (Esman and Uphoff 1984: 115). Conversely, planners believe that dispersed residence is a constraint to development, or more specifically, that dispersed populations can not participate effectively in rural development projects because of a lack of social cohesiveness, common purpose, and cooperation. It is difficult to find published evidence of this positive bias toward nucleated settlement, but it is obvious to those who have worked in international development. Occasionally, these beliefs are reflected by journalists. In his attempt to justify Mozambique's communal village program, Hanlon reports: "Many countries with dispersed populations have realized that there is simply no other way to provide a minimum of services such as health, education, and clean water to the people" (Hanlon 1984:122).

The idea that Africans must live in villages or towns becomes most explicit in the planning and justification of "resettlement" or "villagization" programs in which people are persuaded or coerced to move to concentrated settlements. The following is a sentiment frequently expressed in USAID planning documents and similar sources: "any development effort that goes beyond the capacity of the single household necessitates a geographical concentration of human resources." Yet, resettlement programs have often been unsuccessful. There is typically much resistance to such programs, not only on the part of nomadic peoples (Ebrahim 1984), but also on the part of dispersed, sedentary populations.

Wherever dispersed people are found, one hears of the difficulties encountered in development work, whether it concerns public health, water supply and sanitation, or agriculture. These problems are often described in terms of lack of cooperation, mutual assistance, solidarity, or common purpose between physically dispersed peoples, which in turn inhibits participation in development projects. Accordingly, this chapter focuses specifically on *participatory* development among dispersed, sedentary populations.

Does dispersed settlement exert a significant constraint on development, or is its influence only negligible in that a different style of program administration is needed? Case studies from several African countries will be used to support the argument that dispersal is not a significant constraint to development. Participatory development itself will also be examined, both in relationship to successful development projects and to settlement patterns. Examples used to support the central argument will be drawn from the literature and from the authors' own field experience in development projects, especially those known to depend for their success on the active involvement of local participants.

The relation between settlement pattern and the success of participatory development can be fruitfully studied in Africa for several reasons. First, a broad range of economies and social organizations can be found here, including hunting-gathering bands, nomadic pastoralists, swidden horticulturalists, and mixed agriculturalists--each with its characteristic settlement pattern. Second, there is an extensive ethnographic literature describing important features of African societies, and there is a growing literature on participatory development. Donor organizations and local governments in Africa have been particularly interested in participation because of lack of resources--other than human resources--on the supply side, problems in the delivery of goods and services, and documented failures of centrally planned or "top-down" development projects. Third, the best documented government programs of nucleated resettlement or villagization are found in Africa, and because these are invariably pursued in the name of development, and even participatory development, such programs are important to our analysis.

Although active participation of intended beneficiaries in development programs is generally acknowledged as essential to their success (Cohen and Uphoff 1977; Chambers 1974; United Nations 1975), there is still a great deal of confusion surrounding both the concept and the implementation of participatory development. This confusion is not surprising given the broad spectrum of concepts that must be taken into account in arriving at a working definition. Cohen and Uphoff (1980) have concluded that a precise definition is probably not possible. Instead, they have developed a framework in which the various concepts and field experiences of participatory development can be included. One consistent theme is that development projects should involve the intended beneficiaries in concrete decision-making in order to ensure permanent results. Participation itself has several dimensions that can be sum-marily presented as questions:

1. In what does the population participate? The possibilities range from decision-making to simply receiving benefits.
2. Who participates? Is it just an elite group or is there a broad range of people involved?
3. What is the context of participation? The answer to this question varies according to the agency administering the program, as well as the physical environment and the demographic, social, cultural, and economic characteristics of the population.

Alastair White (1981) expands on the issue by suggesting that pro-jects be examined based on the origin of the initiative for participation. The options range from various governmental and private voluntary organizations to the communities themselves. Advantages and disad-vantages of each type of participation initiative are examined and it is concluded that some kind of agency-community cooperation needs to be established. Technical assistance and help with organization problems should be provided by the agency while the community provides (1) interest and decision-making, (2) financial, labor, and material contribu-tions, and, (3) administration or long-term maintenance of the project. Under these circumstances, chances of success are much improved.

Bugnicourt (1982), in a critical review, discusses the uses and abuses of participation by institutions and political leaders. He is particularly critical of the influence of "modern" education in promoting an "individ-ualistic" attitude among young Africans that works against participation in development.

Dispersed Settlement of Sedentary Populations

Dispersed settlement is positively adaptive to conditions found in much of Africa as well as other parts of the world, at least for societies whose technology and commerce remain relatively simple. As discussed in earlier chapters, dispersed settlement minimizes the physical distance to basic resources such as cultivable land, water, fuel, and building mate-rials. Nucleated settlement, on the other hand, leads to the depletion of these resources. Viewed historically, settlement pattern may change from dispersed to clustered in response to conditions such as warfare and enforced political centralization but this change may be temporary, with settlement becoming dispersed again once people feel secure. As Silberfein (1989) notes, "In the late 1800s many defense villages (in Africa) broke up with the establishment of colonial regimes and the cessation of inter-ethnic group conflict." In addition, colonial policies may have been a force to disperse people. Finnegan (1992: 114) reports that under Portuguese rule, Mozambicans "fanned out to escape taxes and forced labor."

Because colonial governments found it easier to impose taxes, and to conscript for armies and forced labor if people lived in nucleated settlements, policies of coercing people to live in villages were adopted. The basic aim was increased control over the subject population. In spite of these policies, in countries such as Tanzania, Malawi, and Zambia, soil erosion, loss of soil fertility, firewood depletion, and social disharmony, all encouraged the reestablishment of dispersed settlement.

Lewis (1970), Silberfein (1980), and others have pointed out that nucleated rural settlements as well as small towns may not be the idyllic places assumed by some, but the site of dissension, witchcraft, violence, and other forms of conflict. One study describes the small administrative or trading center of East Africa (of between 500-4,000 population), as a haven for "rural manipulators and disaffected persons" characterized by (Asian-run) trade and the political patronage of rural "Big Men" (Vincent 1974: 261). Witchcraft accusation, a common idiom for expressing social conflict in Africa, seems to occur most often among people in close, face-to-face contact, that is, in nucleated settlements (Mair 1969:216). In fact, witchcraft accusation often causes African villages to undergo a fission process whereby they divide into smaller units.

Even in the post-colonial period, independent African governments have attempted to lure or force rural people into villages. This approach has been justified publicly as: (1) making the provision of facilities such as schools, clinics, and protected water supplies more cost-effective, (2) facilitating the provision of services such as agricultural extension and literacy education, (3) fostering mutual assistance among neighbors living in close proximity, as well as stimulating community self-help schemes, and (4) making collective agricultural schemes possible. Left unstated is the government's interest in better control and administration of rural peoples and in the promotion of new, national ideologies

To summarize our argument thus far: dispersed settlement can be seen as a natural adaptation on the part of technologically simple societies to environmental conditions such as the semi-aridity and poor soils that prevail in much of Africa (as well as in other parts of the world where dispersed settlements are found). In spite of government assertions that nucleated residence promotes mutual assistance and self-help activities--or in our terms, participatory development--there is no hard evidence to support this. In fact the improved provision of government services made possible by nucleated settlement may actually undermine the independence and self-reliance of a community (Chambers 1974: 101). In an analysis of the Ujamaa program, Engas (1980) shows that villages which received the most government inputs--in order to make them model or demonstration villages--became "passive" and dependent upon government largess. Finnegan (1992: 217) found similar evidence in Mozambique. A more detailed examination of Ujamaa will carry our argument several steps further.

The Example of Ujamaa

The Ujamaa program is important to our analysis not only because it involved one of the largest and most dramatic villagization program in recent African history, but because this program was specifically justified as promoting participatory development. Indeed, the avowed corner-stones of Ujamaa would doubtless be accepted as basic to any participatory development program: cooperation and mutual assistance, participation in decision-making, self-reliance and independence, and decentralized administration and planning (Engas 1980: 391-393).

Since the literature on Ujamaa is extensive and well-known and since the topic is discussed in detail in Chapters 12 and 4, the basic ideas need not be repeated here. However, it is generally agreed that Ujamaa failed to meet its stated goals of creating successful agricultural and other cooperatives or even establishing communal villages. These shortcomings have been attributed variously to the refusal of bureaucrats and rural elites to share power with peasants, to a "natural individualism" that resists collectivism, to corrupt leadership, to drought, to World Bank policies and macroeconomic forces, to ill-advised agricultural policies, to failure to emancipate or sufficiently empower Tanzanian women, and--of most relevance to our argument--to the coercion of formerly dispersed peasants into villages (Engas 1980; von Freyhold 1979; Green, R. 1977; de Vries 1977; Briggs 1979).

Critics and supporters of Ujamaa alike have shown that mutual assistance, self-reliance, and participation in decision-making were rarely found in the newly-created villages. The inhabitants of the Ujamaa settlements preferred to engage in private, individual rather than collective production; "village planning" often amounted to little more than devising strategies for attracting government largesse (de Vries 1977: 18-21). Villages also tended to resist participation in development projects (Fortmann 1980; Engas 1980). In one voluntarily settled village, a majority of men interviewed said they joined the village in order to get government aid (von Freyhold 1979: 171), suggesting, if anything, a pre-selection of non-self-reliant people.

Case studies of individual villages have also documented how too much government aid can undermine existing levels of self-reliance and instead promote unrealistic expectations, laziness, and dependency (von Freyhold 1979). De Vries (1977: 18-21) has also shown how villagers preferred to leave development related decision-making to government extension workers--even when extension advice conflicted with common sense and practical experience--in the belief that the extension staff were adept at prying funds from government coffers.

The attitudes and behavior of villagers are, of course, just part of the story. Government officials also imposed their will on a peasantry they tended to regard as ignorant, backward, and obstinate (Engas 1980). Our point is that even in villages founded on principles of participatory development, the residents reacted to outside manipulation with passiveness and dependency. One of the present authors (Green 1984: 14) found that in Swaziland, attitudes and behavior associated with participatory development seemed less common in more nucleated settlements, such as peri-urban areas and government-resettled "rural development areas," than in the more traditional areas of dispersed settlements. Although this impression was difficult to quantify, findings from two studies on community participation and health in rural Swaziland documented that women's self-help organizations were considerably less likely to be found in resettled areas than in non-resettled areas (Green 1984; Tshabalala 1983). In both studies, in-depth interviews were conducted with a broad cross-section of community residents, local organizations were assessed, and factors were identified that appear to account for organizational effectiveness.

In short, self-reliance and other basic elements of participatory development, seem not to be especially facilitated by the nucleation of settlement. One could even make the case that village residence--or at least the improved access of government assistance that usually accompanies it-- actually promotes the antitheses of participatory development, i.e., dependency, passiveness, and individual-centeredness.

It is possible to round off our argument by citing some pertinent data from an important survey. In an analysis of participation in thirty-five primary health care projects in developing countries, bolstered by a substantial review of the literature on community participation, dispersed settlement is mentioned as relevant only in so far as travel to meetings or home visits may be difficult, costly, or time-consuming (Martin et al. 1983: 38). However, there is no suggestion that dispersed communities lack the will, esprit, or mobilization potential for community participation.

In an even more pertinent study, Esman and Uphoff (1982) evaluated factors influencing the effectiveness of local organizations. Their operational definition of a local organization is broad, including all types of development organizations in a locality that are accountable to their members and which may be organized around ethnic, religious, professional, or other types of affiliation, but excluding political and purely commercial organizations. One hundred and fifty organizations for which enough data were available in the literature were analyzed. Cases were drawn from Latin America, Asia, and the Middle East as well as from Africa. Of the organizations analyzed, twenty percent were local development organizations, thirty-five percent were cooperatives, and forty-five percent were interest associations. Each organization was scored using a one-five scale to indicate organizational performance. Several types of variables were analyzed to determine if they might be causal, that is, if they might account for variation in the performance of development organizations. Among these are variables that are relatively fixed, such as topography, and those referred to as structural characteristics of the local society, such as a legacy of partisanship. Settlement pattern was one of the structural variables. The results of the analysis show only three factors had a significant correlation with organizational performance: social heterogeneity, social stratification, and community norms. The correlation between settlement pattern and organizational performance was so weak that it could be discounted.

The following section examines social organization and popular participation in development in Swaziland, a country with dispersed settlement and a traditional, monarchial government. A comparison is then made with a program in Mozambique, also a country with dispersed settlement but one which, until recently, had a Marxist government.

Examples of Participatory Development in Dispersed Settlement Areas

Swaziland

The basic social, economic, and residential unit in Swaziland is the homestead (*umuti*). Larger homesteads consist of several households (*tindlu*) or nuclear families that form basic production and consumption units within the homestead. Homesteads are linked to other groups to form wider units much as neighborhoods, wards, and finally chiefdoms, of which there are some 200 in Swaziland. Likewise, homestead members are linked to more inclusive groups through marriage ties, descent group (clan) membership, and regiment or age-group membership.

Homesteads typically consist of a patrilineal extended family headed by an umnumzana, who is usually the senior male of the family. The head may be absent due to wage laboring or to his shifting residence between two or more homesteads in a polygamous situation..It may be noted that "the individual homestead situated at a distance from its neighbor...all of whose members tend to be related to its head" is characteristic of the Nguni and Tsonga speaking groups of Southern Africa, found in major areas of eastern South Africa (Transkei, Natal, kwaZulu and parts of the Transvaal), as well as Swaziland and parts of Mozambique (Shaw 1974: 85).

There are about ten people per Swazi homestead: eight residents and two absentee workers. Since men are employed--or seeking employ ment--much of the time, and since women perform most agricultural tasks and have virtually all responsibility for child-rearing and domestic chores, life in the homestead is largely centered around women. Health, nutrition, cleanliness, and sanitation are among women's responsibilities. Some two-thirds of Swazi homesteads still rely on unprotected water sources such as rivers or exposed springs for their drinking water (Green 1987). Women or girls usually spend at least an hour a day fetching water from a source lying one-half kilometer or more away. Piped water for domestic use has come to be identified as a highest-priority need by homestead members, both because of the burden involved in collecting water and because of increased awareness of the role of contaminated water in spreading disease. About three-quarters of homesteads still lack a pit latrine (Green 1985). Human waste is left in the bush area surrounding homesteads, as are other types of refuse. Although the situation is improving, largely through formal and nonformal education, poor sanitation and lack of safe drinking water combine to make water-borne and diarrheal diseases the primary cause of mortality and morbidity

Although Swaziland lacks villages in the usual sense of the term, there are groups of dispersed, extended-family homesteads that have a clear sense of belonging together and coming under the authority of a recognized leader. The smallest significant unit of this sort may be called a ward (sifundza) or simply a local community (sigodzi), which refers to a group of homesteads that falls under the undisputed authority of a chief's deputy. Wards are named, they have a degree of internal organization, and they have more or less definite boundaries, although disputes over boundaries and leadership are common. Unless a chief's area is quite small, several wards typically make up a chiefdom, that is, the total area and population that comes under the authority of a chief. A chiefdom also has rather well-defined boundaries, a relatively standard internal organization, and it is recognized as a local administrative unit by the

Swaziland government. At the ward level, there are social and ritual occasions such as weddings and funerals when community ties are reinforced and neighborhood spirit is expressed beyond the level of extended family or lineage group (Green 1989, 1992).

A number of local organizations concerned with various aspects of development have emerged in Swaziland, based, in part, the on economic and community development efforts of the colonial period. In 1983-84, a study was conducted to learn more about local development organizations in rural Swaziland (Green 1984). The purpose of the study was to assess community mobilization for development by looking at--and whenever possible measuring--actual participation in development-related activities on the part of rural Swazis. Respondents from ninety-six homesteads in ten geographically representative local communities (wards) were interviewed. Respondents were chosen to represent every socioeconomic level and every level of involvement in development.

All communities were found to have a traditional council (*libandla*), headed either by a chief or a deputy depending on the location. The deputy's council dealt with problems affecting the local community, including the settlement of disputes and the adjudication of most criminal offenses. The councils of both chiefs and deputies dealt with development-related matters such as new agricultural techniques, planning the construction of a clinic, or discussing the need for a protected water system. Councils were typically involved in various types of preliminary planning. Once decisions were made, council members formed a specialized committee to carry out functions such as choosing a site for a clinic or raising money for the construction of a water system. In addition to the traditional council, all communities surveyed had organizations or committees that dealt with development-related activities. An average of 6.6 (and a range of four to eight) committees per community were found to be functioning within two years of the time of interviewing. During the study, sixty-four development-related committees were identified, most of them dealing with the following areas: women's "self-help," schools, farming, cattle dips, health clinics, communal gardens, resettlement, water supplies, crop storage, markets, telephones, electricity, and Red Cross work. Women's self-help committees (sing. zenzele) were found to be the most diverse and multi-purpose of any local organizations. Their activities included pit latrine construction, nutrition, gardening, home economics and income-generating activities such a sewing.

Whereas members of other development committees might have been appointed by local leaders, members of women's self-help committees were always popularly elected by other women. One of the most significant survey findings was that these self-help committees proved to be among the most widespread, enduring, and effective of all development organizations. Effectiveness was measured, in part, by the organization's support by the chief or chief's deputy, contact with an extension agent, and having clearly defined goals that related to a locally-recognized need or problem.

USAID was enthusiastic--in fact a bit surprised--by these findings that demonstrated such a high degree of organization for rural development in Swaziland. As an experimental part of the USAID-funded Swaziland Manpower Development (SWAMDP) Project (1985-1990), local political leaders were exposed to basic development education to see if this would have an impact on at least local-level development.

In mid-1989, an evaluation survey to measure training impact was conducted. Some 188 chiefs and other local leaders were interviewed and the results compared to baseline data from our survey of Swazi chiefs conducted in 1984. It was then revealed that the number of development-related committees in rural communities had doubled during the interval between the two studies. Such committees are regarded as useful impact indicators because, as noted, there is a committee connected with most development activities, and because they are quantifiable. Over two-thirds of respondents attributed the increase in committees to the influence of project-supported workshops.

The issue of dependency on government did not seem to be a problem here. Another evaluation finding is worth quoting:

> When leaders were asked what the main obstacles to development were in their areas, there was a variety of answers that correspond quite closely to the very topics discussed at workshops. Identified obstacles include lack of available funds--including local contributions--for development; lack of infrastructure or facilities (markets, roads, etc.); lack of employment; problems relating to cooperation between people, motivation, jealousy, laziness, alcoholism; lack of training, education and literacy among rural leaders; problems relating to water and agriculture; as well as disunity among chiefs, disputes over chieftaincies and other problems attributed to rural leaders. No leader cited lack of government response as an obstacle, although this was the most common response when the same question was asked in the 1984 baseline. Instead the responsibility for development appears now to be perceived as resting mainly within the local community (Green 1989: 20-21; 1992).

Even before the development education interventions of the latter 1980s, it seemed clear that Swazi dispersed-residence communities were at least as organized and mobilized as those in village-based societies elsewhere in Africa. Popular participation in development activities has been inhibited by the traditional "top-down," authoritarian, ascribed-status sociopolitical structure of Swaziland, although, even these restrictions should gradually be relaxed (see Daley 1995). However, there is no evidence that dispersed residence undermines participatory development.

Mozambique

At the time of independence, most of the rural masses lived in dispersed homesteads (see Shaw 1974: 85). The physical and social infrastructure of Mozambique was as weak as any African nation that had gained independence in the 1960's. The revolutionary Frelimo government, in its attempt to create a modern, non-tribal, non-racial, equitable nation, embarked on a radical program to transform the country's economy and society as quickly as possible. The "traditionalism" of the various ethno-linguistic groups seemed to stand in the way of scientific socialism, and so there was an attempt to abolish traditional practices such as bride-price (*lobola*), polygamy, initiation rites, and land tenure.

At the time of independence, the dominant settlement pattern was one of dispersed villages. The Frelimo government embarked on a program to persuade or force peasants to re-group into communal villages using the typical rationale: sizable villages were necessary for collective agriculture (cooperative farms); for the delivery of health, education and other services; and for the development of mass organizations, the foundation of a socialist state. According to Hanlon, "Frelimo communal villages have an essential political purpose: only when people come together can they learn to take political control over their own lives, and participate actively in the political and economic development of Mozambique" (Hanlon 1984: 122). The government planned some 10,000 new villages.

It is hard to say how much of the failure of Mozambique's villagization was due to weaknesses inherent in such schemes, and how much was due to over a decade of a brutal insurgency led by the so-called Mozambique National Resistance (Renamo). As exemplars of Marxist rule, communal villages became targets of Renamo attacks and subsequent massacres (Finnegan 1992: 59). But it is also true that promised services were not made available; that peasants were often physically forced to move to such villages, often losing property in the process; and that peasants put more effort into cultivating their own plots than collective fields, to mention only a few problems (Finnegan 1992: 114-115; Hanlon 1984).

By the Fifth Frelimo Party Congress (1989), the Mozambique government formally recognized the mistakes it made in its zeal to create a new,
equitable, unified, national society, and it abandoned many of its socialist programs. A number of government officials acknowledged that the
realities of Mozambican society and culture had been overlooked. One
such official commented to one of the authors that Marxism/Leninism
had failed in Mozambique, Angola, and Guinea Bissau not because of any
international forces, but because it had "no roots in African soil." Another
frequently mentioned explanation for the failure of both communal villages and Mozambique's socialist economy has been the highly-central-
ized government, characterized by top-down decision-making and lack
of local participation. The irony is that villagization, collective agriculture, and other socialist programs were carried out in the name of the
People and mass popular participation.

We may now turn to our central question of whether rural Africans,
accustomed to living in dispersed settlements, are amenable to true participatory development. In the interest of space, we will provide only one
example from the recent fieldwork of the senior author. In 1992, he was
asked to head a team charged with the mission of evaluating the Children
and War (C&W) program, a "sub-regional" program administered by
Save The Children (USA) in Mozambique, Malawi, and Zimbabwe
(Green et al. 1992). The program aims to assist children who have been
adversely affected by the war that prevailed in Mozambique from the
mid-1970s until 1992 and sent hundreds of thousands of refugees to
neighboring countries. It does this by documenting "unaccompanied"
children; tracing surviving kinsmen; reuniting children with their own
kinsmen or placing them in foster families when necessary; and providing for the children's psycho-social needs through various interventions.

Instead of the top-down, high-tech, dependency-creating approach
characteristic of Frelimo in the past, the C&W program took a community-based approach based on the following premises: (1) reuniting unaccompanied children with their families is a high priority for war-affected
people but not for government agencies or NGOs, particularly in times of
crisis; (2) no government agency or NGO can be effective in documenta-
tion, tracing, and reunification work without the active support of the
refugees or the dislocated people themselves; and (3) because lost family
members want very much to find one another, there will already be informal tracing systems operating apart from formal programs. Therefore,
child tracing programs, whether government or private, should discover
informal systems already in place, identify local leaders active in these
informal networks, then use their technological advantages (posters, telephones, computer data-bases, and rapid transportation) to assist the

informal networks.

This is precisely what the C&W program did. By mid-1992, it had developed a network of over 7,000 volunteers in local communities throughout Mozambique, and was training and supervising them in tracing and related children's issues. The program played a major role in the reunification or placement of over 4,000 unaccompanied children, or twice that number if "spontaneous" reunifications are counted, some of which the C&W program may have influenced (Green et al. 1992). The program was participatory in the true sense: genuine local-level leaders planned the program in every phase, and volunteers carried out most of the work because the aims and means of the project were their own and not imposed from the outside. These local leaders and volunteers lived in settlements whose populations were typically mixed with dislocated people from other areas due to the upheavals caused by war and--in 1992--severe drought.

By contrast, the C&W program was prevented, for political reasons, from taking this kind of community-based approach in Malawi. There were well over a million Mozambican refugees in Malawi at the time, most living in large camps where they were documented and therefore relatively easy to find. Certainly their populations were highly concentrated. Instead of consulting and planning jointly with community leaders, then animating local volunteers, the C&W program had to rely on a single cadre of Red Cross field-workers to carry out DTR activities. By mid-1992, it had achieved only ten reunifications of unaccompanied children.

Analysis

The examples discussed above should help elucidate the role of population nucleation as a prerequisite to participatory development in Africa. Many observers have remarked that nucleation facilitates the delivery of government and other services, and that it is easier to organize people to participate in development projects if they live in villages than if they live in less-concentrated settlements. We concede that there is some merit to these observations when viewed from the supply side, that is, from the government or service-provider side. For example, health services tend not to be used by populations living at distances greater than ten kilometers (Gish and Walker 1977). Grouping several hundred people in a central village with a health center, a school, a social center, water supply and sanitation facilities, and other government services, should mean a higher utilization rate for those services as well as greater cost-effectiveness of service delivery. Furthermore, when a population is dispersed into family homesteads, the distance to centers may make it difficult for people to attend meetings, especially during the rainy season when roads are in poor condition. A lack of public transportation services may make the problem even more difficult.

However, we regard these difficulties as financial, logistical, and "supply side" problems (or challenges) rather than as deficiencies or inherent weaknesses on the part of dispersed populations. We argue that there is no lack of social organization, no lack of ability to cooperate in joint ventures, and no lack of community or feeling of belonging together among dispersed African populations. Certainly, lack of self-reliance cannot be said to characterize such populations since these groups typically receive fewer government services than village-based groups and therefore must rely on their own resources. As noted earlier, the expanded provision of government services which typically accompanies government-induced resettlement in villages may actually undermine self-reliance and foster dependency on governments and outside organizations. In sum, although there may be financial or logistical advantages to government service provision when populations are concentrated, dispersed populations can and do participate successfully in development projects.

Factors Contributing to Successful Participatory Development

If nucleated settlement is not a significant factor contributing to participatory development, what is? Among the more important factors, in our experience, are leadership, positive previous experience in development, and the strength of local organization (United Nations 1975; Isely and Hafner 1983; Esman and Uphoff 1982; Green 1984). This is not to present ourselves as the first to argue the significance of these factors, nor is it to deny the importance of other economic, political, physical, and sociocultural factors that affect development in general. It is rather to underscore the significance of those factors we have found to be most relevant to the potential for participation.

Leadership

The quality of leadership in a community is an essential element in successful participatory development. Esman and Uphoff (1982: 31) found that planning and goal setting, conflict management, resource mobilization, and resource management--all factors related to leadership--had high rates of correlation with the effective performance of local organizations. Actual authority seems to be less important than the capacity of leaders to command respect and to work with various groups and interests so as to ensure broad-based support (Martin et al. 1983). Leadership ability is complex, depending as it does on factors such as age, education and literacy, and attitude toward development, as well as on a variety of elusive personal qualities that are not well understood, especially in the context of traditional societies. Literacy and education--both relatively objective measures--tend to make a leader more understanding and supportive of development efforts. More difficult to assess are a leader's administrative skill, level of motivation and industriousness, and the degree of respect and trust inspired by the leader's example. However, informal discussions with a cross-section of people in a community can--if done properly--yield information of this sort.

In his study of community organization at water and sanitation projects in Swaziland, one of the authors recorded the following comments about chiefs in dispersed communities with high levels of participatory development: "He supports any kind of development"; "Without the chief's encouragement our community wouldn't look like it does today"; "He congratulates us on our success"; and "He approves projects after his people decide they want them" (Green 1984: 24). Indeed, the strength of community organization, measured by objective indicators as well as by subjective judgments, often related to the leadership qualities of the chief. Development committees were described as effective in communities where the chief was strongly in favor of development and used his authority to compel people to follow certain measures or to donate money for a project.

Previous Experience in Development

Another factor of importance to the success of participatory development projects is the quality of previous experience of the population in community participation. People who have had negative experiences, especially those involving locally-contributed funds that have been misused or lost, will be resistant to new efforts to induce their participation. Conversely, those with successful previous experiences are usually more receptive to new efforts.

To cite an example from Swaziland of negative experience, Ministry of Health extension workers established a community-based health committee after a series of meetings with local leaders and interested people. Raising funds became the first order of business for the new committee; accordingly social pressure was brought to bear on each homestead to contribute money toward a new latrine-building project. Unfortunately, the local shopkeeper entrusted with banking the money reported that the sack containing the committee funds disappeared from the back of his motorcycle. This dampened enthusiasm and for many months thereafter people were very reluctant to contribute money for any other development project.

In a survey of local development organizations in Swaziland, respondents told a surprising number of stories about the disappearance of locally-collected funds. In some cases, the money had in fact not been misappropriated, there were simply delays in making purchases because the money fell short of what was needed. But once people's suspicions were aroused they often refused to contribute further (Green 1984: 21). In their review of factors that relate to successful participatory development, Cohen and Uphoff (1977: 19) also discuss the importance of previous bad experiences with locally-raised funds or with projects generally.

Local Organizations

A third factor essential to the success of participatory development projects relates to the strength and effectiveness of local organizations (Chambers 1974). In Malawi, the success of a twenty-year-long gravity-flow water supply project which has extended over more than twenty years, has been largely due to an effective working relationship between rural water supply technicians and the leaders of local rural groups. This rapport has resulted in active participation by the local groups in the construction and maintenance of the pipelines, reservoirs, and taps (Glennie 1983). Successful participation was thought to be due to a high level of local organization augmented by relative ethnic homogeneity and strong kinship ties within the participating groups.

In any case, the government has emphasized rural development in its agricultural and development planning and the ruling party finds its base in the loyalty of tightly-organized rural communities. A survey of rural communities undertaken in 1983, showed that there was an average of 5.6 different organizations per community. Out of this survey there emerged an impression of rural Malawi as highly organized (Warner et al. 1983).

As this last case illustrates, the degree of organization exhibited by a population is a basic factor in the success of any participatory development project. Organizational cohesiveness is part of the "gestalt" of a village described by Murray (1974), and it is found in nomadic or dispersed sedentary societies as well. It should be ascertained (by careful interviews of key individuals and observations of decision-making) at the community level in both nucleated and dispersed communities before committing significant resources to a project.

Conclusion

The importance of settlement pattern, and specifically a dispersed, sedentary settlement pattern, in development programs appears to be negligible. Resettlement or villagization schemes in colonial and contemporary Africa have often been carried out in the name of promoting participatory development. Therefore, we focused on this type of development only to find that nucleated settlement is not a prerequisite for mutual assistance, cooperation, self-reliance, or participation--the basic requirements for participatory development. These characteristics can be found in communities with dispersed residence. Resettlement schemes have also been carried out in the name of delivering more government services. We concede that goods and services may be delivered more cost-effectively, and with greater logistical ease, to people living in concentrated settlements. But these advantages may be outweighed by such disadvantages as a higher incidence of disease associated with poor sanitation or a contaminated water supply.

We have also noted a loss of independence and self-reliance on the part of peoples induced to settle in villages. Historically, however, it has been the accelerated depletion of local resources such as cultivable land, water, fuel, and building materials that has helped maintain a pattern of dispersed settlement in many parts of Africa. These "ecological underpinnings" of dispersed settlement are still relevant in contemporary Africa, even where technological change has occurred.

A number of factors do seem to affect the potential of a community for participatory development, including the quality of local leadership, previous positive experience with development, and the strength of local organization. Other factors that did not emerge from our largely health-related examples but which may well be relevant include the nature of development policies and programs, the degree of socioeconomic stratification within the community, trade and economic links with the wider society, local and national political organization, and the prevailing type of kinship system (cf. Charle 1970). Dispersed settlement, contrary to conventional wisdom, seems not to be a determining factor of any significance. It thus becomes more relevant to ask, "Does the proposed development project meet basic human needs as perceived by the intended beneficiaries?" or "Have the intended beneficiaries helped plan the project from the beginning?" than, "Do the beneficiaries live in villages?"

Notes

This chapter grew out of an earlier paper Green wrote with the late Raymond Isely, MD (Green and Isely 1988, see ref. below). Green is indebted to Raymond Isely for persuading him to take up the topic in the first place.

References

Briggs, J. 1979. "Villagization and the 1974-76 Economic Crisis in Tanzania." *Journal of Modern African Studies* 17: 695-702.

Bugnicourt, J. 1982. "La Participation Populaire au Developement en Afrique." *Les Carnets de l''Enfance*. UNICEF 59/60: 63-84.

Charle, E. 1970. "Political Systems and Economic Performance in Some African Societies." *Economic Development and Culture Change* 18: 575-597.

Chambers, R. 1974. *Managing Rural Development: Experiences From East Africa.* Uppsala: The Scandinavian Institute of African Studies.

Cohen, J. M. and N. T. Uphoff. 1977. *Rural Development and Participation: Concepts and Measures or Project Design, Implementation, and Evaluation.* Rural Development Committee. Ithaca, NY: Cornell University Press.

____. 1980. "Participations' Place in Rural Development: Seeking Clarity Through Specificity." *World Development* 8: 213-235.

Daley, Suzanne. 1995. "Tradition Bound Swazis Chafing Under Old Ties." *New York Times*. December 16th: 4.

de Vries, J. 1977. *Ujamaa Villages and Problems of Institutional Change with Emphasis on Agriculture Extension and Development.* Dar es Salaam, Tanzania: University of Dar es Salaam, Department of Rural Economy.

Engas, Z. 1980. "Why did the Ujamaa Policy Fail? Toward a Global Analysis." *Journal of Modern African Studies* 18: 387-410.

Ebrahim, M. H. 1984. "Nomadism, Settlement and Development." *Habitat International* 8: 125-141.

Esman, M. J. and N. T. Uphoff. 1982. *Local Organization and Rural Development: The State of the Art.* Rural Development Committee. Ithaca: Cornell University Press.

____. 1984. *Local Organizations: Intermediaries in Rural Development.* Ithaca: Cornell University Press.

Finnegan, W. 1992. *A Complicated War.* Berkeley: University of California Press.

Fortmann, L. 1980. *Peasants, Officials, and Participation in Rural Tanzania: Experience with Villagization and Decentralization.* Ithaca: Cornell University Press.

Glennie, C. 1983. *Village Water Supply in the Decade: Lessons from Field Experience.* London: Wiley.

Gish, O. and G. Walker. 1977. *Mobile Health Services.* London: Tri-Med.

Green, E. C. 1984. *Traditional Leadership, Community Participation and Development Education: Results and Implications of Two Surveys in Swaziland.* Washington, D.C.: Academy for Educational Development.

_____. 1985. "Factors Relating to the Presence and Use of Sanitary Facilities in Rural Swaziland." *Tropical and Geographic Medicine* 37: 81-85.

_____. 1987. "Beliefs and Practices Related to Water Usage in Swaziland." *International Journal of Water Resources Development* 2: 29-42.

_____. 1989 *Local Leaders and Development Education in Swaziland*. Washington, D.C.: Trans Century Corporation.

_____. 1992. "Evaluating the Response of Swazi Traditional Leaders to Development Workshops." *Human Organization* 51: 379-388.

Green, E. C. and R. Isely, 1988. "The Significance of Settlement Pattern for Community Participation in Health: Lessons from Africa." *Human Organization* 47: 158-166.

Green, E. C., Jan Williamson, and Paula Nimpuno-Parente. 1992. "Evaluation of the Children and War Program." (PRITECH Evaluation) Maputo: Save The Children and USAID.

Green, R. 1977. "Towards Socialism and Self Reliance." University of Dar es Salaam, Research Report.

Hanlon, J. 1984. *Mozambique: Revolution Under Fire*. London: Zed Books.

Isely, R. B. and C. Hafner. 1983. "Facilitation of Community Organization." *Water Supply and Management* 6: 431-442.

Lewis, O. 1970. "Tepoztlan Restudied: A Critique of the Folk-Urban Conceptualization of Social Change." In O. Lewis, ed. *Anthropological Essays*. Pp. 35-52. New York: Random House.

Mair, Lucy. 1969. *Witchcraft*. New York: McGraw-Hill.

Martin, P., M. Favin, M. Parlato, and W. Stinson. 1983. *Community Participation in Primary Health Care*. Washington, D.C.: American Public Health Association Primary Health Care Issues, Series 1, No. 5.

Murray, C.A. 1974. "Investment and Tithing in Thai Villages: A Behavioral Study of Rural Modernization." Unpublished Ph.D. Dissertation, Massachusetts Institute of Technology.

Nyerere, J. 1968. *Ujamaa: Essays on Socialism*. London: Oxford University Press.

Shaw, M. 1974. "Material Culture." In W. D. Hammond-Tooke, ed. *The Bantu-Speaking Peoples of Southern Africa*. Pp. 85-131. London: Routledge and Kegan Paul.

Silberfein, M. 1980. "The Evaluation of Rural Settlements: A Tanzanian Case Study." In Singh, R. L. and P. B. Singh eds. *Rural Habitat Transformations in World Frontiers*. Varanasi, India: National Geographic Society of India.

_____. 1989. "Settlement Form and Rural Development: Scattered Versus Clustered Settlement." *Tijdschrift voor Economishe en Sociale Geografie* 53: 258-268.

Tshabalala, R. 1983. "Community Participation in Water and Sanitation and Clinic Construction in Swaziland." Master of Science Thesis, University of London.

United Nations. 1975. *Popular Participation in Decision-Making for Development*. New York: UN Department of Economic and Social Affairs.

Vincent, J. 1974. "The Changing Role of Small Towns in the Agrarian Structure of East Africa." *Journal of Commonwealth and Comparative Politics* 12: 261-275.

Von Freyhold, M. 1979. *Ujamaa Villages in Tanzania: Analysis of a Social Experiment*. New York: Monthly Review Press.

Warner, Dennis B., R. B. Isely, C. Hafner, and J. Briscoe. 1983. *Malawi Self-Help Rural Water Supply Program: A Mid-Term Evaluation of the USAID-Financed Project*. Report No. 105. Rosslyn, VA: WASH Field Reports.

White, Alastair. 1981. *Community Participation in Water and Sanitation; Concepts, Strategies, and Methods*. Report No. 17. Rijkswijk, The Netherlands: International Reference Center for Community Water Supply and Sanitation.

10

The Design of Community and Its Socioecological Consequences: Marsabit District, Kenya

Asmarom Legesse

Anthropologists and human geographers have devoted much effort to studying how spatial and social organizations are related. One cannot be understood fully without reference to the other -- that is a major premise of the two disciplines. However, the designers and builders who base their work on aesthetic and structural considerations as well as the profit motive continue to build the spaces in which we are supposed to work and live without regard to social, proxemic, and ecological needs. They are often unaware of the social consequences of their actions. Most often, they are not members of the community for which they build and sometimes they are not even members of the same culture. They may not, therefore, be aware of the damage that they do until it is too late to introduce remedies.

The problems of the built environment are brilliantly treated in two classic studies: Edward Hall's *The Hidden Dimension* and William Whyte's *Social Life of Small Urban Spaces* (Hall 1962; Whyte 1980). Hall demonstrates how all our senses are involved in the design of older, man-made habitats that co-evolved with the natural environment in contrast to many of the new, artificial urban settings that violate the proxemic needs of humans as well as the ecological foundations of their communities. Willam Whyte, whose work was inspired by Hall's research, demonstrates, with time-lapse photographic evidence, that some of the spaces designed by architects for social activity are empty while other spaces that were never intended for such activity are full of people. Obviously there is a serious proxemic schism between social needs and some types of man-made environments.

These studies have influenced my thinking about the Oromo of Northern Kenya and how inappropriate technology and design contributed to the collapse of community during the years of drought and ecological crisis in the 1970s and 1980s. The most egregious instance of this phenomenon can be found in an area near Marsabit town that was used as a relocation site for Borana and Gabra communities disturbed by wars and droughts. People in this region had to abandon age-old adaptive linkages between the community and the built as well as the natural habitat. As a result, many communities underwent a process of internal disintegration.[1]

The northernmost political subdivision of Kenya, called Marsabit District, is a vast expanse of semi-arid to arid land surrounding two elevated areas: Hurri Hills and Marsabit Mountain (Figure 10.1). The principal Oromo speaking populations, the primarily cattle-herding Borana and the camel herding Gabra, occupy upland and lowland pastures respectively. During the droughts that destroyed so much of the Sahelian region of Africa in the 1970s and 1980s, the subsistence economy of these pastoralists was badly disrupted. Kenya had significant resources which it mobilized to care for the dislocated populations. The country also received much assistance from the national and international humanitarian organizations. Thus, there was little loss of human life in northern Kenya. However, livestock populations were decimated throughout the Sahelian zone and northern Kenya was no exception. As a result, there was a sudden influx of former pastoralists into Marsabit town and the peri-urban areas around the town.

Traditional Communities (Olla)

Borana settlements vary in size, structure, and other properties. This variation is dependent on seasonal and ritual cycles which cause people to agglomerate during the rains and to disperse in the dry seasons when families usually fend for themselves as they migrate extensively in search of pastures. The Borana consider the agglomerated community to be the fundamental settlement or *olla* but, in effect, they have incorporated an annual alternation between clustered and dispersed forms as a mechanism for dealing with a semi-arid environment. The clusters can be viewed on a map or on a photograph that portrays the Marsabit landscape (Figures 10.2a and 10.3).

Ollas range in size from a few families to several dozen. The modal Olla probably consists of about eight to twelve families that include nuclear or polygynous households in which married siblings often form joint family chains. Ideally, married brothers form the core of the residential cluster but married sisters and brothers frequently settle together. There is no mandatory principle of kinship that serves as the basis of the residential community; rather, the *olla* is a voluntary cluster from which any residents are free to relocate.

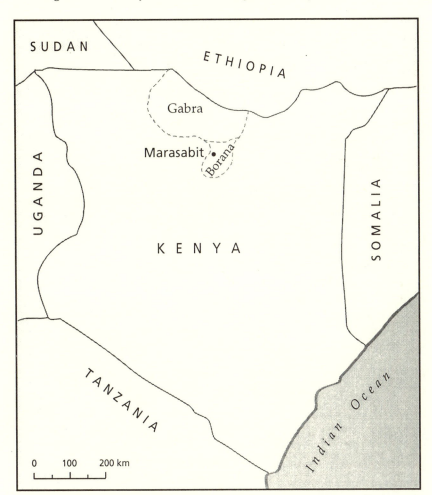

FIGURE 10.1 Location Map: Northern Kenya

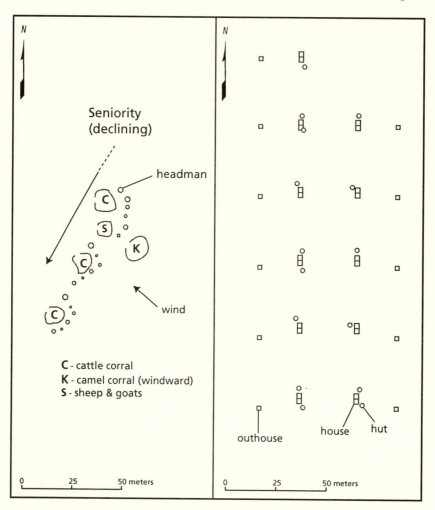

Figure 10.2a Olla Doti: Traditional
Community

Figure 10.2b Olla Hiyyessa: Settlement Scheme

FIGURE 10.3 An Olla in Semi-Arid Marsabit District

Living together in an *olla* does, however, imply a mutual responsibility. There are powerful moral forces that keep the family members together so that they can assist each other in times of crisis. The degree of integration of the *olla* is particularly high if the members have lived together for a number of years. Conversely, it is also true that a Borana feels that he has little obligation to assist the residents of another *olla* unless there are prior bonds of kinship, friendship, or mutual aid.

The *olla* is a relatively self-contained, collaborating unit. Collaboration in regard to herding activities is mandatory because a family rarely has the labor force it needs to perform all the chores of the pastoralist. Caring for three types of animals, cattle, camels, and sheep/goats, requires at least six herders. These three types cannot be herded together because their water requirements, food preferences, and ecological adaptations are quite different. Borana also characteristically split their animals into milk herds (*lon warra*) which are kept in the vicinity of the *olla* and dry herds (*lon fora*) which are moved around in very large nomadic cycles.

Herders also have to be of the appropriate age and gender. The likelihood that a family will have six such persons at any one time is very slight and if they do, it is only a temporary resource until the children grow older, marry, and sometimes move away. Families, therefore, contrive to combine their labor resources in very complex ways that relate to the size and organization of the *olla*; the smaller the settlement, the more precarious the labor situation. Families can also deal with the problem of labor shortage by keeping only one type of livestock, but such a strategy implies other risks; survival prospects and reproductive potential is greater if the herd is diversified.

The most important time for collaboration among neighbors is during a period of crisis. Over and above the annual dry seasons, there are also extended periods of drought that may last for two to three years. In these situations, some families lose their entire herds and become completely destitute. At this point, however, the Borana mutual assistance pact comes into play. The destitute do not necessarily starve or become marginalized and stigmatized. They continue to live in their *olla* where they provide herding to their neighbors in exchange for milk. At the same time, the head of the destitute family goes on a long trek across Borana country to seek help from his clansmen and friends and to borrow animals from families to whom his ancestors had loaned animals in previous years, decades, or generations. The practice serves as a form of insurance. The animals that are loaned out and their offspring are named so as to recall their origin. With these strategies, the Borana have managed to rehabilitate the weakest among them.

The *olla* is not only a unit of collaboration, it also has ecological ramifications. It is located with care so as to be as close as possible to the type of vegetation preferred by milk herds and to a permanent water supply. Since proximity to both resources can be difficult to achieve, the actual location of a settlement usually represents a negotiated compromise between the men who are concerned about the quality of vegetation for livestock and the women who must transport the family water supply on a daily basis.

The *olla* is also positioned so that it will have a natural windscreen in the form of shrubs or trees, access to large trees which offer shade for livestock and the men's meetings, and proximity to particular varieties of acacias that are needed for fence construction. Once a location is selected, all the individual structures are then oriented in a northwesterly direction, away from the wind which generally comes from the southeast. Dust storms are very common and if the door were to face the wind, life could be unbearable.

The arrangement of houses indicates which families have pooled their labor in relation to particular herds. The corrals of sheep and goats and cattle are generally placed in front of the huts whereas those of the camels are always placed in the rear. This arrangement is necessary because of the different degrees to which the animals are domesticated. Cattle are deeply attached to humans; their calves are actually raised indoors around the family hearth. Goats are considered to be more "feral" then cattle, too unruly to be kept indoors, while camels are deemed to be barely domesticated. The Borana express their contempt for camels by referring to them as *binensa* which means wild animal. Camels resist milking and loading, threaten to bite herders, and can panic in response to unfamiliar sounds. Thus, the camel corral must be located behind the huts so that mats, which are often placed on roofs to protect the inhabitants from the elements, won't blow into the cattle pens and cause a stampede.

The factors described here indicate that there is an intimate connection between the design of the traditional community, its internal socioeconomic organization, and its ecological relationships. There is nothing in the design that is arbitrary, nothing that is not determined by proxemic, social, or ecological imperatives.

The New Communities

New settlements have been formed on Marsabit Mountain in response to the great droughts. The spontaneous and planned settlements that emerged in the area make it possible to understand how the structure of homes, farms, and communities works to support or disrupt socio-economic activities. Of particular interest are the following factors: the appropriateness of the spatial arrangement of the houses, their location in relation to the farms, and the construction materials, labor resources, or skills employed in building the communities themselves.

Sedentarization in a Peri-Urban Refuge

Numerous communities have been formed near Marsabit town, some of which are based on the development of new skills, or the application of old skills to new circumstances. One of settlements that established an entirely new production system is Olla Chila, the village of the charcoal makers. It included some of the most destitute people in the district, nomads who had lost their animals to drought and then obtained permission from the County Council to go into the charcoal business. This enterprise provided a meager but steady income, given that charcoal has come to meet a critical and growing need for fuel in the urban community.

The charcoal makers usually go to the foot of the mountain to gather dead wood from scrub land and from trees felled during the clearing of new fields. The forestry department carefully regulates all tree felling in the forest as part of an effort at conservation. It also discourages the removal of dead wood from the forest floor because this material is important to the formation of detritus. The resulting spongy layer soaks up and retains vast quantities of moisture and thus contributes to the viability of the forest and of the aquifers that supply water to the entire mountain population, including the urban residents, farmers, pastoralists, livestock, and wildlife. Furthermore, the forest depends on the type of precipitation which occurs when the trees capture the mist directly from the air, even when there is no rainfall. Hence, the destruction of the forest would be truly suicidal for the mountain population.

Among the residents in and around Marsabit town, there are also skilled craftsmen who provide important services to the nomads in normal times. The most important of the craftsmen are the smiths who make most of the iron tools and weapons which the nomads use for wood cutting, wood carving, hunting, and warfare. In the past, each smith had a quasi-familial bond with particularlineages of herders. He would stay with a lineage for a few weeks each year, and make all the tools and weapons which the community needed. The smith was not paid in cash but was given livestock in exchange for his services. Today, the smiths have abandoned their craft circuit in the nomadic communities as demand has decreased due to the drought, increased purchases of imported tools by the herders, and tool distribution by humanitarian groups. Furthermore, raw materials, which used to consist mainly of scrap metal left behind from World War II, have become more scarce.

The smiths have entered the cash market in town, making the same tools and weapons for tourists and for the urban community that they made for the nomads. They have also expanded their production of copper and bronze jewelry for tourists as well as for townspeople and the herders. They have perhaps had the easiest time adapting to an urban or peri-urban environment since they have readily marketable skills that are applicable in drought years as well as normal years. They have not formed complete villages comparable to Olla Chila of the charcoal makers, rather, their houses are interspersed among those of other urban and peri-urban dwellers.

Both the charcoal village and the neighborhoods of craftsmen evolved over the years in response to a succession of crises. They have, therefore, developed into genuine communities. Neither group experienced the deep dislocation of the nomads who lost their livestock and had to confront urban life without useful skills.

Spontaneous Settlements and Land Acquisition

Olla Duba and Olla Jilo were two of the large peri-urban settlements that emerged spontaneously as a result of the major crises of the 1960s and early 1970s. "Duba" is an elderly, highly respected Borana and "Jilo" is Jilo Toukena, a chief who served the Marsabit Borana for two decades. The Shifta wars in 1963 uprooted many Borana, disrupted their pastoral economy and drove them into the urban environment. The drought of the 1970s repeated a similar round of disruptions that added to the population of impoverished settlers around Marsabit town.

These communities are analogous to the "squatter settlements" that occur frequently around the cities of the Third World. They differ mainly because the Marsabit settlements have been processed by local authorities and thus do not have the extra-legal and sometimes violent history associated with such settlements elsewhere. In other words, there are no invasions of squatters in northern Kenya comparable to those that frequently have been recorded in the peri-urban areas of Latin American cities such as Mexico City or Brazilia (Epstein 1972, Holston 1989).

Many of the Borana who live in Olla Duba and Olla Jilo have acquired land by submitting requests to the County Council. The plots assigned to them range in size from one to forty acres, the median plot size being five acres. Of the 174 households in my sample, eighty-three percent owned less than five acres and ninety- seven percent owned less than ten acres. A few, however, had neither land nor cattle.

The resettled Borana nomads made an effort to combine sedentary agriculture with pastoralism and so provide themselves with a wider range of survival strategies. However, during dry years food production was usually inadequate and, even during average years, approximately two percent of the settlers produced enough of a surplus to be sold in the market. Only when the rains were abundant did the harvest provide settlers with enough revenue to purchase breeding livestock. These animals were then used to reestablish the herds that had been lost to the drought.

The district agricultural office has made some effort to introduce Borana farmers to high-yielding varieties of corn, such as Kenya-bred Katumani maize. Similarly, the National Council of Churches of Kenya and the Consolata Catholic Mission have contributed seed annually to these farmers. The Borana have no hesitation in using these high-yielding varieties and have adopted them eagerly. Their problem does not reflect an unwillingness to adopt new techniques but rather in the unreliability of rain-fed agriculture.

All of the sedentarized populations mentioned so far settled on Marsabit Mountain on their own initiative. They decided where they would live, what kind of housing they would build, who their neighbors would be, and whether labor sharing would take place. Their communities grew slowly and organically. There is a strong contrast between these communities and the planned settlement schemes to which we will now turn our attention.

Planned Settlement: The Village of the Poor

Several schemes were initiated, but the outstanding example of a non-spontaneous settlement is Olla Hiyyessa, the "Village of the Poor." The agency that established this scheme is the Consolata Catholic Mission. The genesis of the community is described as follows by Father John Astiggiani, the head of the mission:[2]

> We set up that settlement. We received aid from CARE. We worked in collaboration with the County Council and Community Development. We told the chief to choose the poorest forty families. From among these, we selected the twenty poorest. The County Council gave them four acres of land each for shambas (farms). We gave each family a house and eight goats. We also gave the village ten oxen to operate the ox-drawn plow. We will give them some more goats soon... We are now very unhappy about this project because the families seem to have developed a high degree of dependence on us. They do not seem to be able to stand up and help themselves. Our aid was intended to made them economically self-sufficient, and yet, we seem to have produced a community of dependent families.

The village is made up of identical houses built out of gleaming corrugated iron sheets with wooden frames and a resting on shiny cement platforms. The houses are built in pairs that are separated from each other by approximately thirty yards. They are lined up on a wide road that forms one of the most prominent physical features of the settlement (Figure 10.2b) The planners thought that vehicular traffic would benefit from such a road but, instead, it was quickly overrun with bush as it evolved into a narrow cow path. The stark, geometric appearance of the village and the houses of iron sheeting can be seen in Figures 10.4 and 10.5.

The housing that was provided for the settlers was a good example of inappropriate technology. First the corrugated iron sheet structures turned out to be quite uncomfortable because they trapped heat inside and because frequent gusts of wind could readily rip off the roof. Whenever this happened, the occupants were forced to obtain assistance from the mission as they hadn't the tools, construction materials, or technical know-how needed to make repairs.

When the houses proved to be dysfunctional, resident families often ceased living in them, using them instead for storage, as a symbol of gratitude to their mission benefactors, or even as guest houses for urban visitors who enjoyed the "modernity" of metal structures. Meanwhile, the settlers began to build traditional structures, each of which evolved into a more liveable annex. It became an extraordinary sight to see a row of perfectly spaced and identical houses gradually being surrounded by thatched huts.

Olla Hiyessa was not just poorly designed, however, it also did not function as a community. Most Borana villages are named after the most senior individual or founder. In this case, since there was no founder as such, the name "village of the poor" remained in place. Although the residents tried to develop a new name and identity, they retained the original name and the stigma that was attached to it. Olla Hiyyessa differed from other Borana settlements in that virtually all the members were escaping disaster. In Olla Fada and the settlements mentioned earlier, some of the migrants came because they were seeking urban employment or services, or they were livestock traders. Such a settlement resembled a diversified traditional village that in turn facilitated labor sharing and the ability of wealthier residents to assist those who were in difficulty.

In 1976, Olla Hiyyessa did something that horrified the Borana; it failed to help when one of its members, a woman named Bone, was dying of starvation. She had declined over a period of several months because she was trying to nurse a severely ill husband and provide enough food for her three children. She had also been pregnant and gave birth to a

FIGURE 10.4 Olla Hiyyessa Under Construction

FIGURE 10.5 A Completed House with Residents:Olla Hiyyessa

stillborn child just before she died. Neighbors who witnessed this development said "Olla knana Bantitti hinqabu!" (This village has no Borana-
ness). It was a situation reminiscent of the Ik of Uganda, an uprooted people lacking structure, a sense of purpose, or a rudimentary moral code
(Turnbull 1972).

There are many factors that contributed to the problems of this settlement. Since the farms were located on the wind-swept side of the
mountain, i.e., the south side, cultivation turned out to be quite precarious. Areas of the mountain that had previously been protected by forest,
bush, and grass became fully exposed to the elements. The top soil was
blown away from the maize fields leaving the roots exposed. The center
of the village was in the worst position; it seemed to be located in some
kind of wind tunnel. When most farmers were growing maize with some
difficulty, the families in the center had no harvest whatsoever. It took
several years to find a solution to the problem; families were encouraged
to plant euphorbia shrubs that would give their crops some protection
from the wind.

Throughout the early 1980s, rainfall was so unpredictable that the
village produced only an occasional harvest. When rainfall was inadequate, the villagers used a variety of other strategies to survive. Among
these, perhaps the most common was making charcoal and selling it in
the urban market as did the residents of Olla Chile. For Olla Hiyyessa,
however, charcoal making was not a means of subsistence but a back-up
resource on which could be relied on when herding and farming activities failed. Initially there was ample firewood from areas outside of the
forest boundary--the areas that were being cleared for cultivation. This
resource gradually dwindled as farmers became more possessive of the
wood obtained from their land, and wood sources shifted to the limited
supplies at the foot of the mountain or further out in the semi-desert.
Collecting, cutting, and firing the wood and carrying the charcoal to town
was considered to be an extreme hardship.

Slowly and with great determination, the village of the poor emerged
from a state of extreme poverty into relative self- sufficiency after 1985.
From a purely economic standpoint, the settlement achieved a modest
level of success. As a community, though, it was still a sociological disaster area. It had no leadership, no name, no internal organization, no
established pattern of collaboration. The symptoms of dependence continue to be obvious even a decade later.

The most puzzling aspect of the relationship between Olla Hiyyessa
and the Catholic mission is the way in which the relief process developed
a life of its own. The mission continued to give out famine relief several
years after the famine had ended and after the families had begun to

grow adequate food for themselves. Some of these families were also growing tobacco as a cash crop and were obtaining a substantial income from it. There were, therefore, no longer poor in any meaningful sense of the word. The donors had created a bond with Olla Hiyyessa which they were reluctant to sever. Each family, which had to merit assistance separately, seemed to put qualifying for relief ahead of the desire for self-sufficiency. There are strong indications that the vertical, paternalistic ties that dominated the relationship between donors and receivers of food aid inhibited the development of horizontal bonds within the community.

There is an important lesson to be learned from the history of Olla Hiyessa: economic aid, agricultural and technical expertise, and good intentions are not enough to effectively rehabilitate uprooted communities. Some attention must be paid to the social and spatial design of communities as well as technological and ecological factors. This reality can be gleaned in part from the sketch of a traditional camp (Figure 10.2a) whose configuration contrasts so strongly with the design of Olla Hiyyessa (Figure 10.2b).

Comparison of Planned and Spontaneous Settlements

When Olla Hiyyassa is compared to other settlements it is obvious that something is lacking. In the traditional camp, the total configuration and the internal subdivisions represent units of collaboration. Relationships develop as people choose each other as neighbors. The village community has a complex organic ground plan which is intimately tied to social networks that determine the patterns of collaboration and the moral code by which they are tied to each other. By contrast, Olla Hiyyassa is remarkably amorphous. It is based on a design destined to produce maximum alienation of the villagers from each other and from the built environment. The houses are like beads on a string and it is a slender string indeed that keeps them together. They are located about thirty yards apart from each other, in contrast with the more clustered traditional community where houses are two to three yards apart. The two mapped villages (Figures 10.2a & b) are about the same size (twenty-two houses in Olla Hiyyessa to eighteen in the other village) but their spatial character is completely different.

Here we must stop to consider an enigmatic situation. The Consolata Catholic Mission which created Olla Hiyyassa is a humane organization that has devoted a great deal of effort to improving the lot of the Borana and Gabra people. They spent decades traveling from village to village on camels to bring education to some of the most remote communities in the territory. They have studied the local language, religious beliefs and, whenever aspects of traditional culture were compatible with Christian beliefs, they incorporated these elements into Christian worship.[3] The Catholic Mass has been so thoroughly Africanized that is sounds more like a Borana ritual then a mass. It is difficult to determine why a mission that has used the philosophy of syncretism so effectively in education, abandoned that philosophy completely in the rehabilitation of destitute families? The missionaries have not made much of an attempt to meld elements of Borana social, ecological, or economic organization into the fabric of the new communities they have created. Nor have they used the material resources or construction skills that are locally available. Finally, and most importantly, they completely ignored the design of Borana communities in planning the lay-out of the new villages.

Some Thoughts on the Design of Community

Technological and Ecological Factors

Marsabit mountain is a volcano which has a large supply of basalt-type rock and a great deal of sand in the dry river beds emanating from the mountain and radiating in all direction. These resources are available to the indigenous population as construction materials that can be used for building houses and other structures. Stone houses are usually build by the Burju and Konso --two people who have settled around Marsabit town and who share their construction skills with the other settlers. The Borana and Gabra herders too, do some construction in stone, particularly at grave sites, dams, and wells, Hence, stonework is not entirely alien to them.

Borana and Gabra are actually much more familiar with wood as a construction material. They like to select the supple branches of such trees as Haroressa (*Grewia bicolor*) to build the exquisitely dome-shaped frame of their huts. They are accomplished wood carvers and use their skills to make various utensils and containers. These skills could easily be transferred to the manufacturing of partitions, doors, windows, and storage spaces for homes in new villages.

Given the various materials and skills that are available on the mountain, it is difficult to understand the rationale for using imported corrugated iron sheets to build the roofs and walls of the houses in the planned settlement schemes. In addition to the environmental problems that such materials create--namely heat and vulnerability to wind damage--corrugated iron cannot be easily fashioned to meet the various needs of the mixed farmers in a peri-urban milieu. Adobe and stone houses can be modified to allow for the creation of partitions and annexes that would permit the herders to keep small livestock, particularly calves, in close proximity with the families. This is important to cattle herders because cattle that are raised in such an environment during a critical period in their socialization become attached to humans and respond to their verbal commands and admonitions. As a result, they can be herded easily by young children. By contrast, camels, are kept away from human habitation throughout their lives. It is easy to see how the design of community has important consequences for the human-animal nexus in a mixed farming community.

Sociological and Economic Factors

An important lesson that we learn from the settlement schemes has to do with the social composition and social structure. Most of the spontaneous settlements on the mountain have a viable community life. Olla Jilo, for instance, developed around the home of Chief Jilo Toukena, the chief of the Marsabit Borana. Even the communities that are predominantly composed of refugees from drought and famine exhibit strong communal properties. Thus, Olla Duba, which grew up near the house of a respected elder, has all the structural properties of a Borana village.

Olla Chile, the charcoal village, shares some characteristics with these communities. It has internal neighborhoods that bind people into working units. Unlike Olla Duba and Olla Jilo, however it has no founder. Its name derives from the humble product that it brings to the market.

The main sociological message of this paper is this: if the destitute ex-nomads were to be mingled with the other newly sedentarized populations, they would be much less likely to develop the symptoms of anomie exhibited by Olla Hiyyessa. The recruitment of such a mixed group would allow for the gradual selection of neighbors. Most importantly, the community design would not undermine the pattern of collaboration which is an integral part of the life of Borana and Gabra communities. Even under the best of circumstances, the Borana or Gabra family rarely has all the workers it needs to look after all the different types of livestock. If, in addition, family members are urged to become farmers and to grow cash crops, more, not less, workers will be needed. Furthermore, education and urbanization are drawing off a growing component of the potential workers, making labor supply issues even more critical.

Spatial and Proxemic Factors

Research on Marsabit communities suggests that a voluntary process has an important role to play in determining the shape and density of communities. If families choose their neighbors as the new com munity is established there is more of a likelihood that the spatial agglomeration will develop strong community properties.

Distances have meaning only in relation to particular cultures. It is impossible to determine what constitutes an appropriate spacing of homes in communities without reference to culture. Among some groups, a sense of community may be fairly strong even if individual houses are miles apart. This was the case, for instance, among Appalachian communities in the United States (Eller 1982). Such societies have compensatory mechanisms that seek to ritually renew ties that might otherwise be weak. Yet, for the Borana who live within hearing and smelling distance of each other during the rains, placing houses thirty yards apart is a form of punishment and a serious barrier to community formation.

This study of the changing pattern of residence in Marsabit has shown the adaptability of a people living in a difficult, relatively remote location. The Borana have survived very basic changes in their production system and basic economy. The study has also shown that overall design and neighborhood social organization is of critical importance in determining the success or failure of a settlement program, although these factors are not always taken seriously. Those charged with changing settlement systems must determine the social and spatial aspects of a community before implementing basic changes in structure and location. A community that is allowed to grow organically will usually have a legitimate name and leader as well as a socio- spatial ground plan which tells outsiders who lives where and why. Much community life is linked to such a plan. Without it, the social fabric of the community can disintegrate.

Notes

1. The research reported on in this chapter is part of a much larger body of data gathered among the Borana and Gabra pastoralists of Northern Kenya. The larger work will be published under the title of "A Pastoral Ecosystem: Field Studies of the Borana and Gabra of Northern Kenya" (Red Sea Press, forthcoming).

2. Personal tape-recorded interview with Father John Astiggiani, Marsabit, 1982.

3. See, for example, the remarkable ethnographic studies of the Gabra by Father Paolo Tablino (Tablino 1980a, 1980b, and 1989).

References

Eller, Ronald D. 1982. *Miners, Millhands, and Mountaineers: Industrialization of the Appalachian South 1880-1930*. Knoxville: University of Tennessee Press.

Epstein, David G. 1972. "The Functions and Genesis of Squatter Settlements in Brazilia." In Thomas Weaver, ed. *Anthropology of Urban Environments*. Washington, D.C.: Society for Applied Anthropology.

Hall, Edward. 1966. *The Hidden Dimension*. Garden City, NY: Doubleday.

Holston, James. 1989. *The Modernist City: An Anthropological Critique of Brazilia*. Chicago: University of Chicago Press.

Tablino, Father Paolo. 1980a. "Babra del Kenia." Bologna: EMI.

____. 1980b. "The Diocese of Marsabit: Some Historical Notes." Marsabit: Catholic Diocese.

_____. 1989. "Time and Religion Among the Gabra Pastoralists of Northern Kenya: A Course." Marsabit: Catholic Diocese.

Turnbull, Colin M. 1972. *The Mountain People*. New York: Simon and Schuster.

White, William. 1980. *Social Life in Small Urban Places*. Washington, D.C.: The Conservation Foundation.

PART FIVE

National Settlement Strategies

11

Rural Settlement Patterns in Zimbabwe and State Manipulation of the Settlement Structure

Lovemore Zinyama

The rural areas of Zimbabwe today consist of four agricultural sub-sectors, each quite distinct in terms of its settlement patterns and population density, levels of output and productivity, as well as the intensity of interaction with the rest of the economy. The four sub-sectors are (1) the large-scale commercial farming sector, (2) the small-scale commercial farming sector, (3) the communal or peasant farming sector and (4) the resettlement areas (Figure 11.1). The large-scale commercial farming sector occupies some 11.3 million hectares of land, which is thirty-four percent of the 33.3 million hectares of the national agricultural land or twenty-nine percent of the total national land area (excluding parastatal-owned commercial farms, which occupy about 0.9 million hectares). The sector comprises some 4,000 farming units, which range in size from less than 200 to over 8,000 hectares, mostly held under freehold tenure. These farms were exclusively owned by European settler farmers and companies, but since independence in 1980 and the removal of racial restrictions on property ownership, newly affluent Africans have acquired some of these large properties. At the time of the 1992 population census, 1.7 million people resided in the large-scale commercial farming areas, or 11.3 percent of the national population of 10.4 million; these consisted mainly of farmers as well as farm-workers and their dependents.

The small-scale commercial farming sector (formerly known as the African Purchase Areas) comprises some 10,000 units of land that were originally set aside during the colonial period for a few Africans who had both the desire and the financial capacity to buy land under freehold or leasehold tenure. These former Purchase Areas were first established in the 1930s as compensation for the Africans' loss of the right to own land in any part of the country in open competition with European settlers. This followed the passing of the Land Apportionment Act in 1930 by the

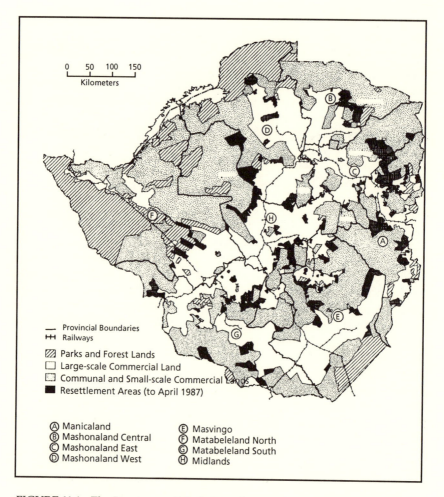

FIGURE 11.1   The Provinces of Zimbabwe Showing Land Use Categories

colonial administration (Floyd 1962). The farms are generally less than 150 hectares each, with somewhat larger sizes in the drier parts of the country where livestock ranching is a more viable option than crop culti-vation. The sector occupies some 1.4 million hectares, or four percent of the agricultural land. At the 1992 census, there were 170,170 people, or 1.6 percent of the national population, in the small-scale commercial farming sector.

The communal farming sector occupies some 16.4 million hectares, or forty-nine percent of the agricultural land. The sector supports about 5.35 million people in about one million farming families, representing 51.4 percent of the national population. The average size of arable land per family in the communal areas is about two hectares held under tradi-tional communal ownership, with each household having only usufruc-tuary rights to the land. Farmers also have access to communal grazing land.

The fourth sector, the resettlement areas, is a post-1980 development, being the outcome of the Zimbabwe government's program to redistrib-ute national resources, particularly land, more equitably between the races (Republic of Zimbabwe 1981, 1982, 1986; Zinyama 1986; Zinyama et al. 1990). By the end of 1990, the resettlement areas were home to some 52,300 farming families on 3.3 million hectares, or ten percent of the agri-cultural land. A total of 426,000 people were recorded in the resettlement areas in 1992. Some 2.7 million hectares (eighty-two percent) of the reset-tlement land has been transferred from the former European large-scale commercial farming sector for redistribution to African peasant farmers over the past decade, while the remaining 0.6 million hectares was vacant state land that the government has used for resettlement purposes. The question of tenure in the resettlement areas remains unresolved to date and the settlers reside as tenants of the state. They are subject to close control and supervision of their land utilization practices by resident gov-ernment officials. Typically, these include both the resettlement officers and agricultural extension staff.

This chapter will focus on the communal and, to a lesser extent, the resettlement areas as it is in these two sectors that the writ of the state has left its biggest imprint on settlement patterns. In both large and small-scale commercial farming areas, the settlement patterns have been deter-mined mainly by the system of land tenure, while the density in any given area is influenced by the size of farm holdings (Figure 11.2). In addition, planning regulations against the unauthorized subdivision of commercial agricultural land have ensured against large increases in population and settlement densities in these areas. In the large-scale farming sector, settlements are generally widely dispersed. On each farm

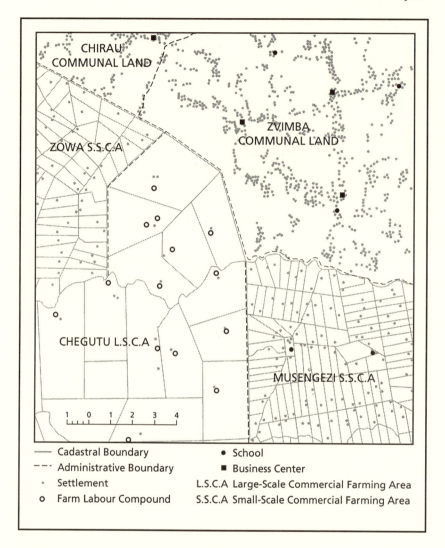

FIGURE 11.2   Rural Settlement Patterns West of Harare
Source: Redrawn from the Marwa (1730 C3) 1:50000 Map Series, Surveyor-General (Harare, Zimbabwe 1982).

are found spacious farmsteads and associated farm buildings as well as clusters of small huts (or compounds) that accommodate the farm laborers. Although settlements in the small-scale farm sector are also dispersed, densities are higher because of the smaller sizes of holdings. On each farm are generally found just the farmstead and associated buildings without a workers' compound, as most African small-scale commercial farmers use family rather than hired labor.

Shortly after independence, the Department of Physical Planning proposed a seven-tier national hierarchy of settlements for purposes of planning and investment (Gasper 1988; Wekwete 1989). The hierarchy comprises (1) cities, (2) towns, (3) growth points, (4) district service centers, (5) rural service centers, (6) business centers and (7) proposed consolidated villages (the latter being above the present villages and dispersed homesteads). `Growth points' strictly refer to some ten or so centers that are expected to develop into new towns in the near future. They typically possess an important resource base, capable of stimulating economic growth such as a large irrigation scheme or mineral deposit (Sibanda 1985). Growth points, therefore, rank above the fifty-five district service centers which are the administrative capitals of the communal areas districts, although it is possible for a district service center to also qualify as a growth point. Government infrastructural investment has been focussed on upgrading facilities at the growth points and district service centers. Below these are some 450 rural service centers and another 2,500 small business centers serving the rural population in the communal areas. At the lowest level, the Department of Physical Planning proposed the establishment of consolidated villages which will replace the existing linear and dispersed settlements in the communal areas. This paper is concerned primarily with rural settlements below the level of growth points.

Two sets of factors have left an almost indelible mark on rural settlement patterns in Zimbabwe (Zinyama 1988). The first set lies in the political history of the country from the time of European colonization in 1890. A series of laws were introduced by the colonial government which, until the attainment of political independence in 1980, discriminated against the majority African population. Colonial policies and laws set the framework for settlement patterns found in those areas that were reserved for occupation by Africans. A second important factor that has influenced settlement patterns in the communal areas is the rapid increase in population during the past half century. The increase has been caused by both the high rates of natural growth and the forced relocation of the indigenous population from alienated lands into the reserves. Growing population pressures in the communal areas have led to increasing land shortage and the expansion of settlement into areas previously reserved for livestock grazing. The post-colonial government has attempted to alleviate the problem of over-population within the communal areas by resettling some of the people on former European-owned, large-scale farms.

Population Growth and Land Use Changes

Until the early part of this century, land was generally abundant and population densities were low over much of tropical Africa. In Zimbabwe, the indigenous people lived in both dispersed homesteads and small villages of not more than a few hundred inhabitants each, taking advantage of the diverse resources-- soils, water, flora, fauna, and security--provided by their physical environments (Beach 1990). They practiced either shifting cultivation or bush fallowing which, given their limited technology and tools, left few permanent scars on the landscape.

The imposition of colonial rule at the end of the nineteenth century involved the demarcation of new national and sub-national boundaries that were used to control the movement of people and their use of land resources. In addition, in cases like Zimbabwe and Kenya, colonization was accompanied by the large-scale alienation of land for European settlement. Consequently, the amount of land available for agriculture and other uses by the indigenous population was greatly reduced. In the following decades, population has grown and larger numbers of people now have to be supported on this reduced land area, with significant implications for settlement patterns.

In Zimbabwe, the African population, which has comprised no less that ninety-five percent of the total population since colonization, increased from an estimated 700,000 in 1901 to three million in 1954 and 7.4 million in 1982. At present, nearly sixty percent of the African population live in the communal farming areas where approximately 30-35,000 new households are being added annually. Kay (1975) estimated that by 1969, fifty-seven percent of the communal farming areas were already overpopulated or grossly overpopulated. Yet, they still absorbed fifty-nine percent of the 3.7 million increase in population between 1962 and 1982, compared with thirty percent who were absorbed in the urban areas and a mere eleven percent in the former European-owned, commercial farming areas (Zinyama and Whitlow 1986). The average amount of land per capita in the communal farming areas decreased from nineteen hectares in 1931 to a mere four hectares in 1982.

The deteriorating man-land ratio, combined with the implementation of colonial government policies, forced the African population to change to a more permanent system of agriculture around their settlements during the first few decades of this century. Unfortunately, the change in land use was not accompanied by a compensating increase in agricultural productivity per unit of land, mainly because African farmers were discriminated against by the colonial administration which sought to protect the agricultural commodities markets and support services for the exclusive benefit of European settler farmers (Ndlela 1981; Zinyama 1986). The adoption of a permanent system of agriculture and the resultant loss of fallow led to a decline in soil fertility and a reduction in crop yields. Faced with a deteriorating man-land ratio, impoverished soils, and a rapidly growing population, farmers in the communal areas have responded by bringing more land under cultivation, including agriculturally marginal land on steep slopes and along watercourses (Whitlow and Zinyama 1988; Zinyama 1988). At the same time, there has been a decline in the supply of fuelwood, the primary energy source in the peasant rural areas.

The problems of land degradation in the subsistence farming sector have received considerable attention during the past decade as the now independence government grapples with the task of developing these previously neglected areas (Mutizwa-Mangiza and Helmsing 1987; Zinyama 1986). A number of national and sub-national surveys on changes in rural land use and settlement patterns and on land degradation have been conducted during the past decade (e.g., Munzwa 1979; Whitlow 1988; Whitlow and Zinyama 1988; Zinyama 1988).

State Policies Affecting Rural Settlement Patterns

The apportionment of land by race, which started with the establishment of the first two African reserves in north-western Zimbabwe in 1894, was institutionalized in the Land Apportionment Act of 1930 and culminated in the Land Tenure Act of 1969 (Christopher 1971; Floyd 1962). Under the latter Act, land was divided equally between the two principal races, with Europeans (including Asians) having exclusive right to 46.6 percent of the land area, Africans another 46.6 percent, while the remaining 6.8 percent was designated national parks and forest lands. The notion of racial equality in the distribution of land did not take into account the wide disparities in the quality of the land allocated to each group. Thus, much of the land made available for Africans was situated in the ecologically marginal areas where the light sandy soils (derived from granite parent rock) are inherently infertile and rainfall is both inadequate and unreliable for rain-fed crop cultivation (Roder 1964; Vincent and Thomas 1962). But the influence of government during both the colonial and post-colonial periods has not been confined to the broad allocation or re-distribution of land between the races. A variety of laws and policies have, over several decades, influenced the distribution of people and settlements in rural Zimbabwe (Table 11.1). These policies and their impact on settlement patterns are discussed in the following paragraphs.

The alienation of land for European settlement and the subsequent eviction of Africans from the alienated lands, precipitated land degradation within the reserves. The impending crisis did not go unnoticed by the authorities. However, the official position was that land degradation was the result, not of land shortage and increasing population pressure in the reserves, but of backward and wasteful farming practices on the part of the Africans (Whitlow 1988). In 1926, an American missionary-agriculturist, D.E. Alvord, was appointed the first director of the newly established Department of Native Agriculture, a position that he was to occupy for the next twenty-three years until his retire- ment in 1949. The primary task of the department was to get African farmers to adopt prescribed soil conservation practices, with extension staff (supported by district administrators) often resorting to compulsion in order to implement these measures.

One of Alvord's initiatives has had an impact on rural areas that has lasted to the present. This was the launching, in 1929, of a program to rationalize settlement and land uses in the African reserves and so put a stop to the practice of shifting cultivation. The effect of rationalization, or "centralization" as it was called, was to replace the traditional dispersed and clustered arrangement of rural people with linear settlements that separated large consolidated blocks of arable and grazing lands throughout the communal areas of the country. The long lines of settlements, usually running parallel to the rivers and watercourses, were located between the arable land above and the wet grazing areas below. This arrangement allowed for crops to be protected from stray livestock during the growing season (November-April); in the dry season the animals were allowed to roam freely and graze on crop residues.

The reorganization of settlements within the communal areas continued for the next two decades and was ultimately incorporated into law with the passing of the Natural Resources Act of 1941 and the Native Land Husbandry Act of 1951 (Beck 1960; Floyd 1959; Yudelman 1964). One function of the Native Land Husbandry Act was to provide for the reallocation of land in the communal areas but only to those families who were cultivating at the time the law was enacted. As a result, people who were absent from an area undergoing reallocation, including migrant workers in urban employment, would cease to have any right to land.

TABLE 11.1: Chronology of Legislative and Policy Landmarks in the Evolution of Rural Settlements in Zimbabwe

1890 Colonization of the country by the British South Africa Company
1894 First African reserves established in the north-west
1926 D.E. Alvord appointed Director of Native Agriculture
1929 Program of `centralization' launched
1930 Land Apportionment Act passed into law
1941 Natural Resources Act passed
1949 Alvord retires as Director of Native Agriculture
1951 Native Land Husbandry Act passed
1955 Implementation of the Land Husbandry Act accelerated
1964 Implementation of the Land Husbandry Act abandoned
1967 Tribal Trust Land Act passed
1969 Land Tenure Act passed
1972 War for independence begins to intensify
1980 Political independence achieved
1980 District Councils Amendment Act passed
1982 Communal Land Act passed

Secondly, wetland cultivation was prohibited because tillage of these lowlying areas was thought to be one of the major causes of soil erosion and the silting of rivers. Communal area farmers had traditionally culti-vated alluvial flats and wetlands under dry season (May-November) crops (e.g., green mealies and rice) and vegetables gardens, as well as practicing ridge cultivation of an artichoke-like edible tuber (*Coleus esculentus*), thereby adding to the overall quantity and variety of the house-hold food supplies.

The Act of 1951 also proposed to change the system of tenure from communal to individual ownership. Land would become a marketable commodity, but with prohibitions on sub-division below a designated minimum size per household (Floyd 1959; Yudelman 1964). The only exception was that widows--as well as second and subsequent wives of polygamous men--were allocated one-third of the standard arable hold-ing. Implementation of the Act began in earnest in 1955 and continued until 1964 when the government was compelled to abandon the program because of mounting opposition from the African population and bur-geoning nationalist movements.

In the years following the unilateral declaration of independence (UDI) by the white minority government in 1965, an attempt was made to introduce a modified form of the South African policy of apartheid under the guise of implementing a community development approach to rural development. Traditional African leaders who were acceptable to the authorities were given the power to run these programs in the local areas (Bratton 1978; Mutizwa-Mangiza 1985). A number of administrative functions, as well as the provision of services and infrastructure, were devolved to chiefs and inadequately funded district councils in the communal areas.

One devolved responsibility was the allocation of communal area land. Under the Tribal Trust Land Act of 1967, this function was legally transferred from the government-appointed district commissioners and trained agricultural extension staff to the chiefs and other traditional leaders of the Tribal Land Authorities (Henderson 1977). In practice, land allocation by the chiefs was not always based on sound ecological and conservation principles. Chiefs and members of the Tribal Land Authorities were also accused of taking bribes and showing favoritism in land allocation. A few of the chiefs, not wishing to be associated with the politically unpopular land policies, made little attempt to prevent the extension of cultivation and settlement onto land that had previously been designated for grazing purposes.

The mid-1960s were, therefore, a turning point in the state-guided evolution of settlement and land use patterns in the communal areas of Zimbabwe (Henderson 1977; Whitlow and Zinyama 1988; Zinyama 1988). The period marks the beginning of the partial breakdown of, and departure from, the strictly controlled and planned linear settlement patterns that had been implemented since the time of Alvord. Unauthorized cultivation and settlement became more marked from the mid 1970s as the war for independence intensified in the rural areas. Both the traditional chiefs (many of whom were regarded as collaborators by the nationalist guerillas) and the civilian district administrators found it increasingly difficult to maintain control over the illegal clearance of land within the communal areas. Many families, especially recently established, landless households, chose to clear grazing areas for cultivation away from the main linear villages. They were responding to the deteriorating man-land ratio, a local administrative structure that was more pre-occupied with the anti-guerilla campaign than with civil administration, and overworked and impoverished soils in the officially designated arable lands.

For some time after independence in 1980, it was not clear who was responsible for land allocation, and hence the resultant settlement and land use patterns in the communal areas. The choice was between the Tribal Land Authorities as prescribed under the Tribal Trust Land Act of 1967 (as amended in 1979) and the newly established democratic local government structures. New legislation, the District Councils Amendment Act of 1980, only prescribed that district councils could be given powers to act as conservation committees and be responsible for natural resources conservation within their areas of jurisdiction. Legally therefore, responsibility for land allocation was still in the hands of the by now ineffectual and largely discredited traditional chiefs. The Tribal Trust Land Act was finally repealed in 1982 following the enactment of the Communal Land Act (1982). This legislation gave the right to allocate communal land for agriculture and residences to the new, democratically elected district councils.

A number of researchers have examined the impact of population growth and state legislation on patterns of settlement and land use in the communal areas, both during the implementation of the Native Land Husbandry Act (Beck 1960; Floyd 1959; Hamilton 1965) and more recently in the post-independence period (Whitlow and Zinyama 1988; Zinyama 1988). In a study of Zimunya communal land south of the eastern border town of Mutare, Whitlow and Zinyama (1988) reported that in 1949, two-thirds of the area was still unsettled, twenty-three percent had densities of less than ten settlements per km^2, while less than one percent had densities in excess of thirty settlements per km^2. By 1981, only thirteen percent of Zimunya, mainly the very steep slopes, was still unsettled, eighteen percent of the area had densities of less than ten settlements per km^2 while the proportion of the area with densities in excess of thirty per km^2 had increased to twenty-eight percent. Although vestiges of the old linear pattern established in the 1950s are still evident, there has been considerable dispersal since 1963, resulting in a landscape comprising a mix of linear, dispersed, and clustered settlements (Whitlow and Zinyama 1988).

The transfer of responsibility for the allocation of land to popularly elected local authorities has, however, not solved the problems of illegal settlement in the communal areas. Throughout these areas, newly established families face the choice of either remaining landless or clearing fields for cultivation on land that was previously set aside for grazing. In response to the problems of landlessness and land degradation, the government, in the 1980s, adopted a two-pronged approach based on the reorganization and rationalization of rural land uses and village re-grouping within the communal areas, and land re-distribution and peasant resettlement on former European-owned commercial farmlands.

The village re-grouping program, which started in the mid-1980s and is still in the pilot stage, is intended to provide for more efficient utilization of land, to curtail unplanned and illegal extension of settlement into marginal and grazing lands, and to facilitate the siting of potable water supplies within easy access of the villagers, particularly in low rainfall regions (Republic of Zimbabwe 1987b; Republic of Zimbabwe 1986). The program involves the consolidation of the dispersed and linear settlements into nucleated villages and the demarcation of arable lands including their separation from communal grazing areas. Village re-grouping is voluntary and implemented only after extensive consultations and with the consent of every household in a locality. The villagers are also encouraged to fence their grazing areas into paddocks in order to improve the quality of their pastures and enable them to practice rotational grazing as well as generally improving their livestock husbandry methods. Since the program began in the mid-1980s, a number of pilot projects have been started in several parts of the country where the local communities have chosen to reorganize their land use patterns with the assistance of government planning officers. By mid-1987, re-grouping was in progress in fifty-nine villages in different provinces throughout the country (Republic of Zimbabwe 1987c).

Unlike the Tanzanian situation where the centralized Ujamaa villages established in the 1970s became the focus of service provision by the government, the principal emphasis of the village re-grouping program in Zimbabwe is on checking the environmental degradation caused by inefficient land utilization within the communal areas. The provision of services in the rural areas is not focussed at the village level but at district and rural service centers as outlined in the following section.

Development of Rural Service Centers

A number of strategies have been adopted by the government since independence to stimulate development within communal areas. These include the improvement of agricultural production and productivity (of both land and labor); raising on-farm incomes through the sale of agricultural surpluses; and the provision of social and economic infrastructure such as agricultural marketing facilities, transport and communications, health and sanitation services, and water supplies. Attention is also being given to the creation of rural off-farm employment in order to reduce the level of rural-urban migration (Helmsing 1987; Sibanda 1985). To this end, the government, in February 1987, gazetted fifty-six district service centers as "growth centers," one in each of the districts into which the communal areas are divided for administrative purposes. These designated places not only serve as the local district administrative capitals, but also as locations at which a variety of economic and social services can be provided by the government, non-governmental organizations, and private investors.

Although the formal designation of these growth centers only came in 1987, a number of incentives in the form of tax concessions and capital investment allowances have been available since 1981 to investors wishing to develop commercial and industrial enterprises at rural centers

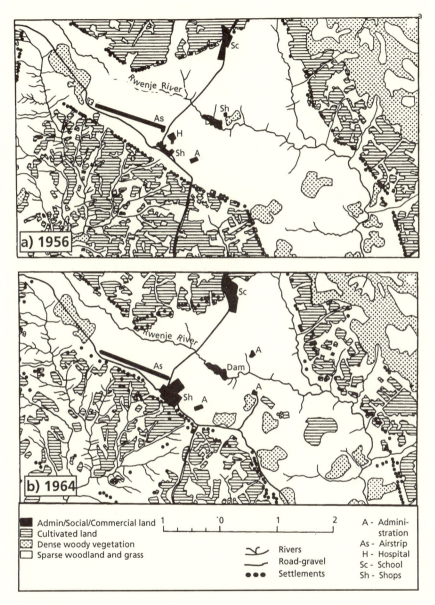

FIGURE 11.3 Changes in Settlement and Land Use in Part of Save North
Communal Area
Source: Adapted from L. Zinyama in *Erdkunde* (Band 42 1988) pp. 55-58.
Reprinted by permission.

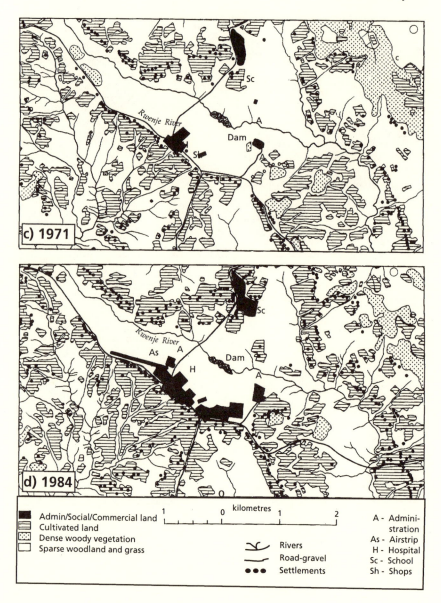

FIGURE 11.3 (cont'd.)
Source: Adapted from L. Zinyama in *Erdkunde* (Band 42 1988) pp. 55-58.
Reprinted by permission.

within the communal areas. A more recent addition to the package of incentives was legislation passed in early 1990 which allowed investors to acquire title to land at designated growth centers rather than having to lease land from local councils. Both current and potential investors in the communal areas had repeatedly complained that the absence of title to land, and therefore the lack of both collateral and security for one's investments, were inhibiting private sector investment at the rural centers.

During the past decade, the government has embarked on a program to develop and upgrade the infrastructure at these centers such as major and feeder roads, market stalls, bus termini, water reticulation, and, in some cases, connection to the national electricity grid. The centers are also intended to be the focal points for social and economic services such as secondary schools, clinics and district hospitals, agricultural marketing depots, and agro-industrial activities (Gasper 1988; Wekwete 1989). However, while the government's aim is the growth of local industries, economic activities at the rural service centers are still dominated by small-scale retailing and informal sector artisanal activities.

Several surveys have been carried out to assess the range of commercial activities at rural centers. According to one survey conducted in the mid-1980s in Mhondoro communal area south-west of Harare, general dealers accounted for twenty-six percent of all activities, liquor stores twelve percent, small diesel-operated maize grinding mills twelve percent, and butcheries eleven percent (cited in Wekwete 1988). In another survey of several centers located in different communal areas carried out shortly after independence by M. Gottlicher (reported in Helmsing 1987), forty-four percent of the activities were in general retailing, twenty percent were grain milling plants, followed by butcheries (ten percent) and liquor stores (nine percent).

However, a few centers located in regions of high agricultural potential have, in recent years, begun to attract investment by large, urban-based retail companies seeking to capitalize on the growing annual income flows to cash crop farmers (Zinyama 1990). Such centers include Gokwe, in the heart of the principal peasant cotton growing region north-west of Harare, and Murehwa, to the north-east of the capital. These favoured locations have other newly created advantages that make them attractive to private corporate investment, including high quality infrastructure (electricity, all-weather roads), banking facilities, and a large complement of middle income public administrative and service employees.

Communal Area Settlement Change: A Case Study

A study of part of Save North communal area around Sadza service center about 175 kilometers southeast of Harare by Zinyama (1988) will be used to demonstrate the changes in settlement patterns that have occurred in one area over the period 1956 to 1984. The case study shows clearly the effect of the interplay of government policies and increasing population pressures (as outlined above) on rural settlement. It is based on data obtained after systematic comparative mapping from panchromatic aerial photographs of the area taken in 1956 (the earliest photographic coverage of the area), 1964, 1971 and 1984, each date more or less coinciding with major government policy directions.

By 1956, "centralization" had been completed in Save North, producing the distinct linear settlements that separated large blocks of arable and grazing lands on either side (Figure 11.3a). Areas of broken relief, particularly in the extreme northeast and southwest, were devoid of settlement or cultivation in conformity with Alvord's strict conservation and land use control measures. These controls were tightened further during the late 1950s and early 1960s when the Native Land Husbandry Act was being implemented in the area. Thus, by 1964, the only intrusion of settlement and cultivation into areas officially designated for grazing had occurred about two kilometers east of Sadza business center where a small religious sect had been permitted to establish a settlement and some fields (Figure 11.3b). The years 1964-1971 mark a transitional period during which government was devolving direct control over the allocation and utilization of land within the communal areas. At this point, the traditional chiefs and the tribal land authorities still exerted some control over settlement patterns. Nonetheless, changes in settlement and land use did occur within the study area during this period.

By 1971, cultivation and settlement had extended quite substantially into areas previously designated for grazing, particularly to the east of the business center where former arable lands were being abandoned on the grounds that their soils had become impoverished due to prolonged cultivation (Figure 11.3c). A more dispersed settlement pattern was being superimposed onto the original linear pattern. Dispersal was even more marked by 1984, mainly as a result of uncontrolled encroachment during the late 1970s and after independence (Figure 11.3d). Another significant change since 1980 has been the extension of the area used for administrative and social purposes. The local business center was designated the district administrative center and now provides a wide range of newly decentralized government services and commercial functions. This has resulted in a threefold increase in the extent of its built-up area between 1971 and 1984. Overall, 350 hectares at the center have been excised from communal to state land for commercial, industrial, administrative, non-farm residential, and other uses. North of the center, the area set aside for educational purposes has also expanded with the establishment of a secondary school adjacent to the primary school.

Rural Land Redistribution and Settlement Change

The resettlement program represents a significant redistribution of the African population and alteration of rural settlement patterns by the state in areas that had previously been alienated for European use. The government has sought to avoid the problems that arise from unplanned and haphazard land resettlement. Instead, rigorous formal procedures have been adopted in the implementation of the resettlement program. These include the identification and purchase of the land, the assessment of appropriate agricultural land uses and agronomic practices for each scheme, the siting of village settlements, the selection of settlers, the provision of economic and social infrastructure (boreholes, schools, clinics, roads, and shops), and so forth. As a result, the low population densities and dispersed settlements of the former European commercial farmlands have, upon resettlement, been transformed into higher densities with nucleated villages (Zinyama and Whitlow 1986; Zinyama 1986).

The more popular plan for this program is known as Intensive Resettlement Model A. Under this particular model, each settler family is allocated an individual arable holding of five to eight hectares (depending on the ecological conditions in the area), communal grazing for a specified small number of livestock (again according to the carrying capacity of the area), as well as a residential stand of 0.25 hectares in a nucleated village. Thus, in the Umfurudzi resettlement scheme northeast of Harare, twenty-two former large commercial farms covering a total of 35,823 hectares (an average of 1,628 hectares per farm), plus another 18,889 hectares of vacant state land, were resettled in the early 1980s with 563 families in twenty villages, plus two co-operative settler farms (Figure 11.4) (Republic of Zimbabwe 1981a; Manyara 1983). At the Chinyika scheme near Headlands, mid-way between Harare and Mutare in the east, eighty-one commercial farms totalling 113,752 hectares were resettled with 3,984 families in 103 nucleated villages. In addition, the scheme, has been provided with twenty primary schools, four secondary schools, and eight service centers (Republic of Zimbabwe 1981b; Republic of Zimbabwe 1987a).

It should be notes that the government has extensively utilized village resettlement, a strategy that has caused problems elsewhere in Africa. The prognosis for the Zimbabwe program is more encouraging,

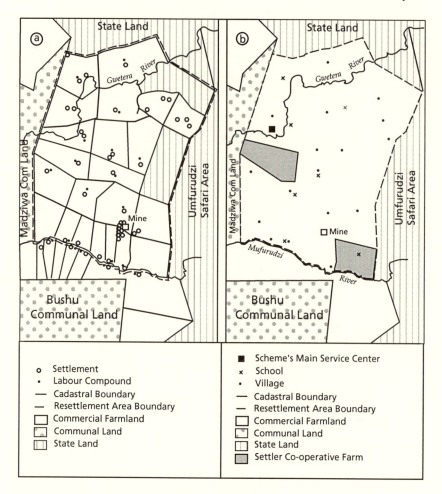

Figure 11.4 Settlement in the Unfurudzi Area, Northeast of Harare:
a) Before Resettlement; b) After Resettlement; during 1981-1982
Source: Redrawn from the Zimbabwe National Map Series 1:50000
Survryor General (Harare, Zinbabwe 1982).

however, for several reasons: (1) Village building efforts seem to be moving forward at a pace commensurate with the resources available, (2) participation is completely voluntary, and, perhaps most important, (3) the siting and design of villages reflects thorough surveys and an effort to match the number of settlers and their farming systems to the environmental constraints of the surrounding area.

Concluding Remarks

The chapter has examined the evolution of rural settlement patterns in each of the four agricultural sub-sectors of Zimbabwe, with particular focus on the communal and resettlement areas. It is clear that the state has had a major impact on rural settlement patterns in the country since colonization in 1890. This is evident at the macro-scale in terms of national legislation, the division of land between the races, and the determination of broad tenure systems applicable to each sub-sector. At the local level, state influence has affected land use and conservation practices as well as the siting and structure of village settlements and service centers.

It has also been observed that both colonial and post-colonial governments have sought to manipulate and change settlement patterns, albeit for very different reasons. During the colonial period, changes in settlement patterns reflected the overall government policy to control the African population and to subjugate African interests to those of European settlers. After independence, changes in settlement patterns form part of the government's strategy to develop the previously neglected African rural areas and to raise living standards for the majority of the population who live there.

References

Beach, D. N. 1990. "The Early History of Harare to 1890." *Heritage* 9: 5-27.

Beck, J. H. 1960. "Yafele's Kraal: A Sample Study of African Agriculture in Southern Rhodesia." *Geography* 45: 68-78.

Bratton, M. 1978. *Beyond Community Development - The Political Economy of Rural Administration in Zimbabwe.* From Rhodesia to Zimbabwe Series, No.6. Gwelo, Zimbabwe: Mambo Press.

Christopher, A. J. 1971. "Land Tenure in Rhodesia." *South African Geographical Journal* 53: 39-52.

Floyd, B. N. 1959. "Changing Patterns of African Land Use in Southern Rhodesia." *Rhodes-Livingston Journal* 25: 20-39.

_____. 1962. "Land apportionment in Southern Rhodesia." *Geographical Review* 52: 566-582.

Gasper, D. 1988. "Rural Growth Points and Rural Industries in Zimbabwe: Ideologies and Policies." *Development and Change* 19: 425-466.

Hamilton, P. 1965. "Population Pressure and Land Use in Chiweshe Reserve." *Rhodes-Livingstone Journal* 36: 40-58.

Helmsing, A.H.J. 1987. "Rural Industries and the Communal Lands Economy in Zimbabwe." *Tijdschrift voor Economische en Sociale Geografie* 78: 139-150.

Henderson, H.J.R. 1977. "Legislation and Land Use Planning in Rhodesia: an Example of Recent Landscape Evolution in the Nkai Tribal Trust Land." *Swansea Geographer* 15: 56-60.

Kay, G. 1975. "Population Pressures and Development Prospects in Rhodesia." *Rhodesia Science News* 9: 7-13.

Manyara, A. S. 1983. "A Study of the Umfurudzi Resettlement Scheme." Unpublished BA dissertation, Department of Geography, University of Zimbabwe, Harare.

Munzwa, K. 1979. "Household Demand for Woodfuel Resources - A Study of Land Use Patterns and the Problem of Deforestation in Ndanga." Unpublished BA dissertation, Department of Geography, University of Rhodesia, Salisbury.

Mutizwa-Mangiza, N. D. 1985. *Community Development in Pre-Independence Zimbabwe - A Study of Policy with Reference to Rural Land.* Supplement to *Zambezia.* Harare: University of Zimbabwe.

Mutizwa-Mangiza, N. D. and A.H.J. Helmsing, eds. 1991. *Rural Development and Planning in Zimbabwe.* Avebury: Aldershot.

Ndlela, D. B. 1981. *Dualism in the Rhodesian Colonial Economy.* Economic Studies No. 22. Lund: University of Lund.

Republic of Zimbabwe. Department of Conservation and Extension. 1981a. *Umfurudzi Intensive Resettlement Area, Shamva District - Final Project Report.* Harare: Government Printer.

_____. Department of Conservation of Extension. 1981b. *Preliminary Project Report: Chinyika Intensive Resettlement Area.* Harare: Government Printer.

Republic of Zimbabwe. 1981c. *Growth with Equity: An Economic Policy Statement.* Harare: Government Printer

_____. 1982. *Transitional National Development Plan, 1982/83-1984/85.* Harare: Government Printer.

_____. 1986. *First Five-Year National Development Plan, 1986-1990.* Harare: Government Printer.

_____. Department of Rural Development. 1987a. *Chinyika Resettlement Scheme - 17th. Quarterly Progress Report.* January-March. Mutare: Government Printer.

_____. Ministry of Local Government. 1987b. *Report on the National Symposium on Agrarian Reform in Nyanga, Zimbabwe.* October 19-23. Harare: Department of Rural Development and FAO.

_____. 1987c. *Parliamentary Debates: House of Assembly.* August 19, 1987: 793-794.

Roder, W. 1964. "The Division of Land Resources in Southern Rhodesia." *Annals, Association of American Geographers* 54: 41-52.

Sibanda, B. M. C. 1985. "Growth Points - A Focus for Rural Development in Zimbabwe." *Agricultural Administration* 19: 161-174.

Vincent, V. and R. G. Thomas. 1962. *An Agricultural Survey of Southern Rhodesia.* Government Printer: Salisbury.

Wekwete, K. H. 1988. "Rural Growth Points in Zimbabwe - Prospects for the Future." *Journal of Social Development in Africa* 3: 5-16.

_____. 1989. "Growth Centre Policy in Zimbabwe." *Tijdschrift voor Economische en Sociale Geografie* 80: 131-146.

Whitlow, R. 1988. *Land Degradation in Zimbabwe: A Geographical Study.* Harare: Natural Resources Board.

Whitlow, R. and L. Zinyama. 1988. "Up hill and Down Vale: Farming and Settlement Patterns in Zimunya Communal Land." *Geographical Journal of Zimbabwe* 19: 29-45.

Yudelman, M. 1964. *Africans on the Land.* Cambridge: Harvard University Press.

Zinyama, L. M. 1986. "Agricultural Development Policies in the African Farming Areas of Zimbabwe." *Geography* 71: 105-115.

_____. 1988. "Changes in Settlement and Land Use Patterns in a Subsistence Agricultural Economy: A Zimbabwe Case Study, 1956-1984." *Erdkunde* 42: 49-59.

_____. 1990. "Retail Sector Responses to Changing Markets in Zimbabwe: Some Geographical Perspectives." *Geographical Journal of Zimbabwe* 21: 32-49.

Zinyama, L. M. and R. Whitlow. 1986. "Changing Patterns of Population Distribution in Zimbabwe." *GeoJournal* 13: 365-384.

Zinyama, L., D. J. Campbell, and T. Matiza. 1990. "Land Policy and Access to Land in Zimbabwe: The Dewure Resettlement Scheme." *Geoforum* 21: 359-370.

12

The Political Economy of Spatial Rationalization and Integregation Policies in Tanzania

Richard J. Massaro

Settlement structure has been a core element of Tanzania's development policy. Specifically, villagization, a mandate that all rural inhabitants live in formally constituted nodalized villages, was a key to modernization, development, and "nation-building" strategies. Together with administrative decentralization, Regional Development Programs (RIDEPs), national industrial location planning in a settlement and service center hierarchy, villagization was to be a major tool in postcolonial institutional, economic, and spatial restructuring within the Ujamaa framework. The aim was to modernize the traditional sector, replace colonial structures that fostered social and spatial inequity, and build a unified, integrated society and territory able to meet its own development needs. Implementation prompted controversy. Villagization was denounced as forced resettlement and blamed for agricultural disruption that contributed to a national economic crisis. On the other hand, it was credited with increasing literacy and life expectancy, reducing infant and child mortality, and improving the provision of productive inputs and services.

The use of settlement structure in development strategies raises questions of villagization's theoretical and practical soundness and the question of how crucial spatial issues are to development. This study addresses those issues by reviewing villagization's origins and aims within Tanzania's overall development agenda and by assessing villagization's contributions to Tanzania's development progress and problems, with examples from Arusha and Tanga Regions. However, depicting the scope, scale, and nature of policy intent and implementation first requires a review of the context of settlement intervention: mainland Tanzanian environments and the ways peoples interacted with and appropriated those environments, forming traditional socio-economic

and settlement systems. Villagization policy was conceived and implemented not in abstract space but over specific widely diverse ecological
formations that were the material basis for similarly diverse indigenous
settlements. What Tanzania aimed to alter was an array of formations
shaped by local environmental conditions and social processes, then variously altered by mercantilism, colonialism, and articulation into national and international structures.

The argument of this chapter is that space is socially constructed.
While environmental factors have always significantly affected where
and how densely people settled and established production systems,
populations, in turn, have altered the landscape and created spatial formations and structures that also influence subsequent change. Setting
the context makes it clear that the implications of villagization were not
uniform, nor were implementation modes and outcomes. Differences
and similarities among groups and places illustrate critical issues in
defining the "development problem" and formulating policies. An examination of villagization aims and outcomes makes it clear that rural
restructuring is far more than a matter of relocating and reorganizing
homes and production sites. It involves intervening in political, economic, and cultural systems that are materially based and concretely
expressed in spatial structures.

The evidence suggests that economic outcomes were affected less by
villagization than by local ecologies, climate, and social formations, other
national policies, and the place of villages within broader spatial structures. Conversely, villagization seems to have been a major factor in
meeting other policy aims, including better access to educational and
health services, creating a national consciousness, establishing widespread and stable political institutions, and building a political and
administrative base for integrating small rural spatial units into a functional national whole. Tanzania's experience of spatial restructuring suggests that, while there can be no "spatial fix" to development problems,
spatial relations as concrete expressions of social and material relations
are a key element in defining opportunities and constraints for growth
and integration from the local to the national level.

Although many traditional systems conform to commonly understood types, significant variations or "intermediate types" warrant a note
on terminology. "Household" is the basic social unit. Nuclear households
consist of a husband and his wife or wives and their unmarried children
while joint/extended households consist of grouped nuclear households
locally defined as a single social unit (Hill 1986: 176). "Homestead" is the
spatial unit on which the household resides (living quarters, outbuild-
ings, and surrounding garden plots and livestock holding areas) distinct

from major production sites (farm fields, pastures, groves, fisheries, etc.). Finally, "settlement systems" refer to how people organize both residential and productive space as they locate homesteads in relation to each other and to household, communal, open, and unused production sites.

Types of settlement systems can be distinguished along two axes: degree of concentration from sparse to dense, and degree of nucleation, i.e., aggregation into formal functional units, from scattered to clustered. Another key factor in defining types is nodalization, the presence of a concentrated production site, leader's compound, or other functional space that serves as a pivotal location for identifying a distinct socio-spatial unit.

"Scattered" or "dispersed" and "clustered" settlement systems are relatively straightforward and have previously been discussed. The difficulty comes with settlements of mixed types. One is the "farmstead cluster village" with homesteads located within their own production sites but highly concentrated. Such homesteads are virtually contiguous, and identified as belonging to a distinct spatial and social entity, a village, spatially separated from other settlements. Another type is the "hamlet constellation village": small clusters of homesteads grouped into hamlets and a group of hamlets, identified as village sections, located within a larger demarcated area. Rather than further discussing types in the abstract, it seems more useful to review processes of settlement system formation and then demonstrate how differences in traditional settlement contributed to wide variations in both the implementation and the ultimate impact of the "villagization" process.

Environmental Contexts and Indigenous Social and Spatial Formations

Tanzania has arguably Africa's most diverse ecology.[1] Much of its topography is associated with The Great Rift. One Rift branch runs down western Tanzania, another through its center with a plateau between, part of which subsided to form Lake Victoria. Most of the remaining half of Tanzania varies from 1,000 to 1,500 meters above sea level. There are also volcanic mountains and highlands and other mountain blocks. Only Tanzania's annual bimodal rains are markedly uneven partly due to its elevated contours. These help produce quasi-regional rainfall variations by casting a "rainfall shadow," up to 200 kilometers wide, on a third of the plateau from Kenya to the Southern Highlands. As rains come in off the Indian Ocean the coastal triangle gets 800-1,000 mm of rain a year and highlands up to 1,400 mm or more. Levels on the plateau then drop below the minimum for agriculture until winds again gain moisture over the western lakes (Figure 12.1).

Varied topography, climate, and soil fertility made for very diverse ecologies. The overall Tanzanian pattern could be characterized as "a bowl of fairly harsh environments at the center, surrounded by a series of better-watered and relatively more fertile areas along the broken rim" (Sheriff 1980: 13). In general, highlands were forested while lowlands were mostly covered with grassland savanna. More specifically, fertile, well-drained savannas with good rain became miombo woodland while dry areas became wooded or bushed grassland. At the local scale, variations in drainage and fertility caused variations on these themes. For example, poor drainage led to infertility or mbuga grasslands in low-lying areas and salinity in some river basins and lake beds. Where there were poor soils, bushland and dense bush thickets evolved. Relief and soils could change markedly and abruptly so that diverse ecosystems were interspersed with each other.

Early humans harvested plants and game with stone tools. Technology and culture developed to exploit savannas and forest- fringes as Khoisan hunter-gatherers spread over Africa's savanna. Other regional cultures emerged: North Afro-Asiatic and Cushitic; Nilo-Saharan; and Niger-Congo, including "Proto-Bantu" who expanded east and south 2,500-4000 years ago as small groups broke off to begin colonies at highland margins.[2] Two millennia ago, Arab coastal traders brought bananas and iron-working, the crops and tools that gave access to fertile mountain forests areas.

By 500 A.D., Bantu had settled Kilimanjaro, Upare, and Usambara. Late in this Bantu expansion, Cushites and Nilotes came down the Rift. The dry grain farming of the Cushites and the pastoral technology of the Nilotes enabled Bantu to settle the savannas, assimilating or displacing most Khoisans. By 1700, except for Maasai migrations, 1700-1900, and Ngoni invasions, 1835-1850, ethnic distributions were set, with over eighty distinct Bantu groups; Nilotic Luo, Barbaig and Maasai; Cushitic Iraqw and Mbugu, and Khoisan, Sandawe, and others.

Small, mobile, hunter-gatherer bands could spread over vast areas but agriculture and pastoralism concentrated populations in areas with good soils and rains. The innovations made in these areas increased the capacity to produce food, made random harvesting secondary, and allowed for permanent settlement. Concentration also created needs for social control. Sukuma and Nyamwezi chose expansion, fragmentation and limited organization. Sons of chiefs led groups to colonize new areas of bush in return for livestock, grain, and labor tribute but social pressure to redistribute surplus limited class formation (Sheriff 1980). Settlement became a system of defined village organizations and distinct bound-

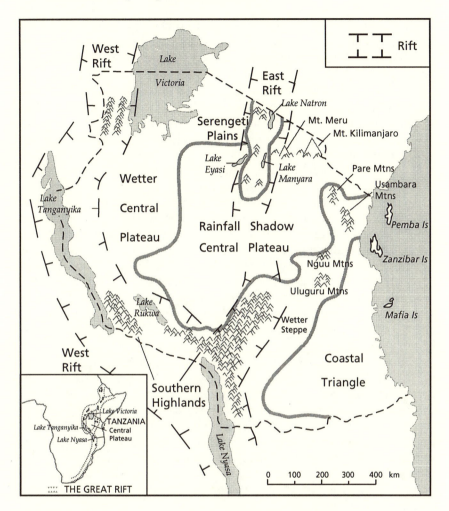

FIGURE 12.1 Topography and Climatic Regions of Tanzania

aries, within which lay dispersed homestead clusters, household farms, and communal pastures. Large villages were divided into age-set sections (Moore 1971), a settlement form termed here "hamlet constellation villages."

In the highlands with less room to expand, control of tools and weapons gave iron-working clans early dominance (Sheriff 1980). This situation had spatial impacts among the Shambaa, who became grouped by lineage and marriage into villages and neighborhoods for defense and trade. Internal trade drew Shambaa together across village and lineage affiliations; whole neighborhoods might rely on one or two iron-working centers (Feierman 1974: 79). As metallurgy spread, land control gained importance. By 1500, the Shambaa had permanent villages ringed with outlying hill plots. Villages were placed on mountain rims for defense while year-round food supplies were ensured by lowland and upland farms. The Shambaa traded with plains groups for famine insurance, and undertook lowland grazing to expand spatial and social links. A local chiefdom system emerged to ensure ecological and social stability as the population increased. By the 1600s, one chief had formed a Kingdom which later extended its domain to the plains and coast and, within 150 years, became a spatially integrated, centralized state (Feierman 1974; Cliffe 1977).

In northwest savannas with good rains but poor soils, Haya used manure and plant debris to manufacture soils and create a banana culture, usually limited to mountain environs (Schneider 1986). Royal clan chiefs appointed patrons to administer nyarabanja estates and allot plot access in return for crop and labor tribute. This set a patron-client relation between the ruling class and cultivators and integrated cultivators into a state system hierarchy of regional administrators rising to one ruler (Sheriff 1980). Haya formed compact villages of individual houses, each surrounded by permanent crops (Moore 1971), an example of "farmstead cluster villages."

In Mbulu, Iraqw based identity and social order on spatially defined relations. Adapting to highlands they could colonize and defend, they had ridge-top settlements, communal slope pastures, and household valley farm plots. Bounded homesteads on a ridge formed a community. Community-clusters formed sections of an *'aya,'* a space marked by natural features and delimited in annual rites to define spatial-social units within which people had mutual rights and duties. To enter or stay in an aya, members had to follow communal pasture and farming rules and social norms. "Territorial boundaries and social behavior are the criteria for membership, not birth, or even language" (Thornton 1980: 118).

Nearby, the rainfall shadow made rain marginal, groundwater

scarce, and soils shallow and needing long fallow. In vast grasslands inimical to farming, Barbaig and Tatoga pastoralists prospered, rotating grazing and sparsely scattered homesteads among seasonal pastures assigned by elders to clan, family, and friendship groups (Klima 1970). Maasai evolved large, autonomous clan territorial sections, with no ruling clan or central authority but with hierarchic male age sets across clans and sections. Elders controlled domestic and group decisions (Galaty 1981) and "transactions which circulate livestock and women within the community in order to ensure the reproduction of the community as a whole" (Rigby 1985: 161). The elders, in turn, formed homestead compounds, grouped into neighborhoods.

Where water sources permitted, irrigation-based systems evolved. Water from spring-fed ditches was allocated to Sonjo fields by a council of elders, the source of these springs kept secret by hereditary ritual leaders. Water distribution became a basis of social control in fortified villages located on slopes above the fields. In Pare, furrows dug by clan members took water from mountain streams to fields and to artificial ponds and a secondary furrow system was used for dry season irrigation. Clan-appointed elders oversaw upkeep and access (Yoshida 1985).

When water was widely available, it reinforced diffuse, loosely organized settlement. On Kilimanjaro, the Maasai blocked Chagga expansion onto the plains, fostering economic and political concentration, and dense, dispersed settlement. Crop rotation, fertilizing, and livestock stall-feeding intensified land use and canal networks made constant cultivation possible (Iliffe 1979).

A Bantu/Arab Swahili coastal culture based on farming, fishing, and some trade developed compact nucleated settlements which became the foundation for a network of port towns (Slater 1977; Sawers 1989). Many remaining mainland societies settled where local ecologies allowed for subsistence farming but not for the surplus to support extensive population increases, concentration, or stratification. For example, the Gogo on the semi-arid plateau, spread homestead clusters over wide areas in polycephalous, clan- based systems with production on individual family farms (Moore 1971; Thiele 1986a).

Ecology, technology, and social forces encouraged differentiation between groups and varied socio-spatial systems. The size and reliability of the surplus affected levels of labor division, social stratification, and political centralization (Sheriff 1980). When surpluses and resources (land, labor, water, etc.) became a "royal patrimony," it created a base for a centralized state (Shorter 1974). Four political forms evolved: (1) feudal--rulers controlled land, labor, or surplus; (2) tributary--mostly surplus control; (3) segmentary--little surplus, loose organization; and

Rural settlements varied in terms of density and relative concentration. Densities tended to be high in wet, fertile highlands and low where conditions dictated shifting cultivation and grazing. Concentration was, in part, a response to the environment. For example, where hillsides and valleys were best for production, homesteads would be clustered on ridge tops. Nucleation was also common among societies utilizing communal agricultural activities and resource management. Otherwise, settlement was scattered unless social factors or defense needs, prompted clustering. The detailed settlement types for farmers have already been described; pastoral types ranged from dispersed homesteads to compounds with varying degrees of clustering and mobility, while remnant hunter-gatherers remained nomads. Tanzania's social contours became as diverse as its physical features with over a hundred peoples in varied stages of creating national identities, state formations, and trade-based as well as other forms of internal and external relations.

Exogenous Factors: Trade and Colonization

External forces altered the indigenous development trajectories. By 1200 A.D., Arabs had formed coastal and offshore island settlements. The inland trade, based on iron and cloth for ivory, covered only short-distances into the 1600s but trade relations and routes grew via a slow widening of older networks dealing in food, livestock, iron, and salt (Slater 1977). Zanzibar became Oman's key outpost, yet trade remained marginal to the mainland until the 1800s when European and American expansion changed its scope.

As higher ivory demand pushed hunting and trade inland, Arabs built caravan posts. Trade control and tribute then became vital to chiefly wealth and power (as well as a base of conflict) and a trader class evolved among the Nyamwezi. Trade also stimulated food production for porters, coastal towns, and export, creating markets for metal hoes and expanding iron industries. In a similar way, coastal salt production was encouraged but indigenous textiles were virtually wiped out.[3]

These dynamics changed when slaves became the prime exports and firearms the major imports. Part of early trade, slaving grew in the 1600s to serve Omani plantations. In the 1700s, demand exploded with the establishment of French plantations on Mauritius and Reunion and Arab plantations on Zanzibar and Pemba. Slaving heightened old and created new conflicts and accelerated centralization trends already fed by early trade as well as the Maasai and Ngoni invasions. "By the time the Germans came, almost the whole country was divided between a small number of tribal empires with organized armies based on possession of firearms" (Coulson 1982: 17-18). Violence, increasing in scale and level of organization, caused political change, such as the replacement of ritual-hereditary rulers with military leaders. The Hehe, for example, built a southern empire based on military organization and "war medicine". Conversely, rival chiefs among the Shambaa, unable to raid better-armed neighbors, raided each other and their own subjects, and destroyed the Kingdom.

Trade inaugurated mainland integration into the international economy with Zanzibar as linchpin, controlling exports and import duties. A new hierarchy emerged: the Sultan; Indians financing inland expeditions; coastal leaders collecting customs; Arab inland traders; chiefs with trade control; African traders, slaver- hunters and porters; and those who grew crops, collected honey, copal, or rubber, and sometimes became slaves. The Sultan's policy made Africans "the porters, rather than the financiers or entrepreneurs, of the caravans to the coast" (Coulson 1982: 27). By 1880, most mainland economies were restructured around export trade. They traded surplus instead of retaining it for internal development, and relied on imported tools, textiles, and arms.

Trade, in turn, caused spatial change. Permanent market centers arose, often at traditional exchange places, "mostly on the plains so that wealth and power tended to shift from skilled agriculturalists to savannah peoples whose economies rested more on cattle, game, trade, or warfare" (Iliffe 1979: 69). Groups like the Zigua abandoned villages after finding that clustered settlement made them slave raid targets. Elsewhere, dispersed groups formed fortified villages as a form of defense. Settlement change reversed processes of bush colonization and ecosystem management. On the coast, "long-dormant towns were resuscitated and...new settlements sprang up...as coastal entrepots for the developing trade with the interior" (Slater 1977: 167). Trade turned paths of local exchange into long-distance lines of mercantile capital, with coastal termini linked to Zanzibar and beyond.

Colonialism "altered the pace and direction of change and forcibly wrested from Africans... (control) of their own evolution" (Temu 1980: 128). In 1891, Germany annexed the mainland in order to make it a source of raw materials and wealth, i.e., to restructure the regional economy, destroy Indian Ocean trade links, and replace internal commodity specialization and exchange with primary product export (Raikes 1978). The Germans set up forts and outposts, made subjugated chiefs and African-police their agents, and built roads and railways to speed extraction, administration, and troop movement. They levied taxes and required cash for taxes and imports as part of a plan to encourage Africans either to produce crops for cash or to work as laborers. Africans near towns, plantations, railways, or roads grew traditional or new crops for local through international markets. Those in remote or less fertile areas, collected beeswax and rubber or sold their labor to colonial enterprises.[4]

Germany pressed restructuring via settler farms, plantations, and peasant cash cropping. Plantation production, which had the highest priority, was based on extensive capital, land, labor, and a few non-African managers (Rodney 1980). Four plantation areas emerged: Tanga, Morogoro-Kilosa-Kilombero Valley, Moshi-Arusha, and Lindi. To supply labor, Germans set district quotas based on population, transport access, and cash crop capacity, making southern and some northwest and central areas into labor reserves. To exploit more land and labor, the Germans ordered chiefs to begin communal farms, but when fierce resistance undermined this approach, individual cash cropping was promoted instead (Coulson 1982). This tactic worked quite well; Chagga and other coffee growers were so successful, they competed with settlers and were forced to limit output. Africans also wanted to grow sisal, but European grower pressure kept it as a plantation crop.

Infrastructural development aided structural change and embedded it in the landscape. A rail and feeder road network replaced the nineteenth century economy's core (caravan routes, trade, and tribute) (Figure 12.2). This network raised extraction levels and intensified external dependence as local manufactures were replaced by imports. Last, it transformed the coast, a result of railroads concentrating exports at their termini. Tanga and Dar became the sole conduits from the entire interior directly to Germany, instead of being two in a system of port towns linked to hinterlands, each other, and Zanzibar. This destroyed the coast's complicated economy, causing large towns like Pangani and Bagamoyo to atrophy and small and mid-sized places to virtually disappear (Slater 1977).

Since Europeans focused on the most densely populated, prosperous areas, productivity and wealth became even more concentrated. Less favored areas produced migrant workers who were paid low wages and thus had little to invest at home to counter increasing backwardness (Cliffe 1977; Rodney 1980). Colonialism also skewed development by promoting export crops, neglecting production for domestic markets, and encouraging Indian rather than African traders. Imports disrupted traditional trade and were a particularly negative influence on local iron and textile industries (Raikes 1978).

Indigenous factors also affected change. Some groups passively resisted tax, labor, and crop laws. Others used cash crops to meet colonial demands and still maintain territory, cultural integrity and limited

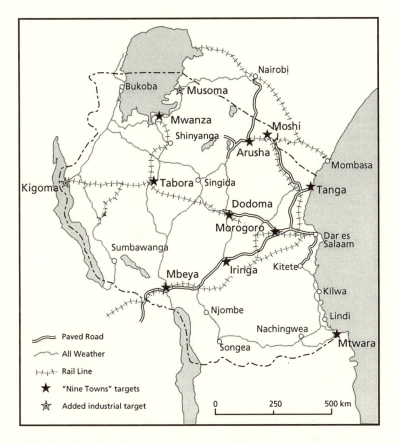

Figure 12.2   Tanzanian Ground Transportation and Urban Infrastructure, in 1990

economic autonomy. In a few cases, old structures were put to new advantage. In 1913, six Chagga chiefs each owned over a thousand coffee trees and, by 1930, five royal clan members had sixty percent of all the trees, although there were over 2,540 coffee growers in the region. As for pastoralists, the colonial government aimed at containment more than exploitation, confining herders to "ludicrously inadequate" reserves where they preserved traditional life at a cost of contracted territory and marginalization (Iliffe 1979).

Colonial spatial specialization and inequality produced four types of regions based, in turn, on (1) peasant cash-crops, (2) estates and plantations that produced crops for export with imported labor, (3) labor reserves, and (4) a peripheral role and location. Mainland areas and peoples were selectively articulated into European capitalism with some being deliberately disarticulated, removed from circuits of colonial development, and blocked from advancing on their own (Figures 12.2 and 12.3).

These divisions continued after World War I when the mainland was entrusted to the British. The new government extended rail and road systems, expanded plantations, and promoted settler estates and capital intensive projects like the Groundnut Scheme. Although peasant cash crops and, later, progressive farmers were encouraged, labor reserves were still maintained and African access to resources and marketing was limited. "Indirect rule" seemed to restore some power to traditional leaders but kept real power in expatriate hands. It also fostered elite formation, as did African incorporation into colonial education and the civil service. These trends were actually reinforced by the cooperative movement, whose leaders were part of an elite that had ousted Asian marketing monopolies.[5]

One policy change of the British period was to stress erosion control. Some officials understood the relationship between erosion and externally induced problems that had ruined the traditional systems/environment equilibrium, but others blamed erosion on traditional farming and grazing methods (Rapp et al. 1972; Watson 1972). Colonial policy advocated technical solutions which Africans resisted since "the agricultural and economic logic behind many of the rules was wrong" (Coulson 1982: 53). Programs designed to control the tsetse fly were equally biased and ineffective. The British built village settlement schemes, purportedly to protect against sleeping sickness and foster development, but the underlying goal proved to be the securing of labor for the Groundnut Scheme, mining ventures, and conservation (Kjekshus 1977). The settlements achieved neither purported or real aims and were eventually abandoned.

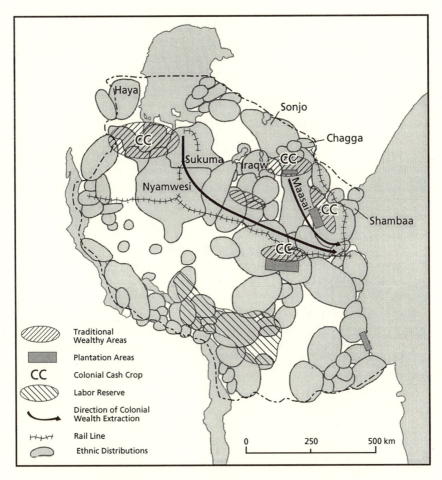

Figure 12.3   Traditional Ethnicity and Wealth and Colonial Restructuring Effects (1895 - 1945)

Roots of Villagization Policy

The drive towards Tanzanian independence was led by three fac-
tions: (1) civil servants and teachers from throughout the territory who
were associated with Nyerere, (2) the co-operatives, which had an economic base, but which were spatially and ethnically concentrated, and (3)
plantation, town, and transport labor unions with a modern sector base,
but few links to the majority. Together they channeled anti-colonial ani-
mosity into a pan-ethnic, pan-territorial movement, presented an image
of unity and political maturity, and convinced the United Nations to
press Britain to withdraw in 1961. What appeared as unity, however, was
shared hatred for foreign rule that masked the potential for open conflict.
Thus, post-colonial leaders made "nation building" a primary aim, i.e.,
securing energetic support for unity above diversity and self-interest, and
support for government as the vehicle to forge a cohesive new entity.

The independence coalition proved fragile as various groups pressed
for their own agenda. President Nyerere was forced to take action when,
after 1965, an economic crisis developed based on falling commodity
prices, a serious drought, and foreign policy disputes that caused cuts in
British, West German, and U.S. aid. On February 5, 1967, Nyerere, acting
against internal factionalism and external domination, made official the
policy of African socialism and self reliance that he had long promoted.

This new policy, known as Ujamaa, aimed to recapture values of
equity, self-reliance, and democracy and build a modern state that used
its resources to benefit all (Nyerere 1968: 238-241). According to Nyerere,
building a society with a few very rich and the masses desperately poor
would be a betrayal of the people and would generate class and ethnic
conflicts (Nyerere 1968: 199). Alongside this populism was a paternalism
that saw peasants as apathetic, resisting change, and needing guidance.
So, efforts meant to foster participation were accompanied by mechanisms to guide the people and restructure traditional and colonial relations. The Party would guide political development, channel participation, and set policy. Under Party oversight, government, the administrative arm, would implement policy and develop the nation by using its
resources for people's benefit. To halt elite formation, Party members and
government workers were barred from capitalist enterprises and from
having income sources other than their own labor or state wages
(Nyerere 1968: 231-233, 248-250; Nyerere 1973: 9, 155, 280-282).

Within this political agenda, policies to transform the rural economy
were driven by prevailing capitalist theories. The aim was to advance in
stages to "take off" to self-sustaining growth via technical innovation
(Rostow 1963; Lewis 1955; Hirschman 1958). Appropriate technology
would be used to make the transitions from improved local resource use

and ox-plows to modern inputs and mechanization, a "revolution by evolution" (Nyerere 1968: 199, 320-325, 340). Ujamaa actually undervalued traditional farming, as the colonial regime had done earlier, and indigenous innovations and adaptations were ignored. Peasant production was considered backward and impoverishing because of ignorance and the scale of production, the remedies for which were modern knowledge and techniques and collective production (Nyerere 1968: 340).

Nyerere claimed that only collective ownership was both efficient and equitable considering the alternatives. Small scale, hand-tool farming produced only a limited output, mechanized farming was beyond family labor capacity, and hiring labor for efficient technology use was exploitative (Nyerere 1968: 305, 345, 355). Because of the belief that collectivization was necessary to achieve economies of scale, rural transformation was defined as inherently spatial, and villagization became a policy focus.

Thus, the material base for development would combine bringing peasants into concentrated settlements and reorganizing production in communal farms. Villages would be all-purpose social, economic, political units, democratically deciding in village assemblies and committees how to meet economic and social service needs and divide labor. Gradually, they would develop small industries with groups of villages joining to provide for common needs, e.g., a service station for tractor fuel and repairs (Nyerere 1968: 320, 351-353, 363; Nyerere 1973: 306).

Villagization was also linked to other spatial issues. Nyerere argued for the rural base of villagization, in part, to counter the economic influence of towns and cities. He felt that any further urban-industrial focus would be planned exploitation (Nyerere 1968: 242-243, 341). Nyerere argued for regional as well as rural-urban equity. He countered charges of tribalism in the civil service by maintaining that the over-representation of some groups was due not to bias but to colonial and missionary activity that had spawned uneven regional development and access to education (Nyerere 1973: 72-74). Policies were designed to help or even favor more backward parts of the country as well as to counter Dar es Salaam's industrial concentration. A system of towns in "a new urban growth poles policy" was introduced and these towns, among other functions, were to supply inputs and services to surrounding villages (Waide 1974: 49; Nyerere 1973: 96-97).

The political principles underlying Ujamaa made villagization a crucial policy piece, a vehicle for addressing a variety of aims. The program was expected to incorporate peasants into the nation building process, accelerate modernization and development, establish state structures at all levels and in all places, reverse the formation of feudal, colonial, and capitalist relations, and be the basic unit in an integrated spatial system. In short, villages were to be the institutional, spatial, social cornerstone of socialist development.

National Planning and Villagization Efforts

The first post-colonial national development plan (1961-64, prepared by Europeans and based on colonial, World Bank, and other studies), aimed to increase agricultural exports while industry was left to private investment. The Bank had proposed transforming peasant farms into capital intensive, mechanized, irrigated systems but the plan focused on aiding progressive, labor-hiring farmers (Iliffe 1979; Coulson 1982). The First Five-Year-Plan (FYP) 1964-1969, shifted slightly toward internal development (Svendsen 1970; Waide 1974) but stressed improvement-approach extension for export crops. Peasants were still seen as "primitive, backward, stupid, and generally inferior human beings" entrenched in systems that had to be changed by force if needed (Coulson 1982: 162).

While the first plans were in operation, Nyerere tried to promote the Ujamaa concept. As early as 1959, TANU was urging farmers into nucleated, communal production settlements to foster economic and political development. After independence, Nyerere urged voluntary villagization hoping for spontaneous mass mobilization. He argued that to modernize, farmers first had to concentrate in "proper villages" to share costs of tractors and services. His speeches prompted some 1,000 "spontaneous settlements," half of which were party initiatives, (Coulson 1982: 238).

Government could not support the initial settlements and few succeeded, but the First FYP used them to justify seventy-four World Bank transformation-approach experiments: nucleated villages based on capital-intensive, mechanized, cash crop production (von Freyhold 1979; Lundqvist 1981; Mlay 1985). They were over-capitalized, badly managed, and created dependence (Nyerere 1968: 44; Nyerere 1973: 66). Most of these schemes collapsed without having spread improvements or spurred local cash crop output (Lundqvist 1981; Mlay 1985). In 1976, a phase-out of program support began for the twenty-two settlements that had been completed.

Villagization remained a formal but marginal policy until 1967 when the Arusha Declaration, the essays "Education for Self- Reliance" and "Socialism and Rural Development" and a policy of Ujamaa Vijijini (Ujamaa in Villages) made rural development and villagization priorities. "Education for Self-Reliance" proposed expanding the education system to the whole country and reorienting it away from training civil servants and elites to providing development skills to the majority. "Socialism and Rural Development" made rural development the planning priority and socialist production a goal. Ujamaa Vijijini made villagization a Party aim and mandated government resources for village development. It also caused the Second FYP to be revised, increased production alone becoming less important than "gradually moving toward integrated rural development" (Nyerere 1973: 82-83).

Until this point, Nyerere still urged a voluntary transition to nucleated settlement and collective production. Since diverse ecologies and traditional formations precluded "one universally applied method", implementation needed to take advantage of local conditions and initiatives and begin with small groups of farmers to ensure long-term viability. Steps to collectivization could include such activities as block farms and seasonal-task working groups, or communal herds started by pastoralists. A major goal was to avoid the mistakes of the large mechanized schemes by keeping machinery, service, and credit expectations commensurate with the resource and administrative capacities of the state. The government/Party roles would be to guide the transition and help meet human and material resource needs beyond village capacities (Nyerere 1968: 349-364; Nyerere 1973: 5-8, 67-70, 91, 306).

Only 180 villages were formed during 1962-68 (Coulson 1982). In 1969, Nyerere directed all government departments to become involved in village formation. He ordered a "widespread frontal approach" to develop Ujamaa villages across the nation, not just in areas like Rufiji and Handeni where vigorous efforts had begun in response to floods and drought respectively (Nyerere 1973: 95; Yeager 1982; von Freyhold 1979). Finally, he decreed villagization to be the top development priority (Coulson 1982).

By 1970, Presidential Planning Teams had been created because of a need for "planning by experts under TANU leadership" (Nyerere 1973: 156-157). A 1970-73 villagization campaign was conducted in Dodoma Region (Thiele 1986a), a rainfall shadow area with scattered population clusters. Elsewhere, officials offered education, health, water, extension, and credit services to entice volunteers to start villages. Still, in June 1971, there were just 271 Ujamaa villages and "more commitment to a future of Ujamaa than to the practice of it" (Nyerere 1973: 306). By the end of the year, only eight percent of peasants lived in Ujamaa villages (Nyerere 1973: 280). Other rural development efforts, such as the use of ox traction and state farms, fared little better (Nyerere 1973: 303-305).

More policy changes came about because of slow, voluntary villagization, economic decline, and the state's need to penetrate rural areas, accelerate development, and prove socialism's superiority. Aggressive villagization was begun in Kigoma, Tabora and Mtwara Regions, The latter an effort to create defense outposts in response to Mozambique's revolt against Portugal (Lundqvist 1981). These initiatives and "Operation Dodoma", moving 200,000 people into villages by 1973 (virtually all Dodoma's rural people by 1975), were so "successful" that in 1973, villagization was mandated on a national basis. All pretense to voluntarism was dropped. (Svendsen 1974; Thiele 1986a). Judged by the number of registered villages, results were indeed "dramatic" (Yeager 1982), "the most extensive attempt at clustering rural people in Africa" (Silberfein 1989: 264). Villages rose from 809 in 1969 to 1,956 in 1970, and 5,628 in 1973, (Lundqvist 1981: 338). Campaigns to sedentarize herders and hunter-gatherers helped raise the number to 7,300 in 1977, encompassing thirteen million people or eighty-five percent of rural Tanzanians (Yeager 1982: 64). By 1979, there were 8,579 settlements and 369 larger rural service centers (Kauzeni 1988: 122). By then, virtually all rural people could be said, at least in some formal sense, to belong to a nucleated settlement.

Overview of Policy Results

Closer examination of the resettlement effort shows first that the numbers mislead. Claims that five million people were moved initially (Hyden 1980), over twice that overall, must be qualified. Relocation varied from a few kilometers to a few meters (McCall and Skutsch 1983). Designated villages in Dodoma, for example, were often places that already had sizable homestead clusters or had long been administrative centers. In two typical cases, villagers moved a mean of 3.9 and 2.2 kilometers, displacing population centers 1.7 and 0.7 kilometers (Thiele 1986a). Many village sites were places of existing concentration due to trading posts, water supplies, mission schools, and health posts, etc.

Some areas of the country saw no movement at all. Urban places, villages that already had 200 families, and some highlands, notably those producing coffee, were exempt (Coulson 1982: 249). Site visits and interviews in 1989 found that in Usambara, as in other highlands, homes were left in traditional clan clusters on ridges throughout the mountains. "Villagization" was a matter of drawing boundaries around existing homesteads, making many villages contiguous, with no space or obvious natural features to mark where one ended and the next began. The major impact on spatial organization was added nodalization as shops, bars and other establishments clustered around village offices.

A similar pattern was found in both highlands and plains in Mbulu District (Arusha Region). Homes remained scattered in clusters up to seven kilometers from the "village"--offices, school, shops, storage facility, and church or mission. Coulson describes forced Maasai relocation in Monduli District (Arusha) but he saw little homestead movement elsewhere.[7] Most relocation took place with farmers who had colonized scattered rangeland areas. In those cases, farmers were clustered and village boundaries were extended to incorporate Maasai dry season settlements that traditionally surrounded farms at a distance of a few kilometers for access to grain reserves.

Villagization even produced an anomaly in Kijungu village, Kiteto, where both agricultural and pastoral populations were fairly large. The farmer concentration became one village and encircling Maasai were constituted as a separate village with its own political institutions, school, and office. In Maasai areas that lacked farming clusters, a village office, school, and other buildings were erected as a village center. These were located near to wells, pumps, water storage, and monthly cattle auction facilities that had been built earlier to improve and commoditize pastoral production. These sites usually corresponded to the traditional neighborhoods where the Maasai regularly stayed longest each year. Conversely, in some Kiteto and Handeni District farming areas, far more regimentation was applied, at times by force, to construct houses in straight rows along village feeder roads.

In Olgira, in an area where Arusha, Morogoro and Tanga Regions abut, villagization combined peasant resistance and government accommodation. In 1975, Oligira farmers were told by Arusha officers to move their scattered homesteads twenty kilometers from a fertile, well-watered area to a large, established village with chronic water problems and low farm yields. To avoid this fate, the farmers first argued they were in Morogoro Region, not Arusha. Then, when Morogoro authorities came, farmers claimed to be in Tanga. Officials discovered and ended the ruse in 1977 and backed Arusha's mandate to move. Local farmers and the surrounding Maasai then sent a petition to district and regional officials and were given permission to remain in place and register as a village.

Both observation and the literature show that the term "villagization" cannot be used unequivocally. Some relocation took place and force was used, and the operations amounted to a massive, nation-wide, formal administrative/spatial restructuring. However, degrees of regimentation, force, and distance moved varied across the country. Given the scope and speed of reorganization and counting intimidation, there was likely more force than Nyerere would admit: "Eleven million people could not have been moved by force in Tanzania; we do not have the physical resources for such forced movement, any more than we have the desire for it" (Coulson 1979: 66). Given promises of services, uneven actual dislocation, and the lack of protests, strikes, marches, and other past tactics, there was likely less force than critics claim. The areas least affected spatially by villagization had common traits. Many were high density, relatively rich areas in which disruption would threaten the non-plantation export base. Moreover, Kilimanjaro, Arusha-Meru, Pare, and Usambara, were among the earliest, most highly, politicized areas, with strong local organizations and, more importantly, cooperatives on Kilimanjaro and Meru. In short, villagization, in terms of spatial reorganization and unprecedented nucleation, was implemented in those areas least equipped with the economic power and political organization to defy the policy.

Other generalizations about villagization require caution and attention to continued diversity. Overall, efforts up to 1972 produced three kinds of village: (1) politicized and committed villages with communal production; (2) villages begun by kulaks so as to get state aid, corrupt from start; and (3) large villages with little or no commitment to communal work and scant idea of the purpose of concentration (Coulson 1982: 242). Type three villages proliferated during the compulsory stage of the program, so much so that a 1975 government act formalized distinctions between village types. Legal status was given to groups of 250 or more families that lived together, established requisite village political institutions, and were confirmed by the registrar. They were also deemed multi-purpose societies (*Vijiji vya Maendeleo* or Development Villages), a distinction that rural people themselves adopted.

The Ujamaa Village title was reserved for villages with substantial communal economic activity, and gave privileged access to services, inputs, and credit (Kauzeni 1988: 111-112). It was clear that in most villages there was more living together than working together (Svendsen 1974). It remained difficult to establish communal production, due principally to the absence of this type of production in established economic systems. Traditional communal activity was limited to managing rangelands, irrigation systems, and other common property resources, to feudal systems, and to short term, ad hoc activities in which individuals arranged "beer parties" to augment family labor (see Chapter 5). Once tasks were done, all returned to individual production and consumption. Aside from some pastoral activities, which also became individualized, there seem to have been no regular, communal production and distribution systems (Lundqvist 1981). Gradually, the government de-emphasized communal production. Some villages continued to have token communal fields, but often sites and layout were chosen for service provision and "ease of access to civil servants in their landrovers and to state transport seeking local produce for export" (Leonard 1984: 158).

The economic development policy that came to replace socialism in the villagization program came from supply-side, induced innovation, Green Revolution models. "The main hope for increasing production was left to the provisions of improved seed, fertilizers, and to projects supported by the World Bank and other multi-national organizations which were given the choice of regions to assist under the "Regional Integrated Development Programme" (Mlay 1985: 88). Yet, neither project officials nor the peasants were ready or able to meet the practical problems of rural transformation, especially with regard to improving productivity. Villagers "had little conception of what they were required to do beyond hoping for receipt of massive government assistance and were neither equipped nor motivated to cope with all the organizational and technical problems" (Kitching 1982: 109).

Given the lack of production-oriented strategies, policy came to focus on providing educational, health, and water services. This was easier for the state than modernizing, much less communalizing, peasant agriculture, and allowed the state to penetrate rural life. To peasants, service provision was more acceptable than interference in production (McCall and Skutsch 1983). A "blueprint" approach emerged whereby each village was to have a primary school and all school-age children would attend. Next came a Universal Primary Education campaign (UPE) to extend literacy to all adults. Finally, to improve rural health care, dispensaries were built, health workers were posted in select villages in each district, and plans were made for every village to eventually have an adequate, clean supply of water.

The analyses of early and medium-term villagization fall into two camps, one stressing success in social development (ILO 1982; Stewart 1985), the other agricultural disruption and economic decline. On the positive side, life expectancy rose from forty-one years in 1962 to fifty-one in 1988, three years above the Sub-Saharan average, and infant mortality fell to eighteen per thousand--five below average. Literacy rose to seventy-nine percent (Boesen et al. 1977), above average in Africa, and comparable to Italy (World Bank 1986).

There were numerous costs that derived from villagization, however, including the loss of the time and labor needed to relocate, build a new home, and travel to more distant fields. Some farmers were moved to less fertile areas or lost control of permanent tree crops like cashews that needed careful husbandry (Coulson 1982; Mlay 1985). Major food crop (maize, wheat, rice) sales fell from 226,300 tons in 1972/3 to 161,000 in 1973/4, and 61,000 in 1974/5, but rose to 169,400 in 1976/7 (Migot-Adhollah 1984: 223). Some analysts have argued that all of the setbacks were temporary and due primarily to drought and the 1974 oil price hikes that reduced inputs such as fertilizer. Cash crop output also fell, and Tanzania exhausted its foreign exchange reserves in 1975, further impeding investment in rural production (Green et al. 1980; Hyden 1980; Migot-Adholla 1984).

Later data indicate that villagization caused no permanent damage and that other factors were responsible for production levels. When, in 1976, 77, and 78, maize prices were raised fifty-eight percent, 2.8 percent, and 6.25 percent respectively so as to spur production, marketed output rose 265 percent, 44.8 percent, and 64.9 percent in corresponding years. Then, as both money prices and real returns for cash crops as a whole fell relative to food crops, so did marketed output (Ellis 1982). This suggests that Tanzanian farmers have "a remarkable sensitivity to prices" and shift production patterns "in response to changes in prices and price structures, not only on the official market but also in the parallel" (De Wilde 1984: 47). The data also supported proponents of supply-side remedies for Tanzania's economic problems (e.g., Lele 1984; Lofchie 1985).

However, maize increases "should not be taken to indicate a mythical high price elasticity of supply for Tanzanian agriculture as a whole" (Ellis 1982: 271). Gauging impacts of prices versus other factors is more complex with other crops. Production and price levels do not readily correlate since it takes a year to increase cotton and tobacco output, and five to six for cashew nuts, coffee, tea, and sisal (Malima 1985).

In other respects, villagization was in fact counterproductive to its aims. Rather than rapidly incorporating peasants into a socialist society and increasing state allegiance and control, "hostility arising from hasty villagization was reinforced by emphasis on cash crops as opposed to food crops and caused alienation, and opposition to Ujamaa" (Ake 1981: 117). Data gathered during and just after villagization fed a critique that villagization co-opted the development and political process, transforming Ujamaa policy "from one of radical democracy to one of state control and commandism" (McCall and Skutsch 1983: 253). It was termed top-down planning in bottom-up rhetoric, paternalistic state control that substituted bureaucracy for mass mobilization and mass responsibility (McCall and Skutsch 1983). To Coulson, it was not worth the cost. "Only a bureaucracy distant from peasant life could have forced through measures as draconian as villagization, and with so little productive effect" (Coulson 1982: 262).

Events and policy trends support critiques that villagization was a major part of efforts to extend state penetration. At the same time, social development efforts suggest that policies were also consistent with Ujamaa's emphasis on humanism and equity. More importantly, the move to establish villages as the basic spatial and socio-political unit, was a crucial step for the goals of nation building and fundamental restructuring. Conceived and implemented in tandem with decentralization and Regional Integrated Development Planning, villagization gave Tanzania a uniform institutional framework for redesigning state structures and redirecting development processes.

Villagization Redux: Peasant Perspectives and Survival

In 1989, as part of a study of Tanzania's Regional Integrated Development Programs, eight villages were visited, two each in Mbulu and Kiteto Districts in Arusha Region, and Handeni and Lushoto Districts in Tanga Region (Figures 12.4 and 12.5). Interviews were conducted with 210 villagers and a similar number participated in structured group discussions, with roughly equal numbers of men and women in each instance. Tanzanian and expatriate personnel at national, regional, district, and village levels were also interviewed. If the research revealed any one insight, it is the following: while the state has been able to press its rural agenda with varied success, as had its colonial predecessors, peasants have been equally engaged in pressing theirs. This intriguing interplay of forces has maintained diversity as Tanzania's hallmark, and has interjected traditional dynamics into modern economic and political structures.

The research uncovered striking similarities and differences among villages. As expected, all had the requisite political institutions and offices. What was surprising was the broad awareness of institutional planning mechanisms. Fully eighty percent of men and sixty percent of women were able to outline, the prescribed steps of village committee meetings, village council and open village assembly meetings, as well as decisions at ward, district, and regional levels, and national approval and funding.

Each village also had a primary school. As an example of how villagers have internalized the state's development agenda, common complaints were not that education was mandatory but that the quality of education was steadily declining, basic materials were lacking, and there were virtually no opportunities for secondary education and access to real advancement in rural areas. Mbulu District had long ago established private secondary schools and people in Handeni District, denied government funding, were starting a District secondary school on a self-help basis. Ironically, despite extensive complaints about primary education, in no village was there an effort or even any impetus for villagers to take improving matters into their own hands.

Orienting peasants toward western health care was another villag-

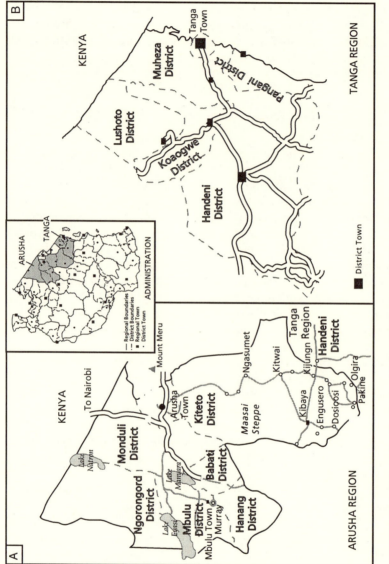

FIGURE 12.4 Tanzanian Regions: A) Arusha Region; B) Tanga Region

ization aim, and again state efforts succeeded. Four villages had government and/or mission health care facilities while building a dispensary was a priority in all four villages that didn't have health facilities. In all eight villages, people complained of the lack of medical supplies in local facilities and exorbitant costs of securing treatment in state and private facilities in large towns and cities.

Where villages diverged was in the way village, government, and development planning structures were used and village project benefits were distributed. Half of those interviewed said that village planning decisions were made by the village council alone, especially by the chair and party secretary. Significantly, villages where decisions were perceived as leader-controlled were the same ones that had complaints of inefficiency, if not corruption, and, in fact, had histories of failed projects. Nearly as many, eighty-one, said no one had benefited from village development efforts. In eighty-three villages, all residents were supposed to have benefitted, but in twenty-six, no specific benefits were named, suggesting they may have been offering politically correct answers. In forty-one villages, only a few people were said to have benefited, twenty-nine of them specifying that the beneficiaries were village leaders. The third of the interviewees who sat on village councils tended to have larger land holdings, broader crop mixtures, and more diverse and substantial livestock holdings than those not in leadership positions.

While interviews suggested that, in general, prior clan and class formations had become incorporated into state structures and undercut development and equity, there were indications that traditional and modern structures could enhance as well as hinder development and equitable benefit distribution. In Murray, in the traditional Iraqw heartland, villagers pointed with pride to their village office and crop storage complex, a cooperative store, and a nearly completed health facility, all built with communal labor under the leadership of a long-standing village chair. When he decided not to run for re-election, village development efforts declined, questions arose about the store's accounts, and the former chief was re-instated.

One Kiteto village provides a classic case of corruption undermining communal activities. The village was formed in 1974, first with a contingent of poor Gogo farmers moving in from scattered homesteads, then with a group of wealthier Irangi farmers. In response to state directives, villagers began a communal farm and used its profits to start a cooperative store and a maize grinding mill, which in turn funded the purchase of a village tractor. Villagers said they stopped working the communal farm when profits vanished and the council ignored requests for accounts. Later, the store collapsed, the maize mill was stolen, and other problems developed which could be traced to the village leadership.

Among the Maasai, traditional propensities for collaboration led to some positive results. In Lolera, the Maasai village surrounds Kijungu, a predominantly Nguu village. Since the economic crisis of the early 1980s, the Maasai have maintained their own cattle dip, collecting fees for services and adding their own funds to buy inputs when government could no longer provide them. They also have a profitable maize mill and a far less well operating communal lorry project in collaboration with the local Catholic mission.

One of the most successful programs in Tanzania was Lushoto District's Soil Erosion Control/Agroforestry Project (SECAP) which demonstrates the capacity of villages to function as vehicles for development. Instead of terracing and other failed, resented conservation measures, SECAP introduced an integrated mixture of approaches. Macro-contour lines, planted with fodder grasses and bushes, checked erosion better and with less labor than terraces and provided inputs for stall-fed livestock. This approach also eliminated open-grazing damage and provided manure for soil regeneration. Severely eroded areas were turned to village woodlots by communal labor, with communal harvesting rights for building materials and fuel. Village nurseries were established to provide fruit, fuel, and lumber tree seedlings for common ventures and villagers' own plots. By nearly every measure, the project made massive strides, expanding to 126 villages in Lushoto with many farmers spontaneously adopting project components and making direct requests for project assistance (Massaro 1993). Yet, although erosion control and tree component benefits were equitably distributed, there was marked difference in livestock component benefits. These were biased toward current village officials and council members and wealthy farmers who also tended to be members of traditionally powerful clans.

Retroduction

Across degrees of project success and differences in form, new settlements had common aspects that suggest both the utility and limits of villagization as a development policy tool. It was never thought that this approach alone could provide a naive, facile "spatial fix" to development problems. Village experiences and overall Tanzanian development performance confirm the complexity of the development task and prove that no such simplistic fix is possible. What villagization shows about the relation of settlement form to development is that clustering, where ecology and production systems permit it, can facilitate local mobilization and common effort. Spatial concentration helped push some peasants to collaborate in building schools, health facilities, and water projects but it was not a prerequisite. Once legally constituted as villages, highland and lowland farmers in scattered hamlets and herders in traditional settlements had the same installations as did the concentrated and regimented villages. Similarly, nucleation was a useful, but not necessary, instrument in implementing communal production efforts. Here, other factors outweighed spatial concentration, specifically the viability of the project itself and, most importantly, the accountability of the village leaders in ensuring that benefits were equitably distributed, with no questions of mismanagement or embezzlement.

The fact that villages all had projects regardless of degrees of clustering, and that success depended on factors other than concentration, suggests that a major requisite for rural restructuring and development is not nucleation but nodalization. This implies the creation of a common functional space that, in turn, facilitates the formation of a common social and spatial identity. Such communal identities and institutions were essential, even if people still lived somewhat apart from each other. The village center, then, functioned as a focal point for fostering that identity and focusing group efforts.

In some areas, especially those with the most sparsely scattered settlements, some relocation and concentration was necessary. Yet, it was not critical to rigidly enforce relocation and a uniform settlement form, particularly where ecological, economic, and political factors made relocation untenable. More important was establishing a space and a community that identified itself as a unit, followed by the crucial steps of establishing village institutions. It didn't matter if homes were tightly clustered and in neat rows, or if a village consisted of separate hamlets in a defined territory. It did matter, however, that people identified as village members and had a place to concentrate development discussions and shared effort. It mattered that people had a project of communally recognized value, its work and benefits equitably distributed. It mattered that leadership was accountable for efficient and honest management of common projects, few of which would have happened without villagization's spatial and social nodalization.

Spatial and organizational factors can become equally important when widespread common effort is needed to address a specific problem, as with SECAP villages. SECAP demonstrates the need for effective institutional mechanisms, within defined spaces, to ensure that destructive farming and grazing practices are replaced by those that allow both the environment and humans to prosper. In effect, SECAP represents a rediscovery of common property resource management, which is possible only when individuals can define themselves as a group, equally responsible for an environmental asset. The same dynamic applies to rangeland management among pastoralists and extends to land use policy in areas with fragile, easily eroded soil.

Where villagization has proved most useful is in fostering broad national political aims. It provided the spatial and institutional foundation for forging a national identity and avoiding the chaos, conflict, and intense class and ethnic factionalism plaguing African nations. Tanzania still represents a rare instance of leadership transition, from Nyerere to Mwinyi, not caused by coup or natural death. There has been a similarly smooth transition from single to multi-party democracy.

In terms of economic restructuring and development, villagization represents, if not a failure, a glaring case of unfinished business. Efforts to transform the space economy have not been nearly as successful as efforts to provide the nation with political stability and a common institutional framework, and, within that, a common social service base. Rural restructuring policy was badly flawed in at least one major area: it was not able to define or demonstrate the superiority of horizontal over vertical integration. Village production projects have not, in fact, been designed to produce advantages of scale or the division and specialization of labor. Despite planning rhetoric, even first-stage agricultural processing remains concentrated in large towns and cities, adding to transport costs of both raw materials and processed goods. In fact, incremental, vertical integration appears to be the more viable strategy if one examines various successes such as SECAP, well-run village stores, water and construction projects, private and district cooperative tractor-hire schemes, and block farms where private fields are laid out contiguously to facilitate mechanization.

Villages have received little help in identifying and developing locational advantages and forming local production and trade relations. There remain severe problems in linking villages to a still-disarticulated, externally dependent urban system. For example, in 1989, both Lushoto District vegetable and fruit producers and Mbulu and Kiteto District maize farmers found themselves unable to sell surpluses because crop collection, processing, distribution, and sales structures were exclusively oriented to an extreme few urban market centers. At the same time both groups experienced shortages of the other's products. Rather than devising state, or allowing private mechanisms to even the imbalances, people in both areas were allowed to remain economically and nutritionally deprived while their surpluses spoiled.

Inattention to intermediate scales is further evidenced by scant, post-primary vocational training opportunities. The few institutes that do exist are urban based and further intensify the rural to urban drain.

Graduates find few opportunities to return to villages in viable enterprises integrated into rural life and production. Similarly, highly successful literacy and universal primary education campaigns were conducted, but they did not include plans to produce and distribute useful materials to read.

Yet, even as village experiences demonstrate defects in Tanzanian development strategies, they are also indicative of the resilience of Tanzania's rural people. As they adapted to colonial demands for taxes, labor, and cash crops without becoming totally subsumed in or destroyed by a new system, so they continue to maintain a local identity and security while taking advantage of, or minimizing the disadvantages of, membership in the modern state. Pastoralists and agriculturalists are extensively involved in markets, both in selling surplus and in purchasing productive inputs and household consumer goods. Recent research demonstrates they are far more heavily involved, if not completely captured, than previously estimated and declines in marketed output through official channels, are more likely indicators of a shift in preferred market outlets than a retreat into a subsistence option (Maliyamkono and Bagachwa 1990). Depleted inventories in rural shops and complaints of shortages of specific goods provide further evidence of peasant willingness, even enthusiasm, to be a part of a modern economy. Moreover, to the extent that there have been retreats into subsistence, they have been temporary, market driven responses that signal an economic, and economically rational, decision to conserve productive resources until returns again reach acceptable levels.

The same applies to political institutions. While village structures and institutions have enhanced local elites' abilities to increase their advantages, they have also, in the words of one expatriate planning advisor, become the means to capture development resources that would not be otherwise locally available. In addition, traditional structures remain important instruments of fostering local cohesion and even efficient utilization of village structures. Iraqw villages still use regular meetings of select elders rather than civil courts to resolve disputes, just as Maasai still use open meetings of all elders. In both cases, decisions are made in an open forum, carry the weight of social sanctions which can't be escaped with bribes, and are far more binding on the parties involved. That same pressure is far more effective in mobilizing local resources for communal projects than are unenforceable government mandates.

In short, as much as Ujamaa idealized traditional society, villagers do demonstrate that there is much in rural Africa that can contribute to creating a modern nation state not based on conflict and exploitation. Despite significant progress, much of the structural context, notably the skewed space economy, remains as it was when villagization began. To continue restructuring, with a now stable national government and firm village base in place, it seems time to shift the focus of development planning. The question is no longer whether development can and should come from bottom up or top down. Both levels have essential functions and limits. If peasants really are as astute and adept as they appear, and if, in fact, some problems are beyond the capacities of villages to resolve, are broader and need to be addressed at wider spatial levels, then, perhaps, it is time to end the question of how the state can capture the peasantry and ask instead how and when peasants, with their insight and energy, can capture the state.

Notes

1. Sources for ecological development include Tanzania in Maps, L. Berry, ed. (Africana Publishing Corporation, New York, 1971) and A Geography of Tanzania, S. E. Durra (Premier Publishers and Distributors Company, Dar es Salaam, 1986).

2. Sources for the early history of mainland Tanzania include works by Shorter (1974); Lamphear (1986); Rigby (1985); and Sheriff (1980).

3. The summary of mainland trade history is based on Coulson (1982); Sheriff (1980); Illiffe (1979); Arnold (1979); and (Shorter) 1974.

4. For a more detailed description of German colonial agricultural production and labor policies, see Iliffe (1979); Temu (1980); Rodney (1983); and Sago (1983).

5. The summary of cooperatives and class formation is based on Migot-Adholla (1984); Saul (1975); Cliffe (1977); Raikes (1978); Iliffe (1979); and Coulson (1982).

6. As in early Russian debates, at Ujamaa's core is a conviction that economies of scale in socialism can be achieved only intra-farm. Marxists argued that horizontal concentration (expanded farm size) produced mechanization and marketing advantages. Family farms limit cooperation, division of labor, productivity, and social progress. Conversely, Chayanov found the peasant scale more appropriate, efficient, and competitive. Limits of nature usually caused horizontal concentration advantages to disappear with vertical concentration. Peasant intensive production was more efficient than capitalist units with their technical demands and expense. By vertical concentration (forming and institutionalizing ad hoc co-operatives), peasants could obtain all scale advantages and still maintain a competitive productivity advantage. Rather than impeding progress, family farms held the most potential for higher production. They lacked capitalist internal contradictions and exploitation and overcame collective production motivation problems (Kerblay 1987; Harrison 1975). In essence, Nyerere took a Marxist stance.

7. From 1975 to 1980, the author was administrator of the Catholic Mission in Kijungu, Kiteto District, Arusha Region and Chaired the Arusha Diocesan Planning Committee which afforded opportunities to make observation and collect data throughout the Arusha Region.

References

Ake, Claude. 1981. *A Political Economy of Africa*. Essex: Longman.

Arnold, David. 1979. "External factors in the Partition of East Africa." In M. H. Y. Kaniki, ed. *Tanzania Under Colonial Rule*. Pp. 51-85. London: Longman.

Asmerom, H. K. 1986. "The Tanzanian Village Council: Agency of Rural Development or Merely a Device of State Penetration into the Periphery?" *Cahiers du CEDAF* 2: 177-197.

Boesen, Jannik, Birgit Storgaard Madsen, and Tony Moody. 1977. *Ujamaa - Socialism From Above*. Upsala: Scandanavian Institute of African Studies.

Bryceson, Deborah Fahy. 1985. "The Organization of Tanzanian Grain Marketing: Switching Roles of the Co-operative and the Parastatal." In Kwame Arhin, Paul Hesp, and Laurens van der Laan, eds. *Marketing Boards in Tropical Africa*. Pp. 53-78. London: KPI Limited, Routledge and Keegan Paul.

Cliffe, Lionel. 1972. "Planning Rural Development." In J. F. Rweyemamu, J. Loxley, J. Wicken, and C. Nyirabu, eds. *Towards Socialist Planning*. Pp. 30-49. Dar es Salaam: Tanzania Publishing House.

____. 1977. "Rural Class Formation in East Africa." *Journal of Peasant Studies* 4: 195-224.

Cliffe, Lionel, Peter Lawrence, William Luttrell, Sjem Migot-Adholla, and John S. Saul, eds. 1975. *Rural Cooperation in Tanzania*. Dar es Salaam: Tanzania Publishing House.

Coulson, Andrew, ed. 1979. *African Socialism in Practice: The Tanzanian Experience*. Nottingham, England: Spokesman Press.

____. 1982. *Tanzania: A Political Economy*. Oxford: Oxford University Press.

De Wilde, John C. 1984. *Agriculture, Marketing and Pricing in Sub-Saharan Africa*. Los Angeles: University of California, Los Angeles, African Studies Center and The African Studies Association.

Ellis, Frank. 1982. "Agricultural Policy in Tanzania." *World Development* 10: 263-283.

Feierman, Steven. 1974. *The Shambaa Kingdom: A History*. Madison, WI: University of Wisconsin Press.

Friedmann, John and Clyde Weaver. 1979. *Territory and Function: The Evolution of Regional Planning Doctrine*. Los Angeles: University of California Press.

Galaty, John G. 1981. "Land and Livestock among Kenyan Maasai: Symbolic Perspectives on Pastoral Exchange, Change and Inequality." In John Galaty and Philip Carl Salzaman, eds. *Change and Development among Pastoral and Nomadic Societies*. Pp. 68-88. Leiden, the Netherlands: E. J. Brill.

Green, R. H., D. G. Rwegasira, and B. van Arkedie. 1980. *Economic Shocks and National Policy Making: Tanzania in the 1970s*. The Hague: Institute of Social Studies.

Harrison, Mark. 1975. "The Peasant Mode of Production in the Work of A.V. Chayanov." *Journal of Peasant Studies* 2: 323-336.

Hill, Polly. 1986. *Development Economics on Trial: The Anthropological Case for a Prosecution*. Oxford: Oxford University Press.

Hirschman, A. O. 1958. *The Strategy of Economic Development*. New Haven, CT: Yale University Press.

Hyden, Goran. 1980. *Beyond Ujamaa in Tanzania: Underdevelopment and an Uncaptured Peasantry*. Berkeley and Los Angeles: University of California Press.

Iliffe, John. 1979. *A Modern History of Tanganyika*. Cambridge: Cambridge University Press.

International Labor Organization. 1982. *Basic Needs in Danger: A Basic Needs Oriented Development Strategy for Tanzania*. Addis Ababa: International Labor Organization Jobs and Skills Program for Africa.

Johnson, E. A. J. 1970. *The Organization of Space in Developing Countries*. Cambridge: Harvard University Press.

Kaberuka, D. P. 1984. "Evaluating the Performance of Food Marketing Parastatals." *Development Policy Review* 2: 190-216.

Kauzeni, A. S. 1988. "Rural Develpment Alternatives and the Role of Local-Level Development Strategy: Tanzania Case Study." *Rural Development Dialogue* 9: 105-140.

Kerblay, Basilie. 1987. "Chayanov and the Theory of Peasant Economies," In Theodore Shanin, ed. *Peasants and Peasant Societies*. Pp. 176-184. Oxford: Basil Blackwell.

Kitching, Gavin. 1982. *Development and Underdevelopment in Historical Perspective*. New York: Methuen.

Kjekshus, Helge. 1977. *Ecology Control and Economic Development in East African History: The Case of Tanganyika 1850-1950*. Berkeley and Los Angeles: University of California Press.

Klima, George J. 1970. *The Barbaig: East African Cattle-Herders*. New York: Holt, Reinhart, and Winston.

Lamphear, John. 1986. "Aspects of Early African History." In Phyllis M. Martin and Patrick O'Meara, eds. *Africa*. Pp. 64-86. Bloomington, IN: Indiana University Press.

Lele, Uma. 1984. "Tanzania: Phoenix or Icarus?" In Arnold C.Harmerger, ed. *World Economic Growth*. Pp. 159-197. San Francisco: Institute for Contemporary Studies.

Leonard, David K. 1984. "Class Formation and Agricultural Development." In Joel D. Barkan, ed. *Politics and Public Policy in Kenya and Tanzania*. Pp. 141-170. New York: Praeger.

Lewis, W. 1955. *The Theory of Economic Growth*. New York: Basic Books.

Lofchie, Michael M. 1985. "The Roots of Economic Crisis in Tanzania." *Current History* April: 159-163.

Lundqvist, Jan. 1981. "Tanzania: Socialist Ideology, Bureaucratic Reality, and Development From Below," In W. Stohr, and F. Taylor, eds. *Development from Above or Below.* Pp. 329-350. New York: John Wiley and Sons.

Malima, Kighoma A. 1985. "The IMF and World Bank Conditionality: The Tanzanian Case" *Africa Development* 10: 286-297.

Maliyamkono, T. L. and M.S.D. Bagachwa. 1990. *The Second Economy of Tanzania.* London: James Currey.

Massaro, Richard J. 1993. "Beyond Participation: Empowerment for Environmental Action in Tanzania's West Usambara Mountains." In John Friedmann and Haripriya Rangan, eds. *In Defense of Livelihood: Comparative Studies on Environmental Action.* Pp. 23-52. West Hartford, Connecticut: Kumarian Press.

McCall, Michael and Margaret Skutsch. 1983. "Strategies and Contradictions in Tanzania's Rural Development: Which Way for the Peasants?" In David A. M. Lea and D. P. Chaudhri, eds. *Rural Development and The State: Contradictions and Dilemmas in Developing Countries.* Pp. 241-272. New York: Methuen.

Migot-Adholla, S. E. 1984. "Rural Development Policy and Equality," In Joel D. Barkan, ed. *Politics and Public Policy in Kenya and Tanzania.* Pp. 199-232. New York: Praeger.

Mlay, W.F.I. 1985. "Pitfalls in Rural Development: The Case in Tanzania." In Fassil G. Kiros, ed. *Challenging Rural Poverty: Experience in Institution- Building and Popular Participation for Rural Development in Eastern Africa.* Pp. 91-98. Trenton, NJ: Africa World Press.

Moore, John E. 1971. "Traditional Rural Settlement," In L. Berry, ed. *Tanzania in Maps: Graphic Perspectives of a Developing Country.* Pp. 124-128. New York: Africana Publishing Corporation.

Nyerere, Julius K. 1968. *Freedom and Socialism: A Selection from Writings and Speeches 1965-1967.* London: Oxford University Press.

____. 1973. *Freedom and Development: A Selection from Writings and Speeches 1968-1973.* London: Oxford University Press.

Raikes, Philip. 1975. "Wheat Production and the Development of Capitalism in North Iraqw." In Lionel Cliffe, Peter Lawrence, William Luttrell, Sjem Migot-Adholla, and John S. Saul, eds. *Rural Cooperation in Tanzania.* Pp. 79-102. Dar es Salaam: Tanzania Publishing House.

____. 1978. "Rural Differentiation and Class-Formation in Tanzania." *Journal of Peasant Studies* 5: 285-325.

Rapp, Anders, Len Berry, and Paul H. Temple. 1972. "Soil Erosion and Sedimentation in Tanzania - The Project." *Geografiska Annaler* 54A, no. 3-4: 105-109.

Rigby, Peter. 1985. *Persistent Pastoralists: Nomadic Societies in Transition.* London: Zed Books.

Rodney, Walter. 1980. "The Political Economy of Colonial Tanganika 1890-1930." In M. H. Y. Kaniki, ed. *Tanzania Under Colonial Rule.* Pp. 128-163. London: Longman.

_____. 1983. "Migrant Labour and the Colonial Economy." In Walter Rodney, Kapepwa Tambila, and Laurent Sago, eds. *Migrant Labour in Tanzania During the Colonial Period: Case Studies of Recruitment and Conditions of Labour in the Sisal Industry.* Pp. 4-28. Hamburg: Institut fur Afrika-Kunde im Verbund Stiftung Deutches Ubersee-Institut, Arbeiten aus dem Institut fur Afrika-Kunde, 45.

Rostow, W. W. 1963. *The Stages of Economic Growth.* Cambridge: Cambridge University Press.

Rweyemamu, Anthony H., ed. 1970. *Nation-Building in Tanzania: Problems and Issues.* Dar es Salaam: East African Publishing House.

Rweyamamu, A. H. and B. U. Mwansasu, eds. 1974. *Planning in Tanzania: Background to Decentralization.* Dar es Salaam: East African Literature Bureau.

Rweyemamu, J.F.J. Loxley, J. Wicken, C. Nyirabu, eds. 1972. *Towards Socialist Planning.* Dar es Salaam: Tanzania Publishing House.

Sago, Laurent. 1983. "Labor Reservoir: The Kigoma Case." In Walter Rodney, Kapepwa Tambila, Laurent Sago, eds. *Migrant Labour in Tanzania During the Colonial Period: Case Studies of Recruitment and Conditions of Labour in the Sisal Industry.* Pp. 29-57. Hamburg: Institut fur Afrika-Kunde im Verbund Stiftung Deutches Ubersee-Institut, Arbeiten aus dem Institut fur Afrika-Kunde, 45.

Saitoti, Tepilit Ole and Carol Beckwith. 1980. *Maasai.* New York: Harry N. Abrams.

Sankan, S. S. Ole. 1971. *The Maasai.* Nairobi, Dar es Salaam, and Kampala: East African Literature Bureau.

Saul, J. S. 1975. "The Role of the Co-operative Movement." In Lionel Cliffe, Peter Lawrence, William Luttrell, Sjem Migot-Adholla, and John S. Saul, eds. *Rural Cooperation in Tanzania.* Pp. 206-211. Dar es Salaam: Tanzania Publishing House.

Sawers, Larry. 1989. "Urban Primacy in Tanzania," *Economic Development and Cultural Change* 37: 841-859.

Schneider, Harold K. 1986. "Traditional African Economies," In Phyllis M. Martin and Patrick O'Meara, eds. *Africa.* Pp. 181-198. Bloomington: Indiana University Press.

Sheriff, Abdul M. H. 1980. "Tanzanian Societies at the Time of Partition," In M.H.Y. Kaniki, ed. *Tanzania Under Colonial Rule.* Pp. 11-50. London: Longman.

Shorter, Aylward. 1974. *East African Societies.* London: Routtledge and Kegan Paul.

Silberfein, Marilyn. 1989. "Settlement Form and Rural Development: Scattered Versus Clustered Settlement." *Tijdschrift voor Economische en Sociale Geografie* 80: 258-268.

Slater, D. 1977. "Colonialism and the Spatial Structure of Underdevelopment: Outlines of an Alternative Approach with Special Reference to Tanzania." In Janet Abu-Lughod and Richard Hay, eds. *Third World Urbanization.* Pp. 165-175. Chicago: Maaroufa Press.

Stewart, Frances. 1985. *Basic Needs in Developing Countries.* Baltimore: Johns Hopkins.

Stohr, W. and F. Taylor, eds. 1981. *Development from Above or Below.* New York: Wiley.

Svendsen, Knud Erik. 1970. "The Present Stage of Economic Planning in Tanzania." In A. H. Rweyemamu, ed. *Nation-Building in Tanzania: Problems and Issues.* Pp. 79-89. Dar es Salaam: East African Publishing House.

____. 1974. "Development Administration and Socialist Strategy: Tanzania After Mwongozo." In A. H. Rweyamamu and B. U. Mwansasu, eds. *Planning in Tanzania: Background to Decentralization.* Pp. 23-44. Nairobi, Dar es Salaam, and Kampala: East African Literature Bureau.

Temu, A. J. 1980. "Tanzanian societies and colonial invasion 1875-1907." In M.H.Y. Kaniki. ed. *Tanzania Under Colonial Rule.* Pp. 86-127. London: Longman.

Thiele, Graham. 1986a. "The State and Rural Development in Tanzania: The Village Administration as a Political Field." *Journal of Development Studies* 22: 540-577.

____. 1986b. "The Tanzanian Villagization Programme: Its Impact on Household Production in Dodoma." *Canadian Journal of African Studies* 20: 243-258.

Thornton, Robert J. 1980. *Space, Time, and Culture among the Iraqw of Tanzania.* New York: Academic Press.

von Freyhold, Michaela. 1979. *Ujamaa Villages in Tanzania: Analysis of a Social Experiment.* New York: Monthly Review Press.

Waide, E. Bevan. 1974. "Planning and Annual Planning as an Administrative Process." In A. H. Rweyemamu and B. U. Mwansasu, eds. *Planning in Tanzania: Background to Decentralization.* Pp. 45-60. Nairobi, Dar es Salaam, and Kampala: East African Literature Bureau.

Watson, John R. 1972. "Conservation Problems, Policies, and the Origins of the Mlalo Basin Rehabilitation Scheme, Usambara Mountains, Tanzania." *Geografiska Annaler* 54A: 221-225.

World Bank. 1981, 1982, 1984, 1986. World Bank Development Report. Washington, D.C.: Oxford University Press and the World Bank.

Yeager, Roger. 1982. *Tanzania: An African Experiment.* Boulder, CO: Westview Press.

Yoshida, Masao. 1985. "Traditional Furrow Irrigation Systems in the South Pare Mountain Area of Tanzania." In Adolfo Mascerenhas, James Ngana, and Masao Yoshida. eds. *Opportunities for Irrigation Development in Tanzania.* Pp 33-71. Tokyo: Institute of Developing Economies.

PART SIX

Conclusions and Implications for the Future

13

The Rural-Urban Nexus

Marilyn Silberfein

At the beginning of this book we set out to examine several questions about rural settlement in Africa. In order to accomplish this task, it was necessary to recognize the difficulties posed by the temporary nature of many homesteads and villages, the use of readily destructible building materials, and the lack of written records to supplement the meager archeological evidence. It was also clear that most settlement theories could not be readily applied to Africa because much of the continent is the complete opposite of the isotropic plain so frequently used in model building. Typical African rural environments are not characterized by large floodplains with expanses of similar soil and terrain conditions; rather, there are frequent changes in slope, soil, and microclimatic conditions that call for complex adaptations by farmers and pastoralists. Given these constraints, our efforts at settlement analysis have focused on identifying settlement types-- clustered, dispersed, and variations in between--and then determining the processes leading to each of them as well as their role in development.

Clustered settlements evolved from dispersed prototypes in many parts of the world during periods of unrest and were consolidated as part of the phenomenon of political centralization. In Europe and in much of East and South Asia, these clusters were transformed into permanent settlements, in part because substantial structures were built from stone and brick, and in part because of a process of socio-political entrenchment. The village became integrated into an accepted way of life, reinforced by the local leadership, especially during periods of strife. Occasionally, as when a region was at peace, a few farmers would venture beyond the village area and establish a homestead or spread out along a trade route.

In contrast, we have found that many rural Africans were able to move their settlements frequently in response to environmental or other stimuli, and even transform their settlement structure from clustered to dispersed and back again. Under these circumstances, settlement change could continue to function as part of the package of strategies for surviving in rural areas under difficult circumstances. Settlement transformation did not take place everywhere; in some cases permanent villages evolved as they had in Europe and Asia, while in some low density or semi-arid regions, clusters never developed at all. In much of Africa, however, settlement flexibility has persisted and the evolution toward nucleation has frequently been disrupted by dispersal.

Several factors have contributed to the continued importance of dispersal in the rural landscape. In Chapter 3, Newman suggested that the movement of farmers into areas of lower fertility made the maintenance of villages too difficult. In effect, dispersal was particularly effective as a "risk minimization strategy in areas of variable rainfall and poor soil" (Gould 1992: 307). Since this type of relocation becomes more important with land scarcity and population growth, there should be a definite trend toward dispersion. Similarly, commercial opportunities, increases in individual land ownership, and agricultural intensification are encouraging dispersal so as to allow for the protection of assets and the closer supervision of field and tree crops. Finally, since lack of security has become a more prevalent rural problem, crops, tools, etc., may have to be protected against thieves by farmers residing amidst their own fields.

As a result of our analysis, we can also say that the way in which people arrange themselves in rural space does not necessarily impede the development process. According to Stone (Chapter 5), Green (Chapter 9), and others, a wide range of economic and social activities can be performed, individually and collectively, by community members who are dispersed across the landscape.

Dispersal is not in itself a negative factor in spite of government rhetoric to the contrary. What seems critical here, is achieving a density level that will allow for some provision of services and marketing opportunities. At one end of the spectrum is Rwanda or Burundi where rural densities were always high by African standards, and where levels of 350 persons per km^2 have been reached. Given the conditions of high density, neither Tutsi or Hutu-dominated regimes have ever agglomerated rural people in order to better control them. As discussed in Chapter 8, services in Rwanda could readily be provided to a threshold population without clustering people in villages.

As densities decrease, however, the provision of goods and services to the majority of rural people in a region gradually becomes more difficult. There are several mechanisms can be used to maintain access to services that will be discussed later. Yet, in spite of these mechanisms, several African governments, searching for approaches to penetrate the countryside and transform the rural economy, have decided to carry out villagization. These resettlement efforts have been beset with problems, well documented in this volume. They have also been unable to achieve the improved productivity that would have provided compensation for the negative aspects of relocation. As Massaro shows in Chapter 13, the Tanzanian Ujamaa program did not increase farm yields, introduce crop varieties, or in other ways improve farm output and income.

The Urban Connection

Up to this point, the focus has been on rural settlement systems, but it is now necessary to look at the interface of such systems and the urban centers that are unevenly distributed through rural space. One of the problems of such a discussion is that rural and urban places are usually studied by different researchers using distinct vocabularies and perspectives. Urban analysts tend to refer to rural places in pejorative terms as being "relatively unorganized and certainly subsidiary to towns" (Lipton 1984: 154). There is often an implication that rural places are there to serve the needs of urban centers, providing basic foodstuffs and raw materials for processing.

Rural-Urban Comparisons

There are definite problems in differentiating rural and urban places. Even the census definition of what constitutes an urban location in Africa varies from one country to another. In some cases, any settlement with more that 1000 persons is considered urban, but the cutoff point may also be 2000 or even 10,000. Other definitions require not just a minimum population but also the presence of functions that are considered urban such as trade, or manufacturing. In areas with a village structure, the overlapping qualities of rural and urban places can make it particularly difficult to distinguish the two types of settlement. Rural villages often grow in size and perform an increasing range of services, especially when located in an accessible position. There is a discussion of this phenomenon by Shilitshena (Chapter 6), whereby places that were still functioning socially as villages had started to behave like towns in economic terms. In a similar vein, many urban residents continue to engage in agriculture.

One other factor that has to be taken into account in determining what is urban. Places that are called towns in an African context may be included in that category not because of size, but because of their dominant economic activities. This is particularly true of centers that were created during the colonial period for local administration or mission stations that included schools and/or health facilities. Later, a few shops or a periodic market may have expanded the range of services. The inhabitants, probably few in number, would often be outsiders, and would have had little connection with the established rural communities. This type of urban places would usually remain a cultural isolate, poorly integrated into the wider region

It is also interesting to compare rural and urban settlements in terms of a series of additional characteristics. While rural places can be impermanent, often passing through cycles, urban centers are not necessarily stable landscape features. Many African cities went through an inexorable decline due to deteriorating environmental conditions, changes in basic economic systems, or warfare. Unlike most villages, the cities left physical traces behind. In a few cases, as at Great Zimbabwe, the urban legacy of stone structures was very substantial indeed.

Rural and urban places both share a connection with the local cultural heritage. Just as the design of homesteads and villages reflects prevailing tastes and preferences, so do those of towns and cities. Both ends of the rural-urban spectrum provide a venue for exhibiting the symbolic aspects of culture. The shape of a homestead, the orientation of a building, or the location of a sacred structure may reflect a meaning that derives from religious beliefs.

Urban centers are less constrained by the physical environment than their rural counterparts, but they are not immune from ecological influences. Towns and cities in Africa certainly require an accessible water source and need supplies of fuelwood as well. Soil appropriate for cultivation (including such factors as good drainage, natural fertility, etc.) may not be as critical, but in many African towns residents do some farming. One of the distinguishing aspects of African cities, remains the continued importance of food production, sometimes as an ancillary activity but sometimes as a dominant source of income.

Finally, while rural places vary from widely dispersed to tightly clustered, urban places belong at the clustered end of the continuum. Yet, such places are not all compact, some tend to spread out along lines of movement and develop a loose structure with multiple focal points. Others are focused on a single central area, with little open space surrounding various residential neighborhoods

Rural-Urban Relationships

The confusion over the definitions of rural and urban is matched by the overlap of rural and urban spheres of activity. This can be most clearly seen in the context of the family. Relatives can hedge their bets by pursuing both urban and rural opportunities, part of the flexibility of African survival systems that was discussed earlier. An extended family, for example, might include one branch that operated a farmstead, a second that maintained a specialized vegetable plot in a desirable river valley location, and a third, based in town, that derived its income from marketing the foodstuffs produced on the family farm among other items. This pattern has been reinforced by such practices as child fostering whereby rural or small town children spend long periods residing with urban relatives or other associates so as to be accessible to schools or apprenticeships. The child is then considered a part of two very separate families in two locations, and ultimately has obligations to both.

Movement between rural and urban bases is a further part of these interconnecting worlds. A rural household might establish a house in town that could be used by any family member carrying out business, attending a ceremony, visiting, or accessing urban services. Travel back and forth could take place as often as allowed by the cost and availability of transport. Families that are relatively well-endowed with resources are able to move frequently between a rural and urban environment.

At the other end of the continuum, migrants who have established themselves in town return home for visits, ceremonies, and often to retire. Circular migration has become quite common in some areas whereby job seekers move to the city for periods of several months to several years, returning to the rural community after earning a target income or failing to secure regular employment.

In addition to back-and-forth movements of people between town and country, money, food, and other items circulate between rural and urban places (Morgan and Solars 1994: 64). There has been much discussion of the role of financial remittances from urban workers in providing resources to their rural counterparts. Although remittances can be a critical source of household income, more typically, they make only a small contribution to rural finances. (Lipton 1984: 148). At the same time, foodstuffs and other rural products are made available in the opposite direction. The relative importance of this type of exchange has varied from one rural region to another, but in some areas, food supplies have been invaluable in protecting recent migrants during a vulnerable stage of their lives.

In general, levels of rural-urban migration have been increasing as young people in particular, dissatisfied with the amenities, job prospects, general income levels, or other facets of life in rural areas, have been looking for alternatives, particularly in the largest cities. This process can create serious labor shortages and a loss in crop output in rural places while cities become crowded, polluted, and overwhelmed by large numbers of the unemployed (Anstee 1990: 197). The migrants are typically young men who live in sprawling slums without regular incomes and become a threat to social stability. The negative implications of high rates of urban growth (over six percent annually for many cities) has led to a search for programs to discourage outmigration from the countryside. Yet, such programs, including villagization, have not been successful in slowing the flow of population in an urban direction.

The Impact of Urban Centers on Rural Areas

The question of remittances is an example of an issue that has fueled a controversy: is the basic relationship between an urban place and its rural region likely to be a positive or a negative one? This topic was discussed in a landmark study that tried to distinguished between parasitic and generative cities in terms of their relationships with their rural hinterland (Hoselitz 1955). Since then, the potential role of towns in rural development has been reevaluated on a regular basis, and opinions have changed along with prevailing development theories.

Initially, in the 1960s and early 1970s, there was some optimism; cities and towns were to be the mechanisms through which services, new technologies, expertise, and capital were moved out into the countryside. Disillusionment followed when resources transferred from urban to rural areas failed to sustain growth or when urban centers remained separate enclaves rather then contributing to rural change (Pedersen, 1990: 89). This was just one part of the failure of the trickle-down (or spread) approach to economic development.

By the 1970s, when a more rural and basic human needs orientation dominated the development literature, cities were often portrayed as points of exploitation though which the resources of rural areas could be removed. Urban centers were seen as extensions of the state, a place where bureaucrats impinged on the rural population in order to collect taxes and exert control. They were also loci of capitalist penetration where both urban and rural elites could take advantage of new opportunities to enrich themselves.

Local rural leaders played a complex role in this scenario; they might obtain services or new roads for their constituents, but in the long run they would serve their own interests which were not always coincident with those of most rural residents. Much of the wealth of this rural elite would be invested in cities where returns were perceived to be higher and where there were such inducements as entertainment and educational opportunities for children. Merchants and traders, in particular, had vested interests. Although they worked closely with rural producers, they invariably tried to maintain a low price for rural exports so as to increase their own profit (Fennell 1988: 270).

Urban places were also seen as disrupting the continuity of rural life, and, in the process, destroying local cultural values (Southall 1988: 5).

Nor did gains in access necessarily compensate for these cultural losses. In fact, towns were sometimes referred to as blockage points because resources sent out from the capital city could be intercepted before they reached the rural areas that were meant to be their destination (Schatzberg 1979: 308).

These and other negative factors were pulled together in an important 1977 study by Lipton on the theme of urban bias. The main contention of the study was that urban areas exerted control over the distribution of a state's resources that was completely out of proportion to the urban share of either population or production (Lipton 1984: 143). These inequities were in part the work of the private sector, but the government was implicated as well.   Purchase prices to the farmer were kept low both for foodstuffs aimed at the urban market and cash crops for the export market. In the latter case, the government, in effect, levied a tax on rural producers by purchasing crops from official buying stations at far below the world market price at which the crops would be sold abroad.

One of the reactions against actual and perceived urban bias, was the emergence of new conceptual approaches to the organization of rural areas in ways that avoided urban expoitation. One such approach was "agropolitan development," based on identifying planning regions, each with populations of approximately 50,000 to 150,000, in which economic decisions would foster local development. Any investments made in urban centers would focus on providing markets and inputs for the farm sector (Friedman and Douglas 1978).

Another construct was termed "selective spatial closure." It called for the identification of regions that were: (1) relatively remote from the dominant core, (2) distinctive in terms of ethnic/cultural traits and (3) in control of resources that could stimulate economic change. These regions were to be cut lose from central government control and allowed to function autonomously (Weaver 1981). As in the case of the agropolitan regions, they would try to generate employment by concentrating on labor-intensive, low tech forms of production that utilized local raw materials for processing and manufacturing.

No African countries implemented these ideas at the time they were generated but they remained part of the development dialogue. The concept of selective spatial closure was later modified, based on the reality that some inputs and technology continue to be required from outside the region, but that as much as possible, an area's own resources should be used in order to generate local economic growth (Yapa 1984).

The negative perspective on the role of cities expressed above, was gradually replaced in the late 1970s by UFRD (urban functions in rural development), a new version of the concept that urban centers had an important contribution to make to rural development. Briefly, towns were seen as places where basic services could be made available, where marketing could take place, where agricultural inputs, supplies and other goods could be purchased, and where there would be off-farm employment options (Rondinelli 1983). An ideal hierarchical arrangement of urban places was envisioned with links between rural places, basic service centers, market towns, and regional cities which would promote rural development (Chetwynd 1984). New technologies would spread down the hierarchy and influence ever more remote locations. Urban and rural growth would then become mutually reinforcing.

It is not possible, at this point, to review all of the positive implications of a well-developed central place structure. Those who support this position claim that areas which lack a fully articulated and integrated system of urban centers will experience rural stagnation because of isolation from needed goods, services, and employment possibilities. Furthermore, any wealth that could be generated under such circumstances, will be drained away for want of local options for investment. The implication here is that the even distribution of urban centers (at each level in the hierarchy) throughout the national territory, "is efficient, equitable, and will accelerate development" (Gould 1988: 89).

Many factors can interfere with this process. The interests of the peasantry and the urban population (or more accurately, with the urban as well as the rural elite) are not always the same. Nor do bureaucrats in the towns necessarily work for the benefit of rural citizens. For an urban hierarchy to function properly, there may have to be specific policies, such as price controls or the regulation of marketing activities, that will limit the potential for exploitation.

Comparative Rural Regions

One of the problems in generalizing about the rural-urban dynamic is that the precise relationship depends on the nature of the rural region and its role in the wider national context. It is necessary, then, to examine several possible scenarios in order to evaluate the potential for complementary rural and urban growth.

Low Density Regions

At one end of the spectrum, are the rural regions characterized by high rates of rural depopulation. Under these circumstances, when employment opportunities have offered a profitable alternatives to rural life, the countryside has virtually emptied out. Gabon is the best country-wide example of this phenomenon. The government has had to purchase food for workers in the mines and forest industries as agricultural production has declined below a level that would justify any investment in marketing and infrastructure

Where low densities reflect not just alternative options,but also such conditions as semi-aridity, poor soil, or isolation from the national marketing network, investment in urban or rural-based activities will probably be very limited. Yet, it is areas like this that would benefit from investment in social infrastructure and efforts to find a local resource or other source of income generation (as in the example of selective spatial closure). In any case, filling in all the gaps in the hierarchy of urban places would be a costly undertaking that would be difficult to justify (Gould 1988: 339).

Medium to High Density Regions

Areas that are more densely settled with some commercialization, potentially allow better access to goods and services. However, linkages to regional and national centers are required, and the local system of production cannot be threatened by pressure on limited resources such as land. Of the types of situations that might prevail here, one in particular is becoming more common in Africa: a situation in which security has been compromised because of an ongoing conflict or even a failure of local law enforcement. For example, the rural region surrounding Masaka, Uganda. combines a median rural density with good potential for commercial production of coffee as well as other cash crops. However, a protracted period of country-wide conflict followed by economic uncertainty has undermined local commerce. Roads have become almost impassable and bridges wash out during two rainy seasons, making marketing difficult and delaying payments for any cash crops that are grown.

Without ready access to a market, commercial production in this area has become minimal and most farmers are engaged primarily in subsistence production. There is a central town but its economy has become stagnant and it does not provide a stimulus for change. The following description conveys this reality:

> The few shops stock paraffin, maize meal, soap, match boxes and bicycle spares. In an area with few sources of cash income, the demand for consumer goods is small. Agricultural extension services and credit are virtually unknown here. The local clinic suffers from lack of drugs and competent staff. Schools are confined to the lower grades and

trained teachers are not easy to recruit (Kayizzi-Mugrerwa 1993: 183-184).

Given this reality, towns are limited in what they can contribute to rural development until the legacy of conflict has been overcome.

In contrast is the scenario in which a rural area surrounds an economically dynamic town. Here land is often in the process of becoming a commodity. It may be lost to farming as urban uses expand or it may be purchased by urbanites for part-time farming enterprises such as growing fruits and vegetables for the urban market (Binns 1994: 122). It is also possible that rural dwellers will purchase or obtain rights to additional land for cash crops at the same time that they search for seasonal or part-time work in town. Thus, both rural and urban residents may engage in a combination of farming and non-farm employment, each group doing some commuting, but in different directions. The same individual may diversify into several activities or the members of a family may each specialize in one activity with income pooling at the end. Terms like rural-urban proletariat are sometimes used to describe the people who become involved in this mixed economy.

Towns that have a growth impetus, whether that growth derives from administrative functions, a local resource, an important role in trade and transportation, or some combination of the above, provide a setting in which near-by rural areas can experience economic growth. The regional dynamic is usually enhanced when a traditional city and its hinterland have developed linkages over a long period of time and there are well established networks based on trading and other relationships. Another advantageous situation is one in which widespread access to land provides both the urban and rural population with a chance to diversify into cash cropping. Unfortunately, when land has become fully commoditized, acquisition may be dominated by an elite, and the only new employment may be in unreliable, low-wage paying agricultural labor (Swindell 1988: 99).

The spatial dimensions of peri-urban regions depends on a series of factors including the size and dynamism of the urban center as well as the physical, social, and access characteristics of the region. Given an appropriate economic structure, towns of 20,000 and up are large enough to stimulate a food production sector that serves those urban employed who are not involved in growing their own food. Towns over 100,000 will usually have a complex rural tributary area that may be sub-divided into zones (Swindell 1988: 98). The market-gardening areas can easily reach out to twenty kilometers beyond the town with further extensions depending on the road network and transport system. There are exam ples of farmers head-loading produce to the urban market over a distance of eleven kilometers (Mortimore 1979). Bicycles easily double this distance while trucks operated by traders or trader-farmers, can provide the option of longer-distance movement of heavier loads.

Current Perspectives

A series of factors are coming to dominate the discussion of urban-rural relations, a reflection of the conditions that prevail in Africa today. Most significant of these is the changing role of the state. Since the mid 1970s, African states have become less effective in carrying out programs, controlling their boundaries, or maintaining security. Increasingly the state is referred to as "failed" or "patrimonial," run by politicians and administrators who are authoritarian, self-seeking, and who selectively favor their clients in carrying out their responsibilities (Lewis 1992).

Along with the deterioration in political conditions that has occurred since independence, the wealth of the state has diminished. This is due, in part, to the prior debt, ineptitude, and corruption that characterize the failed state. It is also due to the sequence of high rates of population growth leading to environmental degradation and a subsequent fall in agricultural productivity as well as to rural-urban migration. At the same time, farmers have been withdrawing from commercial production, discouraged by their declining resource base as well as by poor rewards for their produce at official buying stations, and a lack of accessible markets, services, and needed inputs. Finally, economic conditions reflect changing international terms of trade that include lower prices for the products of African farms and mines.

The international funding sources that used to help fill these gaps have diminished with the end of the cold war and the emergence of endemic economic problems in the industrialized countries. The current flow of aid is precarious, even from those countries tied to Africa by long-standing colonial and post-colonial relationships.

Intervention Strategies

Correcting this situation remains a daunting prospect. The major recent sources of revenue, the International Monetary Fund (IMF) and the World Bank, have establishes conditions for recipients known as Structural Adjustment Programs or SAPS. In order to receive IMF allocations or to qualify for debt restructuring, a country must agree to carry out reforms that result in a decreased role for government in the economy. More specifically, the SAPS call for an austerity program that includes such changes as curtailing the size of the bureaucracy, providing

fewer subsidies to agencies and to the formal sector, devaluing curren-
cies, and providing incentives, such as higher prices, to the agricultural-
sector. This approach does not address the negative implications of a patrimonial system, however, particularly the diversion of resources from
the official state to the "shadow" state, dominated by those who have a
client-patron relationship with the national leadership

Even without the pressure of the IMF, difficult circumstances would
probably have propelled African governments to become less ideological
and more pragmatic, placing greater reliance on the market than on discredited parastatals and other agencies. The challenge becomes one of
creating an environment favorable to producers, processors, traders, and
various types of entrepreneurs, an environment characterized by greater
security and consistency. There is certainly opposition to this strategy
since greater reliance on the market undermines egalitarian economic
goals and can ultimately lead to extremes of wealth and poverty. Furthermore structural adjustment programs have had disappointing results in
terms of generating economic growth and employment at the same time
that the austerity measures have led to numerous problems including the
curtailing of public services.

The decline of the state has also meant less capacity to control territory and implement directives in the provinces. As rural people have
become increasingly discouraged by poor services, low crop prices, and
the acquisitiveness of state officials, they have been more likely to opt out
of the national economy (Reed 1995). This is usually accomplished either
by participating in the underground economy (including smuggling or
selling contraband goods) or, as mentioned earlier, by returning almost
completely to self-reliant production.

In some cases, withdrawal from the state has a strong political as well
as an economic dimension. The process starts when local government
entities or non-governmental organizations (NGOs) ignore the authority
of the central government and begin to create institutions that perform
roles usually assigned to the state. If relations worsen, autonomous activities can evolve into open conflict, a process which is more likely when
there is a history of colonial wars (as in Angola) or ethnic rivalries
(Rwanda, Ethiopia) (Chazan et al. 1992). The Congo Republic provides
one of the best examples of this sequence of events. After a period of
intermittent conflict during the immediate post-colonial period, an effort
was made to tightly control the territory of this vast state. However, after
the mid 1970s, the combination of a collapsed system of service delivery,
deteriorating infrastructure, a failure to regularly pay government
employees and other related factors, intensified a trend toward local
autonomy in the provinces (Young 1994: 263). By 1997, this situation had

evolved further when the eastern region, long economically isolated from the trading networks of Zaire and impacted by the central African refugee crisis, erupted in an insurrection that eventually led to the overthrow of the Mobutu regime in Kinshasa.

The long-term repercussions for Africa of all of these disturbing phenomena can only be the subject of conjecture. It is likely that some African boundaries, sacrosanct since independence and defended by the Organization of African Unity (OAU), will be reconfigured. Yet, on a more positive note, some governments have already begun to respond to these crises by making gestures toward democratization. Such efforts may be only symbolic unless leaders are seriously threatened. The process of liberalization is a complex one that calls for a combination of a willingness of political leaders to sacrifice patrimonial powers and the existence of a civil society able to ensure real public empowerment. In other words, for this process to have a positive impact, government needs to become responsive to public pressure and establish a tradition of accountability (Fatton 1992; Monga 1995).

Part of this phenomenon is the trend toward decentralization, whereby the control of resources, decision-making, and other functions are devolved from the central government to local entities. This may involve reviving district councils and other local governing bodies which, in turn, can raise their own revenue and allocate resources. At the same time, top down programs are being deemphasized by international development agencies and more responsibility is being directed to local groups and NGOs, especially those that have grass-roots support (Hyden 1996).

Yet, in spite of these efforts, African economic and political problems may remain intractable, at least in the short run. A combination of factors makes it difficult for Africa to compete in the world market including the high level of debt and decreasing prices for basic export commodities that were alluded to earlier, the low quality infrastructure and communication systems, and a poorly educated work force. African countries cannot currently emulate the Asian model of economic growth which has produced real gains in employment and income. Asian countries, particularly Korea and Taiwan, prepared themselves to take advantage of opportunities for export expansion by combining relative political stability with investment in education, land reform, and balanced investment in industry and a modernizing agriculture (Calaghy and Ravenhill 1993).

The Impact on Settlement Structure

What do these developments portend for rural and urban settlements? There are some real deficiencies in the literature. Studies have been carried out on connections between rural and urban places but none of them have looked at the specific role of settlement structure in these relationships. There has been no consensus as to how either villages or dispersed structures impact on rural/urban interaction or economic growth.

It can be predicted, however, that democratization and decentralization should enable rural people to resist any manipulation of settlements that goes counter to the demands of their social structure or production system. Furthermore, governments recognize that large-scale villagization programs, like the one implemented in Tanzania, created ecological, production, and managerial problems. Nor are these governments likely to have the resources to carry out national or even regional resettlement initiatives. To the degree that any efforts are made to change rural settlement patterns, they will probably be voluntary and make use of economic incentives to achieve compliance.

Perhaps the best representative of this trend is the settlement program in Zimbabwe discussed by Zinyama (Chapter 11). Efforts to carry out conservation and to improve productivity have been linked to the creation, initially on a pilot basis, of new settlements which in turn are tied to urban service centers. Each of these is carefully assessed to be in balance with its environment to include land for rotational grazing. The program is designed to prevent illegal expansion of settlement into public land as well as drastic overcrowding and land deterioration. Zimbabwe has been able to carry out this policy, in part, because it has more capital and trained personnel than most African countries, but its approach is one that should provide some insights that can be replicated.

For a more typical African country, there still remains the question of revitalizing rural regions. In part this is a matter of encouraging political participation that can translate into bottom-up planning for economic interventions. Some approximations of what was previously called "selective spatial closure" have actually emerged in Africa. For example, in the Sudan, Niger, and Guinea, a few relatively isolated areas have experienced increased autonomy and economic growth by gaining control over local tax revenue and investing remittances from urban migrants (Simone 1992: 163).

Yet, in most rural areas, economic growth also requires improved accessibility and services which, in the absence of resettlement, implies mobile or dispersed services, periodic markets, and improvement of the distribution of urban centers. All of these possibilities depend upon a road network that is upgraded in terms of both quality and quantity, but this is an investment priority in many African countries . Periodic markets, have a particularly long and successful history in Africa and maxi mize flexibility. They are the ideal intervention in a situation where low demand and limited purchasing power are important constraints. Varying the size, periodicity, and location of such markets allows them to adapt to changing circumstances. Periodic markets also make excellent central nodes (as in Massaro's discussion of nodalization), providing an economic focus in areas of dispersed settlement that can also evolve into a site for social and political gatherings.

As for the expansion of the urban system versus manipulation of rural patterns, there has been very little discussion of the trade-offs involved. The only direct reference, mentioned in Chapter 4, was the suggestion made by Friedmann that in Mozambique, it might make sense to create service centers and mobile services rather than moving people off of their homesteads and into villages (Friedmann 1980).

The concept of improving on central place hierarchies has led to a range of programs, from those which would add basic services to small centers to attempts at filling in all the major gaps in the national urban system. The latter condition is not one that can be readily achieved. Careful decisions have to be made as to which areas are underserved by urban centers but could benefit from added urban functions (Gleave 1992).

Those countries that have tried to implement programs of national urban planning have often started with modest goals, such as carefully choosing the best locations for making limited investments. One of the best examples of this approach was developed in Kenya, based on a strategy that involved every level in the urban hierarchy. Before the program began, a survey of all urban places in the country was carried out. The centers were ranked with points assigned for each service. Then, for every center of a certain rank, an assessment was made of economic potential, accessibility, and population density in the tributary area (Taylor 1975: 144).

The level in the urban hierarchy that was most closely associated with rural development was the rural center, a location which was expected to provide farmers with information, credit, transport to market and other basic services. In the Kenyan program, those towns with the best location and the most potential were selected from all of the possible candidates and designated as rural centers. Each of these would then be allocated scarce resources which would stimulate growth in and around the town. The goal was a population of 5000 by the year 2000 which could support a hinterland population of about 40,000. It was hoped that this plan would improve on the use of resources, even if specific goals for the year 2000 were not reached.

The current development context has other implications for rural-urban relations. For example, the structural adjustment programs call for a decrease in the size of bureaucracies and fewer subsidies for the formal sector, thus decreasing the number of urban jobs available (Gould 1988: 212). At the same time, they emphasize improving the position of farmers through better crop prices and more investment in agriculture. Thus, if these types of changes were made, they would have the potential to narrow the gap between rural and urban incomes.

Yet, in much of Africa the elite continues to be dominated by urban interests that only pay lip service to reforms. The residents of the cities, more concentrated and potentially better organized than their rural counterparts, command more than their fair share of government largesse. It will take a combination of the rural resourcefulness amply demonstrated in this volume, outside pressure to distribute resources more equitably, and better settlement planning to finally allow the rural economy to become an impetus to economic growth in the modern African state.

References

Anstee, Margaret J. 1990. "Social Development in Africa: Perspective, Reality, and Promise." In James Pickett and Hans Singer, eds. *Toward Economic Recovery in Sub-Saharan Africa.* New York: Routledge.

Baker, Johnathan and Paul Ove Pedersen, eds. 1992. *The Rural-Urban Interface in Africa: Expansion and Adaptation.* Uppsala, Sweden: The Scandinavian Institute of African Studies.

Binns, Tony. 1994. *Tropical Africa.* London: Routledge

Callaghy, Thomas M. and John Ravenhill, eds. 1993. *Hemmed In: Responses to Africa's Economic Decline.* New York: Columbia University Press.

Chazan, Naomi, Robert Mortimer, John Ravenhill, and Donald Rothchild. 1992. *Politics and Society in Contemporary Africa.* 2nd Edition. Boulder, CO.: Lynne Rienner Publishers.

Chetwynd, Eric. 1884. "Regional Analysis, Market Towns, and Rural Development." In H. Detlief Kammeier and Peter J. Swan, eds. *Equity with Growth? Planning Perspectives for Small Towns in Developing Countries.* Pp. 663-671. Bangkok: Asian Institute of Technology.

Cobah, Josian A. M. 1988. "Toward a Geography of Peace in Africa: Redefining Sub-State Self-Determination Rights." In R. J. Johnston, David B. Knight, and Elenore Kofman, eds. *Nationalism, Self Determination, and Political Geography.* Pp. 70- 86. London: Croon Helm.

Economics Focus. June 10, 1995. "Out of Africa, a Smoother Ride." *The Economist* 72.

Fatton, Robert. 1992. *Predatory Rule: State and Civil Society in Africa.* Boulder CO.: Lynne Rienner Publishers.

Friedman, John and Michael Douglas. 1978. "Agropolitan Development: Toward a New Policy for Regional Planning in Asia." In F. Lo and K. Salih, eds. *Growth Pole Strategy and Regional Development Policy : Asian Experiences and*

_____. 1980. "The Territorial Approach to Rural Development in the People's Republic of Mozambique." *International Journal of Urban and Regional Research* 4: 97-116.

Funnell, D. C. 1988. "Urban-Rural Linkages: Research Themes and Directions." *Geografiska Anneler* 70B: 267-274.

Gleave, M. B. 1992. "Urbanization." In M. B. Gleave, ed. *Tropical African Development: Geographical Perspectives.* Pp. 315-346. New York: John Wiley.

Gould, W.T.S. 1988. "Rural-Urban Interaction and Rural Transformation in Tropical Africa." In Douglas Rimmer, ed. *Rural Transformation in Tropical Africa.* Pp. 77-97. Athens: Ohio University Press.

_____. 1992. "Population Mobility." in M. B. Gleave, ed. *Tropical African Development: Geographical Perspectives.* Pp. 284-314. New York: John Wiley.

Groove, A. T. 1886. "The State of Africa in the 1980s." *Geographical Journal* 152: 193-216.

Harriss J. and M. Moore, eds. 1984. *Development and the Rural Urban Divide.* London: Cass.

Hoselitz, B. F. 1955. "Generative and Parasitic Cities." *Economic Development and Culture Change* 3: 278-294.

Hyden, Goren. 1996. "The Challenges of Analysing and Building Civil Society." *Africa Insight* 26, 2: 92-106.

Kalepeni, Exekiel. 1992. "Population Redistribution in Malawi Since 1964." *Geographical Review* 82: 13-28.

Kayizzi-Mugrerwa, Steve. 1993. "Urban Bustle/Rural Slumber: The Dilemmas of Uneven Economic Recovery in Uganda." In Magnus Bloomstrom and Mats Lundahl, eds. *Economic Crisis in Africa: Perspectives on Policy Responses.* Pp. 181-207. New York: Routledge.

Keller, Edmond J. 1995. "Liberalization, Democratization, and Democracy in Africa: Comparative Perspectives." *Africa Insight.* 25, 4: 1995.

Jones, Barclay Gibbs. 1986. "Urban Support for Rural Development in Kenya." *Economic Geography* 62: 201-214.

Lewis, Peter M. 1992. "Political Transition and the Dilemma of Civil Society in Africa." *Journal of International Affairs* 46, 1:   31-54.

Lipton, Michael. 1984. "Urban Bias Revisited." *Journal of Development Studies* 20: 139-166.

Monga, Celestin. 1995. "Civil Society and Democratization in Francophone Africa." *The Journal of Modern African Studies.* 33,   3: 359-379.

Morgan, Wm. B. and Jerzy A. Solars. 1994. "Agricultural Crisis in Sub-Saharan Africa: Development Constraints and Policy Problems."   *The Geographical Journal* 160: 57-73.

Mortimore, M. J. 1979. "The Supply of Urban Foodstuffs in Northern Nigeria." In J. T. Coppock, ed. *Agriculture and Food Supply in Developing Countries.* Pp. 45-65. Edinburgh: University of Edinburgh.

Pedersen, Paul Ove. 1990. "The Role of Rural Small Towns in Development." In Jonathan Baker, ed. *Small Town Africa: Studies in Rural Development in Africa.* Pp. 87-107. Uppsala: The Scandinavian Institute for African Studies.

Reed, William C. 1995. "The New International Economic Order: State, Society,

328   and African International Relations." *Africa Insight* Marilyn Silberfein
25, 3: 140-148.

Rondinelli, Dennis. 1983. "Small Towns and Cities in Developing Countries."
Geographical Review 73: 379-395.
____. 1984. "Cities and Agricultural Development: The Urban-Rural
Connection." *Regional Development Dialogue* 5: 1-18.
Simone, Abdou Maliqalim. 1992. "Between the Lines: African Civil Societies and
the Remaking of Urban Communities." *Africa Insight* 22, 3: 159-164.
Schatzberg, Michael G. 1979. "Blockage Points in Zaire: The Flow of Budgets,
Bureaucrats, and Beer." In Aiden Southall, ed. *Small Urban Centers in Rural
Development in Africa*. Pp. 297-312. Madison: University of Wisconsin Press.
Southall, Aiden. 1988. "Small Urban Centers in Rural Development." *African
Studies Review* 31: 1-16.
Swindell, Ken. 1988. "Agrarian Change and Peri-Urban fringes in Tropical Africa."
In Douglas Rimmer, ed. *Rural Transformation in Tropical Africa*. Pp. 98-115.
Athens: Ohio University Press.
Taylor, D.R.F. 1975. "The Role of the Smaller Urban Place in Development: The
Case of Kenya." In Salih El-Shakhs and Robert Obudho, eds. *Urbanization,
National Development, and Regional Planning in Africa*. Pp. 143-160. New York:
Praeger.
Taubmann, Wolfgang. 1991. "Rural Urbanization in China." Unpublished paper
presented to the International Symposium on Urban Development in China.
Shanghai: East China Normal University.
Weaver, Clyde. 1981. "Development Theory and the Regional Question: A
Critique of Spatial Planning and its Detractors." In W. B. Stohr and D.R.F.
Taylor, eds. *Development From Above or Below*. Pp. 73-105. New York: John
Wiley & Sons.
Yapa, Lakshman S. 1982. *Regional Issues in Strategies for Increasing Rural
Employment*. Worcester, MA.: Clark University, Regional Cities Project.
Young, Crawford. 1994. "Zaire: The Shattered Illusion of the Integral State." *The
Journal of Modern African Studies* 32: 247-263.

About the Contributors

Robert E. Ford holds the Adamson chair in international studies at Westminster College in Salt Lake City, Utah. He has carried out applied research on human-environment interaction around the world, but with a concentration on Francophone Africa. Among his many publications are "The Population-Environment Nexus and Vulnerability Assessment in Africa" in *Geojournal* (1995) and "The Rwanda Tragedy: A Personal Reflection," in *Hunger Notes* (Summer, 1996).

Edward C. Green in an anthropologist and independent consultant based in Washington, D.C. and southern Africa. One of his recent assignments was with Swiss Aid in Mozambique. His many publications include "Evaluating the response of Swazi Traditional Leaders to Development Workshops," in *Human Organization* (1992).

David Grossman is a professor of geography at Bar-Ilan University in Ramat-Gan, Israel. He has been interested in rural settlement throughout his career and is the author of *Rural Process-Pattern Relationships: Nomadization, Sedentarization, and Settlement Fixation* (1992).

Gerry Krieg, the project cartographer, started working on this assignment as a graduate student at Temple University. He is now based on Long Island as an independent consultant in cartography and computer graphics.

Asmarom Legesse is an anthropologist at the University of Asmara. He recently returned to Eritrea after many years at Swarthmore College. He is well known for his research on pastoralists in Kenya and Ethiopia and is currently completing "A Pastoral Ecosystem: Field Studies of the Borana and Gabra of Northern Kenya" (forthcoming, 1997).

Richard Massaro teaches in the Department of Geography and Planning, West Chester University. He has carried out rural and regional development work in Tanzania and recently published "Beyond Participation: Empowerment for Environmental Action in Tanzania's West Usambara Mountains," in John Friedmann and Haripriya Rangan, eds., *In Defense of Livelihood: Comparative Studies on Environmental Action* (1993).

James Newman is a professor of geography at Syracuse University. His interests include African prehistory, agricultural and nutrition systems, and population geography. He recently completed a book that reflects all of these concerns: *The Peopling of Africa: A Geographic Interpretation* (1995).

David Siddle is a professor of geography at the University of Liverpool, U.K. He began writing on African settlement several decades ago and has more recently become interested in cultural/ historical geography in alpine Europe as well as in Africa. He is the author of *Rural Change in Tropical Africa* (1989).

Marilyn Silberfein is an Associate Professor of Geography and Urban Studies at Temple University. She has a long-term interest in settlement issues in Africa as well as in geopolitics. Her publications include *Rural Change in Machakos Kenya: A Historical Geography Perspective* (1989).

R.M.K. Silitshena is a professor of geography and chair of the department of environmental science at the University of Botswana in Gaberones. He played an important role in the symposium that produced *Settlement in Botswana* (1982) and he has continued to publish on the themes of settlement and urban environmental management. His publications include *Intra-Rural Migration and Settlement Change(* 1993), and the co-authored work, *Development in Context*, Volume 2 (1995).

Glenn Davis Stone is an associate professor of anthropology at Washington University in St. Louis, MO. He has been researching settlement themes among the Kofyar of Nigeria for over a decade and recently published *Settlement Ecology: The Spatial and Social Organization of Kofyar Agriculture*(1996).

Lovemore Zinyama is a professor in the department of geography, University of Zimbabwe in Harare. His primary interests are in settlement and land policy and he has numerous publications on these subjects including "Changes in Settlement and Land Use Patterns in a Subsistence Agricultural Economy" in Erdkunde (1988).

Index